W9-CKI-753

The New Jewish Identity
in America

0822

BY THE SAME AUTHOR

The Real Jewish World
Christians and Jews: The Eternal Bond
Great Religions of the Holy Land
The Jewish Community in Canada: A History
The Jewish Community in Canada: In the Midst of Freedom
What Do We Believe? The Stance of Religion in America
  (Co-Author, with Martin E. Marty and Andrew M. Greeley)
To Understand Jews
Judaism
America Is Different
The Bible Is for You
Bridge to Brotherhood
A Time to Speak
Lines on Life
The Road to Confidence
Man Is Free
The Jewish Community in Rochester
A Humane Society (editor)

The New Jewish Identity in America

Stuart E. Rosenberg

Hippocrene Books
New York

Copyright © 1985 by Stuart E. Rosenberg

All rights reserved, including the rights to reproduce
this book or portions thereof in any form.

For information, address: Hippocrene Books, Inc.,
171 Madison Avenue, New York, N.Y. 10016.

Printed in the United States of America

Portions of *The New Jewish Identity in America* relating to pre-1962
events originally appeared as *America Is Different* (Thomas Nelson &
Sons, 1964) and *The Search for Jewish Identity in America* (Anchor Books,
1965, Doubleday & Company, Inc.)

Library of Congress Cataloging in Publication Data

Rosenberg, Stuart E.
    The new Jewish identity in America.

    Bibliography: p. 279
    Includes index.
    1. Jews—United States—Identity.   2. Judaism—United
States.   3. United States—Ethnic relations.   I. Title.
E184.J5R625   1985   305.8'924'073   84-10938
ISBN 0-88254-997-9

FOR

MURAD and *MICHAEL*

Contents

Introduction

A *NEW* JEWISH IDENTITY? AND WHAT OF THE OLDER ONE, OR OF *ANY* FIXED Jewish identity at all? Perhaps most American Jews have already lost much of their former distinctiveness, now that they have reached into their fourth and fifth generation on the soil of the new world?

Some would indeed say that by now, a clearly shaped "Jewish identity in America" is purely chimerical, merely fanciful and imaginary. They stoutly deny the existence of an explicitly definable American Jewish group identity, seeing it as unmeasurable or, at best, barely discernible. Taking a page from Heinrich Heine, they would argue that in America and the free world, *"wie es sich Christelt, so Jüdelt es sich"*—*as the Christians do, so do the Jews.*

Is there, then, nothing really unique, unusual, or identifiable about American Jews? At the very least, can it not be claimed that "Jews are like every one else, only more so?" Curiously, it would appear that perhaps that was precisely what Robert E. Park, one of the founders of American sociology, was saying about them as long ago as the early 1920s. He had argued that the Jews were "the most American of all groups"; that they exhibit the predominant *American* traits; and that by studying the American Jewish community in detail, all of its citizens would better understand themselves and American culture. He seemed to believe that Jews tend to be more sensitive to the trends in the larger society than others, and that, as a result, they often can anticipate the cultural patterns of the future.

But what was Park really saying? Were Jews the "most American" of all groups because they were the least—or the most—different? If the former, then why not study, instead, more dominant others? If the latter, then why equate their special Jewish way of living as Americans, with all of America? Was Park suggesting that American Jews were both more *and* less like other Americans, at one and the same time? And was it, in fact, a good portent for their future survival for Jews to be "more" or "less" American?

In the early 1960s, an interesting resolution of this dilemma was offered by a sympathetic, survivalist Jew, who was himself a highly regarded American sociologist. While accepting Park's views, Seymour M. Lipset took them a step beyond, in what I would regard as a classical description of the earlier or "older American Jewish identity"—one that had remained in vogue for over sixty years until challenged by a series of events that dramatically began to interlock as the 1960s were coming to a close. In so doing, Lipset, too, fell back upon Heine's Law—but he saw it as a constructive tool to be used by Jews in understanding how best to survive as a group in America. He had suggested that "the only way one (can) understand the variations in the behavior of Jews in different countries (is) by seeing the differences as adaptations to the dominant behavior patterns within the Gentile community." Lipset's view—that the lifestyle and identity of American Jews are best understood when seen as a conscious or unconscious accommodation to American culture at large—had only described the way in which the greatest majority of Jews had already been functioning as individuals.[1] "The less Jewish, the more American"—this had been the underlying *leitmotif* of most Jewish behavior and self-understanding in the Promised Land of America—at least until the fourth quarter of the Twentieth Century. Had he, however, overlooked the possibility that Park may also have had in mind something different: "the *less* Jewish, the *less* American?"

Yet, Lipset was, in fact, reflecting a reality now surpassed, but one virtually enshrined as a fundamental sociological law, which regarded "America" as the principal metaphor through which Jews should structure and define the values and aspirations of their own group life. We may call it the "accommodationist thesis"—*Jews survive in America only by "adjusting" to it.*

Moreover, at the beginning of the century, and for some decades to follow, two different but all-powerful forces had served to diminish any possible hope that America might exceed the monolithic expectations of its federalist motto of *"E Pluribus Unum."* On the one hand, there was what has been called the "liberal expectancy"—the anticipation that in an open and democratic society, features which had once served to divide group from group would soon be erased. It was fully expected that there would be a growing emphasis on personal achievement, not on subgroup loyalty, and that universal public education would rapidly provide the cement for the building of an increasingly undifferentiated American culture. Still others, on the more militant edge of the political spectrum—the radical left—went even further than the liberals. They maintained that only the differentiations of economic and social class would long abide, and that distinctions and divisions would remain, after earlier walls of separation based on language, culture, religion, race, or national origin, would be eradicated. With the coming of the revolution, the radicals believed, even these class divisions would finally disappear, as well. Which explains why Karl Marx and his disciples were—and remain—intolerant of, and impatient with, what they regard as the reactionary character of religious and ethnic loyalties. They held that it was "interest" that should propel rational men into social action—and interest, they believed, was the product of one's *economic* position, not of one's ethnic or religious identity.

But the winds of political and cultural doctrine, as well as of war, do change. By the late 1970s, both Lipset's "law" and the liberal and the radical expectancies were all being challenged by activist Jews and other "ethnics" at the grass-roots level, and by new leaders and scholars—the apostles of the "new ethnicity" which, by then, had already overtaken much of the country. In the wake of the Vietnam war came the "dethronement of America." The substitution of ethnic communities as the new "interest groups" now began to replace the older, more centralized forms of national patriotism. Both Marxism and liberalism suffered serious declines—not only at the popular level, but also among the intellectual élite. A new hour had arrived for America. The serious and separate ethnic interests now served as a new organizing principle for a nation whose only majority would be seen to consist of the sum of its *self-interested* minorities.

By 1977, "the critical question," as one Jewish scholar had put it, was "not whether Jews have historically adapted themselves to the surrounding culture—this is a self-evidently true proposition." There were now more important and relevant issues that had to be addressed. Among these were: "Which elements of that culture have they simply assimilated without change; which elements have they transformed in the process of absorbing them; which elements have they resisted; and which important elements, if any, have they ignored?"[2] This new mood, product of the awareness of an emerging *new* Jewish identity, would seek answers that were radically different from those suggested by the Heine-Lipset law. It would begin with the basic proposition that Jews *were* and *are* capable of more than mere accommodation—and that there were clearly discernible elements of Jewish *resistance* and *transvaluation* to American (or for that matter, liberal or radical) values and cultural or behavioral patterns. Jews now came to believe it possible to ignore American norms and styles in areas which they thought clearly threatened their *integrity as Jews.* But they did so by compartmentalizing their lives. Many American values, ideals, and attitudes could be accepted and even accommodated to, while others were simply disregarded as irrelevant and of no benefit to the Jewish style of life. We may call this the "compartmentalist thesis": Jews can survive creatively by living in two civilizations at once—both the Jewish *and* the American. By *selective accommodation* to only those values in American society which shore up and strengthen the integrity of their own historic culture or religion, they can also achieve their own "self-interest," as do other "peoples" in America.

This *new* Jewish identity was principally abetted in the mid-1960s by the sudden emergence of new American ways of affirming "peoplehood." Until that decade, in the words of Martin E. Marty, ethnicity was essentially "inescapable, automatic and reflexive." As a result, it had come to be identified primarily with self-enclaving subgroups who had virtually refused to accommodate to American culture and society—with all the pejorative connotations such self-induced ghettoization suggested to a nation bent on Americanizing its multiple immigrants, and which prided itself on its free-wheeling openness. Moreover, by that time this kind of unaccommodating ethnicity seemed to have been either dead or dying, since the older streams of immigration to America had virtually dried up. But the "new ethnicity" would be very different in character: it would not be based simply on the transplantation of old world cultures, but on a new way of affirming one's sense of peoplehood. "It was intentional and reflective: the Black who once 'passed' now wore an 'Afro,' and instead of obliterating African traces in worship, now elevated them. The Jew who had his name Anglicized restored the original name and perhaps, turned orthodox and observant. . . A secularized or Reform Jewish coed on a university campus in 1967 might have thrown in her lot with the Arabs. Her choice would have been based on conscious identification with what she thought was the Third World, over against an Israel that looked to be part of American imperialism. As time passed, she would become unsure of herself and her loyalties. Eventually, she might reaffirm Judaism and choose to follow its orthodox forms. . . *An acquired ethnic sense demands a different kind of nurture than an inherited one.*"[3] (Emphasis added.)

Along with other ethnic groups in America, Jews have only recently discovered that identity is not the same as identification. A passport picture identifies the bearer. It pictures one's person, but does not describe, examine, evaluate, or "discover" it. It can only reflect what appears to be. It can say nothing about a more significant, non-physical, non-material reality: what the owner of that document knows about himself and his ancestors, or what he wants his own children to become. Indeed, identity—old or new—is not identification. Its subject is not an external appearance—that photograph, for example—but the "coherent sense of self," as Allen Wheelis calls it, which its bearer wishes to affirm, or seeks to discover.

There is, of course, still another crucial dissimilarity between identification and identity which is especially relevant to the emergence of the new Jewish condition in America. Our identification must always remain changeless: aliases or forged numbers counterfeit it. Our identity, on the other hand, is always dynamic, never static—because we know ourselves differently at different times and under changing circumstances. Identification is something given us by others; identity is something we ourselves must work at. It is always hard to achieve, and in a shifting, changing society, harder still, to maintain.

Jews in America, as I hope this work will demonstrate, were always aware of the fact that for them it was special, different in spiritual texture and quality from all their other diaspora centers, and especially from their earlier European "homelands." Accordingly, even the most ardent among them not only adapted to those aspects of American life they admired, but in many and varied ways enormously helped to build and to enhance its culture, commerce, and community. This is why it is so important to place their own Jewish identity within the context of *American* cultural, religious, and ethnic history. We can not understand American Jews without understanding America itself by relating the Jewish experience here and elsewhere to the comprehensive and changing American scene. A study of Jewish identity in America must thus be as much concerned with what America was and is still becoming as it is with the inner dynamics of Jewish life. As we will later note, for example, the belated awareness of the lingering and haunting meaning of Hitler's Holocaust, and its vital links to threats of Israel's annihilation in 1967 (which contributed so notably to the emergence of the new self-awareness and identity of American Jews) might not have achieved its current crucial hold on Jewish life in America—which has since been completely "Zionized"—were they not also coupled in time to the rise of "Black Power," and the new prominence given to a reconsideration by most Americans of their attitudes to the Third World abroad, and at home to all racial or cultural minorities.[4] When "black" became "beautiful," American Jews, too, sought to strengthen their inner community life in new and important ways. They countered "affirmative action" with affirmations of their own. What they had once sought to forget or repress—even the Holocaust itself—would be raised to heightened levels of American Jewish consciousness only after 1967.

It is thus neither profitable nor relevant to measure Jewish identity principally by "appearances"—in quantitative terms—mainly by projecting or analyzing our very low fertility rates; or the attrition caused by inter-marriage; or even the relatively low national averages of the affiliated. Jews, it has long ago been pointed out, are "Jews by association"; they are infinitely more than what the statistics may say they are, or are not. Indeed, at crucial moments in both the ancient and more recent Jewish past, strong and committed minorities within the community have rolled back and even reversed the often larger numbers of the indifferent, apathetic, or the alienated among them.

Jewish identity in America is a new and throbbing reality today—the more so as a result of the new ways all other Americans associate themselves. Even the unexpected spectre of the new public "armies" of skullcap, or *kippah,* wearers—a new way of showing the "Jewish flag"; or those young people now seeking a "return to Judaism"—the so-called *baalei teshuvah;* or the campus "*mitzvah*-mobiles" of the ubiquitous Lubavitcher Hasidim must all be seen as more than a reflection of the new interest in religious traditions now prevailing in America—and in many parts of the Christian and Muslim worlds. At their base, it can be successfully argued, even these religious stirrings among American Jews today are profoundly part of their new and prideful ethnic identity. It also goes without saying that, by itself, such an identity—even in a most heightened form—can not produce culture. But the obverse is equally true, if often overlooked: without identity, there can be no vital culture or religion.

It seems clear that, by now, many Jews have learned their American ethnic lessons well. Today they constitute a small but increasingly effective and cohesive "interest" group. And day by day there are hopeful and vital signs that a more vibrant Jewish culture may yet emerge out of their recently revitalized and *new* Jewish identity in America.

NOTES

1. See Seymour M. Lipset, "The American Jewish Community in a Comparative Context," in *The Ghetto and Beyond,* ed. by Peter Rose, Random House, New York, 1969, pp. 21–32.

2. See Charles S. Liebman, "American Jews: Still a Distinctive Group," in *Commentary,* August, 1977, pp. 57–60.

3. Martin E. Marty, *A Nation of Behavers,* University of Chicago Press, Chicago, 1976, pp. 164–166.

4. A fuller and far-ranging analysis of the effects of the Holocaust on reshaping Jewish identity in America is required. I am presently completing a new work dealing comprehensively with this special and unique dimension of the new Jewish identity, to be published by Hippocrene Books.

PART ONE

American Ways

CHAPTER I

The New World and the Old

SOME JEWS BELIEVE THAT AMERICA TODAY IS THE HOME OF THE MOST powerful, most sophisticated, enigmatic, complex, and, in many ways, the most innovative Jewish community in the millennial history of the House of Israel. Descriptions such as these can only be the result of a growing awareness on their part that a new and more confident Jewish identity in America is presently emerging—an identity that could not have even been foreseen barely a century ago. Indeed, it has taken more than one hundred years for Jews to come to terms with America itself, and to find a more self-confident place within its changing social order. The story of their self-contradictions, inner ambivalence, and the search for a coherent, confident sense of self, in many ways, is also the story of America itself.

About one-half of the world's Jews now live in America. Yet, had they requested the advice, consent, or blessings of their rabbis, at least two million East European Jewish immigrants would probably have remained where they were, never venturing forth to "godless, tainted, un-Jewish America"—thus extending even more the tragic oblivion that awaited six million of their brothers and sisters only a few years later during Hitler's Holocaust. Six million were slaughtered in Europe—almost six million now live hopefully in America.

For nearly thirty-five years, from 1881 until the outbreak of World War I in 1914, most hometown rabbis of these two million new Americans—Jews from East Europe—had been admonishing them not to "abandon Judaism" by going to alien America. By the turn of the century, however, even their pious ones and their intellectuals were streaming out to the new world, joining the *proste yidn*—the most unlettered Jews—who had already made the break a decade or two before. In spite of the warnings of their rabbis, a goodly part of Jewish Europe was being rapidly transplanted to America.

An understandable fear had gripped their scholarly leaders as their own communities began to empty out. Old Country teachers had cautioned them before their departure that in America they would be tainted by the foreign ways of the Gentiles, openly or unknowingly. Their rabbis had forewarned: If you go to the United States you will not only be leaving home, but also your Jewishness. And, as if examining permitted and prohibited foods in the light of the religious dietary laws,

[3]

they repeatedly judged that "Golden America" was *treif*—not kosher. It was as unfit a place for Jews to live as it would be unfit for them to touch, raise, or—heaven forfend—to eat, pig!

As proof of how seriously they viewed the problem, some of their noted rabbis had ventured across the Atlantic to repeat the message to them, even *after* they were settled in New York and other large Eastern cities. "Return home," they pleaded, by which they meant, of course, that only there, in that closed and cloistered east European community of Jews did Judaism have a chance to survive. Even the recent memory of pogroms past, or the specter of those still on the horizon, did not shake their determination. The threat of the open society in the tinseled melting pot that was America troubled them much more.

Hitler's diabolical "Final Solution"—which could not have been predicted—proved those rabbis to have been terribly wrong. But they surely had good reason to be concerned about the future of Jews in America. Their instincts were unerring: they understood that in a new world, the old might not only be temporarily discarded, but ultimately, completely forgotten.

Those who came to settle in America came to forget, not to remember. Encouraging himself to discard and forget the old, the new American came to believe with perfect, almost naïve faith that he was indeed building a new world. In his view the European lived in the past, he in the future. And to build that future he felt the need to forget that past from which—by God's grace, he often believed—he had miraculously escaped.

Yes, the new American must forget or else his American Dream would be impossible. But can he? Can he always remember to forget? Can he abridge himself as a man by expurgating every vestige of fathers who lived before? Can he rip away all the bonds that connect him to his antiquity—the cultural and religious umbilical cords that tie him to an irrevocable ancestry?

He tries, but cannot fully succeed; inevitably, he must remember as much as he forgets.

This national ambivalence, these shifting moods of rejection and remembrance, constitute a root cause of much that *is* different about America. This curious admixture of feelings has been largely responsible for the development of a unique historical community: an optimistic nation, intent upon succeeding, uncomplicated by morbid philosophical speculation over failure, a people convinced that in the end its "free society" would triumph over any other because it was different from any other.

And this strange, almost fanatical belief in their own uniqueness as a people and their superiority over the nations, grew even stronger across the years, as America extended its influence farther and farther beyond its own shores, in the growing conviction that one day its reach might indeed exceed its grasp. Indeed, as early as the 1790's, Europeans had already discovered to their sheer amazement that Americans sincerely believed that "no one has any brains, except in America."

What accounts for this collective sense of national destiny, the near-divine certainty of their chosenness, which seemed from the earliest days to obsess the American settlers of this continent, and which, to the continuing consternation and displeasure of both friend and foe, keeps growing with the years?

To such an elusive question many learned answers might be given. And yet, there is perhaps a profound meaning available in a simple suggestion. May not what sometimes seems like crude American swagger and braggadocio, and what on other occasions partakes of deep national commitment to excellence and uniqueness, be the product of the recurrent tension caused by the pull of two opposing American mind-sets: remembering and forgetting?

Alternating between remembering and forgetting, the American seemed to come to the conclusion that the only way to retain both moods with any degree of peace of mind was to succeed at both! He remembered that he was an American, forgot that he was a European. He remembered that the European experience had to be exceeded and transcended if he was not to subvert his new purposes as an American. America, suggests Henry Steele Commager, "which displayed the most diverse racial stocks . . . achieved a distinctive and stable national character with an ease that confounded not only the expectations of her critics but all history and experience. . . . Whereas in Europe," he notes, "with its age-old traditions of feudalism and nationalism, the particular triumphed over the general, in America . . . the general triumphed over the particular."[1]

Many of her past and contemporary critics, even those from within, have looked upon this "American virtue," in turn, as a symbol of a cultural, a political, or a religious weakness. The triumph of the "general over the particular"—this peculiarly American triumph—has been laid at the door of the indifference America is said to have to any system of absolute values. It has also been identified as the source of American philistinism: an undifferentiated medley of mobs is too often confused with the "people in general." Lacking a particular philosophy of its own, it can never create a cohesive and organic community.

But is it indifference to values that accounts for the American espousal of the general rather than the particular? Not if, as suggested here, we assign the cause to the clash of moods engendered by the rational desire to forget, and the unconscious will to remember.

Both moods have resulted in peculiar feelings of guilt. The American who came here to forget knew very well that he had left behind him a community of men who lived in the same world as he, whose ages-old ethos was still a living and vital part of their present life. From time to time, in spite of himself, he chose to affirm their lives by living in America as one of them. He prayed in their language, sang their songs, ate their foods. By affirming them in his own life, he came to recognize the need to affirm his immediate neighbors who were doing the same in their own. Thus it was that he came to espouse the value of pluralism: not out of indifference, nor religious skepticism, but as a result of those guilt feelings which his estranged "newness" incited. In the old world, pluralism would have been an affront to God and to king. In America, it emerged in response to the new human situation.

But there were other moments, moments when the toleration that grew out of this commitment to pluralism caused the American to experience feelings of guilt of another coloration. There were times when he seemed to believe that he was "remembering too much," and in the process forgetting that his was a new world, a new way of life, unconnected to what had come before. When this mood overcame him, he moved deeper and deeper into his own narrow confines, and fearing spiritual as well as political "entangling alliances," he looked upon foreign men or ideas with almost paranoid eyes. Ironically, in the very midst of gigantic waves of immigration to America, which ensured the growth and development of an expanding nation, local nativism—hate and suspicion of the "foreigner"—festered and spread throughout the body politic.

On balance, however, the essential result of these two conflicting sets of guilt feelings, which developed out of the remembering-forgetting axis, was the typically American desire to avoid guilt feelings altogether. The way to achieve this happy condition, Americans came to believe, was by avoiding all doctrines. Doctrines, they felt, move a man to extremes and to the espousal of inflexible, unrelenting dogmas. They are self-defeating because they breed what must at all costs be avoided: those disturbing guilt feelings! In the artless manner described by George Santayana they consistently avoided the doctrinaire approach: "We do not refute our predecessors, we pleasantly bid them good-bye!"

It does often seem that the American predilection for ideas-in-general rather than an espousal of a specific, unchanging dogmatic set of values is the result of indifference to essentials. In the main, however, it was fear of triggering inner feelings of guilt that led Americans to avoid debate over doctrine. In adopting this position, unwittingly, and without philosophical premeditation, they slowly came to recognize that toleration and pluralism were indeed built into the "American way of life."

To be sure, this pragmatic approach inevitably produced many strange anomalies. Religion, the Founding Fathers made bold to assure, would never be established, as in European countries. Yet they, and the generations which followed, liked to think of America as an even more religious land than any European country with its state-church. Alexis de Tocqueville, that perceptive mid-nineteenth-century Gallic visitor, accurately remarked: "There is no country in the whole world in which the Christian religion retains a greater influence over the souls of men than in America." Yet, in the very next breath, he was quick to add: "In the United States religion exercises but little influence upon the laws and upon the details of public opinion. . . ."

Inconsistencies like these—and many, many others could be adduced—were not resolved head-on, in logical fashion. Rather, they, too, were the product of America's alternating moods of remembering and forgetting. There was hardly a generation, for example, which did not reflect religious antagonisms between Catholics, Protestants, and Jews— each group attempting to remember who they were. Nor was there a time when these three groups did not give thanks for the unique religious freedom they enjoyed here, each carefully forgetting their deprivations in the old world.

All three groups wished to forget the pains inflicted upon them in their European past. Protestants suffered at the hands of Catholic rulers. Catholics were denied by Protestant heads of state. And the Jews, perhaps more than either, to maintain their sanity, *had* to forget. They had to forget what had happened to them in both Protestant and Catholic Europe: when they distributed goods they were called parasites, but when they made the goods, guilds were closed to them because they were said "to excel their Christian fellow-workers"; papal restrictions and royal decrees forced them off the land, but when they had to become petty traders and money lenders they were despised; set apart in ghettos, as in Poland, they were dishonored as an alien blight, but when they adopted the culture of the majority, as in Germany, they were accused of "controlling" the country.

While each group wished to forget its European past, each sought to remember that it was profoundly part of the American landscape. By believing that it had had a vital role in the making and shaping of America, each group mitigated its own guilt at leaving the old world, and sought to endow its American experience with near-cosmic significances. Protestants, even those far removed culturally and theologically from the Puritan variety, like to feel that America is a Protestant country, historically and spiritually. They point to the first colonizers who came, they believe, to establish the Protestant empire on these shores. "We go," they quote Francis Higginson, one of the first Puritan ministers to reach Massachusetts, "to New England not as Separatists from the Church of England, though we cannot but separate from the corruptions in it; but we go to practice the positive part of church reformation and propagate the gospel in America." Without this Protestant spirit, Protestants believe, America could never have been different; it would have been corrupted by the corruptions of the old world.

But despite this monopolistic claim, Catholics feel that far from forming a community of strangers who arrived late, America owes a debt to the Roman Church whose settlers were here virtually from the beginning. Indeed, in the earliest days, Protestants comprised the preponderant majority of the thirteen colonies. But even forgetting the Catholic-led community of Maryland, Catholics point to the nineteenth century as the really first "American century." Only with the great waves of immigration which brought huge Catholic communities to this country did the western frontier open up to crown America's good "from sea to shining sea." Protestants may indeed have supplied America with the spirit of its countryside. But the influence of Roman Catholics, it is contended by their partisans, is widespread in industrialized America, in the productive cities of the nineteenth century.

And Jews, too, are not to be outdone by the others. While admitting to the paucity of their numbers in early America, they attempt to fuse the spirit of the early Puritan settlers of America with the Judaism of the Old Testament. "Puritanism," they contend, "was, in essence, the rebirth of the Hebrew spirit in the Christian conscience." Village, town, and city bore Hebrew names. Bethlehem, Jordan, Mount Carmel, and Zion are reminders that if Jews were not present in large numbers in Pilgrim America, the Children of Israel were. For did not the first settlers consider themselves the builders of the New Canaan, the New Zion in the image of the Hebrew Bible? And had not even Franklin and Jefferson drafted, as a proposed seal of the new United States, a picture of Pharaoh, Moses, and the Children of Israel at the division of the Reed Sea's waters, with the telltale motto: "Resistance to tyrants is obedience to God"? The basic Pilgrim document, they maintain, the one which more than all others molded and shaped America, was a Jewish document: the Old Testament.

It was this "variety of American experiences" that gave the country so many faces. Because of the variegated and composite nature of its population, each group had the right to view all of America from its own angle of vision. If we add to this need to remember the ambivalence created by the immigrant's desire to forget his own particularities in favor of a general view of America, we will come to see that fluidity of national character is normal to America. It has been said that there is nothing as permanent as change; indeed, the evolving quality of the American national spirit has become a fixed part of its history.

In our day, there have been many studies of the "national character" analyzing the many changes in the years following World War II. In some ways, these years have wrought cataclysmic changes in the social psyche of America. In the main, however, these "new" patterns were not unrelated to all that had gone before, in the three centuries preceding. To be sure, there are new emphases and some revisions of earlier themes, but the seeds of what had already been planted are still to be found in the fruit.

To understand the *Zeitgeist* of our own day, and to locate more accurately the place of Jews and Judaism on the spiritual and cultural map of contemporary America, we should examine three major moments in the evolution of the national character, which placed an indelible imprint upon the face of the land. And although the themes of each of these, as well as those of the present moment, sometimes seem discordant and tangential, they are, as we shall see, more like polyphonous melodies in the changing movements of a masterful symphony, which are repeated and restated in newer climaxes and combinations, but yet retain their integrity to the whole.

As a preface to our examination of the urban-suburban national character of our own day, we should first confront these earlier significant communities: the Puritan world, the frontier community, and the ethnic islands wrought by the large-scale immigration waves.

NOTES

1. Henry Steele Commager, *The American Mind* (New Haven: Yale University Press, 1950), p. 5.

CHAPTER II

The Changing American Character

THE PURITAN WORLD. EVERYONE SEEMS TO TAKE FOR GRANTED THAT THE Puritan community of early America represented a progressive development over the England it was supposed to have rejected. In point of fact, however, its politics were less tolerant, its religion less literate, its culture less intellectual. What is more, while it came to be known as New England, the Puritan community in America never considered that its life constituted an outright rejection of Old England. Rather, the American Puritan believed that his life here was intended to be an extension of the old, not a radical undertaking of the new. In assessing the Puritan impact upon the making and shaping of the American character, all these factors must be kept in view. For if Americans have tended to remain conservative ever since, these conserving tendencies of the very first settlers—their wish to remember their past—must not be forgotten.

Compared with later generations of Americans, the Puritans were indeed religiously oriented. They believed earnestly in the central Calvinist doctrines: the Fall of Man, Human Depravity, Predestination, Sin, and Salvation. But when compared with the English co-religionists they had left behind, these new-world Puritans were more interested in the practical application of Calvin's teachings to the building of their community than to debating the fine points of his theology. While their English counterparts were busy speculating about the nature and the relationship of God, man, and government, they were occupied with the strenuous physical tasks of building the New Zion, not in clarifying the doctrines. As for the doctrines, these, they believed, they already possessed; their singular function was to apply them in strict fashion to the new physical and social situation. They came to clear the wilderness, to build the city of God, secure in their belief that their inherited orthodoxies were sufficient enough, and true enough, to stand all tests. All that the doctrine needed now was a community in which it could take root, uncorrupted and undisturbed by the errors of older institutions.

Curiously, this need to build a community, rather than a concern with ideology, led the early Puritans to harden the doctrine rather than to develop it. While in England ways had to be found to deal with dissenters, in New England these were promptly expelled—they got in the way of progress! If toleration as a theory of modern government was the product of their English contemporaries—of men such as John Milton and even lesser worthies—American Puritans seemed never to have heard about it. Instead, they kept reasserting what they had enshrined as their Cambridge Platform of 1648: "wee desire not to vary from the doctrine of faith, & truth held forth by the churches of our native country . . . wee desire to hold forth the same doctrine of religion (especially in fundamentalls) which wee see & know to be held by the churches of England, according to the truth of the Gospell." This repeated emphasis on their connectedness to the English church, this ardent desire to keep their ties intact, actually kept them from opening up to newer and more democratic ideas that were already beginning to be expressed in England itself. But they were building a theocracy, not a democracy, and they had no need to revise the old Scriptural laws, only the need to apply them to the political life of the new community.

Even the laws they began to enact, while rooted in the Biblical spirit, paralleled the English legislation they remembered from the old country. The Puritans, never forgetting that "wee, who are by nature, English men," sought to prove to themselves that, by a remarkable coincidence, the English law was indeed the same law that Scripture required. When they resided in England, they had made no such equation between Scripture and the local legal and social customs. Far from it. They ventured forth on their long and dangerous journeys to the New World in order to strike out on their own and to establish, in accordance with their own lights, a truly Christian society. Yet, the human need to remember and to stay connected to what we remember is very strong. In many ways, the Puritans were better Englishmen in New England than they had been in Old England.

The myths created by writers of American history textbooks are intended to give the impression that the major contribution of the Puritan community to the future development of America was its rigorous Americanism, its self-conscious awareness of its pioneering role. That they were pioneers there can be no doubt. But it remains to be emphasized that the Puritan pioneers in America, like all the other immigrants from Europe who followed them here, never turned their backs completely on the world they had left behind. If we would recognize this built-in psychological reaction as a normal mechanism that continued to operate in the life of *all* immigrants to America, we will come to undersand more clearly some of the inconsistencies in the later development of the American character.

Sometimes, for example, we find it difficult to understand what happened to the so-called Puritan mind when we analyze the spirit of later American generations. We were taught that the Puritans held fast to the Calvinist view that work was virtuous, idleness a vice, and frugality and thrift the greatest human ideals. What has happened to America since? we often ask ourselves nervously. Who spoiled the grand view of the Puritans?

Or, studying the nature of American politics, we often wonder about its lack of ideology and the static, conservative tendencies of its general course. Weren't the Pilgrim Fathers an adventurous, progressive, and destiny-conscious folk? What has happened to their "liberalism"?

And so, too, when we look out upon the current religious situation in America and decry its notable lack of intellectual and theological content, we often tend to mythologize the earlier America, harking back to the "good old days" when church life in New England was spiritually vigorous.

Yet, whether in the economic, political, or religious realm, the lines that would cast a later shadow were already clearly drawn in early America. The Pilgrims did not bring democracy here aboard the *Mayflower*, nor did the Puritans nurture it later, in their Yankee towns. The Pilgrims of Plymouth and the Puritans of the Cape Cod colony worked hard. But they worked hard not only because of their Calvinist temper, but also because they had to work hard in order to cut through the wilderness and survive in what was often a hostile environment. They were regular and devoted church-goers, to be sure, but of doctrine, theology, and philosophy they knew very little.

Yet, in a paradoxical way, their biblical faith was responsible for building into their lives and the lives of future immigrants fundamental ambivalences and incongruities that still abide and have been responsible for much of the "irony of American history." God Himself, they believed, had called America into being, as a "separated" nation, as His new Israel, to establish His covenant-community in the New World. They felt called upon to establish no ordinary society, for they firmly and fully believed that they had been elected by God as His chosen people. Even before they had actually set foot on these shores, they felt a divine hand leading them, covenanting and contracting with them—as with old Israel in Old Testament times—to create a new humanity, "a new heaven and a new earth." "Thus stands the cause between God and us," began Governor Winthrop's sermon aboard the ship *Arabella,* while yet en route to the New World: "We are entered into Covenant with him for this work. . . . Now if the Lord shall please to hear us, and bring us in peace to the place we desire then hath he ratified his Covenant and sealed our Commission. . . ."[1]

Such spiritual ambitions and yearnings—the self-consciousness of possessing a divine election and vocation—helped to give America "pretensions of innocency" and an acute preoccupation with being a "virtuous humanity." But as Reinhold Niebuhr has pointed out, this "spiritual pride" was also responsible for involving Americans—Puritans and non-

Puritans alike—in ironic incongruities that always followed when their illusions and ideals clashed with the harsh and necessary realities of life.[2]

In this light, we cannot only appreciate the basic contribution of the Puritan mentality to the formation of the American national character, but can also see how that very contribution made for continuing feelings of guilt and frustration. Inevitably, the Puritan was to be concerned not so much with who he was, or where he came from, but with what he must strive to become: a new man in a new and promised land. Nor could he easily become what his illusions had made him long to become, for man's reach rarely equals, let alone exceeds, his grasp. And so, inevitably, he sensed that he could not build his new world without relying upon the old.

And in this fundamental respect, the millions of other immigrants who followed them to America have differed from the Puritans not one whit. A haunting ambivalence was woven into the very fabric of America, a fabric loomed out of the shifting heroic-tragic immigrant moods. "We have to be Americans. We shall be. We shall love America and help to build America. We shall accomplish in the New World a hundred times more than we could in the Old." A sensitive immigrant editor of an American Yiddish paper in 1916 could thus sing his hymn of hope. But then, not even the glory of the new and the bold could make him eradicate the old, as he, like millions of other immigrants to America, called his past into life. For in the very next breath he reminds himself: "But you shall not be able to erase the old home from your heart. The heart shall be drawn elsewhere. And in your solitude, images shall rise up and stare in your face with eternal sorrow."[3]

Immigrant Americans believed that America was chosen, that it was a promised land endowed with divine favor. To ensure their own beliefs against doubt, they had to turn their backs upon the vices of Europe and repeatedly glorify their new beginnings. But even the real virtues of America could never quite catch up with the image of America which their spiritual visions had projected. The result: a new world that could never be altogether new; a new world that could never altogether forget the old.

The Frontier Community. The view that America was different led some historians to turn their eyes away from the cultural heritage that the immigrants had brought with them here. They sought out those special experiences in America itself which they regarded as the fundamental sources of American distinctiveness. More than all others, it was the nineteenth-century American historian, Frederick Jackson Turner, who saw in the "frontier community" all the vital elements which, in his judgment, created a distinguished and distinctive American civilization.

This is an attractive view, a romantic and dynamic one. It links the freedom and equality that Americans cherish as their special contribution to mankind with the vastness of their terrain and its almost unlimited natural resources. It proclaims a romantic connection between the land and the mystique of human wandering: whenever their restless spirits urged them to move on to newer horizons, new worlds opened up. The frontier community was thus made responsible for much that is distinctive in American political life. But in this view the frontier is actually responsible for much more. In addition to providing the new arrivals with a fierce and often irrepressible political individualism, Turner and his disciples believed that in the magical environment of the American frontiers the cultures of Europe, brought there by the immigrants, disintegrated and disappeared within the course of a single generation—never to be heard from again! The immigrant did not only transform the wilderness, the wilderness transformed him, and he became, in Turner's memorable phrase, "a new product that is American." The further he pushed the boundaries of the frontier, the further away he moved from the old world he had left.

The frontier made "the new product that is American" different from the European in still another way, Turner claimed. As the American made his way westward and opened up new worlds, he also established new varieties of American life. The surging spirit of the frontier created "sections" in America, sections that reflected the uniqueness of each of the frontier lands: the middle west, the southwest, the northwest, and ultimately, the far west, came to reflect the local attitudes of their settlers. These varieties, Turner held, were not bad, but good: they reflected the power of the frontier to bring forth distinctive ideas and values from distinctive environments. American regionalism, spawned by the frontier spirit like the frontier itself, was far removed from the European spirit.

But his federal view of American sectionalism is realistic only in terms of its political judgment; it misses the mark in understanding the psychological as well as the cultural and economic components of human behavior. The frontier certainly did unite its immigrant-participants around a political rallying point; it gave them new civic loyalties. But the very fact that it also gave birth to a growing sectionalism with new and narrower concerns should remind us that psychologically the new American was not much different from his European cousin: sectionalism grows out of human loyalties to a particular cultural expression, a particular economic life style, a particular religious espousal. (The Civil War between the States, for example, was not caused so much because of political misunderstanding as by the deep-seated cultural and economic differences between North and South: differences, by the way, which even found their way into the religious life.) Because the immigrant was human, the environmental pull of the frontier could never completely erase the cultural differences that were part of each section and region of America. In the course of time, environment was transcended by culture: by a regionalism that was the product of the combined weight of economic factors and ethnic awareness. The life of the frontier came to be influenced as much by the Old-World cultures brought by those who came to it as Turner believed it had influenced them.

Yet by the mid-nineteenth century this mighty phenomenon, the Protestant frontier spirit, was already in decline, and with its gradual demise, Protestantism "graduated" into a respectable middle-class religion, split into contending denominations. Thus, when Turner was writing his interpretation of American character and purpose, the older frontier spirit was all but dead. Romanticist that he was, he seemed to be calling his compatriots back to the "real America," back to the spirit of the old frontier. He perhaps could not see that the American frontier was already moving elsewhere. Similarly, when contemporary Protestants hark back nostalgically to what they believe is the "real religious spirit" of America, its Protestant Era, it is really to the old frontier days they are returning. Even so urbane a Protestant theologian and historian as Reinhold Niebuhr could claim that "the greatest religious vitality in America developed in the first half of the nineteenth century" and maintained that it "began to wane" after 1850.[4] All these, however, neglect the newer frontiers that were to become even more important in the shaping of the future American character.

That new frontier was the industrialized American city teeming with millions of new immigrants, who brought with them new languages, new cultures, and new religious traditions, thus filling the void created by the passing of the older frontier. In a sense, even as the rugged frontier days had ended, the Anglo-Saxon, Protestant Era in America was over forever.

The day of pluralism was beckoning.

The Ethnic Community. While Turner was intent upon looking the other way, he did seem to have a faint awareness that something new was indeed happening, that a new frontier might yet be rising elsewhere. "The story of the peopling of America has not yet been written," he once lamented, and, in an almost self-critical afterthought, added: "We do not understand ourselves."[5] A generation later, after the giant waves of immigration had virtually inundated the frontier, and the newer immigrants had already built—and their children sometimes partially destroyed—their own ethnic island-communities, another historian was ready to help America understand itself anew. His scholarly gaze was turned in the direction of those immigrants who had settled in America in the course of the hundred years preceding—from 1830 on.

Marcus Lee Hansen believed that "emigration has been connected with as many phases of European life as immigration has of American life."[6] In concentrating principally upon the limited environment of the frontier, he believed that most historians were overlooking an even more important influence on the shaping of American character: the immigrants and their cultural baggage. As a result of Hansen's efforts, a goodly number of his colleagues began to take a new look at America, and what they saw convinced them that the frontier could not be understood apart from the European heritage of the newer immigrants. To be sure, much work remained to be done in analyzing the ways in which the immigrant sought to adjust, accommodate, and translate his heritage to the condition of the New-World community. But the newer emphasis in American historiography since the days of Hansen is unmistakable: Americans remember as well as forget the Old World, and in order to fathom more fully the changing American mind, one must seek to relate the social and cultural "hows" to the psychological "whys" of this process. Indeed, one of the important current axioms of American social history is known as Hansen's Law, after the innovator: "What the son wishes to forget, the grandson wishes to remember." But, of this, more later.

The native American of the 1830s would hardly have agreed, but in historical retrospect it is certain that without the new Irish, English, and German peasants who were then beginning to arrive in large numbers, the frontier could never have become what it was. True, the European newcomers were not frontiersmen, in the American sense. They disliked the primitiveness and loneliness of the wilderness and the backwoods. But this did not deter them from purchasing land from the pioneer farmers who had already cut through with their axes to "create" arable farms.

As they poured into the country in their millions, so millions of native Americans moved westward "in clocklike progression." "When the German comes in, the Yankee goes out." This became a familiar byword, and it would be applied, in succession, to arriving Swedes, Bohemians, and the others still to come. Perhaps, as Hansen sardonically suggests, the American was indeed divinely predestined to inherit the land from sea to sea. "But, as the evidence shows, he was hastened into his inheritance. When an Englishman or a German came with his gold in his hand and asked, 'Will you sell?' there was no hesitation in the reply. He took the gold and went."[7]

Large-scale immigration to the United States in the nineteenth century began to gather momentum in the 1830s, bringing great numbers of Irish, English, and German peasants and laborers to these shores. Prior to and immediately following the Civil War, immigration temporarily subsided, only to climb up again in the 1870's when German and English immigrants were joined en masse by Scandinavian newcomers. East, central, and south Europeans made up the bulk of the third wave of immigrants who began to arrive in the 1880's, and but for the necessary interruption caused by the Great War, they continued to stream in until 1925, when restrictive quotas were enacted into law, putting an end to a century of mass migration. In that time, some thirty-five million had come.

What did these "delayed Pilgrims" mean to America, and what did America mean to them?

Politically, they were secure in their new home; they enjoyed political rights and privileges never dreamed of in Europe. Nor did political assimilation and adaptation take them very long to achieve. The leader of a Jewish workers' association could boldly declare in New York, at its founding conference in 1890: "We have no Jewish question in America. The only question we recognize is the question of how to prevent the emergence of 'Jewish questions' here." And this political judgment after only scant decades of Jewish proletarian settlement in America. So it was with the other immigrant groups; in purely political terms they were 100 per cent American and stood in fear of their rights before no man. Occasionally, petulant and aggressive antiforeign nativist movements arose. But they were far removed from the mainstreams of American political life, and after short lives expired.

It is instructive to understand why these political threats failed and why the mass of the immigrants had so quickly accommodated to American political democracy. The fierce egalitarianism of the frontier had disposed nineteenth-century Americans to an almost naïve faith that any man who came to the United States and lived here was easily capable of exercising the rights of American citizenship. (Indeed, in some states citizenship had not yet been made a prerequisite for voting.) There was about this frontier mentality an air of patriotic confidence: mere exposure to America could quickly transform a man into a democratic and free American whose constitutionally guaranteed rights were sacred and inviolate. It was this political openness on the part of the native population that rapidly created a feeling of reciprocity on the part of the newcomers. They became passionately loyal to, and often deeply involved in, the American political system. Clearly, they reacted so positively because, in terms of their political status, they were received so positively.

But in other realms, in the inside world of their private lives, things went much less smoothly for them. The offer of political equality was a public gift, a bonus given by the world outside. But could they trade in their own interior world, their accumulated patterns of belief and behavior—their whole life-style—merely for the right to vote, a right they did not even have to fight for? Migration to America had given them new rights but it could not easily erase a lifetime of old habits. Their language, their style of thought, their worship of God, were too precious to give up—without fierce defense. It was their own American-born children's alienation from their parents that reflected the triple chasm that isolated the immigrant: now he was separated and estranged from the old world, from American cultural life, and even from his future—his very own children!

Nor were the children secure. Often they were beset by the acute conflict between the natural desire to look up to their parents and the social shame they felt for the exposure of their different ways and their uncertainties and unseemliness in a strange land. It was the foreignness of their parents, they believed, that stood in the way of their own "at-homeness" in America. Now, they too felt estranged; they were alienated from both the old *and* the new worlds. And this insecurity, this morbid sense of alienation, as we shall see, would even be communicated to their children. But this later generation of Americans, spurred by a quest for an at-homeness of a very different kind, would be willing to seek out the meaning of the old ways—ways their own parents never knew—instead of turning their backs on them. The children of the immigrants wanted nothing more than to feel "at home" in America. But the grandchildren *were* Americans. By recalling and recapturing the older ways their parents had forgotten, they would try to fulfill a need their parents never understood: the need to feel at home in the universe.

Their immigrant grandparents had known this cosmic need, too, and when they expended supreme efforts to maintain unbroken cultural continuities with the world they had left behind, they endowed their enterprise with universal meanings. Their admittedly national or ethnic traditions were now elevated to religious and spiritual heights they may never have reached in the natural habitats of the older environment. In spite of the many obstacles of an indifferent or even hostile environment, to serve as willing conduits for the uninterrupted flow of ancestral ways gave their lives profound meaning. It provided the immigrants with a spiritual awareness of their own "courage to be" not unlike the moral power with which the "conquest of the wilderness" had endowed the earlier frontiersmen.

The preservation of their native tongues also served as an important force in the formation of their personal and group identities. Some foreign groups tended to become even more language-conscious in America than before. In 1919, a survey taken of Russian immigrants reported that "out of 312 correspondents only 16 have regularly read newspapers in Russia" while "in America all of them are subscribers or readers of Russian newspapers." In the new world many became regular readers of their foreign-language papers while "at home they used news-papers as cigarette papers."[8] Indeed, it was in America, not in Europe, that some immigrants such as the Lithuanians had established a news-paper in their own language, for the very first time in their history.

Language was not only a protective weapon against the loss of personal identity in the larger American environment, but it also served as a bridge that united the many villagers who came from the different regions of the same European "country." To be sure, by the end of the nineteenth century nationalism had become deeply rooted in the Old World, yet many of these immigrants who had come to America did not come only as Germans, Italians, or Czechs but also as Bavarians, Sicilians, or Bohemians. While in the old country, many of those who left had rarely pictured themselves in anything more than local or regional terms. (If, in their own minds, they had been nationalists or even nationals, they would probably have never emigrated.) But in America they identified their longing for the ways of their Old-World culture with the nationalism of their former "countries," not with the village life of their separate regions. It was the common language they shared with other European immigrants from their "own country" that served to cement their ties to one another. Language thus gave them more than a connection to their personal past, more than a personal identity. It became the bond that united them into cohesive social units bearing a proud group identity. Thus it was that through language something new was born—in America, not Europe—"the ethnic group."[9] And the ethnic group, in turn, became a profound influence in their lives, and in the life of America. Class and social structure, religious and cultural forms, political and economic choices—all these, and more, were for a long time dictated and governed by the prevailing attitudes of these ethnic communities.

In addition to foreign language newspapers, theaters, cultural societies, and mutual-aid associations, the special schools established by these immigrants in the larger communities helped to foster "ethnic consciousness" in their children. Some went to great expense and built their own autonomous schools where they sent their often reluctant and disgruntled youngsters to learn the language and traditions the parents cherished. The German immigrants, for example, were often so ardent in their desire to transmit their own language and customs that they petitioned state legislatures to allow the teaching of German to their children. When such efforts failed they even sought, in 1836, to establish a "Deutschheim" in western Pennsylvania: a separate settlement that would serve as a center for the promotion of German cultural interests, with their own schools, libraries, and societies. But this attempt to establish a "new Germany" failed, as did later efforts to found their own separate cultural enclaves in the states of Missouri, Texas, and Wisconsin. What remained, then, was to build their own private and parochial German language schools. But the pull of the public school was strong and German children, like all other children of immigrants, were tugging away from Europe and in the direction of America.

But by far the most significant institution in the life of the ethnic community was the ethnic church and synagogue founded in America. Although many immigrants shared a common religious affiliation with older settlers, they insisted on building their own churches and synagogues—here too, at great expense for impecunious recent arrivals. But these institutions were not only places of worship: they were a piece of the old patrimony in the New World. In addition to religious worship and education, they embodied a whole community of needs. Familiar language, culture, and customs—even the popular societies for mutal aid and social welfare—were intertwined with religious life. More than all their other institutions or activities, participation in the ethnic church life afforded the immigrant community a visible, vital, and accessible link to the Old World within the reach of the New. To remain "true to the faith" thus meant more than being "religious." When immigrant parents harbored this wish for their children they really meant that they hoped that their American offspring would still be "good Poles," "good Germans," "good Italians," or "good Jews."

As early as 1852, a Catholic missionary priest in the diocese of Milwaukee, Wisconsin, lamented to his archbishop in Vienna that "German Catholic schools are a crying need in this country, because German children, if Anglicized, by some strange fate, generally become alienated from Catholic life." But, he went on to say, "Irish children, if well instructed by their priest in any English catechism generally are saved to the Catholic faith."[10] This same language problem also helped to make "religion" unpalatable for many children of pious east-European Jewish immigrants, now the second generation in America. They were seeking the New not the Old World. They had very little to remember, and what they did remember they wanted to forget. In their eyes, "religion" was a reactionary force forestalling and hindering them from "Americanism" by sheltering an immigrant heritage they were anxious to cast aside. Religion, many of them said, was really not necessary in America; they meant to say that they did not want to remain identified with the foreignness which the piety of their immigrant parents seemed to suggest. They longed for the victory of the general over the particular. They wanted to be "Anglo-Saxons," and like the Germans, but unlike the Irish—or the Scots and the English—a foreign language was an impediment even to their faith.

In addition, as we shall soon note in greater detail, there were those Jewish immigrants who brought with them from east Europe a strong antagonism to the religious way of life. They were already socialists or anarchists in Russia, and in America, where they were freer to federate along these political lines, they struck out militantly against Judaism and its religious teachings. In place of rabbinic and ritual culture they seized upon the Yiddish language and literature as the vehicle for their Jewishness. But, on both counts, their second-generation children were less rabid than these revolutionary parents: they were neither anarchists, nor were they ardent and zealous pursuers of Yiddish culture. The language and the culture of many of these ethnic communities withered as the second generation refused to make them part of its life. And when the parents died, their language and their culture were often interred with them. But in spite of themselves, this was not the end of the matter among the Jews. For even after the demise of the language and culture of their immigrant parents, curiously, it was their religion—not their irreligion—that lived on.

But the children did not come to know this until much later—not until they had children who would remind them. What is more: the surprising "fever of ethnicity" that would later overtake the country—beginning with the late 1960s—would also lead to something even more unexpected among many of the great-grandchildren. It was they who spurred the dynamic drive toward the new and resurgent identity which then began to pervade the lives of a significant number of American Jews.

NOTES

1. See Stuart E. Rosenberg, *The Bible Is for You* (New York: David McKay and Co., 1961), pp. 40f.

2. Reinhold Niebuhr, *The Irony of American History* (New York: Charles Scribner's Sons, 1952), pp. 24f.

3. Abraham Cahan, editor of the *Jewish Daily Forward,* quoted by Ronald Sanders, "The Jewish Daily Forward," in *Midstream,* December, 1962, p. 86.

4. Reinhold Niebuhr, "The Impact of Protestantism Today," in *The Atlantic Monthly,* February, 1948.

5. Quoted in Edward N. Saveth, "The Immigrant in American History," in *Commentary,* August, 1946. Saveth's analysis sheds fine light on the changing spirit of American historiography.

6. *Ibid.*

7. Marcus Lee Hansen, *The Immigrant in American History* (Cambridge: Harvard University Press, 1940), p. 76.

8. See Robert E. Park, *The Immigrant Press and Its Control* (New York: 1922) pp. 7–9 (article by Mark Villchur in *Russkoye Slovo,* New York Russian paper, dated June 10, 1919).

9. The Erse revival (Gaelic) was begun in Boston. The nation of Czechoslovakia was launched at a meeting held in Pittsburgh. For a perceptive description of this American phenomenon, see Nathan Glazer, "America's Ethnic Pattern" in *Commentary,* April, 1953, pp. 401–408.

10. Quoted in John A. Hawgood, *The Tragedy of German-America* (New York: G. P. Putnam's Sons, 1940), p. 40.

CHAPTER III

Recent National Moods

WHEN WORLD WAR II ENDED, RETURNING SERVICEMEN CAME HOME TO find, and to continue to build, an America different from that they had left. Pent-up desires for new jobs, new homes, new cars, new leisure time—for virtually everything new—were suddenly and furiously released. Industrial America, poignantly conscious of the pivotal role of the new "consumers," tooled up frantically to meet the rocketing material demands of the citizenry. The resultant step-up in automation not only helped to mass-produce the new abundance, it also helped to fashion a new American, and a new style of life in America.

Beginning with those recent decades, the American accent has been on bigness. The mass-production mentality impetuously burst the seams of the economic world and rapidly invaded realms previously untouched. It played havoc with both the private and the public sectors of life: virtually industrialized, religion, education, and culture became "big business," as did government and leisure-time activities. America, in David Riesman's phrase, became "other-directed." Few, indeed, could resist the anonymous yet willful dictates of "the lonely crowd."

As accredited members of that crowd, Americans made the will to conform to its rules and tastes into the latter day surrogate of their earlier conscience. Even their Superego was now traded in exchange for a homogenized, coast-to-coast character structure. Personal submission to an impersonal "popular consensus" encouraged new morality-and-habit patterns. A "Gallup Poll ethic" was fashioned: if everybody was doing it, why not you?

This "new look" in the American character coincided with the coming of age of many third-generation Americans whose grandparents had been part of the immigrant tidal waves that began in the 1880's. Twenty years before the G. I.'s came marching home, immigrants had stopped coming in appreciable numbers because of the restrictive legislation that came into force in 1925. The flooding of America by those immigrants had decisively transformed the country from a rural to an urban civilization in little more than half a century. The cities they had helped to fashion teemed with a life of variety and diversity. Each ethnic community continued to add new cultural colors and cosmopolitan flavors to the aggregate. The heterogeneous character of the American city, product of immigrant diversity, gave urban life a frontier spirit and strength that could resist any aimless drift to conformity, to sameness of type. The economic struggles of these new groups also tended to give them a consciousness of kind, an awareness of their separateness from the older, settled population.

By 1945, however, many of these factors were passé. It soon became apparent to Americans that the old slogans and questions had been by-passed. Now, more and more people—the rich and poor alike—were really middle class. With only quantitative, not qualitative differences, they were living alike, eating alike, relaxing alike, dressing alike—and inevitably, thinking, reading, and speaking alike. Yet, great debates had taken place in the earlier decades of the twentieth century regarding the future character of the evolving American. Protagonists on opposing sides of the question were locked in profound ideological battle. On one side stood those who had espoused the cause of the "melting pot"; on the other were the supporters of "cultural pluralism." The more popular of the two was the idea of the "melting pot." This phrase is now so organically part of American speech that few remember that it was first introduced by the British Jewish author and dramatist, Israel Zangwill, whose play, "The Melting Pot," was performed in New York in 1908. His hero, David, cries out: "America is God's crucible, the great Melting Pot, where all the races of Europe are melting and re-forming! . . . A fig for your feuds and vendettas! Germans and Frenchmen, Irishmen and Englishmen, Jews and Russians—into the Crucible with you all! God is making the American."[1]

Some of the immigrants, particularly those who wished to counter the movement—already looming on the horizon—calling for exclusionist immigration policies, seized upon the "melting pot" as some insurance policy guaranteed to protect a foreignness that would soon be obliterated. "Americanization" programs were widely instituted. They were aimed not only at teaching the foreign-born the new language, but were principally geared to fitting them out, psychologically and temperamentally, in the new and precious garments of Americanism.

But with the advent of World War I, Americans awoke to discover that the "melting pot" was a pot in which nothing seemed to melt. Too many of the immigrants seemed still to be Europeans, not Americans, in their active espousal of the cause of one warring camp or the other in the battle then dividing the European continent. To many of the older Americans, it seemed that the foreign-born had merely transplanted their European rivalries to the soil of their country. Even liberal-minded men such as President Woodrow Wilson, who sincerely believed in national self-determination for the minority nationalities in Europe, cautioned against the importation of such ideas to America. Here, he admonished the newcomers, any form of "hyphenated Americanism" must be discarded as a divisive force that threatened the integrity of the

American people. Ominously, the more illiberal, "nativist" groups were gripped by an almost-hysterical fear of foreignness that bordered on racism. They firmly believed in the purity of what they saw as a fixed *American type,* and they warned against being over-run by strangers who were bent on "diluting" America. As a result, immigrants were repeatedly cautioned: they were now officially urged not to remember, but to forget.

Until the eve of the First World War, "America as a melting pot" had thus been the dominant national motif. It was only afterwards that this view of the new world as a continuous fusion of the disparate and surpassed elements of the old, into a single American nationality was finally challenged. In the eyes of the new ideologists of pluralism the "melting pot" was the enemy of democracy, and their philosophy represented a revolutionary departure from the older, conventional ways of thinking about America. Indeed, those who spearheaded this new and challenging analysis of the American national character regarded pluralism as the necessary cultural base for political democracy. Anything less, they contended, would be stifling to minorities—as in Europe—whereas the "American dream" called for a revolutionary understanding of grass-roots democracy as a loose federation of autonomous, self-realizing "nationalities." It should not be altogether surprising that it was a Jewish thinker, Horace M. Kallen, who was the first proponent of the idea that "democracy involves not the elimination of differences but the perfection and conservation of differences." Dr. Kallen, ironically, argued from the very texts supplied by Wilson and others like him who stood opposed to the cultural tyranny imposed by European rulers upon their own minorities. Would America follow the Czar who was forcibly Russifying the Poles, Finns, Jews, and other minorities of his Empire, or the Kaiser who, similarly, was ruthlessly Germanizing the Danes, the French, and the Poles in his?

America is different, he argued, and if it could not constitutionally grant its minorities political nationality rights, as was to be done in a liberated Europe, it should, at the very least, be hospitable to the diverse cultural claims of its heterogeneous citizenry. American democracy, he maintained, would not be harmed, but advanced, by its espousal of what he called "cultural pluralism." The hyphens between such labels as "German-Americans" or "Italian-Americans" were not signs of subtraction, but of addition. They did not divide: they united America!

So much for the theories. But what was actually to happen to the ethnic patterns in the years ahead? And which of the two suggested styles of cultural accommodation to America would actually be followed in the years to come?

As it turns out, neither of the proposals was to become the practiced way of America. True to its pragmatic, non-ideological nature, America chose in the ensuing years to halt between these two theoretical extremes. In practice, Americans borrowed from both—the melting pot idea and cultural pluralism—and, *mirabile dictu,* before very long the threads of the two polar positions were tightly woven into a close, coordinated pattern in the gossamer of America. At least until the end of the 1950s.

It was in that decade, especially during the Eisenhower years, when many Americans began talking about a "return to religion." What they actually were observing was not so much a religious revival, but a vast explosion of church and synagogue building, caused principally by the rapid growth of suburban communities then being located on the rim of America's metropolitan centers. It was intimately connected to the new "baby boom" that followed World War II and the consumerism that came in its wake, during those affluent years. It was not religious fervor but "religious consumerism" those observers really saw—in the guise of a new generation of "belongers," not of "believers." Popular theologians like Will Herberg, who was more of a sociologist than a religious thinker, offered religious descriptions of America which gave the older idea of cultural pluralism temporary shelter among the church and synagogue communities. For even Herberg was ready to concede that ethnic groups eventually lose their separate identities as a result of the tremendous impact of the homogenizing forces built into non-ideological America.

Three melting pots, to borrow a phrase made popular by Herberg, had emerged. These are the three major American religious communities: Protestant, Catholic, and Jewish. But what Herberg overlooked is a fourth "pot," in fact, the catalyst for the other three, which is the spirit of democratic, humanistic secularism. That fourth pot is fed by sources very deep in the American spirit and it continues to long for the triumph of the general cause over the particular and the sectional.

The triple melting pot supposedly represented by the three major religious communities was, in effect, a "pot" in which the older idea of cultural pluralism survived in the new guise of religious pluralism. But the fourth pot, the catalyst that really influenced and invaded the other three, still retained a sometimes invisible identity. It turned out to be nothing less than the old melting pot in which all differences are to be transcended in a great commonalty, the particular melding with the general.

How did these intriguing developments come about?

To begin with, the fundamental constitutional arrangement that separated church from state had made religion in America, from the days of the Revolution, a private rather than a public concern. The Deistic framers of the Constitution knew the European situation very well and, disdaining the idea of an established church, determined that this condition should never take hold here. Thereafter, America was destined to remain officially indifferent to the religious—or unreligious—choices of its citizens. As a result, far from weakening religious life, this situation helped to protect it from the incursions and encroachments of government, as well as from those forces which sought to divest the new immigrants of their Old World trappings. On one hand, the immigrant may have been expected and encouraged by public opinion to merge his national cultural and political will with the general population. Yet, on the other hand, acculturation to the mores of America could be undertaken without guilt; or the immigrant who wished, could retain his own heritage at will. Never was it even remotely expected that he change his religion and join the "right church." Religion was his own affair, not a public matter. This was one of America's distinguishing hallmarks, as one of the newest of nations which, unlike Europe, remained unencumbered by a medieval past.

This built-in toleration of religious pluralism did not always square, as we have already seen, with the cultural monism called for by advocates of the melting pot. But the immigrant slipped through the horns of the dilemma by pouring the ethnic content of his culture into the vessels of his religious life. This almost unconscious transference actually made him believe—and the proponents of the melting pot, as well—that he had indeed shed the old culture and accepted the new. But no such thing really happened: the churches and synagogues of the immigrant were simply made the bearers of the old ethnic traditions. Their language, literature, schools, theaters, and newspapers may have passed away, but the legacy and influence of these precious assets were transferred to the halls of church and synagogue.

Thus, the religiously plural triple melting pot, the Protestant, Catholic, and Jewish communities, have often served as the agents of the cultural pluralism of America. But in the process of ingesting and absorbing cultures primarily secular into their institutional life, the American religious communities sometimes seem to have lost more than they have gained: they appear, too often, more secular-minded than religiously oriented. These newly acquired secular impulses within the contemporary religious communities are further strengthened by that older, unforsaken hope, a hope whose history stretches back to the moods of the Deistic Founding Fathers themselves. For the last two hundred years there always have been Americans who believed that the humanistic elements of Democracy can serve as a spiritual ideal sufficient to unite all Americans in a common quest.

Paradoxically, this unofficial secular religion, which might be called the "Religion of Democracy," is in many respects more powerful and significant than the three "official" partners of the triple melting pot. Its power and significance derive from the fact that it acts as a catalyst upon each of the three pots. It has successfully urged upon all three its glittering view that although religious differences in America are socially and culturally acceptable, the spirit of democracy is enhanced when stress is placed upon the similarities, not the differences between the religions. This double irony, whereby the melting pot preserves cultural pluralism in the name of religion, and where, moreover, each of the three religious melting pots is, in effect, controlled by a Fourth Force from without, is pithily summarized in this cryptic comment of Arthur Mann: "What the Deists hoped to achieve without a church has in large measure come to pass in the land of many churches. Indeed, the idea that religion is handmaiden to democracy has made such headway that American Catholicism, American Protestantism, and American Judaism appear like parallel shoots of a common stock."[2]

It is true that individual Christians in high or low station may nevertheless continue to think of America as a "Christian country," and by this they usually mean a Protestant country. The facts of contemporary American life, however, are otherwise. To be sure, America in federal law was never a "Christian nation." But in the light of social realities the atmosphere of American life, not only in the Puritan communities, on the frontier, and in rural areas, but also in the early twentieth-century cities, was Christian in everything but law. The observations of the French historian, de Tocqueville, were confirmed fifty years later, in the views of the learned British visitor, James Bryce: "Christianity is in fact understood to be, though not the legally established religion, yet the national religion. . . . [Americans] deem the general acceptance of Christianity to be one of the main sources of their national prosperity, and their nation as a special object of the Divine favor."[3] But as a result of the leveling influences of the new urban-suburban values, some of which have been described earlier, there was by the mid-century a "new shape" to American religion, as with many other realms of the national character. It would later be called "civil religion."[4]

This new shape of American religion, the worship of "religion-in-general" in the name and even the forms of the three separate religious communities, went unnoticed by many. But in what may yet become a classical analysis of this relatively recent development, an editor of *The Christian Century*, Martin E. Marty, radically came to grips with it. Like many other Protestants, his nostalgia urged him to remember that the earlier America was built on the models of Protestant pioneering. Yet he boldly recognized that we had now reached the "post-Protestant era" in American life. We are cautioned to discard the notions that rural, Midwestern Protestants or the few remaining pockets of the Anglo-American religious tradition are a true reflection of America as a whole. As a thoughtful Protestant, he would remind his co-religionists of the special meaning of their own religious heritage. Yet, the "new shape," he suggested, seems here to stay. Everything he said led to the conclusion that, in a fundamental sense, each of the three religious groups could be seen as constituting either co-equal majorities or co-equal minorities. Marty apparently assumed the latter to be true, for he was convinced that the secularist fourth pot, the Religion of Democracy, had achieved the upper hand over the other three. He writes:

> The spokesmen of the "Religion of Democracy" school are reaching for and appropriating an authentic parcel of the American past. They are more accurate in their reading of the founding fathers than are the unthinking Christians who try to make Protestants out of them and who try to theologize all the basic documents of our national history on Christian lines. They are taking aspects of a consensus which the "three great faiths" support and elevating them to ultimacy.[5]

Marty concluded, however, that all three faiths were suffering basic insecurities and inner tensions as a result. He noted "the insecurity of Protestantism as it recognizes the *fait accompli* of its new 'minority status'; the minority complex with quasi-majority responsibility of Roman Catholicism; the quest for definition by Judaism; and the confusion of all three in the presence of the secular, national, natural, humanistic, religion of democracy."[6]

The triumph of the secular position may indeed be the basic cause for the failure of the so-called religious successes of the 1950's to achieve a real religious revival. Despite mammoth organizational achievements of the three religious communities, the new buildings and sprawling religious "plants," the outward appearances seemed to be primarily a reflection of the Americanization patterns of the third generation under the approved auspices of the triple melting pot. There can be no doubt that for many members of that generation churches and synagogues performed the same function as did ethnic clubs and associations for their grandparents. Many joined church or synagogue, not as a sign of their religious living, but as a symbol of appropriate religious *belonging.* Nevertheless, while the ethnic church had lost its place in America, what it had lost in ethnic content it more than made up in new recruits from the third generation, whose "Americanized" parents had wanted no part of the immigrant church their own parents had founded.

Yet, despite these anomalies, there were other signs on the horizon not even the most skeptical could ignore. The third generation, if we recall Hansen's description, was also in search of a heritage; it wanted to retrieve what the second generation was anxious to discard; it wanted to remember. Why, in spite of the nihilistic call of the wild, assorted varieties of beatniks, were so many others of that generation interested in the possibilities of a "return"?

There are surely many reasons and subreasons for this, a detailed analysis of which would take us far beyond the scope of this volume. Here, we can only hark back briefly to the urban-suburban values created by the "new consumer" of the postwar years. His success striving, his status symbols, his will to conform to other-direction, his shift from the rural world to the city, and then again to the suburbs—all these rapid changes had left him with a basic feeling of insecurity. These dramatic changes deposited insecurity in American hearts primarily because they led the average man to experience, in spite of growing affluence, a gnawing sense of powerlessness in directing his own life and the life of his family.

In such a situation it is not unusual that, in some circles at least, there was a desire to achieve greater personal stability. It was this desire that led some to seek to re-examine the meaning of human life and the significance of human existence. Secular in outer spirit and public activity, there were yet those whose middle-class, urban-suburban insecurities led to open windows on the spiritual worlds their own parents had passed by. They were Americans; but this, many felt, was no longer enough. In the classical religions and in the religious traditions that had nurtured older worlds for so long a time, some began seeking the answers to their insistent, human questions. Religious existentialism came into vogue; many were seeking to resolve the "absurdities" and the "*angst*" with which their wordly successes, they feared, had loaded them down.

So it was that the "return to religion" of the 1950s did become something more than a "religious edifice complex." But it was not powered by a rediscovery of ethnic roots—*that, for Jews at least, would come a decade or more later.* It was a search for selfhood in a struggle against anomie— "meaningfulness," "self-realization," and "commitment" became the new religious code words. Many Americans, bored by their middle-class "pleasures," now thought they could find a cure for their malaise in religious styles and traditions that had weathered earlier storms of history. Yet, it was not principally a group identity they were seeking to reinforce by re-entering the religious institutions of their ancestors. It was, rather, their very own *personal identity* that was at the heart of their search. Those religious stirrings of the 1950s, where they did exist, were essentially private searches taking place in the public domain. They represented, in effect, a reassertion of personalism and individualism in the form of institutional religious affiliation. In fact, most of these "seekers" were clearly in retreat from loyalty to "mere" ethnic groups. Their brand of religion, they said, had to transcend culture, even their own. Indeed, they contended, it was the folk culture—the life of a dominating ethnic group—which had depersonalized, trapped, and thus victimized them, in the first place.

It so happened that they were, in any case, coming into churches in an America where the ethnic elements had been increasingly absorbed by the religious content. But if not for all Jews, then for Judaism as a religious system, there was the danger that in such an America, it could become estranged from its own historical nature. After all, it was not the synagogue *per se* that had carried the Jewish people through history, but the organic Jewish community which had, in fact, kept the synagogue alive. Unlike Christianity, Judaism is a religion of a specific people—the Jewish people. Much of its religious culture, custom, and tradition is interwoven with the national history of the Jews. Judaism is not a church with a body of doctrine and a single system of theology: it is, in effect, the national, religious civilization of a corporate, covenantal community—the Jewish people. In the 1950s, ironically, the strengthening of the synagogue was often accompanied by a diminution of one's ties to the larger Jewish community.

This paradox is understandable only if one realizes that the new Jewish identity which began to emerge only a decade and more later—based both on the centrality of the state of Israel as well as on a reawakened awareness of the Holocaust's devastating implications for the future of *all* Jews, America's included—was still not deeply engrained in the collective psyche of the community in the 1950s. It is a remarkable, if lamentable, fact of American Jewish life: the two most overpowering events in modern Jewish history, the slaughter by Hitler of six million European Jews and the establishment of Israel in 1948, did not become crucial driving forces in Jewish life in America, until the Six Day War in 1967, when most American Jews feared that the surrounding Arab states would make good on their promise "to drive all Israelis into the Sea." One astute observer described what seemed to have been the mood of American Jews during the 1950s, and even later still:

> Vast sums of money were raised for the relief of European Jews and for the establishment of the Jewish state. . . (but) when collections began to fall after 1948, it was in part because of the conflicting demands for money to build local institutions, largely synagogues. . . Those who desired to build synagogues were thus in direct conflict with those who wished to send money overseas to help the survivors of Hitler's massacres and the state was taking hundreds of thousands of them. . . When Israel was established, there was much talk about what this would mean for American Jewry. It was largely an expression of ebullient feelings. What happened after the state was established was that the major Zionist political organization . . . rapidly declined. The establishment of Israel meant little for American Judaism (before 1967) specifically.[7]

The Six Day War changed much of this. Now, American Jews began to identify with the new image of the Jew—one who could turn back five Arab armies in six days—and no longer only with the lamentations and tears that were enshrined in their earlier recollections of the slain six million. Before 1967, American Jews seemed to repress these painful memories; afterwards, the "Holocaust" itself was turned into a challenge to survive. To remember the helpless, martyred dead was now also to vow that it would never happen again. A strong Israel, many American Jews came to feel, was the only guarantor of that. The shame—or unrequited guilt—which had long kept most American Jews from thinking about, or even discussing the Holocaust, was, it seems, suddenly swept away. In near-mystical manner, many of them now came to regard their own future in America as inextricably tied to a stable, secure, and undiminished Israel.

Perhaps the tersest summary of the new mood that began to overtake Jews in North America in 1967 was made by one who later became a leading theologian of the Holocaust, Professor Emil Fackenheim. In 1983, looking back to the events of 1967, he described his own new Jewish identity as a result of this spiritual oddysey:

> For about twenty-five years (before 1967) I . . . held to a definition of Jewish faith in which, systematically, all historical events were considered irrelevant. (But in 1967) I formulated the only statement I ever made that became famous: that there now exists a six hundredth and fourteenth commandment—Jews are forbidden to give Hitler a posthumous victory . . . if we live as if nothing had happened we imply that we are willing to expose our children or their offspring to a second Holocaust—and that would be another way of giving Hitler a posthumous victory . . . I think that I have been rightly understood by *Amcha*—the (whole) Jewish people."[8]

In a word, since 1967, many Jews have transformed private, personal *angst* into anxieties of their own group survival.

But there were other *American* events which came upon the scene about the same time which would make sheer ethnicism—open and unabashed loyalty to one's own minority group—a new, and dominant factor in American life. For Jews, this major turn in American political and cultural life, provided additional reasons for new confidence in their own Jewishness, and unparalleled, positive motivations for the strengthening of their personal ties to all things Jewish—everywhere in the world. America's rather sudden return to ethnicity now made minority status a proud label to bear: indeed, the very idea of a "majority" now came to mean the "sum of all minorities."

Lurking on the horizon, as the 1970s beckoned, was this new "fever of ethnicity" which came to grip most Americans, both inside and outside their religious institutions. "Black Power" became a new trigger for rekindling all sorts of sub-group loyalties, and reassociation with one's own "kinsmen" was no longer regarded as "parochial," or "anti-American": it was the new fashion. It had not only succeeded in rallying passive Negroes—transforming them into militant, "beautiful Blacks"—but it fed new energies into most other ethnic sub-cultures that had lain dormant for decades, or had seemed to have been fully absorbed into the various melting pots of America. "Affirmative action" and various "catch-up" operations, designed to appease or to satisfy vocal and assertive Black demands for a greater economic and political share of the country, now led other minority groups to reconsider their position in this "new America"—with its rapidly changing power alignments, political lobbies, and voting blocs.

For those Jews who had long before cast their lot in support of the "melting pot," those new days were shocking and traumatizing. Good liberals that they were, they had believed, in Jeffersonian fashion, that the rights of the individual were pre-eminent, and that a separate group-life was dispensable—or at least not urgent—so long as the private, inalienable rights of each person were protected and assured. But now, in the mid 1960s, Blacks succeeded in their attacks upon the American Anglo-Saxon Protestant elite, charging them with being anti-democratic by their thwarting of pluralist ideas basic to a land populated by diverse immigrant groups. What is more: "Wasps" now became an epithet of derision—they were regarded as the manipulators and destroyers of every legitimate American minority.[9]

The "dethroning of America"—as the ideal democratic nation—was now under way. James Baldwin asked: "Do I really *want* to be integrated into a burning house?"[10] The obvious answer was not only negative, but went on to suggest, in the words of Stokely Carmichael and Charles Hamilton, that "before a group can enter the open society, it must first close ranks . . . By this we mean that group solidarity is necessary before a group can operate effectively from a bargaining position of strength in a pluralistic society."[11] Their new "politics of liberation" would soon find echoes far beyond their own Black community.

The unwanted, unpopular Vietnam War also produced, at the very same point in time, widespread alienation with the older America, and helped launch still another front on which the battle for minority dissent of almost every variety would now be fought. The older idea of the "melting pot" was angrily cast down, and the validity of a new ethnic and social pluralism—not merely religious diversity, as before—was now boldly asserted. There were some, like Michael Novak, a leading Slovak Catholic intellectual, who trumpeted the new and widely acceptable theme: "The Rise of the Unmeltable Ethnics."[12] In 1972, he wrote, with devastating insight:

> The emergence of "rational" universal values is dysfunctional since it detaches persons from the integration of personality that can be achieved only in historical symbolic communities. The "divisiveness" and free-floating "rage" so prominent in America in the 1960s is one result of the shattering impact of "forced nationalization" upon personality integration. People uncertain of their own identity are not wholly free. They are threatened not only by specific economic and social programs, but also at the very heart of

their identity. The world is mediated to human persons through language and culture, that is, through ethnic belonging.

The function of ethnic belonging is to integrate a person's sense of reality, the stories that tell him how to live, the symbols that move him. These are the matrix in which his conscience receives instruction. By contrast, the American system of individualization and rationalization leaves all but a certain human type profoundly deprived—deprived of initiative and symbolic thickness, unable to function in the nonconnected way demanded by the ethnic symbols of Wasps: individualism, competition, and merely rational interest.[13]

It is of particular interest to note that again and again, in repetition of his theme, Novak used the historical experiences of the Jewish community in the lands of their dispersion as a paradigm for his own vision of "ethnic America." "People, uncertain of their own identity," he took pains to reiterate, "are not wholly free."

Yet, for all his encomia to Jews as a model "ethnic group," who, according to Novak, still served as a shining example of "a people who without governmental or coercively structured economic institutions nourished in their midst strong persons, strong cultural selves," are Jews merely or only another small ethnic group in the larger mosaic of secular, political America? Jewishness alone, as we shall see, never fully comprehended or exhausted all of Judaism. Nor had modern or even ancient teachers believed that the Jewish group experience should be regarded as only an end unto itself. The purpose of Jewish life was grander than mere group survival—or else Jews would have become merely another quaint sect. Judaism was always linked to heroic moral and spiritual visions that transcended self-perpetuation. After all, they were the People of the Book, and even the most particularist or defensive teachers of classical Judaism in antiquity had linked Jewish spiritual life to *world survival*—not only to *Jewish* survival: the "covenant community" was established to serve as a "light unto the nations." While modernist rabbis and teachers may have trained their sights on much smaller targets—on the individual, and the community, not the whole world— neither have they parochialized Judaism by reducing it to being either a small and insular sect, or to the status of a tiny ethnic sub-group. Robert Alter has poignantly suggested that "B'Nai B'Rith bowling leagues, Temple Sisterhood fashion shows, lox-and-bagel breakfasts (are) . . . empty and limiting, a cultivation of clannishness rather than the matrix for the development of a secure and open self."[14]

Despite their own sense of community in America, even the most affirmative Jews had always sought to be regarded as persons in their own right—as "secure and open selves"—and not merely as sectarians or as minuscule ethnics. Indeed, it was this very self-assessment which had impelled impecunious immigrant Jews to come to America, the "golden land," where their children could receive higher education; then, as a result of their own new station and personal merit, they would be able to break down all remaining barriers, quotas, and group restrictions. It was this passionate commitment of American Jews to "meritocracy" that had powered their personal drive toward self-development and improvement. The results of this fundamental belief in the "primacy of the individual"—and not merely in tags or labels denominating them as Jews—have not only produced Nobel Prize winners, but helped change the face of American business, science, arts and letters, and the academy, to mention but a few of the many areas which have benefited from the slow but steady acceptance by the American body politic of Jews, *as individuals*. The commitment of Jews to self-improvement was based on their firm espousal of American democracy as a spiritually oriented system, offering all of its citizens—as private persons, not as members of a particular church, race, or minority—equal rights to enjoy life, liberty, and personal roads to happiness. The individual, both in the classical and the modernist versions of Jewish thought and belief, was not only the vehicle of group life and culture, but always regarded as sacred and unique; a precious creation, whose human needs could never be overlooked or forgotten. For all of Novak's and others' use of Jews as a model for the future America, Jews *did not,* as these writers extravagantly suggest, discard the person in favor of the community; rather, they saw themselves always in balance—as "persons-in-community."

What fate would await them in a changing America, where individualism seemed to have become only a function of group life, and group life appeared destined to be chopped up into endless fractions—the parts becoming more important than the sum of America?

Indeed, as the final quarter of the twentieth century began, nothing less than a vast change in national self-definition was rising to the surface. One by one, earlier and older versions of "Americanism" were being toppled and replaced: melting pots in all their shapes and combinations seemed no longer acceptable. Individualism was not altogether forgotten, but, as Novak had put it, many now believed that "individuals realize themselves, and become whole, only through the group that nourishes their being." The "open society" seemed to consist principally of special minorities jockeying for economic and political position.

To be sure, the "unmeltable ethnics" were increasingly affirmed and not denied, but these now faced a proliferating variety of new and legitimate groups who spoke and behaved as sub-cultures; they not only crossed the lines of the ethnics, but also competed with them. To mention only the most visible: there now were "women's lib" groups; supporters of gay rights; "right to life anti-abortionists"; environmentalists of all stripes; assorted varieties of neo-conservatives; radical right groups, crossing swords with their embattled antagonists, the remnants of Kennedy liberals; and the politically-inspired "Moral Majority," religious fundamentalists in a new guise who now began spreading out from their regional Bible Belt in the South, clear across the country. Liberalism was in disarray and in full retreat in both the Democratic and Republican parties. Everywhere in the land—even in the trade unions—postures could be seen moving from left to center, and from center to the right. In this atmosphere, the mind of America was in a state of vast cultural confusion and ferment, and not unlike other moments of transition in world history, ironical social and cultural paradoxes could be seen co-existing together—often mindlessly and uncritically.

This revival of political conservatism, trumpeting the return to "traditional American values"—the rights of the "private sector," both individual and corporate—over against Big Government and Mass Culture, inevitably rubbed off on religious groups as well. Even among the most liberal Protestant denominations there could now be observed an almost-universal tilt towards religious traditionalism. The short-lived "liberation movement" within the Roman Catholic Church, spawned in the early 1960s by Pope John XXIII's ecumenism, began to recede even in America, where it had been most warmly welcomed not only by lay people but also by the hierarchy.

New life now also entered Orthodox Jewish communities that had been in severe decline in liberal America, generation after generation, as we shall later analyze in greater detail. The return to proud ethnic avowals coupled to the more respectable place now accorded traditionalism in America most keenly benefited the Orthodox. They began to reap an unexpected harvest of rising expectations. To be Orthodox was no longer regarded as "un-American." Rather, it often came to be seen as the fullest, surest way to ensure Jewish survival. Indeed, the "fall and rise of Orthodoxy" also helped to re-ethnicize and re-traditionalize other, more liberal synagogue groups.

For Jews there were also other reasons to "return." After the traumas of the "Six Day War" in Israel in June, 1967, the clarion, antagonistic calls of an assortment of Black leaders and the liberal-left were perceived by them as warning signals of a new order aborning in "democratic America." They, too, were about to "close ranks"—and reaffirm their own minority status as "beautiful"—as they faced the eruption of the "new pluralism" on all sides. Religion, as a private experience which could provide "meaning" to the individual in search of his personal identity, was now an American Jewish experiment that had run its course. The day of "Jewish individualism" seemed to be over.

Jews could not fail to note that all over America new forms of political expression were being seized upon by other minorities: new strategies were adopted and new choices made. Whereas power and privilege were formerly denied many persons as individuals, they now saw that these could more easily be secured through their own ethnic group. As Daniel Bell put it: "Claims are made on the basis of ascriptive or group identity rather than individual achievement, and this is reinforced by the nature of the political process which emphasizes some group coherence as a means of being effective in that arena. *What takes place, then, is the wedding of status issues to political demands through the ethnic groups.* . . . The politicization of the decisions that affect the communal lives of persons makes the need for group organization more necessary, and ethnic grouping becomes a ready means of demanding group rights or providing defense against other groups."[15] It was a time for engaging in "status politics," a strategy hardly ever before practiced by American Jews.

The late 1960s thus ushered in a new period and a new point of departure: the central theme would be "Jewish self-liberation." Group solidarity—not merely the private rights of Jews as individuals—has since become a throbbing and real personal experience for virtually all American Jews, even for those who had long before tossed their lot into the "melting pot," actively desiring to forget, even to destroy, Jewish memories. Jewish artists, writers, intellectuals and academics, previously in the vanguard of the "privatists" and "universalists," now stomped "home"—militantly and adamantly returning to their own "source," the Jewish community.

Nathan Glazer put it this way:

> . . . Judaism in America had been for a long time not much more than ethnic loyalty on one hand and "liberalism" on the other. If anyone asked Jews what it meant to be a good Jew . . . the chief answers suggested simply support of the liberal view of the world—fairness, nondiscrimination, peace, good works. But the other side of the content of Judaism was ethnicity—support for Israel, for fellow Jews. The amalgam that was Judaism in the 1950s in America began to come apart in the 1960s, and after 1967 it came apart even faster. To be "liberal" in 1967 might mean to support Negro interests against Jewish interests, to support leftists who wished to see Israel destroyed, to oppose American aid to Israel. Liberalism and ethnic loyalty thus came into sharp collision . . . Increasingly Jews chose the ethnic component in the disintegrating amalgam. And in response to 1967, ethnic loyalty became even more paramount as the significant content of Judaism.[16]

Yet things were really not that clear or neat, or for that matter, that simple. Jewish identity and experience is a checkered, intricate, and often, a paradoxical cluster of conflicting goals and desires. Jews have indeed responded to the new America by falling back—as do all the other old or new minorities—on their community and culture. But deep down beneath their surface—inside the collective "Jewish psyche"—to be Jews in America had never merely consisted of the simple sum of ethnic loyalty wedded to a liberal political outlook. To believe this about

Jewish identity is to oversimplify, and to empty out its profound and complex historic content. It is to say of American Jews that their Jewishness really amounts to nothing more than fighting anti-semitism; or that since 1967 they serve only as "American colonials" of Israel, protecting it from its enemies and critics.

Jews do sometimes forget their unique historical identity; but they also remember. Often, like jugglers on a high wire, they do both at the same time. They also do many other paradoxical things: they espouse the common culture of the nation while also countering that culture as severe critics and demythologizers. Having been denied citizenship in all their dispersions, then winning it *only* little more than a century ago in Europe, they are understandably committed to patriotic ways in their new homelands. And in the United States, where citizenship was never an issue, but handed to them as freely as to all other immigrants, they often became super-patriots—which helps explain why they often passionately believed that America was different for them. And there were few prouder progeny of immigrants than America's Jews. Yet, before and after the Six Day War of Israel in 1967, they began to remember the Holocaust in new ways, and these memories served to remind them of their potential aloneness. It was those Holocaust memories which provided them with strong reasons to suspect that it was because of their Judaism and its essential apartness from Christian America—and not their ethnic Jewishness—that they, too, may always be different, singled out as eternal outsiders. These anxious feelings would stay with them despite their acceptance as authentic "ethnics" in a country where ethnicity had come into vogue.

Once it was their own Americanism which caused them to forget their Jewishness. Paradoxically, however, now that ethnic loyalties have become acceptable and popular in the ferment of contemporary America, it is doubtful that Jews will give exclusive loyalty to their ethnic identity alone. Although, in a curious way, ethnicity makes them like all other ethnics, they still face the special problem of the uniqueness and otherness of their Jewish *religious identity.* Whether they confront the "civil religion"—a secularized "American religion-in-general," with its Protestant overtones; or revitalized, traditionalized Christian churches—who are again seeking to become the religious majority—they know that as Jews they can never fully share in the "we group" feelings of most American Christians.

Nevertheless, there is still reason to wonder whether Jews will foster a stronger Judaism, now that they need not—and, apparently, will not—forget their Jewishness. Will they remember that their only uniqueness as "ethnics" is rooted in their ancestral religious tradition? The "new ethnicity"—the extension of the rights of the individual to whole and diverse subgroups—could arise only in a post-ideological era, after all the earlier debates concerning the meaning of democracy had left a previously Anglo-Saxon, monistic America exhausted—and seemingly ready to experiment with the idea of social pluralism. But Jews, it appears, will always seek more than the civic "right to be." They will also need to "philosophize" about themselves—to justify and to find rationales for what they really require: their right to be spiritually different in a society organized by Christians, and buttressed by their churches. Other ethnic Americans may lose interest in religious ideologies—those, after all, are "belongers," in a nation of many different belongers; they are not necessarily "believers" in ethnicity. Jews, however, will still have to seek and find satisfying ideologies and meaningful answers to their own unique ways of *believing*—even if not for their ethnic *belonging*.

Will they succeed in this ongoing, taxing enterprise? Or will their new and revived group identity merely serve to make them behave like most other self-interested American ethnic groups? Will they become intent solely on group survival—concentrating only on fending off attacks which smack of defamation or anti-Semitism, or on zealously guarding the interests of Israel in the American political arena? Will they merely live out their Jewish lives by "reacting" to forces which appear to threaten their group integrity, but without grander cultural and spiritual actions of their own? A deeper probe of older, classical challenges to their survival may help shed light on possible answers.

It is time to let Jewish history speak.

NOTES

1. Israel Zangwill, *The Melting Pot* (New York: Macmillan, 1909), p. 37.

2. Arthur Mann, "Charles Fleischer's Religion of Democracy," in *Commentary*, June, 1954, p. 557.

3. James Bryce, *The American Commonwealth* (Two vols. New York: Commonwealth Publishing Co., 1908), Vol. II, p. 650.

4. Although Robert Bellah is generally credited with having "invented" this apt description (see his "Civil Religion in America," in *Daedalus* 96, (Winter, 1967), Mordecai M. Kaplan had long before described it, labelling it as "folk religion." Martin E. Marty had also pre-dated Bellah, labelling the phenomenon as "civic religion."

5. Martin E. Marty, *The New Shape of American Religion* (New York: Harper, 1959), pp. 84–85.

6. *Ibid.*, p. 87.

7. Nathan Glazer, *American Judaism*, (Second Edition) (Chicago: University of Chicago Press, 1972), pp. 115–16.

8. The Hebrew Bible has a total of 613 commandments. See Emil Fackenheim, "To Mend the World," in *Viewpoints: The Canadian Monthly* (Oct.–Nov., 1983), Toronto, pp. 2–3.

9. See Harold Cruse, *The Crisis of the Negro Intellectual,* New York, 1967, pp. 456–57.

10. James Baldwin, *The Fire Next Time,* New York, 1963, p. 108.

11. Stokely Carmichael and Charles V. Hamilton, *Black Power: The Politics of Liberation in America,* New York 1967; p. 41; p. 57.

12. See Michael Novak, *The Rise of the Unmeltable Ethnics* Macmillan, New York, 1972.

13. Novak, *op. cit.,* pp. 229–30.

14. Robert Alter, "A Fever of Ethnicity," *Commentary,* June, 1972, p. 70.

15. See Daniel Bell, "Ethnicity and Social Change," in *Ethnicity: Theory and Experience,* ed. by Nathan Glazer and Daniel P. Moynihan, (Cambridge: Harvard University Press, 1975), pp. 170–1.

16. Nathan Glazer, *op. cit.,* pp. 181–82.

PART TWO
Modernizing Jewish Culture

CHAPTER IV

The Jewish Melting Pot in America

IF THE EXCERPTS FROM THE FOLLOWING LETTER, WRITTEN BY A DUTCH JEW living in Holland in the eighteenth century, were read aloud in the company of contemporary American Jews, it would likely be met with a mixture of comic disbelief, scornful amazement, and unhappy laughter. But the man who wrote the letter was simply revealing, with straight and serious mien, the accepted and approved mores of his community and all other Jewish communities of Europe. "If a Portuguese Jew in England or Holland [a Sephardi] married a German Jewess [an Ashkenazi]," he wrote in 1763, "he would of course lose all his prerogatives, be no longer reckoned a member of their Synagogue, forfeit all civic and ecclesiastical preferments, be absolutely divorced from the body of the nation and not even buried with his Portuguese brethren."[1] And in tones less harsh or in terms less punitive—only because the religious community no longer possessed such sweeping powers—the same words might have been repeated in the mouths of Ashkenazi or Sephardi Jews all over the world, and even in some parts of America until well into the twentieth century.[2]

The walls erected by the nations of the world preventing Jews from entering into normal social intercourse with them seem wrong enough to the present generation of American Jews. How could Jews themselves have built barriers between one another? Inevitably, however, reflecting the pride that forms the basis of their self-consciousness as American Jews, they would doubtless conclude with some such self-assured claim: This could not happen here—the *American* Jew is different.

The self-same divisive and destructive qualities of regionalism and sectionalism that Turner had decried in the European nation-states were absorbed by the Jews who lived in them. This insularity and self-protectiveness was endemic to all Europe, particularly when the prevailing moods of national preoccupation and local provincialism could be intensified by the limited opportunities for travel and the virtual absence of systems of communication.

The American environment, however, has erased the lines of regional or national demarcation among Jews—lines of divisiveness caused by their Europeanization. If other immigrants who came here wanted to be Americans as well as loyal members of their own ethnic or religious groups, then the Jewish arrivals wanted in addition not only to be

[43]

Americans, and not only Jews, but something new as Jews, "American Jews." At the side of the melting pot which was supposed to make the various immigrant groups into good Americans, there was another melting pot in the Jewish community—one which made the Jews who came here from a host of different European countries and regions into that new phenomenon, "The American Jew."

Nowhere else and in no other time in their history (save perhaps the sociologically similar process in the 1950s and 1960s in the State of Israel) had so many Jews, from so many parts of the world, come together to form a single community. If Puritans had believed that New England would become a New Zion, America in many respects would serve for the Jews as a New Jerusalem. Today, in the Sephardic congregations founded in the seventeenth and eighteenth centuries by the early Dutch Jewish settlers in America, the children of Ashkenazim (German and east-European Jews) predominate. And what is more: if you asked many of them, "What are you?" expecting them to reply "Sephardi" or "Ashkenazi," they would be more likely to answer, "I'm a Democrat!" (In the suburbs, they might say: "I'm a Republican!") Only the American Jew of today could make so egregious an historical *faux pas,* and, even after being corrected, still be proud of it!

How did it happen that America should become the great melting pot of the historic Jewish communities? What happened here to break down the hard and fast lines of communal division among a people whose passionate espousal of a way of life-in-general was fortified by an inbred defensiveness that resulted from fierce regional loyalties cultivated for centuries?

As a result of the widely spaced three-stage immigration pattern—an accidental design of history—Jews in America experienced these regional clashes typical of their European counterparts for only one or two generations, at most. As a result, they came naturally by their awareness as American Jews, and with relatively little internal stress. The first Jews to settle in America were of Sephardic descent, Dutch Jews who traced their lineage to Spanish Jewish forebears. The second Jewish immigration wave, from German-speaking sections of west and central Europe, began long after the Sephardic Jews had been Americanized, 150 to 200 years later. And the mass migration of Jews to America, those from eastern Europe, who, in fact, constituted the overwhelming majority of Jewish settlers here, did not begin coming in large numbers until the 1880's and later, some time after the German Jews had already made a basic adjustment to America, and already considered themselves to be at home as American Jews. Thus, each new group to come to America, for the most part, found Jews here who were no longer Europeans intent upon preserving their sectional heritage, but Americans. This fact contributed immeasurably to the relatively smooth transition each of the later groups underwent en route to their coveted destination: their ultimate arrival as American Jews.

The earliest history of Jewish communal settlement in America is in reality not history, but group biography, for up to the eve of the Revolution they numbered no more than 3,000 souls. And these 3,000 in a total population of more than 3 million were, in turn, scattered throughout the thirteen colonies: about half in the North, the other half below the Mason-Dixon line. Even as late as 1848, when the first of the settlers hailing mostly from Holland were to be joined by new co-religionists from the German-speaking sections of west and central Europe, the total Jewish population of the then United States consisted of about 15,000 people.

In 1654, twenty-three Jews comprising a small group of Sephardic families came to New Amsterdam. Their forebears were expelled from Spain and Portugal in the last decade of the fifteenth century. Now it was their turn, in the new world, to seek a haven from the same Portuguese tyranny which, in the old, had driven their ancestors from the Iberian peninsula to safe refuge in Holland. Before coming to New Amsterdam, these Sephardic Jewish families were part of a prospering Dutch community in Amsterdam: Jews were well treated, and some were even allied to the new-world colonizing programs of the Dutch West India Company. In Amsterdam, the Jews were successful merchants, traders, storekeepers, and artisans. They also had their share of learned and scholarly men. But those who were eventually to leave Holland for the new world would be primarily the traders and petty merchants. They were attracted to venture beyond the seas—like their fellow Dutchmen—by the positive pull of beckoning commercial opportunity, and not impelled, as was so often the case with other Jewish communities elsewhere, by the negative forces of persecution and expulsion. Together with their Dutch compatriots, they came first to the Dutch settlements in South America. But not much time elapsed before they, too, would know what their own immediate ancestors had known. In 1654, the Portuguese reconquered Recife, and Jews ran for their lives. Some returned home, others made their way to Dutch colonies elsewhere, in the Caribbean and in North America.

Arriving in New Amsterdam that year, the first Jewish settlers were met with the hostility of the local Dutch governor, Peter Stuyvesant. With the aid of their own co-religionists back home, some of whom were important shareholders, the directors of the Dutch West India Company finally overruled Stuyvesant and established the right of Jews to settle and to trade. As merchants they found it necessary to seek out new customers and to look for new trading opportunities. Before very long they were dispersed throughout virtually all the colonies, now ruled by England.

The life of these traders was never easy, stable, or settled. There were some, to be sure, who became exceedingly wealthy and lived lordly, squirelike lives, undistinguished in social habit or custom from their Christian counterparts. Most, however, suffered the changing fortunes heir to the pioneering, petty trader. But what they had not acquired in worldly goods they already possessed in the freedoms they enjoyed, in fact and in law. Long before the Declaration of Independence would proclaim all men to be equal, Jews in colonial America were enjoying more liberty than had been known by any other Jewish community since Roman times.

Yet they did not forget their religious traditions. As practical business-minded men, their spiritual life was uncomplicated by theological speculation and unburdened by weighty intellectuality. But everywhere they settled they reproduced the synagogue life they knew in Holland. Soon, Sephardic congregations were to be found in New York, Philadelphia, Savannah, Newport, Richmond, and Charleston. By 1800, however, there were more Ashkenazic Jews in these communities than Sephardic. Not only were members of Amsterdam's Ashkenazic community coming here in increasing numbers, but many groups of individual Ashkenazic Jews—no mass migration, by any means—principally from Württemberg, but also from other German-speaking states, had also come to settle even before the 1800's. But the impact of the new world was already apparent: there was nothing in their behavior here that would even hint at the European divisions described by that letter-writer of 1763. Ashkenazic Jews in early America, unlike their modern American counterparts, knew very well the wall that *should* have divided them from their Sephardic brethren. But that was meaningful only in the old country: here, they were part of the new world, and the class-conscious, aristocratic ways of the old were quickly discarded. They could do what east-European Jews could not do a century later, when they would refuse to join the congregations founded by German-speaking Jews only a generation or two before they had arrived. They mixed freely with the settled Sephardic community and quickly became part of a united Jewish community.

Perhaps the best and most relevant way to understand their unique situation is to compare them not to any community known in the past, nor even to the typical urban American Jewish life of our day. Strange as it may seem—with some obvious exceptions caused by time and place—both their inner life as Jews and the way the external world viewed them parallel very closely the situation of those few Jews who reside today in the small, rural communities of America, and who also comprise but a tiny fraction of the local Christian population.

In the first place, for both groups the mere statistics are crucial. Not only is their total number so very small but, in contrast to the Christian majority with whom they live as intimate neighbors, they virtually do not exist as a community. Nor does the paucity of their number afford them the luxury of subdividing into several organized groups: there can be either one united Jewish effort or none. This dearth of numbers also creates a situation, unique in Jewish history, in which their Christian neighbors see them not as members of an organized group, but as individuals. When one is viewed on his own terms, as a single human being rather than as a reflection of a group stereotype, it becomes exceedingly difficult for group prejudices to take root.

This opportunity for attitudes to be built on the firmer base of face-to-face relations rather than on generalizations formed by abstraction helps people to get to know each other in ways almost impossible in the mass society of a large modern city. As a result, Jews in early America were, by and large, able to dispel certain stereotyped views their neighbors may have held regarding Judaism in general. John Wesley, noted church leader, was unhappy over his apparent religious failures with his fellow Christians in Georgia, but of the Jews he had met there during his 1737 sojourn he could write: "I began learning Spanish, in order to converse with my Jewish parishioners, some of whom seem nearer the mind that was in Christ than many of those who call him Lord." Wesley may have had it in his mind to convert these would-be parishioners to his own faith, but his equation of the "mind that was in Christ" with the mind of Judaism he encountered in these Jews hints at his own surprise at the personal influence the individual Jews he came to know had upon him.

Similarly, Jews living today in rural America often report their success in personally influencing and recasting many of the distorted images of Judaism previously held by their Christian neighbors. And this process often takes place in towns where the Jewish population is so small that it will have either a single synagogue or none. Apparently, the absence of an organized, institutional religious form is far from a hindrance in making Judaism publicly known in a small town. A sociological study of Jews living in the rural communities of New York State with populations under 10,000 noted that 50 per cent of these Jews "designated a Christian person as their closest friend." This fact, plus the customary pattern of informal neighborly visits—Christians and Jews regularly coming into each other's homes—seemed to provide very effective opportunities for reshaping older "Christian images" of Jews and Judaism.

To be sure, in the pre-Darwinian society of colonial America religion was accorded a more vital place in the personal life of most men than is true of contemporary America. It is therefore not unusual, in such a setting, for Jews to retain a fundamental loyalty to their ancestral faith, despite their very small numbers. Occasionally, isolated individuals may have left the fold by converting to Christianity and marrying Christians. But seen from our current frame of reference, one is impressed, not by the number who defected from Judaism, but by the great majority who continued to remain loyal to the faith, despite what amounted to their submersion in a ghettoless, non-Jewish world. Apparently there are in such a community only two live options: either one leaves it or, staying within it, retains strong attachments in spite of his minority status.

Contemporary Jews residing in rural America live, of course, in the same modern world as do all others: a world in which the incursions of naturalism have loosened the authoritarian hold of the traditional religions upon their adherents. Additionally, as we have seen, the secular humanism now so pervasively a part of the general American scene often makes it possible, even for those who are religiously oriented, to regard other religious traditions as acceptable variants of their own. One might therefore expect these rural Jews who have achieved so large a measure of social integration and whose physical remoteness keeps them out of easy reach of the synagogue tradition to kick over their Jewish traces entirely. Some of course do, and even if they do not convert to another religion, will live out their lives in religious indifference and with their Jewish identity barely showing.

Yet, again, as with the colonial Jews, the majority of their modern rural coreligionists maintain deep sentimental attachments to Judaism. Identifying with Judaism, some studies show, seems to play a major role in the attitudes of Jewish parents toward their children. "Small-town Jews, like their urban co-religionists, are anxious for their children to keep the faith and marry Jews. As a result, they send them to Jewish summer camps and, when they are through with high school, encourage them to attend large, metropolitan universities."[3]

By 1825, the numbers of American Jews had more than doubled the 3,000 of colonial days. There were enough Ashkenazim now to allow for the founding of more than the one congregation that had already been functioning as the lone synagogue of many cities for more than a century. Despite this new development, the total Jewish community was still small enough to maintain many of its earlier ways and to preserve its unique American character. The newcomers were quickly absorbed into its patterns, and in very short order adopted America as a suitable homeland for Jews and Judaism.

The promise of the 1848 "Revolutions" was linked to the surging hopes of European national liberation. Increasingly, however, it became clear to many Jews that the spirit of the *Volkerfruehling*—the "springtime of the nations," the banner and rallying call of the Revolution—had bypassed the Jewish quarter. Many Jews in western and central Europe believed that the liberal sparks of the rebellion were extinguished even before the flame of freedom was kindled. In the wake of their political disillusionment, some began to look to America as their best hope for freedom. These were not the adventurers or the lower-class Jewish traders who had filtered into America from Bavaria during the 1820's and the early 1830's. For the most part, they were a better educated, politically oriented group. Their determination to settle in America was based on a rejection of the European system of government coupled to a conscious espousal of the American way. To be sure, the total number of European political refugees who came to America as " '48ers" must not be exaggerated: in all, they probably numbered no more than a few thousand.[4] And as for "Jewish '48ers," research to date has uncovered only a group of twenty-eight men who actually arrived in that year. But while "there is no evidence whatever for the commonly accepted supposition that large numbers [of "Jewish '48ers"] came to the United States," in a profounder sense "practically all German-Jewish immigrants, whether they arrived in 1835 or 1865, came . . . in search of the personal opportunity, economic freedom, and political equality which were denied them in Europe."[5]

Their intellectual spokesmen were riveting attention upon what they felt to be an urgent, pressing need: the mass emigration of the Jews. The almost rhapsodic attachment they felt to America as "the land of promise" found poignant expression in articles, poems, and essays published for circulation in many European communities of German-speaking Jews. One well-known and widely respected poet, Ludwig Kompert of Munchengraetz, called out to them in these ringing, telltale tones:

> God is our witness that we have held our heads ready for every blow, that we have trembled at every frown of our tyrants great and small—until now in the hour that has brought freedom to our land we have no other desire than to flee from this freedom. . . .
>
> To America! . . . It is to . . . America that our longing goes forth!
>
> Be farmers, merchants or craftsmen, peddlers or Congressmen, brokers or vice-presidents of the United States; be cotton planters or sugar refiners. . . . In your adopted fatherland . . . a man is worth what he is, and he is what he does. Before all else, be free—and go to America.[6]

Not all his compatriots agreed. As in so many other times, and in still later days of political peril, many would concur with the thesis but not with the application. He was right as far as America was concerned, but not, some felt, with regard to their fatherland. While Kompert was calling for the emigration of German Jews from western Europe, many of his fellow leaders, strangely unmindful of what was happening at home, were issuing urgent calls for the resettlement of Russia's persecuted Jews! Dr. Zacharias Frankel, Rabbi of the community of Dresden, and a noted scholarly forerunner of Conservative Judaism, wrote: "For the Russian Jews there is one way out: namely, to emigrate and settle under a sky where human rights are recognized by law." Needless to say, Dr. Frankel remained in Germany.

But many thousands did not remain. They began to stream toward America from the German states, Austria, Hungary, and sections of Bohemia. In 1849, the Prague correspondent of Israel's *Herald*—New York's first Jewish weekly—was excitedly reporting the exodus of Jews to America in these glowing and inviting terms:

> It is conspicuous that despite the emancipation, the desire for emigration, especially to North America, increases here from day to day. Hundreds of Bohemians emigrated even this year. The second-class cabins of the boat that is leaving Bremen on April 15 are completely taken by Jews from Prague. The captain is prepared to supply *kosher* food if desired. The number of those from Prague alone who are to emigrate this year is estimated at about four hundred. One can see that there is little faith in the future of Austria. From Hungary, too, a large number is emigrating to America.[7]

Immigration of Jews from the German-speaking states of Europe continued unabated, save for the Civil War period, until the early 1870's. Jews from eastern Europe were also coming during this period, but only in small numbers and not as part of a large-scale immigration movement. In those years, mass emigration was impossible for Russian Jewry since passports were most difficult to obtain, except in exceptional situations. And Rumanian Jewry, although suffering immense disabilities, decided not to undertake a mass exodus. Despite the most extraordinary efforts on the part of the American government to intercede in their behalf, and despite President Ulysses S. Grant's personal interest in their plight, they refused the American offer to accept a large-scale immigration, made directly to them by Benjamin Franklin Peixotto, Grant's Jewish appointee as American Consul-General in Bucharest. In spite of these supreme American efforts on their behalf, and despite the willingness of the Rumanian cabinet to permit their exit to America in large numbers, the leaders of the Rumanian Jewish community, at a special, secret meeting in 1872, unanimously rejected the opportunity to leave, on the grounds that emigration to America would simply discharge the Rumanian government of its political obligation to extend civic rights to its Jewish population. A small number of Rumanian Jews continued to leave for America, but again as individuals, and not as part of large groups. Thus, until the 1880's, the bulk of the nineteenth-century Jewish immigrants were German-speaking Jews whose coming to the new world was linked to their hopes of realizing the dreams of American liberty, to enjoy the democratic way of life of a freedom-loving country.

The largest number of these western-European "German" Jews came to America with very few worldly possessions, and because many had consciously severed their old-world connections, they had few contacts with trading groups in Europe, as had many of the first Sephardi settlers. The long-standing legal tradition preventing Jews from owning or working the land ill equipped them to turn to farming in the new world. Nor could they easily enter into trade since they were without benefit of capital, credit, or commercial connections with European merchants. As a result, large numbers of them placed packs on their backs and roamed the hinterland surrounding their towns, as peddlers. Often, they would peddle in the countryside from Sunday to Thursday, returning home in time for the Sabbath meal with their families, each Friday evening. Saturday, the day of rest, was spent at home and in the synagogue. On the morrow, the week's weary travels would begin again.

Whenever the general population began to move, westward beyond the Appalachians and farther west with the Gold Rush and the building of a continental railway, these German Jewish peddlers were sure to move with it. Soon, some settled in the thriving little towns that sprang up near canal terminals, mining camps, riverboat wharves, or railway depots. There they exchanged their peddler's packs, which had carried their drygoods and general merchandise for so long, for the small shops they now established and where they displayed and sold similar wares. Some of these very shops, particularly in the middle and far west, were the primitive forerunners of many of America's department stores of today. They stand as silent but eloquent testimony of the successful efforts of these commercial pioneers. They had set down deep roots along the path of the nation's expanding frontier.

Oscar Handlin has said: "Once I thought to write a history of the immigrants in America. Then I discovered that the immigrants *were* American history." Close to the heartlands of the new American frontier of the middle and late nineteenth century, these German Jewish traders and merchants were, in fact, Americans, both consciously and unconsciously. Moreover, the fact that most of them dealt directly with the public, native and immigrant, first as peddlers and then as shopkeepers, helped to accelerate any possible lag that may have retarded their rapid acculturation. To be sure, as we have seen, many of them came here despite dire economic circumstances to free themselves of their fears of rampant European nationalism and to adopt free America as their chosen fatherland. In combination, these three factors, the political, psychological, and the economic, were vital elements in the peaceful yet revolutionary changes their Americanization would evoke. Unlike the first two centuries of American Jewish life, where the paucity of Jews had allowed their Americanization to go hand in hand with the old religious ways, the German Jewish community chose to translate its belief that "America was different" into a new way of Jewish life that would conform to that description. If America is different, they seemed to be saying, then surely American Judaism must be different, too.

They did not, however, arrive at this conclusion by shedding their German ties all at once. While they wished to forget the political disabilities of the homeland, they were not willing to forget its cultural riches. In league with fellow Germans of Christian background who were also coming to America in great numbers at this time, they often looked down upon the cultural life they found in America. Germans generally seemed to believe that theirs was a superior culture and they approached this side of American life condescendingly. Indeed, the relative isolation afforded those who settled in the rural areas helped them keep alive their own language and cultural traits for a rather long time. In the cities, too—and most Jews were urban dwellers—the German immigrants usually formed literary associations and cultural societies whose avowed purposes were to maintain vital connections with their old world language and culture. But the culturally centripetal, homogenizing force of city life proved too formidable, and despite their valiant attempts to preserve their language and literature, the efforts of the urban German groups were less successful than those of their rural counterparts. Before long, even their literary associations were bereft of specific German content; unwittingly or consciously, they, too, were caught up and carried away by the sweeping waves of Americanization. The day of ethnic legitimacy had not yet arrived.

Nor did their unique religious accommodation to the American way of life take shape without stringent initial efforts to maintain the older traditions. Two popular misconceptions abound: it is often believed that *all* German Jews adopted Reform; it is also erroneously assumed that German Jewish immigrants imported their "German Reform" religious ways from the home country. In the first instance, it should be noted that many German Jews continued to retain staunch religious loyalties to the tradition and refused to accept the innovations of Reform Judaism. Under the leadership of their gifted rabbi, Dr. Samson Raphael Hirsch, the Jews of Frankfurt broke with the reformers and in 1845 organized the "Religious Society of Israelites," which for many years continued to have a wide following in other parts of Germany as well. It is true, of course, that it was in the German provinces that the first major modern attempts at a reformulation of Jewish religious law had been undertaken by some rabbis, at a series of rabbinical conferences, in the early decades of the nineteenth century. But theirs was an intellectual reworking of Judaism, geared to propositions borrowed from the new "science" of historiography and the findings of scholars in such fields as philology, comparative religion, and Biblical research. They were motivated principally by the desire to make Judaism compatible with the modern temper. Thus, they sought to document their faith that the Jewish religion had developed progressively in the creative periods of the past by producing scholarly proofs that evolutionary change was normative to historical Jewish practice. As occidental men, they sought to remove the oriental mold into which they felt Judaism had been unnecessarily cast, owing to the vagaries of wandering and migration. The universal validity of the Jewish teaching and the Hebrew prophetic message were what they sought to revive. In the service of these ideas, they set about erecting a scholarly monument to their intellectual vitality, which came to be known as the *Wissenschaft des Judentums:* the scientific and scholarly investigation of the history of the Jewish religion.

Generally, however, their new findings had not yet formed the basis for a new or widely accepted religious movement among the Jews of Germany—certainly not by the time that these German Jews were coming to America. To be sure, such rabbis as Abraham Geiger, Samuel Holdheim, and Michael Creizenach were advocating scholarly reasons for religious reforms, but most German Jewish immigrants who came here were, in the main, unaware of this intellectual search, being largely untutored in such matters. For their part, they were not seeking a "science" of Judaism, but a new way to live the old way—a practical Judaism. Their earliest synagogues, in the 1840's and 1850's, were hardly to be distinguished, by their major forms of public worship, either from the orthodoxy of the Sephardic congregations or of the western European synagogues of the period. Slowly, however, as their general cultural patterns became more American and less German, we can note a parallel desire to convert their synagogues into American houses of worship. By the close of the Civil War, at the time when the young, native-born generation was already growing into maturity, most of these congregations succeeded in making two significant changes almost concurrently: the German language, in which the sermon and some few prayers were recited, was dropped; new prayer books were introduced, which substituted modernized versions in English for much of the traditional Hebrew liturgy. These changes served as symbolical as well as concrete evidences of the new *élan:* their synagogue was to reflect neither the European experience they had known nor the ancient land that had cradled Judaism; it was to be neither German nor oriental—but American. To be "American," in the view of many of these pragmatic businessmen, religion, too, had also to be adapted to their ambivalent mood: the wish to forget the past while remembering it.

This mood was at the heart of their religious arguments; their religious debates concerned issues which were geared to the practice of religious forms, not to theoretical or theological speculation. Religious ideology, as such, hardly played a role in these lay-dominated schismatic movements. It was rather a concentration on the external forms—the practice of the public religion of the synagogue—on which they focused their zeal. True to the post-immigration spirit, these same debates would be re-enacted some fifty or sixty years later, when east-European Jews in America would be attempting to meet the religious needs of their nativeborn youngsters in "An American way." They, too, would respond in a similar manner: pragmatically, not ideologically. They seemed blithely to overlook the obvious fact that the form was itself content. But when the first large waves of east-European Jews began coming in the 1880s, immigration from Germany had already come to a halt and the older Germans were now Americans. Many of the things they no longer remembered as Jews, these Jewish newcomers had not yet had the time to forget.

In 1882, the exodus of Jews from east-Europe began. It would not cease until 1925, when restrictive quotas aimed at barring south- and east-Europeans were put into effect. In 1882, the Jewish population of the United States was about a quarter million; today it is close to six million. It is clear that the latter figure would not have been possible were it not for the urge to abandon east-Europe unleashed by the violent pogroms against Russian Jews, beginning in the spring of 1881. One million Jews from all parts of east-Europe came to America, from 1882 until the end of the century. And then, in each year until the outbreak of World War I, almost a hundred thousand new Jewish immigrants poured in, until by the era's end, in 1925, a total of one and a half million had entered America in the century's first quarter.[8]

Looking at this statistical phenomenon in still another way, we may draw the necessary deductions from even these admittedly incomplete figures of the Bureau of the Census: in 1880, there were 270 synagogues in America; in 1890, 533; in 1906, 1,769; and in 1916, 1,901. Statistics—even when they are somewhat incomplete—are often, in themselves, the crucial data. Compared to the sprinkling of Sephardic Jews in the first two hundred years of Jewish settlement in America, and even contrasted with the larger German Jewish group, the east-European Jewish community was clearly destined to become *the* Jewish community of America.

For at least one full generation, or sometimes two, these Jews shared the same pains of immigrant transition—some of which we have already noted—experienced by the other ethnic groups who were also arriving in very large numbers at the same time. But their accommodation to America was more complicated than for the others. In addition to facing up to the national, cultural, and religious patterns of the new country, for the first time they also had to contend with the problems created by *Jewish* pluralism. The established Jewish community was already American in everything but religion, and in the eyes of these east-Europeans, even their religion seemed American, not Jewish.

From their perspective, they were right. As products of the environment of east-Europe, they made up a community whose way of life was intensely Jewish, and in its own way different from any other community in Jewish history.

They traced their Jewish style-of-life back to Talmudic times, believing that their own ways were authentically Jewish because they had wholly appropriated the customs, traditions, ethics, and social habits ordained by the ancient, authoritative rabbinic sages. The Talmudic rabbis, in the Diaspora of Babylonia, had indeed established patterns for Jewish living that were intended to make possible the survival of the Jews as a culture within a culture.

When, in the seventh century, many Jews left Babylonia for North Africa and Spain, Jewish life continued to flourish under Islam, and the Near Eastern and Mediterranean Jewish communities together with the fellow Sephardim in Spain (*Sepharad* means "Spain" in Hebrew) produced a unique intellectual culture in which scientific investigation— spurred by their intimacy with Muslim culture—grew at the side of mysticism, theology, philosophy, and poetry. In that relatively "open society," it was possible for Jews to experience a "Golden Age" of creative cultural growth, until they came upon the evil days of the Inquisition, and in 1492 were expelled from Catholic Spain.

The Ashkenazim, meanwhile (*Ashkenaz* means "Germany" in Hebrew) had been living in western Europe under Christian rule, and their life was one of relative isolation from their neighbors. While the Sephardim were basking in the sun of Moorish culture for almost six hundred years, the Ashkenzim were living in Europe's "Dark Ages." Thus, one looks in vain for worldliness in the Ashkenazic literature of medieval Europe. Cast out from the world of Christianity, they made their domain the world of the Torah and the Talmud; their law, science, art, and philosophy were all part of one fabric: the word of God as revealed to their ancestors at Sinai. The scholars, of course, wrote in Hebrew, the "Holy Tongue." But some time in the late Middle Ages the mass of Ashkenazic Jews absorbed the medieval German language and made it their own, by liberal additions of Hebrew words. This Judeo-German language came to be known as Yiddish, and from those years until only one American generation back, this was the universal *lingua franca* of most Ashkenazi Jews.[9]

In response to the increasing terror inaugurated by the Crusades, the Ashkenazi Jews of western Europe began searching for a new home. They traveled eastward, and by the fifteenth century had already established communities in Poland, and still later throughout most of east-Europe. In Russia, they came upon old Jewish communities they knew nothing about, whose settlement went back to Byzantine days; these were Jews whose brothers and sisters had gone westward to North Africa and then Spain, a thousand years earlier. In Kiev, "mother of Russian cities," a community of Jews from the Middle East had settled even before the eighth century, antedating even the Russians. Ironically, east-Europe became the meeting ground, in the late Middle Ages, of two separate streams of the Diaspora community: one which harked back to those who had come there directly from the Near East through the Black Sea; the other, the newer refugees from western Europe, who now fled eastward. But unlike what was later to transpire in America, the latter group, the Ashkenazim, would not unite with the former, the older community of Sephardim.

In many ways, the Ashkenazim, now settled chiefly in Poland and Russia, made a unique contribution to Jewish history. Of all Jewish communities, before or after, they were the most prolific. Until 1650, the Jews of Europe probably numbered no more than 650,000 out of a total world Jewish population of close to one million. By 1850, however, the number of Jews in the world had climbed to 4,250,000—more Jews than ever before in history! Of these, 3,700,000 were European Jews, most of whom now lived in Russia and Poland. In barely 200 years, these Ashkenazi Jews were largely responsible for multiplying the total number of Jews in the world by almost six times!

But even apart from their unique numerical strength, they succeeded in establishing and crystallizing a cohesive cultural structure that would withstand even the violence of the pogroms of the 1880's. (But not, unhappily, the madness of Hitler.) That structure was enshrined and institutionalized in the life of the Jewish *shtetl*—the small town—of east-Europe. The *shtetl* was often an all-Jewish or predominantly Jewish town enclave set in the midst of a non-Jewish countryside. Its culture often seemed to be totally unaffected by the life-style of the non-Jewish Slavic or Balkan world on the outside. In a remarkably perceptive volume summarizing this way of life, Mark Zborowski and Elizabeth Herzog describe the mind and the essence of the man of the *shtetl:*

> Yiddish means Jewish. . . . To Jews in other parts of the world, Yiddish culture means specifically the culture of Eastern European Jews, and the Yiddish language is the language spoken by this group. . . . To the shtetl folk . . . when they think of Klal Isroel [the world-wide Jewish community], they think of a world-wide shtetl where speech and even thought is in Yiddish.
>
> To the man of the Shtetl, "Jewishness" is "my way of life," in which religion, values, social structure, individual behavior are inextricably blended. It means the way of life as lived among "us," and "us" means the shtetl. There is no conscious rigidity or purism in this, it is merely taken for granted. We are "the" Jews, our way of life is "the" Jewishness, and the word for it is Yiddishkayt.
>
> That word is charged with the joy and pride that are complementary to the "yoke." "It is hard to be a Jew and it is good to be a Jew." The word Yiddishkayt carries all the associations that make it good.[10]

And this way of life, to the man of the *shtetl,* is not subject to the natural historical laws of growth and decay. It will go on forever:

> Whatever question may be raised about the genesis and interpretation of the continuum, a continuity has been maintained through long centuries.

However the tradition may be defined, however its persistence may be explained, whatever future may be predicted for it, it has survived from biblical antiquity to the shtetl.[11]

Thus, when the east-European immigrants from the *shtetl*-community came to America, their Jewish world was not only far removed from the Americanized Jews they now found, but even the "Jewishness" they carried with them was of a profoundly different character from the Judaism these former German Jews had brought here when they first came as immigrants. The "Germany" the latter had known was essentially an ethnically homogeneous society on the verge of becoming a modern national state, possessing but a single nationality. In such a community, Jews obviously regarded themselves as nationals, whose principal divergence from their fellows was one of religion. Like Catholics or Lutherans, they too were potential Germans.

Clearly, the Jews of east-Europe could never feel this way. The *shtetl* came to be regarded, as we have seen, almost as a divinely ordained community, whose way of life was the only proper way for *all* Jews. And their own self-conceptions were bolstered by the political and cultural structures of east-European life, in general. In that part of the world, not the Jews alone constituted a separate nation, but so did many other groups. There, a man's religion, nationality, and culture were inseparably united.

Although they had often regarded the *shtetl* as near-sacred, their attraction to the *goldene medina*—the golden land—called America, was uniformly magnetic: an all-powerful tug had drawn them, from the diverse lands and regions of east Europe, to start life over again in the promising New World. It has been noted that the "element of European Jewish society which we may designate as the *proste* (crude and common Jews) came . . . in very large numbers (to America). Indeed the *proste* came to dominate the Jewish community. Some have contended that America is the revenge of the *proste yidn* upon the *scheine yidn* (the 'beautiful,' or cultured, Jews) . . . Up to 1914 . . . emigration to America . . . was especially attractive to individuals in modest economic circumstances and in relatively modest status positions. It is apparent that many immigrants who came to the United States lacked the strong ideological commitments of those who stayed behind. This was especially true in the area of religious commitment."[12] As a result, it was relatively easy for them to adjust to a world they themselves had chosen. They had come, after all, not to remain impecunious Europeans, but to succeed as Americans.

Yet these east-European Ashkenazim, a diverse and divided lot, continued to constitute and perpetuate what amounted to separate Jewish subcultures in America—at least until the mid-1920s. By and large, they consisted of two camps. The larger, comprised Jews from the Czarist areas who carried with them scorching memories of recent pogroms and persecutions. A smaller number had come from the lands of the Austro-Hungarian Empire—most particularly from the impoverished sections of its Galician Province. By 1925, half of America's four million Jews lived in the great metropolis of New York, most of them on "the Lower East Side." This section of the city was usually their "area of first settlement," and it was divided into two clearly distinct Jewish neighborhoods. Delancey Street served as the Great Divide: Russian Jews and Austro-Hungarians hardly "invaded" each other's territory. As part of the Russian Jewish enclave there were several "satellite" sub-communities: Jews from Lithuania, Rumania, and Poland. The Hungarians and Galicians were divided, much like the Empire itself. Both groups were staunchly loyal to King Franz Joseph, and their younger children were often devotees of Austro-Hungarian culture, with Vienna as its center. The Hungarians, on the other hand, were still intoxicated with Budapest and regarded themselves as Magyar Jews, and, if you believed them, "Magyars were the salt" of all nationality groups in that Empire.

A perceptive observer has described some of the more telling aspects of the uniqueness and particularity of these groups—which had helped keep alive their own sense of self and promoted their mutual apartness as sub-enclaves, at least until a new generation arose in the mid-1920s:

> The Galician, like the others, brought his habits to America. Like all aspiring provincials, he affected courtly manners . . . A Galician of even the most common variety used two kinds of Yiddish, one which set him apart in a manner he did not desire, and one by which he deliberately set himself apart. The first was an idiomatically rich but peculiarly accented daily speech. The other was a kind of high Yiddish, in reality ungrammatical German, which he used in correspondence and in addressing the intelligentsia—physicians, pharmacists, notaries . . .

> The Rumanians, among the Russian satellites . . . had no sense of clan . . . In 1919, they owned 150 restaurants, twenty wine-cellars, and thirty coffee houses in New York City. Most of these were concentrated on the Lower East Side, featured "Rumanian" in their names, and were no doubt responsible for converting the American palate to pastrami, corned beef, horseradish and sour pickles, knishes, blintzes, matzoh balls, and noodles . . .

> . . . The Lithuanians were dispersed inside the Russian quarter where, however, they maintained their own synagogues . . . they were an ascetic, conceited enclave, and made no attempt to pass as Russians, which at any rate would have been difficult because of their characteristically lisping speech . . . The Lithuanian would treat a slice of bread and herring as a full meal, but he would not suffer fools. Even the most common garden variety Litvak could turn out to be a scholar, possessed of quick wits, a stinging tongue, the ability to argue both sides of a case with equal skill, and to invent a third side which he argued even more persuasively. His sons and grandsons became mathematicians, physicists, and professors of law and philosophy . . .

. . . The Poles, who were probably no less numerous than the Russians, suffered from a fragmented collective personality. The several partitions of Poland had left them confused about their speech and sense of place . . . They spoke in accents ranging from Galician to Lithuanian and rejected the Polish label . . . There were many . . . Polish marranos who affected Russian or even Lithuanian accents . . .[13]

Yet, the plural and divisive sub-cultures established by these east Europeans in America began to crumble and wither away by the time their own children were maturing, in the mid-1920s. Drawing them closer, even while they remained separated and distinctive, were the powerful centralizing forces of the Yiddish stage, press, and literary world, which slowly, but steadily, had been bringing them together. But, curiously, it was also those *other Jews,* the Germans, who had ruled the roost as long established "Americans," who served to cement these *öst Juden*—the east European Jews—into a common bloc, and to melt down the differences that had previously kept them apart. Polish, Russian, Rumanian and Galician immigrants naturally regarded American Jews of German background with a mixture of radical amazement, curiosity and scorn. If they, the newcomers, were called "greenhorns," they only laughed back at the Germans, dubbing them as "Yahudim"—not really Jews, but only caricatures of their ancestors. They not only kept their personal distance from those "snooty Jewish Yankees," but also stayed away from their "establishmentarian" Jewish organizations. By the 1920s, they were already able to boast of a large network of organizations they themselves had established *together,* in order to hold the fort against the older Jewish order. Unwittingly, then, German Jews had helped to meld this disparate variety of east Europeans into a new American Jewish community. No longer only Polish, Russian, Galician, Hungarian, or Lithuanian, by then, they too were slowly becoming "American Jews."

What the earlier Ashkenazim had done, they could not do: it was unthinkable that they should fuse with the settled community and become as they. They—the "German" Jews—were Americans; we—the true Jews of the *shtetl*—would be Jews. And the more they clung to their religioethnic interpretation of their group life, the more the settled but now threatened American Jew found it necessary to divorce himself from them. And his desire to disassociate from them increased his will to fall back upon a purely denominational approach to Judaism, as a means of removing any taint of ethnic foreignness. As a result, Reform Judaism in America, encountering the fundamental ethnicism of the east-European Jews, moved farther and farther away from the specific national and cultural elements of their faith, and for a generation or two came close to becoming another small religious sect, with very little to differentiate it from Protestant Unitarianism.

How the clash between these two different "Jewish cultures" helped to create the emergent patterns of Jewish communal and religious life in twentieth century America, we shall soon have occasion to see. Yet, despite the one or two generations of their radical estrangement, the "Jewish" melting pot of America was at work. In the decades that were to follow, neither the "German" Reform of the early 1900's nor the *shtetl* mentality would survive. Each interacted with the other, and, in turn, the changing spirit and environment of America profoundly altered both.

What is even more: the "new ethnicity" of the late 1960s, coupled to the fears of Jewish annihilation generated by Israel's "Six-Day War" of 1967, combined to set in motion newer moods that would virtually obliterate all of these older divisions. Their divided and split identity in America was about to be "patched up," even if it could not be fully integrated in a Jewish community that was still pluralistic. In ways that could neither have been divined nor anticipated only a decade or two earlier, a "new" American Jewish community—showing a unity-within-diversity—began to emerge in the 1970s.

But we are getting ahead of our story. First, we should examine the ways in which their older ideologies and self-definitions—and not only their varied lands of origin—had served to splinter and divide them, long after America, and the world around, had helped to unite them. Some of these marks of division still linger and have not yet been forgotten or transcended. Jewish identity in America would still remain "a coat of many colors."

NOTES

1. Quoted in Salo W. Baron, *A Social and Religious History of the Jews* (New York: Columbia University Press, 1937), Vol. II, p. 166.

2. For a description of how the settled Jewish community, dominated by Polish and Russian Jewish immigrants, viewed the arrival of Sephardi Jews from Turkey, Serbia, and Yugoslavia as late as 1919, see Stuart E. Rosenberg, *The Jewish Community in Rochester* (New York: Columbia University Press, 1954), pp. 187–188.

3. Peter I. Rose, "Small-Town Jews and Their Neighbors in the United States," in *Jewish Journal of Sociology*, Vol. III, No. 2, December, 1961, pp. 174–191. See also Lee J. Levinger, "The Disappearing Small Town Jew," in *Commentary*, August 1952; and Louise Laser, "The Only Jewish Family in Town," in *Commentary*, December, 1959.

See also, Peter I. Rose, *Strangers in Their Midst*, Richwood Publishing, 1977. Later studies of Jews in rural middle America, unlike Rose's study of New York State, point to the conclusion that Jews in those rural sectors were highly integrated, not "strangers" in a host society. See "Small Town Jews," in *A Coat of Many Colors, Jewish Subcommunities in the United States*, ed. by Abraham D. Lavender, Greenwood Press, Westport, 1977.

In 1963, Erich Rosenthal believed that at least 60,000 Jewish families (200,000 souls), those living in the rural areas of America, were faced with a complete loss of identity. (See his "Studies in Jewish Intermarriage in the United States" in *American Jewish Year Book, 1963,* Vol. 64 [Philadelphia: Jewish Publication Society, 1963], p. 41.) Rosenthal's prediction stems from his study of Jewish intermarriage in the state of Iowa (1953–1959), where he found that the rate of intermarriage among Jews increased with the decreasing size of the Jewish community. In cities of 10,000 and over, the rate of intermarriage was 34.2 per cent; in towns with a population of 2,500–9,999, the rate was 64.1 per cent; and in rural areas, the rate increased still further, to 67 per cent.

Yet such sweeping generalizations about *all other rural American Jews* do not even accord with Rosenthal's own disclaimer: Iowa is not necessarily typical since "a high level of intermarriage is traditional in the state of Iowa" (p. 39). It is probably true, however, that those rural Jews living in states or areas like Iowa— but unlike the denser Jewish population centers of the east and parts of the midwest—where even cities do not have large Jewish communities, may well vanish, as they go beyond acculturation to total assimilation.

It should be borne in mind that the mobility patterns affecting America generally—the growth of new *far-western and southern urban centers*—can also affect the rural Jew, positively. Indeed, by the 1980s, the number of 200,000 rural Jews postulated two decades earlier was estimated to have declined to less than 60,000 souls.

4. Marcus L. Hansen, *The Atlantic Migration: 1607–1860* (Cambridge: Harvard University Press, 1940), p. 274.

5. Bertram W. Korn, "Jewish '48ers in America," in *American Jewish Archives,* Vol. II, No. 1, June 1949, p. 5.

6. Quoted in "Cedars of Lebanon," in *Commentary,* Vol. 7, Number 3, March 1949, pp. 273–275.

7. Quoted in Guido Kisch, "Israel's *Herold,* the First Jewish Weekly in New York," in *Historia Judaica,* New York, October, 1940, p. 84.

8. In 1930, the Jewish population of the United States made up 3.7 per cent of the total population. Fifty years later, in the 1980s, the Jewish component in America had declined to 2.7 per cent. (See Chapter 13.)

9. For an interesting description of the growth, spread, and diversity of the Yiddish language, see Uriel Weinreich, "Mapping a Culture," in *Columbia University Forum,* Summer 1963, Vol. VI, No. 3, pp. 17–21.

10. Mark Zborowski and Elizabeth Herzog, *Life Is With People* (New York: International Universities Press, Inc., 1952), p. 428. Used by permission.

11. *Ibid.,* p. 429.

12. Marshall Sklare, "Jewish Acculturation and American Jewish Identity," in *Jewish Life in America,* edited by Gladys Rosen, Ktav Publishing House, New York, 1978, pp. 175–176.

13. See Judd Teller, *Strangers and Natives,* (Delacorte Press, New York, 1968), pp. 7–10.

CHAPTER V

Jewishness versus Judaism:
European Roots

JEWISHNESS VERSUS JUDAISM!

A strange contest, it seems, but a conflict, oddly, that was brought here by east-European Jews.

In the minds of some contemporary Jews, the pragmatic, materialist ways of America are the evil forces responsible for "de-Judaizing" the Jews, after a history of two thousand years of unbroken, unremitting religious loyalties. They naïvely retain the romantic notion of a uniform, all-pervasive piety in east-European Jewry whose spiritual devotion to the *shtetl* religion was undermined here by the spirit of American secularism. These uncritical critics suggest, in addition, that the material success of the settled "German" Jews and their abject conformity to the American way served as still another negative force in uprooting the religion of the east-European Jewish immigrant. Here again, they blame the American environment: if Jews had not had to leave eastern Europe, they would never have encountered such "de-religionizing" of the old religion in Poland or Russia!

They are, however, confusing *Jewishness* with *Judaism.*

This confusion poses problems for outsiders as well in assessing the meaning of American Jewish life today. They sometimes put the matter politely and say that American Jews seem to be in quest of self-definition. But viewing the multiform and diverse activities, secular *and* religious, often carried on by the same Jews, they are confused as to what constitutes the central meaning of American Judaism. They have reason to be confused. Jewishness—the ethnic-emotional awareness of a cultural, communal, and even political indivisibility—and Judaism—the religious matrix of Jewish personal and corporate life—crisscross, interlock and interpenetrate.[1]

Before secularism entered Jewish life in eastern Europe (of all places!), these two aspects of the Jewish historical expression were one and indivisible. But when Jewishness was wilfully divided off from Judaism by the secularist elements in east-Europe, they were forced to make sharp and precise divisions: their Jewishness had to war on their Judaism. When they came to America, they discovered that some Jews of the settled "German" group had lost their Jewishness, but retained their

Judaism. This, the east-Europeans could not do; they could understand Jewishness without Judaism but not Judaism without Jewishness. As a result, in America they became even more determined to save their Jewishness. They discovered later, however, that without Judaism they could not save Jewishness in America.

Americans, as we have seen, have been successful in living a double life, often unawares. Secularism and religion—two violently clashing forces elsewhere—have both been harmoniously integrated in the American character. Uncritically, and often even unconsciously, Americans have continued to mix these opposing systems, thus by-passing the ideological warfare that they have unleashed in other societies. While human intolerance inevitably continues to persist, this wondrous and perplexing achievement of America has been responsible for its amazing ability not only to regard all men as equal, in law, but to recognize all religions as equal, in fact. In the history of truly or nominally Christian countries, this has never happened before.

In a curiously parallel way and influenced by the American spirit, the Jews, for whom secularism is a modern and foreign phenomenon, have successfully grafted this strange growth to a religious style-of-life. With similar disregard for such an ideological incongruity, they too move with ease from one pole to the other, only rarely aware of the oddities or the tensions implicit in such an amalgamation.

Yet, we must not fall into the popular error of assuming that secularism in Jewish life is the product of America. What did happen was that the secularism Jews brought here from east-Europe was Americanized. Even as their religious practices and institutions came to reflect their new American environment, so the secularist philosophies and movements of east-European Jews of the nineteenth century have been revamped and reoriented in twentieth-century America. In modern Jewish history, America is unique not because it fostered the growth of secularism but, on the contrary, because it put a brake on it, by tempering and reshaping its east-European mold. The creation of a cultural climate in which secularist and religious Jews would not only stop attacking or attempting to destroy one another but could even coalesce and merge—this could only happen to American Jews, because this was precisely what was transpiring in America itself.

The contemporary American Jewish community, like America itself, is not always sure where secularism leaves off and religion begins. In this land, it can select elements of one and the other, Jewishness and Judaism. Americans, too, when they stop to think about the problem, note that they are doing much the same thing. Supreme Court decisions affirm that America is a religious nation and yet proceed to rule on church-state questions in the spirit of secular democracy. In the emergent American environment, the Jewishness brought by the east-

European still persists very strongly, but in keeping with the new social and cultural patterns of the general community, it is being absorbed by American Judaism; and in the absence of an ideological battle, no sharp lines are drawn. We can perhaps now understand how the unique American process in which elements of secularism and religion are merging makes it difficult for Jews to remember that Jewishness and Judaism were once bitter enemies. We may see how the ambivalent character of this novel amalgamation makes it difficult for them, or for others, to give precise or fixed definitions to the meaning of Jewish life in America today. This is a typically American problem, which Jews share with all others, and it has been created, in part, by the wish to remember and to forget the old world at one and the same time.

We must go back to the beginning to understand many of the residual flavors and nuances of the east-European brand of Jewish secularism which still abides here today—less visibly in America than Israel, but perceptibly, nevertheless. In the first place, how was it that Jews in that part of the world could even permit themselves to adopt secularism as a philosophy of Jewish life? In retrospect, it seems almost inconceivable that a community that could produce the religiously tight and culturally homogeneous world of the *shtetl* could also father an aggressive, often antireligious secularism. And why, we have good reason to wonder, did this movement grow up among the Jews of east-Europe, and not in the German Jewish community, where the spirit of modernism expressed itself in religious and not in secular terms?

The picture of east-European life is incomplete if we do not look beyond the *shtetl* to see what was happening in the world, and in Russia as well, beginning with the middle of the nineteenth century. The spirit of Enlightenment, which had begun to rise in Europe as early as the days of the Renaissance, did not descend upon east-European Jews until the beginning of the nineteenth century. Put differently, one might correctly say that, for these Jews, the Middle Ages lasted two hundred years longer than for the rest of Europe. For those others, the temper of modernism was a slowly developed process, and they could thus adjust to its spirit in gradual steps, over many generations. The Jews, however, had to speed up their readiness for Enlightenment; in one generation they had to leap out of the medieval world into the modern. Inevitably, such an explosive, enforced maturation resulted in conflicts within the Jewish community, which were spared those who were given time to adapt more gradually to the novel world. Those Jews who accepted modernism did so, most radically; those who could not make so rapid a leap resisted it, most tenaciously. In this situation, as in many others, Jews proved to be just like everyone else—only more so!

In western Europe, by the middle of the nineteenth century, many Jews were already located in the rising middle class, and like all other

members of that group, they were much at home in the bourgeois manner and style of life. They not only spoke the same language as their
middle-class neighbors, but, as we have seen, they had also adopted their
mentality and cultural outlook. The business interests of the rising middle class were linked to a political attitude that identified the whole
nation with the one state. Historically, in western Europe, the economic
nationalism of the middle class served as a mighty engine in feeding
power to the new states forming under the flag of a single political
nationalism.

These changed economic and political conditions were reflected in the
new attitudes of many western rabbis toward the scientific and rational-
istic philosophies of the day. Instead of maintaining a posture of defensiveness, they were willing to erect intellectual bridges to span Jewish
religious thought and the new knowledge. This rabbinical openness not
only permitted the spirit of modernism to be absorbed into the religious
life of some of these communities, but it also had a most significant
result: since rationalism was acceptable to these religious leaders it could
not easily be used as an antireligious weapon. Instead, the mid-
nineteenth century in western Europe saw the beginning of efforts to
reform Judaism in terms of the new philosophies, rather than attempts
to attack it on atheistic, irreligious grounds.

In eastern Europe, however, the situation was wholly different. Far
from becoming an ally of religion, there the Enlightenment forged Jewish movements new to their historical experience—nationalist movements indifferent to religious sanctions, and even radical, antireligious
movements. There were several basic reasons for this interesting development, and, ironically, virtually all were in some way related to the
iron grip held by traditional religion over all Jewish life. For almost a
thousand years in east-Europe, the authority of rabbinical interpretation
went unchallenged in a fenced-in environment made even stronger by
its social and cultural isolation.

Their very large numbers in eastern Europe helped the Jews to
achieve a high population density in many areas. This made possible a
large degree of conformity to Jewish religious law. And this law, in turn,
was helped to become the unrivaled support of Jewish life by the harsh
and cruel policies of Czar after Czar. From 1812 on, there were imposed
upon Russian Jewry—and then on the Polish, Ukrainian, and Lithuanian communities as well—a continuing series of imperial edicts, which
instead of crushing their internal life as intended only served to make it
even firmer, as they were forced to recede farther and farther away from
contact with the world around them.

In retrospect, it seems clear that the powerful fortress of religious
traditionalism might never have been so widely breached, had not the
mad anti-Semitic policies of these Czars resulted in several major coun-

terreactions among the younger Jews. The more it was denied them, the more they sought modern secular education. To be sure, once some had tasted of the forbidden fruit, either secretly at home, or at universities abroad, they went to the extreme of converting to the Orthodox Church. But most of these educated Jews did not long to become "Russians," as had the educated German Jews to become accepted as Germans. They could not become Russians: they continued to feel that they were still the hated Jews. But they did now have, they believed, several important, and vital, and new options: they could ally themselves with all the downtrodden proletariat and help build a program of Socialist activism. Or they could pour their zeal into the building of an activist political program based upon Jewish nationalism. Or they could turn upon the medieval stagnation of Jewish cultural life, and open its windows wide to the world of modern thought, making it come alive, not as a library of spiritual rule-books and codes of religious conduct, but as a flowering, modern, national culture, like all other national cultures.

But they could look now only with jaundiced eyes at the rabbis of their communities who had stoutly opposed their higher secular studies, and who thus unwittingly lined up with the Russian authorities in keeping them from achieving the very education they ardently prized. From the rabbis they could gain neither courage nor support for any of these activist programs, and so they turned their backs on the Jewish religion. Jewishness, yes; this was the keen source of self-awareness that was at the heart of their cultural, political or economic projects. But, Judaism, no; they could only see in it the rabbinate they knew: a passive, suffering, and compliant leadership, well versed in the useless art of martyrdom, which kept repeating the timeworn religious clichés that divine help for the Jews would indeed come, but in God's good time.

Among these younger intellectuals, those who were less politically oriented primarily seized upon the need for a cultural reformation as a necessary prelude to any political emancipation of the Jewish community. They felt that the centuries of ghettoized life had caused a hardening of the spiritual arteries of Jewish culture. Into what appeared to them to be the almost cadaverous body of Jewish literature, they began breathing a new spirit, which reflected the westernized, humanistic values of the Enlightenment. Nature came back into Jewish literature. Odes to beauty, erotic love songs, hymns to the hope of the soil, and self-conscious epic poems lauding the "genius of the nation" were the new discoveries of the young authors and poets. For such themes they could find little inspiration in either the Jewish community they knew or in the shrouded spirit of the medieval years of exile and servitude. Little wonder, then, that they skipped over two millennia, in their search for what they felt were the authentic sources of Jewish cultural creativity, and focused their attention and their longing on the Bible and its language.

For them, Hebrew would no longer remain the esoteric language of liturgy alone. It was the tongue of fiery prophets and embattled warriors, of virile shepherds and sweet singers, of mighty kings and happy lovers, of a people dwelling on its own soil, working its land, naturally and creatively. The ancient past with all its cultural glory had to be recovered, the Bible read with new eyes, the treasures of the Jewish spirit cleansed, once and for all, of the debris of alien lands that had encrusted them and had made them unrecognizable, even to Jewish eyes.

These alienated young writers and intellectuals were unable to live in the present, and this is why they shied away from political programs. They retreated from the Jewish life they saw around them and found meaning only in the recapture of the heroic national moments of the Jewish past. They consciously secularized the "holy" Hebrew tongue, and gave it a new life apart from its entombment within the religious rituals of the synagogue tradition. They wilfully humanized a national culture which, for two thousand years, had read into every line of its history only mystical or theological meanings, and attempted to give it a relevance to the modern world. Thus, despite their retreat and their own inability to come to practical terms with the environment they despised, they paved the way for others who would exploit their cultural revolution and who would build it into their political theories and programs of modern Jewish nationalism.

Since the early 1860s, these cultural nationalists had rallied under the flag of a movement they called *Hovevei Zion*, the Lovers of Zion. This offered an outlet for the romantic expression of their longings for a national cultural reformation. It did not, however, clothe itself in a program for political action. But when the wild pogroms of the 1880s were unleashed upon Russian Jewry, the Lovers of Zion realized that their "romance" had now to be translated into concrete and realizable goals. "O house of Jacob, come ye, and let us walk!"—these words of Isaiah (2:5) became their slogan—and they labeled their organization *Bilu*, using the first letters of the words of the Hebrew verse.[2] Only a small number of Jews responded to their call for an exodus to Palestime, the ancestral homeland; the largest number went westward to America. Nevertheless, they set in motion the beginnings of a radical Jewish idea, political Zionism, a movement that was to capture the attention of thousands of Jews (and the interest of some non-Jews) in the years immediately to follow, and which, in still later years, would become the most significant and successful of all modern Jewish movements.

Political Zionism based itself four-square on the modern concept of nationality: since Jews formed a separate nationality (at least in eastern Europe) they had the right to polical normalcy, and they could achieve normalcy only if they would become a nationality like all others, with a publicly recognized territory or state of their own. But while Zionism borrowed its political theories from the modern world, its attachments to Palestine as a national homeland stemmed from deep sources, which flowed out of the religious teachings and traditions of Judaism. Long before the dawn of the modern political concept of nationality, religious Jews from various parts of the world continued to return to the Holy Land. There, at the end of their days, they would have the privilege of burial in the sacred earth of the sacred land, in anticipation of the resurrection that would be theirs with the coming of messianic days. In addition, even before the Russian *Bilu*-ists, beginning with the early decades of the nineteenth century, a number of colonizing schemes were originated among west-European Jews, linked not to the idea of nationality, but to the historical tradition of religious attachment to the "land of the Fathers."

But the political Zionism of the young Russian Jews was not synonymous with the religious urgings of these earlier "pilgrims." Nor were they motivated as strongly by the same stirrings as western Zionist leaders such as Theodor Herzl, whose Basel program, launching the World Zionist Organization in 1897, stressed the international legal aspects of the movement: "to establish for the Jewish people a publicly and legally assured home in Palestine." To be sure, they joined with fellow Zionists from other parts of the world in order to secure the juridical right of Jews to re-establish their ancient land. For them, however, the inner dynamic of Zionism was linked to their quest for Jewish normalcy.

It was this quest for normalcy which, more than all else, animated their lives as Zionists and as Jews. They had for so long been cowed by the mad rantings of Russian anti-Semites that inevitably some of the accusations of their tormentors took root in their own psyche. This happened in a curious but understandable way. The Russian hatred for Jews had brought the whole people to its knees: they were locked into ghettos within the restricted Pale of Settlement; kept off the land; artificially reduced to a nation of peddlers and shopkeepers; debarred from education; and left to the mercy of their own reactionary religious leadership. But while they, in turn, despised the Russians for what they had made of their people, their sense of shame and hurt was aggravated even more by the fact their own people seemed to accept these conditions as normal, and refused to rebel. Normal? Was it normal, they asked, for what was once a great people to make peace with the abnormal and the degrading? Ironically, the love they had for their people's past made them hate most of those whom they saw now. Defiantly, yet tearfully, looking out at their abnormal people, the poets and writers among them unconsciously echoed words they had surely heard elsewhere: "Jewish life is a 'dog's life,' " cried out David Frishman, their poet; "Not a nation, not a people, not human," mocked Berdichevski, their essayist; "Gypsies, filthy dogs, inhuman, wounded dogs," so Brenner, their novelist, held them up to scorn.

Ironically, the very same Zionists who so caustically criticized their own people were so certain that anti-Semitism was here to stay that they built their political platform on this basic assumption. In fact, their own criticisms were possible only because they were trying to understand the Jewish problem objectively: by seeing the Jews through Gentile eyes. They had come to the unwavering conclusion that anti-Semitism was the natural result of the unnatural Jewish condition: the abnormal patterns of their social and economic stratification in the structure of a foreign community. The outside world would regard Jews as pariahs so long as they persisted in living in societies where they could perform no constructive economic function. Therefore, they concluded, hatred for Jews would never vanish in the Diaspora, where Jews were doomed to remain perennial strangers or, at best, unwelcome guests. Only by establishing their own national community under their own flag in Palestine, where they could be masters of their destiny and character, could they normalize their social and economic patterns. Only there could Jews avoid the inevitable discrimination that was inherent in their anomalous existence elsewhere. And this negative attitude toward the Diaspora grew even stronger as these Zionists actually started to build the Palestinian community. Once arrived, their disdain for the Jews of the exile knew few bounds. Speeches such as the one given in 1933 by a high official of the Histadrut, the Jewish Labor Organization of Palestine, were typical expressions of the psychology which motivated their strenuous efforts to achieve normalcy:

> What is self-preparation? . . . First of all, preparation for Gentile jobs, the self-preparation of the Jewish worker to become a Gentile . . . to do Gentile work . . . to make a profit the way Gentiles do. . . . The Jewish village girl shall live like a Gentile country lass. . . .[3]

But there was another mind among those young Jewish intellectuals in Russia, equally secular and equally desirous of normalcy, but one which violently disagreed with the conclusions reached by the political Zionists. These were the Jewish Socialists, who were fired by the revolutionary ardor of those who would some day be the founders of the Russian Social Democratic Party. They, too, regarded the Jewish religious leaders as stumbling blocks to progress, and saw the impossible economic stratification of Russian Jewry as an abnormal condition, which demanded revolutionary changes. On one major point, however, their differences with the Zionists led them to oppose their nationalist program. They could not agree that anti-Semitism was an eternal phenomenon of the Diaspora, which would not be solved except by emigration to Palestine, where a new national social structure could be erected. Far from it, they argued: only when Jews submerge themselves willingly in a cosmopolitan and classless society and help to build a proletarian-dominated Socialist community would they—and all others—achieve true and lasting normalcy.

At first they had scorned any idea of urging the continuance of a separate Jewish culture in Russia, for fear that they might provoke a charge of chauvinism. Before very long, however, they came to the conclusion that the maintenance of Jewish cultural autonomy was desirable, and they sought to gain recognition of this principle from their fellow Socialists among the Russians. When this position was rejected, the Jewish Bund—as the Jewish Socialists of Russia called their organization—relaxed their ties to the Social Democrats and proceeded assiduously to cultivate "a proletarian Jewish culture."

This meant that Yiddish, not Hebrew, was to be the vehicle of their Socialist-cultural expression. The Bundists regarded Hebrew as the bourgeois-Utopian language of Zionism, and fought its development and acceptance at every turn. It was an artificial, even an immoral attempt, they felt, to make use for secular-cultural needs of a language that was so clearly identified with the reactionary religious life and history of the Jews. Yiddish, on the other hand, they stoutly believed, was the true language of the downtrodden Jewish masses—the folk creation of the internal life of the Diaspora which, unlike the Zionists, they were seeking to reform, not to discard.[4]

These two groups—the Zionists and the Bundists—were thus locked in violent ideological battle: nationalism versus internationalism; Jewish economic and social idealism versus Marxism; building Palestine or creating the world revolution; a renaissance of Hebrew language and literature or the flowering of Yiddish culture: all these issues, and more, were viciously fought over by the respective antagonists. And there is no fight like a fight among brother idealists.

As often happens in such situations, a variety of permutations and combinations grew out of this dialectic, new attempts to synthesize or transcend the antithetical elements in each opposing position. Within a few decades, there were Zionists who were adapting Marxism to their own brand of Socialist nationalism; Zionists who simply wanted a state where Jewish culture would thrive and who were not particularly antagonistic to religion; there were even religious Zionists, those who emerged from their insular synagogues in response to the new intellectual ferment, and who grafted political Zionism to their religious orthodoxy. And there were also two new types of Jewish nationalists; those who were known as "Territorialists" and who sought to establish a Jewish state in some yet-unsettled territory, and not particularly in Palestine; and others, called "Diaspora nationalists," who believed that Jews could be incorporated as a separate minority nation within other European nations, and who sought to have such rights granted legally.

On the antinationalist side, in addition to the Bundists whose Socialism was linked to their desire to achieve legally assured cultural rights for the Jewish minority, a new voice was to be heard. There were Jewish Socialists who would have the separatism of neither Bundism nor Zionism. They were apparently in agreement with Marx that once capitalism would be abolished, the Jews, who were tied to that outdated system, would simply fold up their tents and disappear. And, of course, there were always those secularists who refused to adopt any of these organizational stances. They simply wanted to be assimilated as noiselessly as possible into the Russian environment, if only they could.

What was to become of this welter of secular ideologies when the east-European Jews would pack their bags and head for America? Would they withstand the rigors of transplantation in a new soil and a radically different environment?

NOTES

1. It is only in modern times, as Jewishness divided off from Judaism, that some have sought to make a clear-cut distinction among Jews, based upon their religious beliefs. Thus, the British Jewish scholar, Raphael Loewe, regards those Jews "who recognize that their emotional ties are with their fellow-Jews, earthbound, and not with Judaism itself" as "recalcitrants, who are not Jews, or at any rate are *temporarily* not Jews, even though the non-Jewish world may doggedly insist on so regarding them. . . ." He goes on to say that "If such as these abdicate their Judaism . . . they (and perhaps their progeny) may carry with them sundry residual characteristics, which judged by purely humanistic standards may be desirable ones or undesirable ones. In either case, the *residuum* is, from the point of view of Judaism and its theology, irrelevant, since the indispensable Jewish sanction for them is absent." See Raphael Loewe, *Judaism: Privilege and Perspective* (Barley, England: The Parkes Library), 1962, p. 9.

Traditionally, however, even among the most pious Jews, it has been considered proper to regard even errant Jews as members of the religious community, "the household of Israel." A Talmudic warrant for this view may be found in the rabbinic dictum that " though an Israelite sin, he remains an Israelite nevertheless."

2. The manner in which they truncated even the Biblical source they chose as their acronym is revealing. The full verse was shortened, leaving out the words "in the light of the Lord." They would walk (or go) to the Land, but on their own: they did not look to divine assistance.

3. Quoted in Yehezkel Kaufman, "Anti-Semitic Stereotypes in Zionism," in *Commentary*, March, 1949, p. 243.

4. Ironically, the anti-Zionist, traditionalist rabbinate in east Europe also espoused Yiddish as the carrier of the tradition-oriented community. It regarded Hebrew as "the holy tongue," to be used *only* for sacred purposes—the language of textual studies and ritual ceremonies—not for mundane or profane discourse or literature.

CHAPTER VI

Sacred *and* Secular:
An American Hybrid

EVEN AN UNCRITICAL GUESS, UNINFORMED BY WHAT WOULD ACTUALLY transpire, could surmise that in America the secularism of these east-European Jews would be no less profoundly altered than the all-embracing rigid orthodoxy of their religiously oriented brothers. For the first time, both groups were to live in a country where organized religion was dominated by the principles of voluntarism and pluralism, and where secularism had no need to be militant, since religion was a matter of private conscience. As a result, not only would Jewishness and Judaism come closer together, but they would soon signify something other than they had represented in the Jewish milieu of eastern Europe. There would emerge a paradoxical but typically American expression: a *secularized Judaism* interpenetrated with a *religionized Jewishness*. In such a situation, those secular ideologies—like the various brands of cultural and political Zionism—which could accommodate to a religious-minded community, would play an increasingly important part in the development of American Jewish life. Those, however, like the atheistic socialist movements, would, despite valiant attempts to adjust their views, be all but forgotten by the middle of the twentieth century.

The Jewish radical movements in America were crowned with successes in the first decades of the twentieth-century east-European immigration, but these achievements, curiously, were an omen of the later failures. Hundreds of thousands of these Jewish immigrants, very soon after their arrival, found themselves working in the teeming factories and sweatshops that lined the city streets. For their very large families they eked out a very small living. Like many another urban immigrant of the time in America, they became new recruits of the industrial working class. While some of them had indeed been members of the Bund or of other socialist groups in Russia, for the most part the largest number of these east-European Jews were, on their arrival here, still far removed from a tradition of proletarianism and from the militant socialistic concepts of the class struggle. Yet, even many of those who were remote from Socialism in Europe quickly allied themselves with the aspirations of the working class even while secretly dreaming of becoming the "Boss," one day, in "golden America."

[73]

In the service of these aspirations, a new and burgeoning culture was almost totally harnessed: American Yiddish literature. Yiddish writing in America, which later blossomed into full flower, was first launched in a series of journalistic enterprises that finally began to take root in the 1890s, following two decades of faltering, abortive attempts. Almost all the early works of fiction and poetry that later found their way into Yiddish books were first published in these daily and weekly periodicals. Their journalistic origin, with their appeal to the popular needs and tastes of the immigrant workingman, placed an unmistakable stamp on their style and mold. For the most part, these Yiddish writers dealt with the alienating influences of the detested sweatshop and the frustrations caused by the inadequate pay of "the job." It was a literature heavily freighted with the complementary qualities of both nostalgia and disillusionment. It overidealized the life of the old-world *shtetl* community as it recoiled from the harsh and often cruel reality of immigrants caught in the clutches of the late nineteenth-, early twentieth-century American industrial juggernaut. The early Yiddish novels of Sholem Asch, for example, did not deal with the universal and spiritual themes of his later search, but rather with the "declassed" Jewish immigrant who must give up his old-world cultural values in a money-grubbing society where industrial servitude destroys his human dignity. It was only in later decades that Yiddish writing in America began to move away from its early alliance with social and economic radicalism and came to emphasize aesthetic and cultural values that stemmed from the Jewish tradition itself. But even from the start, this socioliterary alliance was strained by many inherent anomalies which, a few decades later, when the immigrant worker would himself become a factory owner or storekeeper, would lead to the failure of the Jewish radical movements in America. One writer pithily describes an early source of late disaffection: "It was not uncommon for a Jewish worker to read an anti-religious Yiddish newspaper, vote Socialist, join a socialist union, and yet attend the synagogue weekly, or even daily, and observe most of the Jewish law."[1]

Even those who were not regular attendants at synagogue services often found more than passing interest in the various ethnic groups formed around the "home-town" associations—*landsmanschaften*—the fraternal lodges, or the immigrant benefit societies. While they may also have been dues-paying members of their trade unions, they were often more attracted to and interested in these other groups, where the militant common cause of Socialist ideology was forgotten and the relaxed fellowship of old friends and neighbors was the dominant mood. While the union was important to them, because the "job" was important, somehow, in their home-town associations, they sensed the possibilities of achieving at least two desired goals which the union could not. In addition to holding onto "the job," most of them harbored a twin hope: to become Americans and to remain Jews—the familiar theme of most other immigrants, too, who wished to forget but also to remember. True, the union was also "America"—but it was dissident, fighting America! The union was "Jewish," too, in its Yiddish-speaking locals, but its secularism was sectarian, divorced from the synagogue, the "benefit" societies, and the common core of the Jewishness many of them wanted to preserve.

The union and the radical Jewish movements in America posed a dilemma for them. Their dilemma was not unlike that of political parties which have repeatedly failed to gain a majority in the legislature. One day they do attain long-sought political power. But their attachment to their accustomed role as the opposition makes it impossible for them to legislate positively: they have always been against, never for. So it was with many of these Jewish immigrants. If they espoused the programs of Jewish radicalism, might they become so attached to a posture of opposition that they might come to reject what they really wanted to have: a share in America, *and* a warm feeling of Jewishness?

Moreover, while the radical movements may have succeeded with some of their antireligious tactics in the Russian Jewish world, their blatant attempts to scandalize the religious-minded would only boomerang in America. Abraham Cahan, the outstanding leader of the American Jewish labor movement, understood this well. In spite of his Socialism, he appreciated the new realities of American life and repeatedly called attention to the fact that the antireligion of Jewish radicalism was not in keeping with the spirit of America. In 1911, as editor of the *Forward,* the important Socialist Yiddish newspaper in New York, he reminded his readers:

> The most comical and at the same time, saddest thing is to see an atheist turn his irreligion into a cold, dry, unfeeling, heartless religion—and this is something most of our unbelievers used to do. One must not sit at a Seder; one must extend no sympathy to the honest, ignorant mother who sheds tears over her prayerbook; one must deeply wound traditional Jews by eating and smoking on Yom Kippur in front of the synagogue. Verily, the former unbelievers were, in their way, just as fanatical, just as narrow-minded, just as intolerant as the religious fanatic on whom they warred.[2]

But America was destined to become a middle-class nation. This was still another barrier in the way of the pervasive acceptance of Socialist radicalism by the immigrant Jews in America, and perhaps the single most important obstacle to its success. Ironically, this phenomenon would prove to be a bane to the radicals, but a boon to the Zionists. And this, even though it would still take Hitler's Holocaust to shake up many of the immigrants who had, after all, come to America to achieve success—and even to forget their Jewishness. (They had not emigrated from Russia to then swamp-ridden Palestine, *where they would have to remember!*) The east-European immigrant Jew, moreover, had achieved middle-class status—or at least acted as though he had—long before the country as a whole. And with good, if unusual, historical reason.

While the Czarist repressions had tended to proletarianize them, the immigrant Jews who became industrial workers in America did not bring with them long-standing peasant or proletarian traditions, as did most of the other Europeans who were arriving at the same time. These Jewish workers were either the sons or grandsons of scholars or petty merchants, and the "middle-class ambition" to "improve their position," so that they could move upward on the social and economic ladders as rapidly as possible, was an ever-present hope. To be sure, they were still members of the lower class, in terms of their actual location on the economic map. Nevertheless, the general life-style of these Jewish workers already revealed many of the traits associated with middle-class behavior. In their family patterns and habits, their participation in organizational work, the educational choices they made for their children, and even in their leisure-time activities, in terms of their *real, social patterns*, they were already located in the middle class.

By 1930, about half the immigrants were still in the working class and most of their American-born children had not yet risen beyond such positions as office workers, salesmen, or clerks. By the mid-fifties, however, as a result of the general prosperity that followed World War II, the children and grandchildren of the immigrants of 1881–1925 had risen perceptibly in the socioeconomic scale. Virtually all the younger generation had received secondary education, and a large proportion had even gone on to higher education. By then, a majority were either business or professional men. All that had gone on before, in those earlier years of settlement, by way of preparation for their actual entry into the American middle class, was now almost completely consummated. Indeed, by the 1980s, it was clear that as a group, American Jews were far better off, and had greater "household income"—almost 40 per cent more—than any other European ethnic immigrant group in the country.[3] And by that time, too, virtually all young Jews of college age were receiving a university education.

It is clear that the striving for and the ultimate attainment of middle-class status would help prevent the spread of secular Jewish radicalism among east-European Jewish families in America. But why should this very development have proved to be a spur for the successful diffusion of the Zionist ideology, as we have intimated? In probing this unusual relationship, we will also come to see how, in adopting American middle-class values, American Jews were unconsciously establishing different criteria for the expression of their Jewishness and impelled by new motivations for their Jewish belonging.

The twentieth-century, urban American middle class is nominally religious, but because success-striving still lies at the core of their lives, material attainment has first priority. Religion was "used" primarily as an item for "conspicuous consumption." In middle-class America, Christianity had been mixed with the secularism of a materialistic culture and many Protestant churches became little more than social organizations which had, in fact, little to do with satisfying the spiritual needs of the community. They served principally as centers of civic, or folk religion, more than they were emblems of faith or theological concern. (In some ways, as we have seen, this was the heritage of the period of the ethnic church, but by the mid-1940s the middle-class mentality of their members was an even greater cause for this development.) Yet, religion as such could never be warred upon or given up; it was often regarded as a necessary outer coat to conceal the inner heart of an acquisitive society. Many east-European Jews who could no longer accept the traditions, rituals, or even the God-belief of Judaism, yet regarded it as counter-American to discard the religious life altogether. Some, as we shall yet see, joined Conservative synagogues or temples, which they only rarely attended, but which in their eyes—because these seemed more acculturated, "more American"— offered relief from the excessive demands of the tradition. For many, however, Zionism came to serve as the moral equivalent of Judaism—and this was equally true of many American-trained rabbis, until the 1950s.[4] Zionism was able to conceal their escape from the rigors of religious commitment, since, historically, Jewish nationalism had never been divorced from the religious tradition. Despite their lack of traditional religious faith, except, perhaps, for some vague, generalized, cosmic equation of Jewish survival with God Himself, Zionism helped them appear as faithful Jews, both to themselves and to others.

Middle-class Americans tend to be optimistic, even idealistic. Whether this mood is related to the earlier frontier heritage of America, to the zeal of immigrants in their "land of promise," or to the psychological need for materialists to sublimate the meaning of their success, is difficult to know. Perhaps it is the result of a combination of these that has helped the middle class give its stamp to the almost naïve American faith that all will yet go well because the best is yet to be. But if the middle class thrives on this uncomplicated optimism, it, nevertheless, resists the idealism of revolution. It can accept an idealism that is good-in-general, or even one that promises radical changes for the unenlightened, non-American areas of the world (that they, too, might enjoy the equivalent of American benefits), but not the kind that would threaten its own style of life.

On these middle-class grounds, too, Zionism appealed to many in the American Jewish community. To be sure, from time to time some of the older Jewish families who had not been part of the east-European migration fought against Zionism on the ground that it created a divided loyalty and was therefore an illegitimate expression of Americanism. Yet, in the main, the Zionist efforts of the east-European immigrants and their children were repeatedly endorsed by Congressional resolutions, and were applauded by their fellow Americans of all faiths, save those who were consistently anti-Semitic. American Zionism, in the first half of the twentieth century, fitted well the established American patterns. It was part of the same American outlook that favored the expenditure of energy and money to help the Chinese coolies, or the Polynesians, or to spread Christian missionaries throughout the world, or to encourage support for the independence of Ireland or Poland. Americans took satisfaction in the knowledge that they were participating in someone else's democratic revolution, or that they were contributing to the world-wide spread of democracy, by helping to encourage the self-determination of other nations. In supporting the development of Palestine as a Jewish homeland, Jews could indulge their American pride in a vicarious battle again Arab feudalism and the intransigence of the British mandatory government. That they could conjure up American frontier parallels to the Palestinian Jewish effort to settle a rugged terrain in order to make room for persecuted Jewish refugees from all over the world helped immeasurably, as well.

For such reasons as these, Zionism was not only regarded as wholly in keeping with the spirit of America, but its success among Jews here had much to do with the fact that it came to serve an important psychological function: it was the socially acceptable Jewish radical movement of the middle-class American Jew! The bourgeois children and grandchildren of the earlier Socialists now had an American outlet for their secular Jewish humanism.

Virtually the same political-ideological vacuum that characterized the American middle class came to dominate the American Jewish community. Generosity of spirit replaced political philosophy; philanthropy and benevolence became substitutes for a commitment to policies of radical economic change. The ideologists of a Zionism linked to programs of social and economic reform in the new Jewish community in Palestine, or even of an Orthodox religious Zionism that sought to re-establish the homeland as a "Holy Land," had relatively small followings in America. The overwhelming number of those who finally came into the American Zionist movement were "General Zionists"; they shunned the "sectarian" Zionist organizations of labor groups—*Poale Zion*—or the Orthodox—the *Mizrachi*. During the first three decades of the twentieth century, when the Zionist movement in America had not yet become as pervasive as in the years to follow, the leftist labor and rightist Orthodox, combined, probably outnumbered the General Zionists. But in the forties, when Zionism became a "mini-mass" Jewish movement, it mirrored the mass mind of a middle-class community and avoided partisan ideologies that might commit its members to anything more than a general desire to share in the rebuilding of the Jewish homeland. Indeed, many joined the movement on the assumption that to be a Zionist meant to help support Palestinian Jews to build schools and hospitals, drain swamps, plant forests, or rescue European refugees from the jaws of doom.

In America, political Zionism thus became "benevolent Zionism," and in the vanguard of this typically middle-class movement were the women. In twentieth-century America, "the supremacy of women could be read in the statistics of property ownership, insurance, education, or literature, or in the advertisements of any popular magazine. Women ran the schools and the churches; they determined what would be heard over the radio. . . . Traditionally, women had ruled the home, but only in America did they design it, build it, furnish it, direct its activities, and fix its standards."[5] Jewish women, traditionally the "strong but silent" partners, now reflecting their American counterparts became even stronger, but were no longer silent. They made Zionism a mighty force in Jewish life, and Hadassah, the Women's Zionist Organization of America, became probably the largest and most powerful Jewish organization in the world. Yet its average, dutiful member, zealous and indefatigable as she was, had little relationship to the political ideology of Zionism. In the spirit of her middle-class mood, she saw herself as the benevolent provider of medical and educational facilities for an underdeveloped Jewish community that through her efforts and those of others would someday enjoy the same standards as America.

American Zionism reflects, as well, the cultural attitude and condition of the American middle class. To the continued consternation of foreigners, the American middle class appears to be strangely devoid of cultural taste or imagination. Europeans often complain that most Americans seem to have read only two books, the Bible and the telephone directory, and that even with these they have but a passing, occasional, and only practical acquaintance. Yet it is becoming apparent, even to the foreign critics of the American middle class, that certain new "aspirations for culture" have been emerging among them. "It seems that American society," said one of these observers, "after passing through a long stage of materialism and fascination with the dollar and the good things it buys, is gradually growing toward an aspiration for culture, art, ideas, perfection and enrichment in the intellectual and spiritual domains."[6] This "aspiration for culture" still takes many strange forms, however. One, in particular, is the mass habit of appropriating to oneself the cultural achievements of others, a process wherein the "consumer" of culture comes to believe that he is, in fact, the "producer" of culture. The wide appeal of such typically American phenomena as "books-records-art-of-the-month clubs," whose members "acquire" culture, and the increasingly fashionable practice of discussing the latest "best-seller" (even without having read it) are testimony to the middle-class penchant for "vicarious cultural atonement" in a materially affluent society.

In this realm, too, the Zionism of American Jews was linked to their middle-class habits. In Palestine, and later in Israel, their fellow Jews were not only pioneering the land amidst physical hardships, but, apparently, simultaneously capable of producing a cultural revolution by actually creating culture. There, modern literature, art, and music were being produced in abundance, and the renaissance of Hebrew culture was everywhere known and discussed. Hebrew, the "language of the Bible," was coming alive in new and exciting forms. While some American Zionists did make strenuous efforts to learn this "modern" language or to teach it to their children, the great majority continued to speak glowingly about the language, but never in it. Yet in Zionism they discovered a new source of cultural pride: once again, Jews were "The People of the Book." It mattered not that the "people" they referred to were not actually themselves. Their Zionism made them think of Palestinian or later of Israeli Jews, not as "them," but as "us."

Yet, none of these social or economic factors of American middle-class life would have been sufficiently strong, either alone or in combination, to create this sense of "we-ness." The ethnic ties of American Jews to their people all over the world were still strong, even if they seemed somewhat attenuated, by the late 1930's. But the awful facts of contemporary European Jewish history, which were only more fully revealed at the close of World War II, had a profound effect on American Jewish life. The Hitler-Nazi holocaust, the near-fruitless search for refugee havens in the West, Britain's refusal to open wide Palestine's gates to the Jews, the spectacle of the relentless hunting down of Jewish refugees by mighty navies on the high seas, the sight of their creaking, sinking boats making their perilous way to Palestine, and finally, in 1949, the victory of the little David of Israel over the mighty Goliath of Araby—all these desperate but adventurous moments helped to invigorate, unify and ultimately, to politicize Jewish life in America. In those historic years, a sweeping tidal wave of ethnic empathy erupted in every sector of the American Jewish community—often an ethnic emphathy with religious and personal overtones. Hardly a Jew in America could avoid the feeling of "there, but for the grace of God, go I!"

Ironically, the major premises of political Zionism had to wait to be proved right by the testing of its theories in a most horrible and horrifying reality. For, despite its growing acceptance in America, Zionism did not achieve mass Jewish approval here until after World War II, when the revelations of Jewish persecution and wandering rallied broad sentiment to its cause. When this occurred, there was no American Jewish movement, organization, institution, or agency that was not vitally influenced by the spirit of Zionism. Synagogues, Jewish community centers, religious schools, and virtually all the organizations and societies that comprised the American Jewish community, came to espouse the Zionist cause. By the combined efforts of Jews throughout the free world, several million of their people have been brought to the ancient homeland, from the time the State of Israel was established in 1948. And in the pursuit of these goals of the physical redemption and rehabilitation of their fellow Jews, American Jewish organizations alone had raised more funds than had ever been subscribed for such purposes by any nongovernmental, private group in the history of civilization.

The Jewish welfare federation—the American version of the centrally organized charity of the premodern European Jewish community—was the principal vehicle for these successful fund-raising drives in each of the local communities. The voluntary, democratic character of America, with its emphasis upon the separation of church from state, not only led to a broad religious diversity, but had also encouraged the unique development of welfare and benefit societies on the part of the various denominations in America. In Boston, for example, there were such groups as the Scots Charitable Society, the Episcopal Charitable Society, and the Irish Charitable Society. Thus, in the new world, the earliest Jewish settlers were encouraged to continue their historical and traditional efforts in connection with the social and human welfare of their co-religionists. In the less complex and less populous Jewish community of colonial America, the synagogue-community itself had assumed the obligation of maintaining the Jewish charity in each area. As congregations multiplied, however, it was considered useful to co-ordinate some of these activities on a national rather than a local scale. In 1859, the Board of Delegates of American Israelites was founded, principally, to be sure, as a result of an outbreak of anti-Semitism overseas, but, also, "to bring about the union of American Israelites for their common welfare." That the Board functioned for not even twenty years, and was forced to disband in 1878, was evidence of the newer conditions created by the growing complexity of the American Jewish community. A relatively homogeneous community in which the synagogue or a group of synagogues would serve as the central co-ordinating agency for welfare projects had to be replaced owing to the multiplication of new immigrants from eastern Europe. In every city there was a proliferation of new benefit societies, welfare associations, and *landsmanschaften,* each organized to promote its own mutual-aid programs.

The Community Chest movement in America did not come into being until 1914. But as early as 1895, the Jews of Boston had already moved in that direction when they established their Federated Jewish Charities. This new concept in social welfare work brought together into a single fund-raising apparatus five important affiliated agencies: a general relief society, a children's orphanage, a free employment bureau, a women's sewing society, and a free burial society. This "federation" of agencies who still retained their organizational autonomy into a central fund-raising structure was not only destined to become the model and chief instrument for the welfare undertakings of the American Jewish community, but served as a major contribution to the developing concept of community responsibility for voluntary social welfare work in the general American community as well. With the passage of years, as the overseas needs of Jews became more pressing during the Hitler period and in its aftermath, the local welfare funds and federations were to become more and more crucial in the life of the Jewish community. In 1935, a national Council of Jewish Federations and Welfare Funds was organized, to give direction and leadership to the local constituent communities. Increasingly, ever since, both on the national and local levels, these groups have been exerting a major influence in the shaping of total Jewish community life: not only upon fund-raising campaigns, but also upon social services, Jewish education and culture, and community and interfaith relations.[7]

In a country whose Jewish population would gradually disperse from coast-to-coast, no central "New York office" could long continue to exercise complete control over day-to-day decisions in the welfare area. True, as the 1980s began, there were still five Jewish centers—New York City, Los Angeles, Nassau County (N.Y.), Philadelphia and Chicago—which comprised close to 60 per cent of the country's total Jewish population. Yet there were at least 800 other organized communities scattered across the nation. Their local welfare efforts were structured into about 225 federations or councils, and of these, twenty-seven had a Jewish population of more than 20,000, while only ten could boast of more than 100,000.

New York still looks—and often acts—like the American Jewish capital, comprising as it does about 30 per cent of the total national Jewish population. Decentralized regionalism, however, would become a growing factor in the local-and-area management of the social and cultural services that have become the hallmarks of the Jewish community in the United States. Even a quick glance at the shifting distribution of the country's Jews—and their new centers of gravity—tells an important tale about the growing regionalism increasingly at work in the American Jewish communal process.

Their overwhelming concentration in the Northeastern sector continues to diminish with each passing year. While in 1900 almost 60 per cent of America's Jews lived in this highly populous area of New York, New Jersey, and Pennsylvania (in contrast to the less than 30 per cent of the total American population), since 1930 there has been a continuous westward move. And beginning with the 1960s a perceptible shift toward the sun-belt areas of the country would also be clearly noted. Jews joined other Americans, the aged or the retired, as well as younger professionals in search of success, and headed to warmer—and often less costly—climes. As a result, Los Angeles would become the center of organized Jewish life west of the Rockies, while Atlanta, Georgia came to play a similar role for Southeastern Jews. In the "middle" of the country, Chicago, once the "western anchor" of American Jewry, still remained its nominal midwestern capital. By the 1970s, however, its dominant position as the "second city" was already lost to Los Angeles, together with large numbers of its former Jewish residents.

In all of these communities, it was the local federation, council, or welfare fund that sought out the newest Jewish residents, and successfully harnessed many of them to the "team-work" of the local community, in support of its social, educational and cultural services. Of course, since 1967, they have worked hard on behalf of the growing annual campaigns in support of the State of Israel and its citizens. But the history of success is also the history of failure. For, as a result of the intense challenge of these crisis years, the American Jewish community appeared to be unified around a new center, with a new point of departure. The successful and even the less-than-successful businessmen zealously entered the ranks of Jewish organizational life, in response to the need for massive fund-raising campaigns, beginning in the forties. The result has been that since that time fund-raising, almost as an end-in-itself, seems to have become the key function and purpose of Jewishness and Judaism. In order effectively to harness an entire local Jewish community, and to rally its people behind a central fund-raising campaign for Jewish needs, Jewish welfare funds and federations by their very nature tend to emphasize fund-raising techniques as the measuring rod of Jewish achievement, and they often steer clear of Jewish ideological commitments. They have attracted the most enterprising and most successful men and women, whose talent for the solicitation of funds is now considered the chief asset for their leadership of the Jewish community. A guide to Jewish communities, recommended to them by the national Council of Jewish Federations and Welfare Funds, lists "nineteen points" intended to help each community "go over the top" in its fund-raising campaign. Some of the points, obviously valuable as techniques, shed light, however, on what have now become the *desiderata* for Jewish community leadership:

1. Leadership giving and working is indispensable for successful fund raising. Did *leaders set the top example with their own gifts and work?* Did they do it at the beginning of the campaign? Where were the weak spots?
2. Big gifts are always the big priority. Individual cultivation is needed, *throughout the year.* Of prime importance *were the big givers involved as campaign leaders and workers? . . .*

5. Evaluate workers—who was effective and dependable—who was not? Who were the best to be selected for bigger jobs? *Who were the deadwood, to be weeded out?* What new workers can be lined up and educated early? . . .

15. Co-operation of Jewish organizations—*the synagogues,* the social and cultural organizations, the country clubs—have been of great help in a number of cities. How can their further efforts be encouraged? . . .

18. *A sense of success and achievement:* has *appropriate recognition* been given those who contributed to the community's success? . . .[8] (Italics mine.)

It goes without saying that many sensitive Jews were deterred from offering themselves as candidates for Jewish leadership as a result of crass attitudes such as these. Few put down their dilemma as pithily and perceptively as Daniel Bell:

> In the *embourgeoisement* of Jewish life in America, the community has become institutionalized around fundraising, and the index of an individual's importance too often is the amount of money he donates to hospitals, defense agencies, philanthropic groups, and the like. The manifest ends are the community functions being served, but frequently the latent end is the personal prestige—*yichus.* This kind of institutional life may even lend itself to historic forms of corruption: of simony, when those who have risen high in Jewish organizations receive their awards in appointive office in Jewish life; and of indulgences, when leadership is the simple reward of wealth. And in performance of charity as a way of Jewish life, self-satisfaction may take on the face of righteousness. The most sensitive of the Jewish agency professionals, lawyers, and business men have often deplored this situation, yet are trapped by the system.[9]

Aggressive methods such as these have led to the achievement of enormous fund-raising goals which the community has voluntarily set. Since 1946, with the first post-war year, American Jews mobilized the rich and the comfortable, in dramatic, imaginative, and sometimes bizarre ways that had never been employed during the almost two millennia during which Jews have engaged in voluntary self-taxation, as a "welfare community" within a host nation. From that year until 1984, communities across the country, through their central "United Jewish Appeal" annual campaigns, have raised the remarkable sum of over ten billion dollars. The share of these "gift dollars" alloted to Israeli needs usually amounted to three-quarters of the total raised in each community; the remainder was used to support local "bread-and-butter" needs. Added to these charitable gifts to Israel, were funds raised annually through the State of Israel Bond Campaign. Since its inception, in 1951, well over six billion dollars in Bonds have also been sold, at a very nominal rate of interest. Moreover, if one were to add up all the funds contributed by American Jews to Jewish charity campaigns for domestic purposes—including buildings—as well as for Israeli institutions, reliable estimates suggest that the sums would exceed an amount of two billion dollars, annually. For a group constituting less than three per cent of the entire population of the United States, it is little wonder that such extraordinary achievements have become the envy of many other American charities. But to achieve results like these, Jews have had to see their efforts as more than voluntary charity. They were regarded as a self-imposed form of "Jewish taxation."

In the course of time, however, as with similar American efforts like the Red Feather Appeals or the United Community Chests, the "leaders" and the active supporters of these city-wide Jewish enterprises tended to forget about the purposes, programs, and even the existence of the individual organizations which were now subsumed in a giant, over-all Community Fund. All eyes were on the campaign goal, and what little energy remained after the campaign was rarely invested in an effort to think about Jewish commitments or ideologies, but in preparing for next year's drive! The sheer magnitude of the needs seems to have compelled the Jewish community to organize itself in the pattern of the large American industrial enterprise, and often the materially oriented, success-striving values that attach to such efforts have been equated with "success as a Jewish community."

As a result, secularism in contemporary American Jewry has been subjected to an intellectual and aesthetic crisis. On the one hand, the leaders of political Zionist thought in Israel have reminded the leaders of American Zionism—who, in effect, are the leaders of these central fund-raising organizations—that Zionism is no longer a theory but a living fact. If you claim to be Zionists, they repeatedly harangue the Zionists of America, why do you not join with us here in Israel, and help build "our" secular, humanistic, democratic Jewish state? But they went on to admonish, if there is no room in your scheme of values for settling in Israel—which is the ultimate fulfillment of Zionist Jewishness—then you will be left with only a truncated, deculturated Judaism. America, they conclude, is not different in this respect from any other Diaspora Jewish community. (Shades of the political and cultural Zionism of late nineteenth-century Russian Jews!)

The crisis for these secularist American Jewish leaders and their followers arises because they are not willing to say "Yes" to the Israelis, and they must now carefully consider the implications for their Jewishness of saying "No." By saying "No" and staying in America, they must discover a way of infusing their materialistic secularism, which concentrates on means and forgets about ends, with the cultural humanism of the Israeli Zionist ideologists. But can they do this in America, where secularism is possible only when wedded to religious values? Can they express their Jewishness here, if it remains outside the influence, the traditions, and the thought of Judaism?

Moreover, their current expression of Jewish secularism is far removed from its counterpart in modern Israel, or its earlier antecedents in the east-European Jewish community. Unlike the others, contemporary secularism in the American Jewish community is spiritually moribund, for it lacks not only the visible institutional channels necessary for its cultural transmission, but it has lost touch with its own radical cultural history. Thus, while secularists still persist, secularism as a vital, creative, and revolutionary Jewish movement has withered for lack of ideological nourishment and personal commitment. For the Jewish secular ideology to thrive in America, it cannot take refuge under the mythical banner of "cultural pluralism" while its own partisans actually remain monocultural—little more than Anglicized, middle-class conformists whose "secular Jewish culture" consists of raising funds or offering encouragement in support of "Jewish culture" in Israel. Nor can it long subsist even in its organizational forms if, in the private lives of its adherents, Jewish secularism is equated with mere ethnicism and fails to reflect the uniqueness of its cultural and ideological components.

The crisis of the secularists has been further sharpened by the questions their own children are now asking: If we are Americans, what meaning to Jewishness? As Americans we represent one third of this nation, spiritually; what do we have to say to this nation, as one of its major religious partners? And in the search for answers, they have been forced to seek out the synagogue again. Yet, thus far, it appears that their return to the synagogue has had a strange result: instead of the synagogue influencing them religiously or culturally, they seem to be wielding their practiced, secularizing influence over the synagogue.

Will the picture change? When Israeli Jews come to their own economic and cultural maturity, the American Jew, freed from the burden of consistently raising huge funds to keep Jews alive elsewhere, may find personal meaning in the modern Jewish renaissance. Alive to his dilemma as an American Jew, and seeking to define himself in more spiritual terms, he may yet, consciously and wittingly, pour new and enriching ethnic content into his *Judaism,* and find new and vital spiritual meaning in his *Jewishness.* Considering the increasing Israel-centeredness of American Jewish life, however, and the precariousness of that beleaguered state caught in a web of Arab hostility to its very existence, there is grave doubt—as we shall yet see—whether Jews in America will ever be fully freed from their role as "brothers' keeper." The mantle they wear—as supporters and defenders of Jews everywhere—is surely a robe of honor. But does it also serve to cover over some of the inner emptiness of *their own* Jewish lives? Does it act as an almost-permanent shroud that successfully veils a continuing and ambivalent secular leadership which loudly proclaims its Jewishness but has not yet come to terms with Judaism?

There are, indeed, signs on the horizon that these questions are finally being raised and, in some significant quarters, are also being resolved. Yet, before we proceed to examine those newer winds that blow, there is first another question we need to address: How much of American Jewish behavior is really the product of non-Jewish hostility or misunderstanding—other-directed, not inner-motivated?

NOTES

1. Nathan Glazer, *American Judaism* (Chicago: University of Chicago Press, Revised Edition 1972), p. 67.

2. Quoted by C. Bezalel Sherman, "Secularism and Religion in the Jewish Labor Movement," in Theodore Friedman and Robert Gordis (eds.), *Jewish Life in America* (New York: Horizon Press, 1955), p. 116.

3. See Christopher Jencks, "Discrimination and Thomas Sowell," in *New York Review of Books,* March 3, 1983, p. 34; also Thomas Sowell, *Ethnic America,* Basic Books, New York, 1983.

4. A study published in 1945, but based on material gathered in 1937, found that the theological attitudes of 81 per cent of the Conservative rabbis and 80 per cent of the Reform rabbis in the sample could be regarded as *naturalist,* rather than *supernaturalist.* In the Conservative rabbinate, in particular, 81 per cent of the respondents regarded "Zionism as a major solution of the Jewish problem." This combination of views, which favored naturalist positions and nationalist solutions, virtually made Zionism a substitute religion, even for many of these rabbis. See Joseph Zeitlin, *Disciples of the Wise* (New York: Bureau of Publications, Teachers College, 1945), p. 83; p. 100.

5. Henry Steele Commager, *op. cit.,* p. 424.

6. Alfred Max, editor of the French magazine, *Realités,* as quoted in *Time,* August 3, 1962, p. 41.

7. For a full discussion of the history, development, and orientation of the Jewish welfare federation movement in America, see Harry L. Lurie, *A Heritage Affirmed: The Jewish Federation Movement in America* (Philadelphia: Jewish Publication Society of America, 1961).

8. Quoted in *Community News Reporter,* Jewish Telegraphic Agency, New York, July 19, 1962, pp. 1–2.

9. See Daniel Bell, "Reflections on Jewish Identity," in *The Ghetto and Beyond,* ed. by Peter I. Rose, Random House, New York, 1969, pp. 471–472.

PART THREE
Jews and their Host Nations

CHAPTER VII

Roots of Anti-Semitism

CAN AMERICA TRANSCEND THE TWO-THOUSAND-YEAR-OLD HERITAGE OF anti-Semitism? Can it succeed where all others have failed?

Paradoxically, the American pattern of public cooperation between the major faith groups is uniquely the contribution of its secular humanistic heritage. No other part of the theistic world has exceeded its extraordinary achievement. The spirit of secular democracy has exerted a benign influence upon the public behavior of the three religions of America, and in turn the Catholics, Protestants, and Jews of America share a sense of joint obligation for the preservation of the common democratic life. Their official spokesmen repeatedly come together, leaving their separate worlds to meet in the arena of communal concern. They share in a combined pursuit of liberty in order to ensure the guarantees of religious freedom to each, and to all. Such open-handed cooperation between the faiths did not, and will not, take place in countries with an established religion or church.

The growing success of these enterprises has indeed led some Americans to seek the extension of the principles of political equality to the realm of religious interrelation. If all men are equal under God and before American law, they maintain, then, surely, all religions must be co-equal in the sight of the Lord and in the eyes of man. Often, however, it is just at this explosive point that the influence of secularism ends, and the theologies of religion take over. As a result, the "interfaith" programs jointly undertaken by the three religious groups could only be successful if their enterprises were geared to secular purposes. There has thus emerged a strange and curious phenomenon: "interfaith" achievements have been possible only when they have lacked grounding in "a faith." The most ardent supporters of such "interfaith" work, therefore, tend to be those clergy or laymen who are the most secular-minded. They have at least seen the value of working together in the realm of civic enterprise, if not as a religious commitment, then surely as a symbol of the democratic purposes of America.

For Jews, this still represents a major development in the history of their relations with the non-Jewish world. For the very first time, they appear in public as partners with the other religions, and not as religious rivals or outcasts. Television and radio networks often accord them opportunities equal to—or nearly equal to—the Catholic and Protestant communities, for the exposition of their views on morals and related spiritual matters. Newspaper editors, seeking the reaction of America's religious leaders to events that suggest religious or moral significances, call on local rabbis for their opinions, in addition to the priests and the ministers. The army, naval, and air-force academies, symbols of the secular democratic national government, house chapels for worship, which include synagogues, as well as Catholic and Protestant altars. So, too, halls of state and federal legislatures echo with Jewish invocations and blessings, as well as the benedictions and prayers of Catholic and Protestant clergy. In virtually every significant arena of "official" American life, not only are Jews regarded as co-equals, but Judaism is seen as one of the normative religious expressions of Americans. For the first time in the history of the Jewish Diaspora, Judaism has come to be generally regarded—at least by those who wield secular influence—as a full partner with Catholicism and Protestantism in America.

There are even more radical signs of the uniqueness of America for Jews: the revolutionary and even daring attitudes to Judaism recently proclaimed by some influential non-Jewish religionists, as well. History, as we shall soon note, has consistently indicated its verdict on the subject of Jewish equality. In the past, Jews may occasionally have been successful in achieving political equality as fellow citizens. Yet, as long as Judaism was considered a strange, competitive, or degraded form of religious belief, inevitably Jews lacked, in practice, the civil and social rights accorded them on paper. The question that history poses is thus clear: Can Jews be truly equal where Judaism is not? And this very question, and the answer to it, are at the heart of the problem posed at the very beginning of this chapter.

If one scrutinizes closely the American scene he will note that in addition to the secular influences of the "religion-of-democracy" which have given Judaism a status of equality, there is a growing conviction, held by responsible and intellectually oriented churchmen, that the historic mission of Christianity to the Jews should be abandoned. This is another way of saying, that religiously, not only politically, Jews are equal—because Judaism is equal, too. Whether this revolutionary and unique mood is the result of a poignant sense of Christian guilt linked to the wanton murder of six million European Jews, whether it stems from the recognition of the emergent Jewish vitality represented by the rebirth of a Jewish State, whether under the influence of Karl Barth's (and others') teachings that salvation comes not *to* the Jews, but *from* the Jews, or whether as a result of the strong influences of the secular attitude toward Judaism, it is difficult to know. The crucial fact remains: a major revision of their relationship to Jews and to Judaism is taking place in the Christian thinking of some outstanding American church leaders. For the first time, the voice that now speaks up for the equality of Judaism calls out in the name of Christianity. For Jews, it is this aspect of their relationship to the non-Jewish world that truly represents a major breakthrough. It is this side of the situation—the religious side—that may yet be responsible for America's overcoming the heritage of anti-Semitism, bequeathed to her by the Christian civilization of the West.

Modern historians or sociologists have tended to elaborate their simple or their complicated theories of the origins of anti-Semitism, on the basis of economic or political factors, apart from or in combination with local social structures. It is, of course, true that in the later Middle Ages, Jew-hatred was clearly related to economic questions, and that, still later, in the modern period, anti-Semitism was linked to the political nationalism of the emergent nation-states. Yet, they sometimes seem to overlook the central fact embedded in the history of anti-Semitism: Jews were disliked because Judaism was disliked! If, in addition to this religious matrix, those who controlled the economic policies or others who wielded the political power could exploit this situation, so much the easier for them to succeed in their evil machinations.

It is not easy to talk about such things, surely not for Jews, in the presence of Christian friends. After all, the contemporary American Christian does not like to feel that his Christianity is linked to the historical antipathy of Christianity to Judaism, any more than his Jewish neighbor wants to be blamed for what some Jews are reported to have done to Jesus. Yet, unless one goes beyond the learned sociological and psychological treatises that deal with the anti-Semitic question, and comes to grips with what has been the root-issue from the days of antiquity to the present—the religious difference of Judaism—the so-called good will now being practiced by Christians and Jews may ultimately falter and be dissipated. Unless, in the spirit of faithful religious dialogue, Jews and Christians can learn to speak truths to each other, the small beginnings now being made as a result of the aforementioned avant-garde Christian theologians will be wasted.

What, then, are the religious facts at the core of historical Jewish disabilities? How can a knowledge of this vital dimension of the problem help us to come closer to that day when American secularism will be joined by American Christendom, in a fundamental repudiation of anti-Semitism, by according to Judaism, as well as to Jews, fundamental equality with their own religions?

In the pre-Christian years of the Jewish Diaspora, what there was of a "Jewish problem" was directly related to the fact that their unique religious life and customs caused them to stand out as a conspicuous minority. To be sure, some of the Ptolemaic and Seleucid kings of the Greek-speaking empires, as well as a number of Roman emperors, had offered them special privileges and immunities, in order to allow for their religious needs.[1] Yet, by their nature, these decrees evoked the ire of the general population, because they granted to the Jews rights which they themselves did not have.

Unlike the various oriental cults springing up in the Roman Empire, Jews would not allow the fusion of Judaism with the practice of emperor worship, which many of the other groups had eagerly adopted, in the hope that such arrangements would assist the spread of their religions. The Jews consistently resisted every attempt to translate their God into an earthly divinity by giving Him visible forms. They continued to remain separated from their pagan neighbors because the prescribed laws of the Mosaic code required that they remain in a state of ritual purity. While there is evidence that their religious ideology and practice proved attractive to numbers of Romans—particularly the aristocracy—who voluntarily converted to the Jewish faith, clearly, it was the Jewish religion which served as the major source of antagonism and friction between Jews and many Roman pagans. In time, leading Roman writers and thinkers began spreading derogatory ideas about Jews which were based solely upon their "base," "abominable," "depraved," "mean," and "preposterous" religion.[2]

Even in pagan society, it was the unique nature of the religion of the Jews that singled them out for conspicuous contempt. And this basic religious factor continued to serve as the stumbling block in the relations between Jews and the new Christian religion, which sprang from their loins. Christianity, of course, began as a Jewish religious sect. At first, its followers were loyal Jews, worshiping together with their brethren in the synagogues, and studying together the same religious texts. But after the Temple of Jerusalem was destroyed in the year 70, the rabbis began to look upon these "Christian-Jews" with greater suspicion, since they saw in them a threat to the necessary unity of the Jewish community in its troubles with the Roman authorities. By the end of the first century, these Christians had been ejected from the Jewish community, and soon thereafter there was an unmistakable shift of emphasis in the relationships of Christians and Jews. Judaism was left behind by the growth of Christianity as a new and distinct religion, and soon enough, anti-Jewishness became a fundamental feature of the Christian attitude.

The cause of this attitude was only partially connected to a mood of retaliation for the anti-Christian feeling among the rabbis of the first century. True, the attitudes of the rabbis was negative to those first Christians, but their hostility was not directed to the gentile Christians but only to the Jews who still claimed to be Jews, despite the fact that they were also members of the new Christian sect. The effective cause for the elevation of anti-Judaism to the level of Christian policy was basic and central to the new theology of Christianity. It was the writings of the first Church Fathers—the patristic literature—that positioned Christianity into an anti-Jewish stance on theological grounds. The Fathers of the

Church laid claim to the fact that the Church was the true Israel, the divine group to which the promise of the "God of Israel" was really given. To prove this contention, they were constrained to show that the old Israel had, indeed, been rejected by God. Why did God reject the old Israel and decide upon the need for a "new Israel"? The Jews were handy proof of the reason: had they not rejected God's son, and had they not gone so far, so some Church Fathers claimed, as to urge upon the Romans that Jesus be crucified? Indeed, by so doing, they were in effect the executioners themselves! Thus, the new theology could argue, God was displeased with His chosen people and, despising them, sent the Romans to destroy their Temple. In their place, the Church would now rise as the new and the true Israel.

Objective Christian historians have now come to recognize that anti-Jewish dogmatism was built into Christianity in its earliest days. James Parkes, the eminent British scholar, blamed the early Church Fathers for providing "a foundation . . . for the theological conception" upon which "an awful superstructure has been reared." He considered all the other possible factors—the cultural, social, or economic origins of anti-Semitism—as being "at best minor, and the main responsibility must rest upon the theological picture created in the patristic literature of the Jew as a being perpetually betraying God and ultimately abandoned by Him."[3] In a manner not dissimilar from the thesis being presented here, Parkes believed that the latter manifestations of anti-Semitism in its modern national forms could never have achieved either widespread acceptance or virulent expression, without the sanctified sanction given to anti-Jewishness by the theology of the early Church Fathers.[4]

Religious reasons may thus be seen to be at the core of the historic Jewish status of the Jews as western society's outcasts. But religious reasons also operated in ways which sometimes had caused Jews to appear in a different role: as rivals to Christianity. As Christian churches and converts became increasingly more numerous, the pagan Roman rulers relaxed their anti-Jewish laws and set upon uprooting Christianity. They declared it to be an illegal religion and publicly demonstrated their opposition to its spread. The martyrdom of thousands of faithful Christians at the hands of their Roman persecutors is an unforgettable chapter in the early history of Christendom. But as the political position of the Christians deteriorated in the Roman Empire, some of those pagans who were seeking a monotheistic faith preferred to go over to the monotheism of Judaism, rather than to be converted to Christianity.

That for four centuries Judaism seemed to be a dangerous rival to Christianity is not known to us from Jewish sources, but from discussions recorded at one Church Council after the other. Invariably, in that period, the Councils dealt with the apparently widespread problem of the "Judaizers," denouncing those whose Christian practices still retained vestiges of the Judaism of the earlier Christian community. If one were to judge from what these Councils forbade, it would appear that the religious doctrines which had claimed that Judaism was a "rejected religion" were not yet altogether accepted in practice. The fear that some Christians might relapse into Judaism was apparently very real, if the Church Council discussions on this subject are consulted. Again and again, Christians were discouraged from entering Jewish homes and, generally, from having personal contact with them of any kind.[5] Those Christians who ate unleavened bread on Passover, or continued to frequent synagogues, were repeatedly warned that such "Judaizing" practices could not be tolerated by the Church. So historic a Church Council decision as the adoption of Easter as a "movable feast," arranging its dating so that it would never coincide with the first day of Passover, was directly linked to the desire of its leaders to obliterate any ties that Christians or prospective Christians may have seen between Judaism and Christianity. But when the Roman Empire effectively adopted Christianity, Judaism no longer appeared in the role of rival, and the Jew, once again, reverted to his older guise as the outcast.

We need not tarry long on the well-known havoc this status wrought for the Jews in medieval Europe. Popes and kings vied with one another in an uninterrupted series of unhappy exploitations of their perennial Jewish victims. Public disputations were held, as if in the form of religious dialogue, in which priests of the Church and rabbis "debated" the respective merits of their religions. But the rabbis could never "win." The dialogues were not dialogues at all: they were useful public techniques, in the hands of a powerful religious majority, to discredit and heap abuse upon a "captive" religious minority. Invariably, penalties to the Jewish communities followed in the wake of each of these "public dialogues."

By the time anti-Semitism came to east-Europe in the eighteenth century, it had had a long and successful history in the west. In Russia, the two older themes would coalesce, as Jew-hatred became an instrument of government policy: Jews were soon to be seen as both outcasts *and* rivals. The earliest Russian rulers believed with Empress Elizabeth that "our loyal subjects can expect nothing but evil from the haters of our Savior Christ," and sought to preclude their settlement in Russia, unless they would "consent to embrace the Greek Orthodox faith."[6]

As a means of restricting their movement throughout the country, in 1791 Catherine II established the Jewish Pale of Settlement, which thereafter would become the basis of all future governmental oppression of Russian Jewry. The Pale of Settlement kept the Jews from easy access to the Russian people, and for more than a century its effect was to create and maintain attitudes of suspicion and feelings of prejudice between the Christians and Jews of the country. These edicts of the

Czars, moreover, were regarded by the Russian people as the very will of God, and they succeeded in placing the authority of both government and Church behind an unrelenting national policy aimed at making and keeping the Jews as the outsiders and the outcasts.

But in the latter part of Alexander III's reign, another element was introduced into the anti-Jewish policies of Russia: the earlier theme of the Jew as fearful rival! Now, Jews were no longer passively suffered to remain on the outside, but bloody, physical violence, pogroms, were unleashed against them, in which the government was the chief conniver and protagonist. In 1881 alone, there were pogroms in 215 Russian towns, villages, and cities. Many pogromists obviously believed that their attacks on the Jews were in the nature of a patriotic duty to their "little father," the Czar.[7] The official, international interpretation placed upon the source of these outbreaks was stated by the Czar to be the work of the revolutionary anarchists, who were equally the enemies of the government. Yet the private report of his own commissioners was closer to the truth. The source of the violence in their view was none other than the Jews themselves! The pogroms were caused, they said, "by the systematic and incessant exploitation of the local Christian population by the Jews and their unlimited aspirations and eagerness to acquire riches at the expense of their Christian neighbors.[68] Indeed, later, when the liberal 1905 Revolution attempted to mitigate the autocracy of the Czar, the open reply of the government served as an invitation to the slaughter of even more Jews. "Kill the *Zhids*—save Russia and the Czar!" government officials cried. In this way, the monarchy made the Jews appear as traitors to Russia and as the arch-rivals to the established Russian authority. A few days later, during Passover of 1905, the pogroms began again, and before the year was over, more than 700 organized attacks took place against Jews in various parts of the country.

It was in this atmosphere that the infamous Russian anti-Semitic hoax, the so-called Protocols of the Elders of Zion, was spawned. In 1903, there appeared in a St. Petersburg newspaper a series of nine articles under the telltale title: "A Jewish Program to Conquer the World." These newspaper articles, later reprinted in pamphlet form by the Russian Army Staff of the St. Petersburg Military Region (and since, in many languages, many places, and many, many times!) purported to be the stolen record of the plans of a so-called secret world Jewish organization, which was said to be plotting the overthrow of all Christian governments in order to wrest power for Jewish hands. They identified these "leaders" of the "Jewish world organization" as the "chiefs of the twelve tribes of Israel," accusing them of making ready to blow up all the capitals of Europe in pursuit of their ambitious program. In 1917, after the Czarist archives were opened, it was discovered that the Russian monarch himself had actually been supporting the spread of anti-

Semitic propaganda, with money from his own personal fortune! Then, in 1921, the London *Times* exposed the "Protocols" as a cruel and vicious forgery, but, apparently, this still did not prevent many people around the world, even such influential Americans as auto-maker Henry Ford, from regarding them as true.[9] The hatred of Jews and the fear of Jews went hand in hand; the outcasts were also the rivals. The Russian infection had spread thousands of miles from home.

It has been reliably estimated that the number of Jewish lives lost at the hands of the Russian anti-Semites during all the years of the pogroms, from 1881 until 1914, was not in excess of two thousand. Russian anti-Semitism was cruel, vulgar, and often passionate, but by comparison with the "scientific anti-Semitism" later practiced by Hitler Germany, its gory products were meager indeed. There should hardly be any need here to rehearse the history of the Nazi terror, not after the evidence produced at the Nuremberg trials of Nazi war criminals, and the Jerusalem trial of Adolph Eichmann. It is true that, essentially, Hitler warred upon all religions, and all forms of democratic political expression, and in this respect, Nazism came to be recognized as humanity's ultimate barbarism. But only regarding the Jews had he dared to formulate what the Nazis hopefully called the "final solution to the Jewish problem." His racist theories, of course, were not developed in Germany alone, but were borrowed from other "scientific" sources, elsewhere, and expeditiously improved upon in Berlin, in the dexterous hands of Nazi-German scientists and philosophers. The "doctrine" was ridiculously elementary: the Jews are an inferior race, parasites who defile and exploit. Borrowing a page from a Russian book, Hitler warned the Christian peoples that the Jews were bent upon world domination and, unless exterminated, would succeed in contaminating all the human race.

In neither the Russian nor the Nazi-German form of anti-Semitism was there any attempt at sophistication, nor any desire to clothe their Jew-hatred in urbane, suave, or scholarly garb. It was fanatical, filthy, bloody, and violent; it appealed directly to the violent urges; it was openly and crudely incorporated into national policy and made a focal point of the nationalist propaganda. But in America, Jews would discover that prejudice against them was of a totally different kind and character. In the colonial days what little anti-Jewish sentiment appeared was linked directly to the problem of religious differences. Later, in frontier America, religious toleration gained the ascendancy. For a brief time, in mid-nineteenth-century America, nativist, antiforeign movements sprang up, but they were directed by the Protestant majority, as much against the Catholics as against the Jews. Indeed, even the later outcropping of the Ku Klux Klan was principally geared to the anti-Catholic, anti-Negro feelings of the American South, and not specifically at the Jews of America. Throughout all the years of the anti-Semitic terror in east-Europe, from the last decades of the nineteenth century well into the first decade of the twentieth, the people and the government of the United States were the staunch supporters and defenders of the Jews against their overseas tyrants. We have already seen what was offered the Jews of Rumania; even greater moral and political help was given to the Jews of Russia, during the travail of the pogroms. In fact, it must be objectively reported that not until the advent of Hitlerism in the mid-1930s were there anti-Semitic *movements,* as such, in America. What organized Jew-baiting had existed was almost always linked to movements that were essentially anti-Catholic.

With the emergence of Hitler in the 1930's, there began to grow up in America a number of "lunatic fringe" organizations, the German-American Bund, the Silver Shirts, and their like, which attempted to gain support in America for the Nazi race theories. The "New Deal" of Franklin D. Roosevelt was a favorite target of their attack, and they mocked it as the "Jew Deal." The economic depression, too, offered unusual opportunities for the acceptance of their demagogic appeals in circles of America that had never before participated in anti-Semitic activity. Even some outstanding public figures, in that period, deigned to identify themselves publicly with their programs. In the late thirties, before America's entry into the war against Germany, large sections of the American Middle West, long isolationist in their world outlook, came under the influence of the "America First" organization, and not infrequently were tarred with the brush of anti-Semitism. Because they saw no threat in Nazism, many of these people were led to believe that if America went to war against Germany it would serve—and save—no one but the Jews.

By and large, however, the anti-Semitic movements of the United States have been basically different from those in Europe. In the Old World, organized Jew-hatred was principally a political phenomenon supported by a popular base of public opinion, while in America it was primarily a manifestation of psychopathological groups hovering on the fringes of public respectability. The anti-Semitism of modern Europe, in Russia, Germany, and elsewhere, was set into a nationalistic, political framework, and it sought to achieve definite and specific country-wide social and economic reforms on the basis of its anti-Jewish motivations. Jews were either to be reduced to second-class citizenship, denied common civil rights, jailed, expelled, or as we have seen, even actually exterminated. These wild calls of nationalistic anti-Semitism have never been heard from the spokesmen of the accepted political parties in America, but only from the frothy lips of the lunatic fringe: the irresponsible, impulsive, and fanatical hatemongers. That the "call of the wild" is still frightening, and its sounds to those against whom it is directed are ominous, cannot be denied. Yet, it remains a far cry from the endemic, built-in, politically-and-governmentally fostered anti-Semitism of the European Jewish experience. Here it does not, as it had in the Old World, pose a basic threat to the fundamental security of the American Jewish community.

On the other hand, what might be called social anti-Semitism, in contrast to political anti-Semitism, has not yet been eradicated in America. True, to be publicly identified as an anti-Semite is thought to be distasteful, even scandalous. Yet, social discrimination is still widely practiced against Jews in underhanded, unpublicized fashion. It is still accepted as standard procedure in such areas as housing or in real estate transactions, in hotel accommodation, and even in some sectors of the industrial world. The "five o'clock shadow" still falls across the face of America when Jews and Christians leave their factory benches or their office desks and return to their separate, socially sectarian worlds, not to meet again until nine o'clock the next morning. Even colleges, universities, and professional schools were often more difficult for Jews to enter— even for Jewish applicants with higher marks—than for the average non-Jew. Jewish students have been denied admission to such schools on the grounds that they were not Christian, for these institutions, it has been politely claimed, are intended for the training of "Christian gentlemen."[10] Clearly evident in such situations is the secularization in America of the ancient and medieval Christian practice of Jewish ostracism: the substitution of nonreligious forms of discrimination for the religious ideology of older times. Unconsciously, however, this modern, secular "metaphysics" is of a piece with the older theological fabric. The Christian gentleman no longer designates a religious type, but an Anglo-Saxon social ideal. Yet it is by no means accidental that it should still be invoked to conjure up the mental picture that is actually in the minds of many who discriminate against Jews.

On the corporate front, where power and status operate at full steam, the throttling of talented Jews by a predominantly Protestant organizational elite was as much in evidence in the 1980s as it had been decades earlier. Jews were still excluded from the major boardrooms and social clubs of the nation. It was well known that both of these areas were clearly, if discreetly, interconnected. "The clubs are a repository of the values held by the upper level prestige groups in the community and are a means by which these values are transferred to the business environment," Reed Powell, a sociologist at Ohio State University concluded, after surveying the scene. Other researchers report: "One thing is certain when it comes to Jews. There still are not very many of them in these clubs. Of more than 4,000 Jews we studied as directors of prestigious Jewish community organizations or members of elite Jewish social clubs, only 24 were members of the 40 elite corporate clubs we examined around the country. Among 127 Jews who were corporate directors, only nine were members of one or more of these clubs . . . Generally speaking, Jews who (do) sit on corporate boards and belong to non-Jewish social clubs are less likely to list their Jewish affiliations than Jews not serving on boards." What happens to those Jews who get through the discrimination that still exists in some corporations and many social clubs and become part of the corporate establishment? In the words of Laurence Tisch, "a first generation member of the super-wealthy class . . . (who controls) the giant Loews Hotel conglomerate, 'they become less and less Jewish.'"[11]

To be sure, the American Jewish experience remains a far cry, indeed, from the real terror of east European Jews. They had to hide for their lives behind locked doors when Catholic neighbors were returning home from a Holy Week mass which vividly described the Jews as clamoring for the execution of Jesus. Frequently enough, the blood bath of a pogrom was the outcome of a religious service which had stressed that "not only the Jews of Christ's time, but Jews of all time were guilty of having killed Christ, the God-man; theologically speaking they were deicides . . . The sufferings of the Jews were to be understood as part of their punishment for the crime of having rejected Christ and their original destiny—Judaism was a useless thing, an invalid ethic, an invalid way of life, an invalid method of worship, which had been rendered pointless by the advent of Christ . . . The Jews were allied with the devil, they were always entering into conspiracies—with Freemasons, with Communists, with atheists, with secularists—for the sole purpose of destroying the Church and wiping Christianity off the face of the earth."[12] Little wonder that even liberal Christians, like Martin E. Marty, would understand, after reflecting on such a history, that "the American Jew is better off in a ripely pluralistic America than he was in Protestant, or would be Protestant-Catholic America. In many instances he will ally with the avowedly secular, for good reasons."[13]

Jew-hatred in America remained essentially apolitical, and its expressions were principally ideological and social—with economic overtones. These, nevertheless, were unmistakably rooted in the negative imagery inherited from and reinforced by standard Christian teachings about the nature of Jews and Judaism. As a result, anti-Semitism in the United States, however and whenever expressed, often consists of a "barrage of untruths and half truths that seriously compromise the Jew's collective personality, question his behavior, and undermine his role in society." Michael N. Dobkowski has described how these serious distortions operate to justify the inherited Christian view that *because of their obstinate allegiance to Judaism,* Jews are really not the equals of Christians:

> The opponents of nationalism saw Jews as uncompromising nationalists, with a nationalist God and a nationalist Torah; the nationalists saw Jews as

internationalists with allegiance to no country. Political liberals denounced the Jews as an instrument of reaction and pharasaic authority; political reactionaries denounced him as a threat to the stability and order of the state. Religious Christians expressed their disfavor with Jewish pedantry, science, and atheism; and the free thinkers among them never tired of accusing the Jews of superstition, ignorance, and religious fanaticism . . . some radicals and social reformers described the Jew, resentfully, as bursting with self-interest and egoism, the capitalist par excellence who is the bearer of the biblical civilization that is based on slavery, oppression, and parasitism . . . For the living, the Jew is a dead race with no future; for the natives, an unassimilable alien; for property holders, a radical who would dismantle society; for the poor, an exploiter and international millionaire; for patriots, a man without a country; for all classes, a potential rival.[14]

There is a tendency among many sociologists and psychologists to lump anti-Semitism together with "prejudice in general," and to treat it either as a symptom of other flaws in the American social structure or as an aspect of a general tendency in the character structure of certain people. Millions of dollars have been expended on studies dealing with the nature of human prejudice. At regular intervals, one comes across learned investigations bearing some such titles as these—titles which reveal their point of departure: "Personality Factors in Anti-Semitism"; "Anti-Semitism and the Authoritarian Personality"; "The Loss of Status and Anti-Semitic Attitudes"; "The Psychodynamics of the Anti-Semitic Mind"; etc., etc. Undoubtedly, social and psychological factors are at work in the formation of all value judgments, and prejudiced thought and behavior are surely not exempted from such influences. What seems, too often, to be lacking in many of these studies, however, is an awareness of the crucial importance of the *history* of anti-Semitism, in addition to its sociology and psychology. From that history, even as only briefly indicated here, all signs point to a major and fundamental conclusion: the religious elements have been the constant and therefore the crucial factors. The other explanations may be functional, descriptive, or operational. They are not causative. Yet, "without the use of history," as C. Wright Mills reminded us, "and without a historical sense of psychological matters, the social scientist can not adequately state the kinds of problems that ought now to be the orienting points of his studies . . . History is the shank of social study . . ."[15]

Moreover, students of anti-Semitism, including historians, who focus almost exclusively on the personality traits of anti-Semites, on the psychoanalytic basis of their hatred, or on the social milieu, are often guilty of actually disconnecting anti-Semitism from its target, which, of course is, the Jewish people. Ironically, studies motivated principally by psychological or social-economic considerations such as these, usually run the risk of producing conclusions that overlook the central, essential fact: *it was the Jews who were the victims.* Indeed, they may even lead to absurdities, which end up by de-Judaizing anti-Semitism, itself.[16]

Even the social and educational discrimination against Jews as a religious minority in America can be traced to the root-cause of theological doctrine. The very political freedom that the republican form of democracy had given to various religions here could sometimes be put into the service of religious intolerance. Catholics, in America, have known very well that the absence of government restraints in the private area of religious choice also made it possible for Protestants freely to denounce them as Papists or as agents of a foreign power, the Vatican. Similarly, the separation of church from state in America guaranteed a free church, but it did not prevent some free churches from preserving and even extending their built-in theological systems—even when these were clearly intolerant of the religious ways of others. Ironically, the separation principle often worked in a counterdemocratic fashion: it precluded the federal government from any possible role in forcing the elimination of the religious discrimination of religious groups. (Even now, years after the definitive Supreme Court school-desegregation decision, some church-schools still refuse to integrate on so-called religious grounds.)

While it is true that in many ways the secular agencies of America have outstripped the various religious groups in their espousal of genuine pluralism, vestiges of older religious biases still remain deeply embedded within them, nevertheless. Investigations of social studies texts used in American elementary schools reveal that these books are biased in favor of Protestantism over Catholicism and of Christianity over Judaism. The Reformation is usually described from the point of view of the Protestants; the Catholic Church is often seen as evil, corrupt, and cruel. Virtually all of post-Biblical Jewish history and Judaism are ignored and no mention is made of the contributions of Jews to the growth and development of America. Even more discouraging is the fact that on so sensitive a religious question as the Crucifixion, many texts used in American public schools—which, in Justice Felix Frankfurter's words, "should keep scrupulously free from entanglement in the strife of sects"—often buttress rather than eliminate sectarian dogmas that have helped to keep anti-Semitism alive.[17]

It is, of course, among the religious groups themselves that Americans discriminate most. Observing the contemporary scene, one discovers a curious American paradox: religious pluralism, which is so often regarded as the great American aspiration, is also often a source of inter-religious hostility! Protestants still regard America as "their" country. It is for the Jews, however, that this situation has the most ironical meanings.[18] When they had shed their status as just another ethnic or cultural group that had been absorbed into America, and emerged as a "co-equal" religious community, they sometimes moved into direct competition with the members of the other two religions of America. They appeared to be "too equal," in the eyes of those whose religious fervor moves them into moods of anxiety and insecurity. New fears that their Protestant or Catholic convictions are threatened by the existence of a third religion, Judaism, now arise, fears that had not been experienced so long as Jews could be regarded as only an ethnic, and not as a resurgent, dynamic religious community.

In a most sensitive area, the religious classroom of the church Sunday school, where many of the earliest impressions of Christian teaching are often permanently and indelibly imprinted, much damage has also been done to Jewish-Christian relations. The results of a study conducted at Yale University of some Protestant attitudes to Judaism and Jews, as reflected in standard textbook material used by the various denominations, elicited this comment from Dr. Reinhold Niebuhr: "The evidence of the study has convinced me that the religious and racial sources of anti-Semitism are at least equal, and perhaps the religious source may be the more powerful."[19] And his colleague, then Dean of the Faculty at Union Theological Seminary, New York, Dr. John C. Bennett, agreed, noting that the Christian teaching in many contemporary church textbooks in America "does contain elements which stimulate anti-Jewish prejudice."[20] Dr. Bernhard E. Olson, who conducted the study at Yale, had himself noted the difficulties:

It is as impossible . . . for a Christian teacher to communicate the Christian message without reference to Judaism as it would be to teach American history without referring to England and the founding fathers. . . .
This inevitable Hebrew involvement in religious instruction makes the Jew something more than just another minority which happens to get mentioned in Christian teaching. While a lesson writer might disregard the Negro, unless the outline guide specifies otherwise, he cannot ignore the Jew. . . .[21]
. . . While nothing essentially invidious . . . inheres in the marked prominence of the Jew in Protestant texts, there is in it an ever-present danger. As a minority which inescapably figures in the foreground of Christian thought—and remains an accessible minority in a society which contains deep strains of anti-Semitism—the Jewish community easily becomes a vulnerable target. There are instances cited in this study where the Jew is used as a convenient whipping boy for human ills and failings, simply because he is "there" in the biblical material and therefore was suggested to the writer as the most relevant object of criticism. That the writers may have in mind only biblical Jewry does not make the problem less serious, since this distinction is seldom made. For the Jew to be under the continual scrutiny of the pupil and teacher with their open textbook is to expose him to potential hazards; in the Christian era the Jew has infrequently escaped these dangers unharmed.[22]

Dr. Olson's "Yale Study" was a pathbreaker, and it helped to establish the need for textbook revision of Christian teaching concerning the Jews. The new books produced since that study were much improved in this area. Yet, researches conducted in both Protestant and Catholic schools about a decade later revealed that their textbooks still contained an inordinate amount of references to Jews which "included some of the most vile references made of any religious group." The charge of deicide was still frequent, the Jewish covenant was often declared to be ended, and the Pharisees were described on many occasions as sub-human creatures.[23] Clearly, the method of teaching Christianity, in its relationship to Jews and Judaism, must be constantly reviewed by Christians, if they are not to convert religious freedom in America into license for intolerance.

Yet, we must not overlook the new and revolutionary Christian attitudes of some outstanding American churchmen and theologians, to which we have referred earlier. It remains to be seen, however, if the Christian religious community of the United States is willing to follow the same road. Will the rank-and-file member of the average Christian church in America heed the call of the American Christian avant-garde?

What, in fact, have these theologians been saying? First, there is a fundamental suggestion that if America is truly to lead the world, if it is to be really different in its relationships with the Jewish community, then the forces of Christian religion must now come to grips with the ancient theological bias of Christianity, and, in the best sense of the word, Americanize those teachings. Second, implicit in their new teachings, there is an invitation to the development, on the local, grass-roots level, of the spirit of true religious dialogue, by means of which Christian clergymen may explain Christianity in terms of this proposed relationship to Judaism—at least to rabbis.

In 1960, a clearly worded "preface to dialogue," laying down six basic ground rules for this new religious approach, was set down by Dr. Robert McAfee Brown,[24] then of the (Protestant) Union Theological Seminary, New York:

1. Each partner must believe that the other is speaking in good faith;
2. Each partner must have a clear understanding of his own faith;
3. Each partner must strive for a clear understanding of the faith of the other.
    This implies:
    a. his willingness to interpret the faith of the other in its best light rather than in its worst; and
    b. a continual willingness to revise his understanding of the faith of the other.
4. Each partner must accept responsibility in humility and penitence for what his group has done, and is doing, to foster and perpetuate division.

5. Each partner must forthrightly face the issues that cause separation, as well as those that create solidarity.

6. Each partner must recognize that all that can be done with the dialogue is to offer it up to God.

The cast of this new theological thinking was clearly molded out of a more objective, more scholarly approach to Christianity than has heretofore been the case among many Christian theologians. The Christian academicians—for most of those in the forefront of this new trend are teachers at various theological seminaries—make it clear that for Christians, Judaism need not be seen either as a false religion or as one in which the true God is worshiped in ignorance. The relationship of Christianity to Judaism, they aver, is unique and intimate. Christians must never doubt that the God who spoke to Israel is the God who spoke to Jesus. From time to time, in the past, there were those like the Marcionites, who have tried to deny this. But all such efforts are doomed to failure: the God of the Old Testament is the God of the New Testament. The words of a recent Pope were thus crucial, when he declared that "spiritually, we are all Semites."

It is therefore possible, these Christian teachers continue, to speak of a Judeo-Christian tradition and a Judeo-Christian ethic, despite the many different emphases each group must give to these doctrines. The Old Testament, or Torah, was given to Israel that men might live by its precepts, in conformity to the will of God. The New Testament, which proclaims the good news of the advent of the Messiah of Jewish expectation, was given to the world that men might have salvation: the inheritance of eternal life in this world and in the world to come. The Jews were chosen by God to serve as a special people that should make known His ways. The New Israel, the Church, was chosen by the same God to serve as a witnessing community rooted in Christ, whose obedience to the Law of Judaism would now be surpassed in its allegiance to Christ.

Where, then, in their scheme of things, does this leave Judaism?

As God's agent of Salvation, they would answer, Israel came into being as a national community, with the revelation at Sinai. Although, at different times the Jews have opened wide their doors to receive proselytes, the essential Jewish community is that community of Israel and their descendants, which came into being at Sinai. To be a Jew, then, is not only to be part of a religious congregation, but also to be a member of a nation which, at Sinai, became the agent of God's purpose. It should thus not be difficult for Christians to understand how it was that in Judaism, nationhood and religion became inextricably interwoven. Therefore, one must not ask the members of this religio-national community to seek God in any other way than they themselves have encountered Him. Christians, they thus conclude, have no moral or religious right to seek the annulment of Judaism. And they couple this significant climax of their thought to the complementary view that Christianity is, in effect, the Judaism of the Gentiles, the transnational fulfillment in Christ of the Law given at Sinai.

From the Jewish side, these new Christian teachings have evoked an interesting response. While historically Jews have held fast to their own religious views and, with good reason, steered clear of engaging in religious discussion with Christian divines, recent events in America point to the beginnings of a serious theological interchange between the two groups. One hears in America today—from the formerly theologically reticent Jewish religionists—ideas equally unusual. Some noted Jewish theologians and rabbis are now suggesting, too, that both covenants— the Old and the New—are revelations of the One God. The continued existence of the people of Israel, they point out, its undimmed consciousness of its own covenant two thousand years after the coming of Jesus, serve to reinforce the view that the Jewish witness to God has never been annulled. The two covenants, therefore, must not be seen as standing in opposition to each other, but as in parallel affinity. Both are valid, and valid absolutely—one for Judaism, the other for Christianity. Therefore, they believe, neither Jews nor Christians may deviate from the absoluteness of their separate witness to God's truth. Neither religion is wayward or spurious.

It was the Roman Catholic Church, often regarded as an unmovable, traditional monolith, that had first set forth on paths that would lead to some of these new religious positions. In his search for "church renewal"—*aggiorniomento*—Pope John XXIII convened the Second Vatican Council, in October, 1962. It could not have then been foreseen that this "new ecumenism" of the Catholics would ultimately stretch beyond their fellow-Christians, the Protestants, and embrace "strangers" and "outcasts"—the Jews—as well. Yet, by 1965, the Vatican issued a landmark decree, known as *"Nostra Aetate," No. 4,* or more popularly, as "The Jewish Declaration." In it, "displays of anti-Semitism staged against Jews at any time by anyone" were condemned for the first time on so high a level of Church authority. Moreover, the document asserted that not only had the Church received the Hebrew Bible from the Jews but that it still draws sustenance from Judaism, "the well-cultivated olive tree on to which have been grafted the wild shoots, the Gentiles." It was a sweeping, major attempt to wipe away the dark chapters of almost two thousand years of Church-sponsored anti-Jewishness. The decree proclaimed that the Jewish religion possessed continuing validity, for the covenant God had made with the Jewish people had never been annulled: "He does not repent of the gifts He makes or of the calls He issues." Further, the Declaration took pains to emphasize the *Jewishness* of Christianity, itself. "Brotherly dialogues" with their fellow Jews soon became the order of the day in the American branch of the Roman Catholic Church. To help foster these undertakings, "The American Catholic Bishops' Secretariat for Catholic Jewish Relations" was established in 1967, located in Washington, D.C. A goodly number of Bishops—especially those in the Northeast, where Jews were still most populous—created their own diocesan commissions in order to implement the dialogue called for by The Declaration.

In 1975, a newly established "Vatican Commission for Religious Relations with the Jews" issued its own "Guidelines and Suggestions for Implementing the Conciliar Declaration *Nostra Aetate,* Number 4." These "Guidelines" attempted to fill in certain notable voids that were missing, or glossed over, in the earlier Jewish Declaration. More particularly, they discussed questions dealing with the relationship of Jews and Judaism to the land and State of Israel, as well as sensitive areas touching on Christian proselytizing of Jews. The American Bishops picked up the thread of these Vatican guidelines and issued their own "Statement on the Jews," the same year. On Israel, they noted that "An overwhelming majority of Jews see themselves bound in one way or another to the land of Israel. Most Jews see this tie to the land as essential to their Jewishness. Whatever difficulties Christians may experience in sharing this view they should strive to understand this link between land and people." And on proselytizing, they applauded the Vatican Guidelines: "Dialogue demands respect for the other as he is; above all, respect for his faith and his religious convictions." The American prelates explicitly rejected all efforts on the part of Catholics to convert the Jews.[25]

There is little doubt that this novel American trend in Christian-Jewish relations is a function of the mood of dialogue, which became a new and welcome attitude in many areas of Protestant-Catholic relations. Some observers, however, have called attention to the fact that the much publicized "dialogue" between Catholics and Protestants is far from a reality, and that their basic pattern of mutual suspicion is still very much part of American life. They consider, too, that the triple melting pot is, in reality, a triple ghetto because, for them, mounting self-segregation and increasing absence of true interinvolvement represent the real characteristics of the three religious communities. Some would maintain that it really represents a negative, not a positive situation: the failure of Americans to accept the comprehensive, structural assimilation of its minorities. While most third-generation Americans have assimilated the American style in their outward behavior—which is to say that they have been acculturated—social barriers still prevent the descendants of non-Anglo-Saxon immigrants from entering into private, personal, and intimate relations with members of the "host" culture. These social structures—one might almost call them strictures—are virtually invisible in the impersonal interplay of general civic life. But they stand as well-armed sentries guarding the homes, recreation centers, and clubs of the Anglo-Saxon types and carefully prevent "outsiders" from entering into too intimate contact with them. Third-generation Jews may demonstrate a high rate of *cultural* assimilation, but this is also accompanied by a low rate of "accommodation." (Accommodation denotes the amount of social distance that exists between individuals or groups.)

Since the American church—and particularly the suburban church—is no longer a place of worship alone, but virtually serves as a private club for the family's intimate social and recreational activities, it can effectively mask the built-in barriers of the social structures in the hallowed name of religion. What we are really witnessing, then, warn some sociologists, is the deepening of social and cultural cleavage, not the growth and intensification of religious interaction and understanding. The churches and synagogues, in this view, serve as respectable islands of social retreat, institutions perpetuating and dignifying social and ethnic distance, more than as the spiritual instruments of community solidarity. If indeed these sociological observations are valid and represent more than mere academic speculation, they pose a distinct challenge to faithful interfaith dialogue.[26]

Nor was it accidental that many of the new Black leaders were recruited from the ranks of the Christian clergy. They surely knew from their religious training that Jews were vulnerable in the eyes of many of their fundamentalist, "Bible-believing" parishioners. Despite a long-standing history of cooperation between the two groups, and despite the many special efforts which Jewish community leaders had pioneered in favor of Black-sponsored colleges and in support of the civil rights movement, since the late 1960s that old coalition has virtually evaporated. Moreover, the problems facing Israel can, curiously, also continue to drive a wedge between these two communities. Increasingly, Black leaders identify with the Arabs as fellow Afro-Asians and regard Israel as an intruder into "their" world. On the other hand, as Jews find themselves rebuffed by American Blacks—or even as the targets of Black dissatisfaction—they will turn their attention away from support or cooperation with them and rally their interest even more strenuously in favor of Israel, in self-defense against the political attacks of Blacks. These "Black-Christian" developments will be further exacerbated should the Black-Muslim movement in the United States continue to grow in the years ahead.

There were other serious challenges to the integrity of Jewish life which had their source in the Christian churches of America, and which despite—if not as a result of—the "new" Jewish ethnicity, have erupted since 1967. As noted, that year became a watershed in the history of Jewish consciousness. Jews who had already wandered far from "home" began streaming back, as Israel's annihilation was threatened by Arab states, while the rest of the world—churchmen included—kept silent again. For almost all Jews, the spectre of two Holocausts within a single generation was too much to bear. The record of the American churches during the Nazi years was one of ambivalence and almost total indifference. Many hid their faces, or, worse still, placidly accepted the doom of the Six Million in Hitler's extermination camps as a divine judgment for the "Jewish rejection of Jesus." Yet, by June, 1967, when the Six Day War broke out in Israel, there had already been all these "revolutionary" Christian pronouncements about the urgency of arranging "fraternal dialogues" with Jews, and the need to understand, and not to reject the otherness of Judaism. Thus, the profound Christian silence at that fateful hour of modern Jewish history produced a double trauma in the hearts of most American Jews; shock and disbelief that responsible, seemingly liberated Christians could remain aloof from their life-death agonies; and a deep sense of having been misled and seduced by those very recent Christian protestations of love and understanding. There was widespread disillusionment of Jews with the Christian community.

The mainline "liberal" Protestant churches, as symbolized in their country-wide canopy organization, The National Council of Churches, further menaced good Christian-Jewish relations. Not content with its apathetic, quiescent attitude when "the lights were going out" in Israel in 1967, the "N.C.C." continued to side with the Arab states, and to disregard Israel's need for security in the face of the belligerent "no-peace," "no-recognition," "no-negotiation" stance adopted by all Arab countries save Egypt. One astute Christian observer, Franklin H. Littell, pithily summarized the "problem" Jews will probably continue to experience with these liberal Christian groups: "The thing, the nineteenth century Liberal Protestant, the Christian humanitarian, cannot grasp is the Jew who is a winner, a citizen soldier of liberty and dignity, who does not have to beg protection of a patron or toleration of a so-called Christian nation . . . This is precisely the reason why Israel is a stone of stumbling, and why also the generally covert anti-Semitism of liberal Protestantism can be just as dangerous as the overt anti-Semitism of the radical right."[27]

Indeed, the rise of "born again" Christianity and the growth of militant, right-wing evangelical cadres which "television religion" has helped to foster, also continue to threaten good Christian-Jewish relationships. Although these groups bear a variety of different names, they often speak out as one—with a strident, nationalistic voice as "Christian America." Essentially, they are the self-same fundamentalist Christians, who, via television, have now made the whole country into their potential "Bible Belt." Whether denominated as "The Moral Majority," or by other names of their choosing, they are at heart seeking to politicize Christianity by calling into action those dormant Wasp forces which feel threatened by liberal pluralism, and the multiple life-choices offered by the "new ethnicity." Often, they may speak out in behalf of the State of Israel, as "Concerned Christians" who reject the frequent pro-Arab pronouncements of their avowed adversaries, the liberal Protestant churches. Yet, sensitive Jews are not unaware of the fact that these "evangelicals" are also essentially triumphalist Christians whose "Christian Zionism" cannot conceal their hope that Israel will fade away with the "second coming" of Jesus as the acknowledged Messiah of the Jews. Nor do many of these "neo-fundamentalists" take the liberated step of renouncing the validity of the Christian mission to the Jews. The conversion of the Jews remains an integral part of the theological position of most evangelical churches.

In addition, because Black Christian churches have been a leading force in the life of Black America, a religious dimension has been added to the growing number of issues which began to divide Jews and Blacks, approximately from the time of the Six Day War, in June, 1967. One community worker has summarized the new "factors behind Black anti-Semitism" after a period of about one hundred years of peaceful coalition between the two groups:

1. The movement of Blacks into neighborhoods that had previously been largely Jewish and the ensuing competition between those Jews who remained and the Blacks.
2. Reports of crimes against persons and property in these areas and differing views over law and order held by Jewish shopkeepers and Black residents.
3. The move by Black militants to take over the direction of the civil rights movement and to exclude Jews from participation.
4. The growing employment of anti-Semitic and anti-Israel rhetoric by these militants.
5. The developing professional and economic conflict caused by Blacks moving into vocational fields such as teaching and social work that had previously attracted large numbers of Jews . . .
. . . There were of course other and deeper seated factors involved in Black anti-Semitism. These had to do with the character of American society. Blacks who have suffered from a sense of inferiority due to the exploitation and oppression of the dominant white majority could, by manifesting anti-Semitic attitudes, identify with that majority. There is little reason to doubt that some militant leaders seized upon this psychological mechanism already active in their communities. Such leaders knew full well the history of anti-Semitism in America and were cognizant of the anti-Jewish attitudes widely prevalent in white society.[28]

Finally, the thorny and unresolved problem of church-state relations is still another stumbling block on the road toward interfaith understanding. Tensions between Catholics and Protestants, which inevitably overflow to the Jews, must follow in the wake of increasing Catholic pressure to narrow the gaps between church and state, by insistently seeking to level the historic wall of separation. And as Protestant groups respond to these incursions, they tend to become more and more defensive, and their counterpressures to bring religion to the public school often results in distorting the common ground they do share with Jews. The result of all these efforts often ends with Catholics withdrawing further from the secular public school and building their own parochial systems; with Protestants attempting to counter the success of Catholic parochial schools by seeking to make the public school more "religious," if not more Protestant; and with Jews, who are essentially committed to the public school system as a vehicle of the total community, emerging from the contest looking like agnostics, if not as downright atheists, as a result of their legal efforts to maintain the wall of separation.[29]

It may be, however, that American Protestants have not been adequately conditioned by their previous history to deal properly with the new confidence of Roman Catholics, whose Americanization is now almost complete, and whose previous sense of inferiority, in the presence of Protestant America, is now waning. Perhaps the abandonment of their self-consciousness will help American Catholics eliminate the need to keep aloof and remote from Protestants. There is also the possibility that more Protestant denominations may come to recognize what many of their own liberal groups already claim: that the forces of religion are weakened, not strengthened, when they seek to rely upon the agencies of government. Many could agree with Dr. Franklin H. Littell, a leading Protestant church historian, that the "whole image of early America as a 'Christian nation' (i.e., Protestant-controlled) is a lie which must be struck down." Only in "pluralism and voluntarism," Protestants like Dr. Littell maintain, can Americans "find unexpected strengths—political as well as religious," and only in these principles can all Americans achieve "a new lease on life and spiritual energy."[30]

On the other hand, one now hears conservative voices in the Jewish religious community speaking out against what they regard as an unwanted alliance between American Jews and the extreme secularists. They are calling for a new social theology which would re-examine the "Jewish rigidity" on church-state issues. These they fear, have put Judaism into an untenable position in a three-religion country. All this present uneasiness and ferment may perhaps thus be seen as a necessary transition state before arriving at the moment for real dialogue, which may not be as far away as some critics think. As for the Jews of America, however, there is little doubt that if the historic religious antagonisms of the Protestants and Catholics cannot be overcome here by the forces of religion themselves, then the roots of anti-Semitism, embedded in historical religious bias, can never be eradicated by those selfsame religions.

One thing is clear: for the first time in history—in the history of

America and of the world—interfaith discussions are beginning to be grounded in faith, and not linked to noble but secular-minded civic and national purpose. Even if it is only a beginning, it is no exaggeration to claim for this a major place in history; and no extravagance to believe that it can and will mature and grow. The hope of the American Jew depends upon it. But more: the hope of America, as a unique land.

NOTES

1. In the *Antiquities* of Josephus, there have been preserved several descriptions of Roman decrees in the time of Julius Caesar. Here is a typical decree:

"In the presidency of Artemon, on the first day of the month of Lenaeon, Dolabella, Imperator, to the magistrates, council and people of Ephesus greeting. Alexander, son of Theodorus, the envoy of Hyrcanus, son of Alexander, the high priest and ethnarch of the Jews, has explained to me that his coreligionists cannot undertake military service because they may not bear arms or march on the days of the Sabbath; nor can they obtain supplies of the native foods to which they are accustomed. I, therefore, like the governors before me, grant them exemption from military service and allow them to follow their native customs and to come together for sacred holy rites in accordance with their law, and to make offerings for their sacrifices; and it is my wish that you write these instructions to the various cities." Josephus, *Antiquities of the Jews*, Book XIV, Ch. 10, paragraph 12.

2. Trogus Pompeius, the Roman historian in the age of Augustus, wrote:

"And because they remembered that it was through fear of contagion that they had been driven out of Egypt, they were fearful that they should be hated by the inhabitants [of Arabia] for the same reason, and took care that they should not come into contact with foreigners. And this custom, which arose from a specific occasion, he [Moses] gradually changed into a fixed institution and religious principle." See Trogus Pompeius (Abridgment by Justinus), Book XXXVI, Chapter II.

Tacitus, the widely admired Roman historian, described the horrific nature of Jewish religious practices in these words:

"The . . . customs of the Jews are base and abominable, and owe their persistence to their depravity. For the worst rascals among other peoples, renouncing their ancestral religions, always kept sending tribute and contributions to Jerusalem, thereby increasing the wealth of the Jews; again, the Jews are extremely loyal toward one another, and always ready to show compassion, but toward every other people they feel only hate and enmity. They sit apart at meals, and they sleep apart, and although as a race they are prone to lust, they abstain from intercourse with foreign women; yet among themselves nothing is unlawful. They adopted circumcision to distinguish themselves from other peoples by this difference. Those who are converted to their ways follow the same practice, and the earliest lesson they receive is to despise the gods, to disown their country, and to regard their parents, children, and brothers as of little account. However, they take thought to increase their numbers; for they regard it as a crime to kill any late-born child, and they believe that the souls of those who are killed in battle are immortal; hence comes their passion for begetting children and their scorn of death . . . the Jews conceive of one god only, and that with the mind alone: they regard as impious those who make from perishable materials representations of gods in man's image . . . Therefore they set up no statues in their cities, still less in their temples; this flattery is not paid their kings, nor this honour given to Caesars . . . the ways of the Jews are preposterous and mean." See Tacitus, *The Histories*, Book V, Paragraph V (Loeb Classical Library).

3. James Parkes, *The Conflict of Church and Synagogue* (New York: Meridian Books, 1961), p. 373; p. 375.

4. Parkes wrote (*ibid.*, p. 376): "Ritual murder, the poisoning of the wells, the profanation of the Host, all these are natural outgrowths from the picture created by a Chrysostom or a Cyril. And the falsification of Jewish history itself persisted, and has persisted up to the present time in popular teaching. Scholars may know today of the beauty and profundity of the Jewish conception of life. They may know that '*some* Jews' were responsible for the death of Jesus. But the Christian public as a whole, the great and overwhelming majority of the hundreds of millions of nominal Christians in the world, still believe that 'the Jews' killed Jesus, that they are a people rejected by their God, that all the beauty of their Bible belongs to the Christian Church and not to those by whom it was written; and if on this ground, so carefully prepared, modern antisemites have reared a structure of racial and economic propaganda, the final responsibility still rests with those who prepared the soil, created the deformation of the people, and so made these ineptitudes credible."

5. The religious separation fostered by the early Church helped to harden the firm lines of social segregation between Jews and Gentiles in the centuries to follow. Jacob Katz shows how "the relationship between Jews and Gentiles is at all times a reciprocal one. . . . Every attitude of the Jew towards the non-Jew has its counterpart in a similar attitude of the Gentile towards the Jew." Jacob Katz, *Exclusiveness and Tolerance* (New York: Schocken Books, 1962), p. 3.

6. Quoted in Mark Vishniak, "Antisemitism in Tsarist Russia," in *Essays on Antisemitism*, Koppel S. Pinson, ed. (New York: Conference on Jewish Relations, 1946), p. 122.

7. In one village, "the peasants demanded from the village mayor a written certificate that they would not be prosecuted by the authorities for *not* participating in the 'killing of the Jews.' The mayor complied with their demand but for the sake of their own safety the peasants nevertheless plundered six of the Jewish houses." *Ibid.*, p. 131.

8. *Ibid.*, p. 132. The report was prepared by Count Kutaysov on the basis of investigations in South Russia. His report also claimed that there was a widespread feeling among the population that the Czar himself had sanctioned the pogroms.

9. See John Shelton Curtiss, *An Appraisal of the Protocols of Zion* (New York: Columbia University Press, 1942).

10. See Michael N. Dobkowski, *The Tarnished Dream*, Greenwood Press, Westport, Conn. 1979, pp. 158–9. See also John Higham, *Send These to Me*, Atheneum, N.Y. 1975, p. 154 ff.

11. G. William Domhoff and Richard L. Zweigenhaft, "Jews in the Corporate Establishment," *New York Times*, April 24, 1983; see also their *Jews in the Protestant Establishment*, Praeger, New York, 1982.

12. F. E. Curtus, (a pseudonym of a Roman Catholic observer at the Vatican Ecumenical Council), in "Vatican II and the Jews", *Commentary*, January, 1965.

13. Martin E. Marty, *Religion and Social Conflict*, (ed.) (New York: Oxford

University Press, 1964) p. 188. Also see Harold Quinley and Charles Glock, *Anti-Semitism in America,* Harper and Row, New York, 1979.

14. Michael N. Dobkowski, *op. cit.,* pp. 239–240.

15. C. Wright Mills, *The Sociological Imagination,* Oxford University Press, New York, 1959, p. 143.

It is interesting to note that quantitative studies, too, often produce similar ahistorical results. A statistical study published in 1982, based upon work by the Yankelovich, Skelly and White organization, while recognizing the general decline in American religious life, from 1964 on, is only partly willing to admit the Christian religious connection to *what it has defined as anti-Semitism.* It maintains that "the association of (Christian) religion and anti-Semitism is (also) due to the effects of age, education, and race. After we control for these three demographic factors, the association of both religious conviction and Christian fundamentalism with anti-Semitism disappears." See Gregory Martire and Ruth Clark, *Anti-Semitism in the United States,* Praeger, New York, 1982, p. 76.

A professional observer of anti-Semitism in America, Nathan Perlmutter, has demonstrated how far off the mark many of these studies are. See his *The Real Anti-Semitism in America,* Arbor House, New York, 1982, especially the chapter "What the Studies Reveal and What They Don't," pp. 71–102.

16. For an elaboration of this trend among historians and others, see Jacob Katz, "Misreadings of Anti-Semitism," *Commentary,* July, 1983, pp. 39–44.

17. See Judah J. Harris, "The Treatment of Religion in Elementary School Social Studies Textbooks" (New York: Anti-Defamation League, 1963). See also *The A. D. L. Bulletin,* February, 1963, pp. 2–3. Also see Charles E. Glock and Rodney Stark, *Christian Beliefs and Anti-Semitism,* Harper and Row, New York, 1965.

18. Protestant Church historian Wilhelm Pauck has aptly described this difficulty: "The Jews are unable to maintain the particular traditions they cherish except by stressing the particularistic pluralistic tendencies which are also characteristic of democracy. On the one hand, it is an integrated, unified public order, embracing all members of society; on the other hand, it permits individual groups to remain among themselves and to stress their own peculiar ways. . . . Yet when Jews insist on stressing the pluralistic possibilities of democracy which allow them to cultivate their own tradition, they are resented. . . . Insofar as it [social prejudice] is cherished by Protestants it proves that they are shaped in their thinking not chiefly by spiritual considerations but by middle-class interests that reflect their way of identifying themselves with American democracy." See Wilhelm Pauck, "Our Protestant Heritage," in *Religion in Contemporary Society,* Harold Stahmer, ed. (New York: Macmillan Paperbacks, 1963), p. 113.

19. Quoted in an editorial in *Religious Education,* March–April, 1960.

20. *Ibid.*

21. Bernhard E. Olson, "Intergroup Relations in Protestant Teaching Materials," in *Religious Education,* March–April, 1960, p. 129. In this same issue, there are also reports by Catholic and Jewish educators, detailing some of the work done in similar studies of their own religious textbooks, at Dropsie College (the Jewish study), and at Saint Louis University (the Catholic study); see also James Brown, "Christian Teaching and Anti-Semitism; Scrutinizing Religious Texts," in *Commentary,* December, 1957.

22. Bernhard E. Olson, *Faith and Prejudice* (New Haven and London: Yale University Press, 1963), p. 24.

23. For material concerning the Catholics, see John T. Pawlikowski, O.S.M.,

Catechetics and Prejudice, Paulist Press, New York, 1972; for similar studies of Protestant textbooks since the "Yale Study," see Gerald S. Strober, *Portrait of the Elder Brother: Jews and Judaism in Protestant Teaching Materials,* American Jewish Committee, New York, 1972.

24. Robert McAfee Brown and Gustav Weigel, S.J., *An American Dialogue* (New York: Doubleday, 1960), p. 32.

25. For a brief survey of these materials, see Leonard Swidler, "Catholic Statements on Jews: A Revolution in Progress" in *Judaism,* Summer, 1978, pp. 299–307.

26. See Milton M. Gordon, "Assimilation in America: Theory and Reality" in *Daedalus,* Spring, 1961, pp. 253–285; Eugene J. Lipman and Albert Vorspan, *A Tale of Ten Cities: The Triple Ghetto in American Religious Life* (New York: Union of American Hebrew Congregations, 1962).

27. See *Congress BiWeekly,* February 20, 1970.

28. Gerald S. Strober, *American Jews: Community in Crisis,* Doubleday, Garden City, N.Y. 1974, pp. 131–133.

29. For an informed description of the competing viewpoints of the Roman Catholics, the "Protestant dissenters," and the so-called secular humanism of the Jewish community in matters relating to church-state issues, see Leo Pfeffer, *Creeds in Competition* (New York: Harper & Brothers, 1958).

30. Franklin Hamlin Littell, *From State Church to Pluralism: A Protestant Interpretation of Religion in American History* (New York: Doubleday Anchor Original, 1962), p. xx.

CHAPTER VIII

In Search of Liberty

IT WAS A DELIGHTFUL PLEASANTRY, ACCORDING TO THE OBVIOUSLY APOCRY-phal tale, that Emperor Franz Josef exchanged with Czar Nicholas I. The two monarchs met, and in the course of their regal banter the Russian suddenly turned upon the Viennese with apparent anger: "In our country we do everything to thwart the Jews. We deny them all civil rights and political privileges. But you, on the other hand, are planning to emancipate them! You are even ready, I hear it said, to make them equal to the Christians. Cousin! Why do you strengthen them?" To which, Franz Josef is reported to have laconically replied: "You, of course, are free to destroy them in your way. You will forgive me, I hope, if I choose to destroy them in my own manner."

Not many years after this mythical royal meeting, a leading Russian Jewish essayist, Ahad Ha-'Am, still lacking the civic and political privileges granted to his west-European brethren long before, thought of himself as a free man, in contrast to their "slavery within freedom." Emancipated, he asked? Yes, emancipated from Judaism! For him, the price they had paid for that "freedom" was too high. He preferred to remain a free man in the midst of slavery—free to preserve his unique Jewish heritage, despite his political bondage in a land of tyranny. In 1891, he wrote:

> I try mayhap to give my weary eyes a rest from the scene of ignorance, of degradation, of unutterable poverty that confronts me here in Russia, and find comfort by looking yonder, across the border, where there are Jewish professors, Jewish members of Academies, Jewish officers in the army, Jewish civil servants; and when I see there, behind the glory and the grandeur of it all, a twofold spiritual slavery—moral slavery and intellectual slavery—and ask myself: Do I envy these fellow-Jews of mine their emancipation?—I answer, in all truth and sincerity: No! A thousand times No! The privileges are not worth the price! I may not be emancipated; but at least I have not sold my soul for emancipation. I at least can proclaim from the housetops that my kith and kin are dear to me wherever they are, without being constrained to find forced and unsatisfactory excuses. . . .
>
> In a word, I am my own, and my opinions and feelings are my own. I have no reason for concealing or denying them, for deceiving others or myself. And this spiritual freedom—scoff who will!—I would not exchange or barter for all the emancipation in the world.[1]

[117]

Looking back at the history of the Jewish struggle for civic emancipation in western Europe, at the beginning of the modern period, one notes a curious, but evident, relationship between anti-Semitism and assimilation. On one hand, Jews were faced with the problem of surviving in the teeth of an open hostility that threatened to destroy their group life. Yet, on the other hand, their newly acquired emancipated status was no less a challenge to their survival as a group. Now, the question was: how does one retain his Jewish loyalties in the face of the temptation to "become just like everyone else"? The hand of welcome, no less than the face of hostility, threatened them with the loss of their identity.

The emancipation of the Jews in western Europe triggered a most amazing psychological phenomenon. Many Jews had apparently been listening very intently to what some anti-Semites had been saying about Jews and Judaism, and oddly, they, too, seemed to agree! They agreed because they were seeking to be Frenchmen, or Germans—full nationals, for the first time in the history of the Diaspora. And obviously, as neophytes in such undertakings, they did not find it possible to be both Frenchmen or Germans *and* Jews. One or the other they believed, but not both.

To leave the ghetto and to be transplanted overnight into western culture was, understandably, a traumatic event in the life of the Jew. The psychological wounds inherent in so rapid a passage from one world to another are great, and perhaps even incurable. In such circumstances, it is not unusual that those who sought to acquire—and even more important, to keep—this new status would regard Judaism and vital Jewish group life as unwanted sources of further alienation from the glittering world now beckoning to them. Nothing less than their full and unconditional surrender of both these irritants would do: Judaism and Jewishness would have to be expunged and their influence in their lives eradicated from memory. They lived by exaggeration: exaggerating glories of their civic equality, they found it necessary to exaggerate the inappropriateness of Judaism.

They were to discover, however, even if they did not always face up to their discovery, that the anti-Semite would shift his ground and accord to the emancipated, de-Judaized Jew no different a response than to his ghettoized fathers. Despite the success of many in jettisoning the Jewish intellectual and spiritual baggage accumulated over many centuries, the new anti-Semitism in France and Germany still hounded them. It could no longer ground its antipathies in the fact that Jews were aliens, and therefore different, but it could, and did, object to Jews because they claimed to be the same as Christians—and, in fact, were not. The west-European anti-Semite, by the last half of the nineteenth century, had had enough! He was tired of Jews who were Jews but who had been so successful in ceasing to be Jews that they were becoming no different from himself. He was suspicious of their exaggerated patriotism, their over-eagerness to associate only with non-Jews, their disdain of their own people, their unwelcome *parvenu* demeanor.

"The predicament of emancipated Jewry," Jacob Katz has pungently explained,

> and ultimately the cause of its tragic end, was rooted not in one or another ideology but in the fact that Jewish Emancipation had been tacitly tied to an illusory expectation—the disappearance of the Jewish community of its own volition. When this failed to happen, and the Jews, despite Emancipation and acculturation, continued to be conspicuously evident, a certain uneasiness, not to say of outright scandal, was experienced by Gentiles. The internal contradiction at the very heart of Jewish Emancipation—the granting of civil rights to a people, in the hope that they would disappear—began to exact its cost. If gaining civil rights meant an enormous improvement in Jewish prospects, at the same time it carried with it a precariously ill-defined status which was bound to elicit antagonism from the Gentile world.[2]

The case of Alfred Dreyfus, the French Army captain wrongly and falsely sentenced to life imprisonment by a military tribunal in 1894, may serve as a single, yet significant, reflection of the situation. Dreyfus, the Jew, was of course innocent of the high crimes of which his anti-Semitic Army superiors had accused him. Ultimately, as a result of the help of such liberals as Clemenceau and Zola, the sentence was annulled, and he was acquitted. But in the minds of those Frenchmen who had seized upon the Dreyfus incident as an opportunity to cry out *"mort aux juives!"* the guilt of the Jewish Army captain did not in the first instance really lie in the actual charges, true or false, that had brought him before the Army court. Dreyfus was guilty of something else; and that guilt no court could pardon. A French writer has crisply described the real "crime" of Dreyfus in the eyes of the average Frenchman. Dreyfus, he explains, and thousands of other emancipated Jews like him, had too strong a "desire to assimilate completely to Gallic modes, to live on intimate terms with our old-fashioned families, to occupy the most distinguished positions in the state." But not these factors alone disturbed the French. Jews like Dreyfus, this French author concludes with disdain, had only "contempt for the recently naturalized Jewish 'Polaks' of Galicia, and were, in effect, traitors against their own race. . . . The Dreyfuses of 1894?" he mocks. "Why, they were anti-Semites!"[3] By a strange irony, the "anti-Semitism" of the emancipated Jews of western Europe was an important feedback in nourishing the "new" anti-Semitism of the enlightened, modern Westerner.

In the wake of this process, the modern, emancipated Jew of the West soon came to suffer a double alienation. He had sought distant horizons, and failed. The Jewish community was, by now, equally remote from him, and he discovered what every self-imposed exile knows: "You can't go home again." Yet, not always was this twin-sided sense of alienation poignantly felt or brooded over. Fortuitously, the emancipated Jew was temporarily saved from the meaninglessness of his own life. He gained this reprieve because the century marking these efforts to achieve Jewish emancipation coincided with the very years in which new materialist hopes were rising in the West. Following the peace treaties of 1815, Europe would know of no major war for one hundred years. Buoyant philosophies and secular religions of all kinds were now crowding the scene and clamoring for attention. This was an era of discovery, of the growth of industry, trade, and empire. The horizons of Western man were stretching in new and exciting directions. He was eager to cast off old traditions and fit himself out for the spirit of a new age.

In this age of materialist ascendancy, the values and philosophies of the past were crumbling for all men. For the emancipated Jew, however, this situation seemed to provide a very special opportunity. He could lose himself in a welter of new "isms," and by giving allegiance to these political, philosophical, or psychological theories and movements, he would also lose—or believed he could—his sense of alienation. As a result, despite the failure of emancipation to eradicate anti-Semitism, the west-European Jew never gave up even his weak hold on his new status, nor did he fully affirm Judaism. He may sometimes have felt uneasy, but when he did, he could attempt to submerge himself even deeper in the "new secularism" of nineteenth-century Europe, and seek to cover up his real loss of identity.

Could the emancipated Jew of America be any different? Or would he, in the unique environment of the New World, foster a "new emancipation"? Would he open up new highways for Jewish self-expression, as a free man in a free society, and, in the words of Ludwig Lewisohn, initiate "a new emancipation from the sordid fallacies of scientific materialism, from the ominous identification of the state with society, from the cowardice which will not criticize our Gentile environment, as civilized Gentiles do daily, from that inner servility which consents to our being merely the object, never the codeterminants of the historic process in which we are involved.' "⁴ But answers to such questions cannot be adequately evaluated, unless they are first seen in the light of history—a history beginning with the faltering and uncertain steps taken a hundred and fifty years ago by the Jews of western Europe, in their passionate quest for equality and emancipation.

In the eighteenth century, as west-European states, particularly France and Prussia, began to make more and more encroachments upon what had been the private realms of the public life, the powers of many hitherto autonomous bodies became less and less. The emergence of the central state, as we know it today, as the absolute and single governing force, is, in fact, one of the main hallmarks of the death of medievalism. The modern era in European political history may be said to have come into being when the privileges of the nobility, the clergy, and even of the Third Estate, long cherished and kept by these groups as their private rights, were dissipated by the rising authority of absolute central government. All these private pockets of autonomy, hangovers from the medieval tradition, would now be required to give way to the modern, bureaucratic state.

With this progressive deterioration of the older structure of society, the continued existence of a separate, corporate Jewish community (which in many ways had functioned as a "state within a state") was also placed in great doubt. No less than upon the other corporate groups, modern political theory inflicted the same heavy blows upon the cohesive integrity of the Jewish community. Jewish communities under Isalm or in eastern Europe, where the economics of a burgeoning capitalism and its concomitant political theory of the nation-state were still in the distant future, would be spared their communal autonomy for some time. But not in the West. There, if the unification of the state was to proceed, the ghetto walls had to be torn down and Jewish self-government dissolved. An integral unity that had been preserved for centuries and possessed unusual powers of social control was now crumbling. However, Western Jews optimistically believed that the political emancipation soon to be theirs would surely serve as a superior replacement for what they were now required to give up. Indeed, as a result of new social contacts with their non-Jewish neighbors, hastened by the development of capitalist enterprise that opened up doors previously closed to Jewish traders, many were already becoming less deeply attached to their own community and its religio-national values. Little wonder, then, that many Western Jews were not saddened, but delighted by the exciting prospects: the fall of the Jewish community in exchange for political emancipation.

On September 28, 1791, the French General Assembly made Jewish history: on that day they accorded the Jews of France full rights of citizenship. The rejoicing among Jews knew no bounds. But their happiness appeared destined to be short lived. Their newly acquired status, product of the Revolutionary spirit of "Liberty, Fraternity, and Equality," was to be attacked and even partially withdrawn under the impact of the royalist, counter-Revolutionary forces, whose star was rising again. They condemned the Revolution, of course; but they also condemned Jewish emancipation as the "sinister" force behind the Revolution. Jews should be restored to a position of *status quo ante,* they demanded, and shorn of their political rights and citizenship. Jews, they insistently repeated, are forever unassimilable, aliens who would always constitute "a nation within a nation." The great hopes of French Jewry now seemed to be dashed. If only they could prove their loyalty to France; if only they could demonstrate how weak their ties to their own "nation" really were! The opportunity to do just this was fortuitously granted them by that shrewd ruler, Napoleon Bonaparte. He would soon set into motion exceptional and radical procedures in dealing with the Jews of France— and later, following his example, in other parts of western Europe, Jews would also feel the impact of his daring.

"My policy," Napoleon had bragged to his Council of State in 1801, "is to govern men as the great majority of them wish to be governed. . . . It was as a Catholic that I won the war in the Vendée, as a Moslem that I established myself in Egypt, and as an Ultramontane that I won the confidence of the Italians. If I were governing Jews, I should rebuild the temple of Solomon." The opportunity to "govern" the Jews—to make them into a loyal minority subservient to his wishes—came in 1806. He summoned an Assembly of Jewish Notables to Paris, a hand-picked group of over one hundred Jewish businessmen, financiers, traders— and even some rabbis. To these Jewish leaders, twelve basic questions were posed. Napoleon demanded that they give him the Jewish views on marriage and divorce, intermarriage, the function of Jewish law, the role of the rabbinate, the permissibility of usury, and finally, whether, as Jews, they could indeed regard France as their motherland. After their answers were reported back to the Emperor, Napoleon seemed pleased that he possessed an official expression of the Jewish loyalty he sought. Now, he would proceed to his most significant undertaking: if Jews would act on their professions, by enacting these views into their religious law, he would then indeed be satisfied that they were fit for the fullest measure of equality. There was but one thing for Jews to do: they must reconstitute their ancient Sanhedrin and enact into Jewish religious law all their verbal expressions.[5]

The Sanhedrin, the Supreme Council of Rabbis of Jewish antiquity, had, of course, not been convened since the people were driven from Palestine, when the Temple of Jerusalem was destroyed by the Romans. There were many profound impediments to its reconstitution—even today, with the re-establishment of the State of Israel, these religious obstacles still prevent Jews from calling a Sanhedrin into being. But the French Jews were not to be daunted: The Emperor had commanded, and they were to obey.

On October 6, 1806, they sent this proclamation, written in four languages—Hebrew, French, German and Italian—to the "whole Jewish world":

A great event is about to take place, one which through a long series of centuries our fathers, and even we in our own times, did not expect to see, and which has now appeared before the eyes of the astonished world. The

twentieth of October has been fixed as the date of the opening of a Great
Sanhedrin in the capital of one of the most powerful Christian nations and
under the protection of the immortal Prince who rules over it. Paris will
show the world a remarkable scene, and this ever memorable event will
open to the dispersed remnants of the descendants of Abraham a period of
deliverance and prosperity.

When the "almost-messianic" event actually did take place—not in
October as planned, but in the spring of the following year—it was, in a
sense, anti-climactic: all the answers already provided by the "Assembly"
were quickly approved. What ensued, however, has often happened
since, when weak-kneed, modern, "emancipated" Jews feel called upon
to prove their loyalty to the state, to the world, or even to mankind! They
were more than 100 percent "loyal"; they were "110 percent loyal" and
then some.

After strangely pleading that rabbis no longer exercised power over
Jewish communal life, they stressed the view that in any case the authority of the Jewish community over its members had broken down by lack
of organization and lack of funds, ever since communal dues had become voluntary after the French Revolution. They were really telling
Napoleon, themselves, and the rest of the world, that the "Jewish people" as a corporate entity had ceased to exist. And to prove the point, in
case it had been missed, they proceeded to adopt a rarely quoted but
very tell-tale declaration. Thus did they decree: "A French Jew considers
himself in England as among strangers, although he may be among Jews
. . . To such a pitch is this sentiment carried among them, that, during
the last war, French Jews have been fighting desperately against other
Jews, the subjects of countries then at war with France." Little wonder
that east European Jews, who never forgot this sentiment of their
"emancipated" brothers in the West, scornfully regarded the "freedom"
they had sought, as nothing less than a new form of slavery. That is, until
some later came to America themselves and unwittingly made it possible
for their children and grandchildren to behave no differently, in their
own lust for recognition as loyal Americans—even if they themselves,
did not.

Strangely, all their fawning on him, and their protestations of utter
loyalty, did not prevent Napoleon, just one year later, from issuing a
decree against "his" Jews for "lack of patriotism," accusing them of
shirking war service and of espionage on behalf of his enemies. But this
was only a temporary measure which was soon modified. The trend had
already been set toward more and more public Jewish displays of their
desire to live as fully respected citizens of the state.

Napoleon, however, had succeeded in receiving the assurances he desired. The Sanhedrin formally declared that French courts were to have
priority over Jewish courts of law, since the Mosaic Law was exclusively

religious, and not political in application. It went on record and gave expression in "official" religious terms to the imperial desire that Jews give up their own community system, conceptions of their own nationhood, and even their ages-old religious dream of a restored Zion. The net effect of the new "definition" of Judaism was to declare that, henceforward, Jews no longer constituted a people, in their traditional sense, but a "church"—an ecclesiastical religion, alone. One year later, Napoleon enacted into law an "Organic Regulation on the Mosaic Religion"— no longer was it even *Jewish*—and declared Judaism to be an "official religion" of France. Soon, the Jews in all the German provinces and in Italy as well—wherever the influence of Napoleon was felt—were the equal beneficiaries of the Napoleonic French decree. And by 1826, British Jews, too, were accepted as candidates for naturalization as citizens.

With the establishment of the "bourgeois monarchy" under Louis Philippe, the last vestiges of public discrimination against Jews seemed to have been eliminated. In 1846, Louis Philippe himself, shrewdly and ironically observed that he, too, had recognized "the capability of the Jews to become civilized. Regardless of the religious tie which unites them in the various lands, they have succeeded in becoming Frenchmen in France, Englishmen in England and so on . . . They were almost wedded to the good qualities, sometimes even to the faults of the nations in whose midst they lived."

Yet, the situation in America was fundamentally different, from the very start. Long before Napoleon had arrived on the European scene, and almost a full century before such rights were accorded them in the mother country, Jews in the British colonies of North America were by an act of Parliament in 1740 granted naturalization as citizens. As we have noted in the case of France, the emancipation of Jews in Europe was always a political question, related to movements of revolutionary change. As a result, the "counterrevolutionary" forces would always seize upon it, and convert it into one of the major targets of their political attack. "To confer or not to confer" equal status on the Jews—this was for long periods a large, national political issue in Europe. But in America, the status of Jews was never actually contested, as was, for example, that of the Blacks, over whose political emancipation a Civil War had to be fought. Indeed, as it later turned out, much could be made of the point that the existence of so large a Black group in America served to deflect some antiminority hostility away from its preoccupation with Jews. In a similar way, anti-Catholicism in America often served as "the anti-Semitism of the liberal."

America was different, for still other reasons. The Jews of Europe had populated that continent even before the Germans or the Italians; they were an old and widely spread minority. The emancipation of westEuropean Jewry came after their institutionally established status had already been an integral part of the traditions of the continent for eighteen centuries. Only the dramatic rise of the modern revolutionary spirit could alter their time-worn, habitual condition, and then only after years of great effort and struggle. And this new status, even when offered, would be conditional: emancipation yes, but only if in exchange for it the Jews would give up their own unique community life. In America, on the other hand, until the twentieth century there were never enough Jews to warrant consideration of any special problems concerning their status. Besides, like all the other immigrants, they were emancipated from the European political traditions merely by their coming to America, and in a few short years, it was generally assumed, they would be "Americans" anyway.

Yet, in many ways, these very unusual American conditions created unique dilemmas for Jews. In Europe, the price for their emancipation was the destruction of the institutionally established corporate Jewish community. But the American Jewish community was never "established"; never was it an official or even quasi-official autonomous body, along European lines. American Jews were thus always free from the restraints of inner communal sanctions, and what Jewish affirmations they chose to make were solely a matter of personal choice and responsibility. American Jews were free, not only without having to struggle for political emancipation, but also without having to give up something they, in fact, had never had here.

Yet to the eye of the outsider, they have nevertheless demonstrated a remarkable cohesiveness as a community, despite the voluntary nature of their free association in America. However, for many years Jewish communal loyalty seemed no more than an external appearance, more the product of the hostility against them than the result of inner conviction or attachment. And this, too, was the by-product of the unique American environment. America never coerced the Jew to give up his Judaism; it merely enticed him to become an American! For some decades, during the period of large-scale immigration, the east-European Jews, who had never known emancipation in Russia or Poland, attempted to transplant their communal style and institutional life. But it soon became apparent even to them that the Jewish community could not be sustained in America on the basis of the older social sanctions or controls. Moreover, despite the fact that cultural or ethnic pluralism was offered as a theoretical solution to the dilemmas of their Americanization, in practice, as we have seen, the second generation turned their backs on what they regarded as cultural ghettos, and sought to adapt completely to the "American type," the Anglo-Saxon ideal. By the mid-1930s the members of that generation, not unlike the scions of the older Sephardic and German Jewish settlers, were already far removed from the Jewish way of life. Even many of those who did not stray altogether passively stayed "closer to home," principally because of their real or imaginary encounters with anti-Semitism.

Napoleon had set a precedent for the modern west-European demand that Jews give up the national-cultural elements of the Jewish religion and become loyal "Frenchmen of the Mosaic Persuasion." Russian Jews, looking back on what their emancipated Western co-religionists had "gained," called it a loss and a betrayal. But ironically, in an America that was different, where Jews were never called upon officially to divest Judaism of its Jewishness, a strange thing happened. The natural patterns of adaptation to the environment tended to produce the same attitudes in the children of the east-Europeans here that their own grandfathers had condemned in the west-European Jews. The nineteenth-century west-European had acceded to an official formula. But these American Jews adopted voluntarily the same definition of their status. Before very long, it became clear that by ridding themselves of the cultural elements of their ancestral religion they had destroyed the distinctiveness of Judaism. When that happened, it was no surprise that they, too, should have been addicted to "Jewish anti-Semitism." They were shot through with the acids of self-hate and their "negative chauvinism" was not too difficult to understand: since Judaism was of no special or unique account, why should they labor to preserve the very thing that stood in the way of their acceptance by the Christian world? (History, someone has aptly said, teaches that history teaches nothing!)

American life, if not American law, posed still another embarrassing dilemma to these second-generation American Jews. To become fully American, they believed, Jews really should give up their religious traditions. Not so for the other religious groups, they felt, because those seemed much better adapted to survive the challenge of the American environment. In some respects they were right. By the mid-1930s, many Christian churches were already absorbing the earlier cultural elements of the Italian, the German, or the Irish ethnic groups. The "little Italys," the ethnic island-communities, were giving way before their own second-generation, Americanized children. Yet, although they were losing their cultural hold on their offspring, those immigrant parents surely had no fear that the religion of the fathers would be completely cast aside by the children. Both were Christians, and Christians both would remain.

But with Judaism it was different. When the children of the immigrants sloughed off the ethnic elements of the Jewish religious tradition, in effect they cast aside more than a culture; with the jettisoning of their Jewishness, their Judaism too was unloaded. There was no other way out for them, it seemed. The uniqueness of Judaism—the lone religious relic of the ancient worlds of Babylonia, Egypt, Rome, and Greece, where creed and culture were united—stood out like a sore in an America where church was not only separated from state but also from culture.

Unwilling to struggle in order to retain what, in any case, seemed for them an impossible religion in America (and yet temperamentally and historically unconditioned to conversion to Christianity), many quietly became "inverted Marranos." When viewed by the outsider, they appeared to be Jews—not being Christian, what else could they have been?—but in their private lives they were secretly practicing non-Judaism. Their views on Judaism, ironically, were not far removed from that older Christian attitude, which regarded the Jewish religion as surpassed and transcended. Apparently, they forgot to remember history's lessons: if Judaism is unequal, so too are the Jews.

Despite the fact that many second-generation Jews still remained within the fold, this loss of their self-esteem as Jews was responsible for a series of curious paradoxes. They remained members of congregations they very rarely attended. As students or young idealists they often exhibited rare courage in fighting the cause of other depressed minorities, but consistently shied away from speaking up on behalf of Jews. And what is even more telltale of their psyche: even Jewish education became a negative rather than a positive factor in their rejection of folk and faith. What little and inadequate Jewish education many of them did receive, instead of serving as a force for their group-cohesion, often succeeded only in alienating them even more from Jews and Judaism.[6]

But beginning with the 1940s, and growing in intensity ever since, an unusual combination of factors has brought about major changes in the self-understanding of many American Jews. Jewishness came into a new vogue and slowly started to revive, beginning with the time that Hitler's attacks on European Jewry were made known in America. Some of the ardent hopes of the old emancipation now came to be viewed as wistful, wishful thinking: the treatment and the fate of the Jews, even in the emancipated West, seemed no different, after all. Nor were the Nazi diatribes and attacks reserved for European Jewry alone; they struck terror into the hearts of American Jews, too. For the first time, many who had come to believe that they were primarily Americans, and only incidentally Jews, now realized that their American culture seemed to provide them with a fate no different from the immigrant generation— alienation from the majority groups—a fate which they assumed that foreignness had caused for their "greenhorn" parents. Hitler's fiery fulminations enkindled dormant embers in America and succeeded in feeding fuel to latent antiminority feelings. Many of these second-generation Jews now realized that for all its democratic protestations, by and large, America had still not freed itself of its self-image as a "white, Anglo-Saxon, Protestant country."

This startling exposure, of course, brought about great trauma. Many had believed with the Jewish hero of Myron Kaufman's novel, *Remember*

Me to God, that they could gain acceptance into the inner circle of America and enjoy primary, face-to-face relations with their college friends or their business associates. He had eagerly hoped to get in—to be "one of the boys" at Harvard's undergraduate clubs. "If only I can go the last few steps in Ivy League manners and behavior," he says, "they will surely recognize that I am one of them and take me in." But as one sociologist has noted, the "invitation was not really there in the first place, or to the extent that it was . . . it was a 'look me over but don't touch me' invitation. . . . Brooks Brothers suit notwithstanding, the doors of the fraternity house, the city's men's club, and the country club were slammed in the face of the immigrant's offspring."[7]

As a result of such new and sudden awakenings, many who had believed that they could find stability and security outside of the Jewish group now came to feel no different from the Jews of Babylonia or of the *shtetl:* every Jew is responsible for the other, and all Jewish communities are brothers, defenders, and guardians of the others. But they felt this way for different reasons: not because of ideological commitments or spiritual values, but principally as a result of the dynamics of discrimination and prejudice. Those who most keenly felt the barbs of rejection were particularly the more acculturated and the more affluent Jews: those who had been moving closer and closer to the non-Jewish world and farther away from the Jewish community. Ironically, these were the very groups who had formerly sought to cast out the ethnic factors from Jewish life in America; now they were returning to the Jewish community, but not for religious or cultural reasons. They could not "make" the Gentile country club, so they "made" their own—a "Jewish country club." Needless to say, such clubs and associations were "Jewish" only by reason of the fact that Jews alone were invited to membership. Unable to break into the charmed Gentile circles of their desire, they simply aped those whom they could not join. A strange paradox emerged: the very people who had once regarded ethnic isolation and exclusiveness as a baneful aspect of Jewishness in America were now retreating to their own community. They were bent upon making it into a powerful ethnic stronghold capable of sustaining them in the midst of their worldly rebuffs. But clearly, such a community could not be much more than a *traditionless ghetto.*

Then, when for the first time in two thousand years, with their own hands, Jews wrested victory from history and proclaimed the establishment of a sovereign Jewish state atop the rubble of the Nazi holocaust, even the most ardent of the "inverted Marranos" came out of hiding. The specter of a beleaguered Jewish community in Palestine successfully defending itself against the combined Arab attack made most American Jews feel closer to the Jewish people as a whole. To be a Jew, in these new terms, no longer seemed to project the image of a cringing, withdrawing, medieval ghetto dweller, who was essentially irrelevant to modern life. The heroic and epic qualities of the Hebrew Biblical world seemed now to be leaping into life, and the wish to be identified with this new expression of Jewishness became the dominant desire of virtually all the Jews of America. Thousands upon thousands who had previously shied away from membership in Jewish organizations hastened to join, to give tangible proof of their new pride and conviction. Membership in Jewish organizations increased from 807,000 in 1935 to 1,085,000 in 1941, and in 1945 jumped to 1,436,000.[8] Even those who had formerly resisted any open manifestation of Jewish cultural expression, out of fear that this might turn the clock back to an unwanted, ghettoized world, now encouraged it. They began to regard such activities as virile signs of the birth of the "new Jew" rather than as monuments to a dead and uncreative past. And in a most telltale, personal way, the creative signs of their self-recognition as Jews could be seen in the names many young couples were giving to their new-born children. While they still shied away from the "ghetto-sounding names" (sic!) of Abraham, Isaac, Jacob, or Rebecca, many did seem to avoid the earlier "Americanized" versions of these: Alvin, Ian, John, and Roberta. Biblical names with "nonguttural" sounds came into a new vogue: there were now little Davids, Jonathans, Michaels, Judiths, and Deborahs by the thousands. And there were even young Jewish parents who went so far as to "import" some of the modern Hebrew names that were popular in Israel: such names as Aliza, Dana, Sharona, Ethan, or Jordan.

Paradoxically, their new involvement with Jewishness now seemed to satisfy the American mood, even as their earlier march toward total integration and assimilation often met with negative response. Not the least among the reasons for their new positive attitudes toward Jewishness was the belief that their American neighbors of all faiths were encouraging and applauding the "new Jewish look." In the non-Jewish sections of America, a radical re-evaluation of the vitality of the Jewish people seemed to be taking place.

It has been contended by some that the approach of the Jew to the Gentile world is determined, in the first instance, by his approach to Judaism. Those Jews, it is claimed, who have divorced themselves from Jewish traditions, tend to seek their security in the non-Jewish world, and as a result are likely to value and prize the attitudes of the external world toward Jews even more than their own. To a large extent this is true. But it is equally true that no Jew, no matter how deeply he may himself be attached to Judaism and Jewishness—because he inevitably regards his culture and religion as a minority expression—can remain unaffected by what the external world thinks. And this mind-set was particularly true of the mid-century American Jew because, ironically, his new Jewishness was partly the result of his frustrated experiments in assimilating to the American majority. Thus, apart from all the vital psychological reinforcement of his "Jewish ego" provided by the exploits of the Israelis, the fact that American non-Jews were positively impressed by the "new" Jewish nation was perhaps the most crucial factor in his readoption of Jewishness as a legitimate avenue for his self-expression in America. To test the truth of this assertion, one need only imagine what might have happened if, instead of applauding Israel and recognizing its positive values, the American people and government had gone to the opposite extreme and had refused to recognize, arm, or assist the Jewish state in any way. One need hardly be gifted with clairvoyance to realize that under such conditions, despite the dogged determination of a minority of Jews to retain an unimpaired connection with their Jewishness, the largest number would probably have put it aside as an impossible goal in America.

How long into the future the drama of Israel's rebirth will be able to excite the Jewishness of American Jews remains, of course, a moot question. Yet it is no small thing that the highly acculturated and the often de-Judaized Jew of the 1940s was stopped cold in his assimilating tracks, and what seemed like an inexorable, progressive process of submersion in the general culture was reversed. A new burst of self-interest was dramatically manifested in his search to repossess his own particular culture. More important, then, than any attempt at prophecy, by predicting the possible longevity of this amazing phenomenon, is the phenomenon itself. After many another ethnic group had almost forgotten its ancestral culture, American-born Jews of the third, fourth, and even fifth generation were now seeking to remember. For if by the mid-1960s the earlier novelty of the rebirth of the State was losing some of its shine, and no longer impelled some Jews to repossess their Jewishness, the dramatic days before and after the "miraculous" Six Day War in June, 1967, helped to re-galvanize them. It stimulated their consciousness as a people whose destiny was unitary and whose communal will could overcome even "history" itself. This time, however, something new seemed to have begun to develop: Jewishness itself was virtually given the status of religion. To survive as a people was no longer regarded as "mere secular survival." It became, even among some Jewish theologians, a cardinal principle of Judaism itself.

Inevitably, because of the inseparable connection between Jewishness and Judaism, this new, significantly spiritual preoccupation with the former served to spark interest in the latter. The earlier process was now repeated, but in reverse: by the 1930s Judaism in America was on the way out, because Jewishness seemed irrelevant; beginning with the late 1960s, as a self-conscious, self-directed Jewishness revived, Judaism, too, was given a new lease on life. To be sure, the attestation of the Jewish will-to-survive and its remarkable powers of renewal, which in 1967 were incarnated in the "saving" of Israel, provided the average American Jew with a new appreciation of the spiritual strength inherent in Judaism. Some, in fact, now sought to interpret the rebirth of the land and the people in purely religious terms, as the beginning of the long-promised divine redemption. God was "hiding His face" no longer, and the "Great Ingathering" of the oppressed exiles seemed to be a sure heavenly portent of a restored Zion.

But generally the revived interest in Judaism, like that of Jewishness, was also intimately affected by the prevailing winds of the American environment in the 1970s. As some Americans began to doubt the ultimate significance of much of their material success, small beginnings toward a spiritual quest were undertaken, at the side of the affluent secularism. Many of these efforts, as we have intimated, ended on the road that led to an espousal of "religion-in-general." But there were also those Americans for whom religion meant tradition, as a countering influence to what seemed to them to be an uprooted, unstable, traditionless society. Theology came into a new vogue, even among nontheologians. Many Protestants turned back to the past, in search of new insights from the Reformation and the Bible—two realms that some, ironically, had consistently disregarded for long decades. Traditional liturgies were reclaimed, and found their way back to places of honor in many Protestant services, where concocted, *ad-hoc* American rituals had previously become part of the accepted order of worship. Even church architecture seemed to be struggling with the need to produce houses of worship that were more than just contemporary buildings, but ones in which traditional forms would be stylistically blended with modern materials, to represent the "old in the new."

Whether this return to the older traditions to replace some of the "traditions of the new" was only a passing phenomenon related primarily to the emotional needs of the materialistic, middle-class mentality of America was difficult to determine. Yet, there were abundant evidences that, on the intellectual level, as well, there were groups of Americans who were now ready to open up to some of the traditional teachings of the different religions. Many of these were impelled to a consideration of these teachings as a result of the failure of their other gods: communism, psychoanalysis, liberalism-in-general, and the like—to prevent what they believed had transpired: History gone wrong! Others, perplexed and worried by the mass assault on personal character and individual integrity by Big Society, were willing to investigate the possibilities of religious faith as a guide in gaining new insight and power to deal with the crucial, personal decisions implied in their human existence.

This ferment coincided with a most significant moment in the history of American Jews. It came at the very time that their self-affirmation in terms of their Jewishness seemed assured. No longer were they plagued by the dilemmas of the second-generation Jews who had turned away from *Judaism* because they were anxious to discard *Jewishness*. The new confidence of their renewed Jewishness needed more than ethnic outlets; even if they had desired it, in America they could not constitute a "nation within a nation." Nor could their Jewishness be long supported if its principal source of strength derived only from a sense of identity with other Jewish communities, elsewhere, or even from a mystical-ethnic communion with the whole of the Jewish people. There now dawned upon some American Jews an awareness that the future of Jewishness was bound up with the meaning of Judaism. And consciously or unconsciously they came under the influence of the same *Zeitgeist* that was impelling a significant number of Christians at that very time. Like these others, these American Jews, too, came to recognize that the questions before them were larger and more ultimate than they had realized. If they were to give spiritual meaning to their Jewishness, they would have to give spiritual meaning to their own lives as persons. And, as Jews, they could do this best if they would seek out their own religious tradition, Judaism, and on the basis of a personal commitment to it as a spiritual way of life, attempt to discover new insights in its old teachings.

True, as we shall have occasion to note in greater detail (see Chapter XIII) the corrosive forces of assimilation were not altogether without their influence in de-Judaizing some members of the third generation. Studies have sometimes resulted in conflicting data on intermarriage, but clearly, if its rate of growth did not always seem alarming, neither has it been arrested. Yet one phenomenon is little noticed: each year, in America, at least 2,500 persons are converting to Judaism. Almost all of these are Christian women (Christian men comprise only about 20 percent of the total) who are marrying Jewish men and establishing Jewish homes. While this number is not of major proportions, the phenomenon itself is most significant: it was never this way in the old country. The fact is that conversion to Judaism is taking place in the face of negative popular Jewish opinion and without benefit of real rabbinical encouragement. Yet in a free American society Jews can easily "opt out" of Judaism and convert to Christianity when they marry across religious lines. That there are increasing numbers of Christians who are accepting Judaism, in a situation in which the Jewish partner could have gone the other way, does say some things that are significant. It demonstrates that in America, unlike earlier experience in Europe, there are Christians today who regard Judaism as a fitting personal choice. It sheds light, too, on the vitality of Judaism, even among those who otherwise appear to be only marginal Jews.[9]

Indeed, after many years of pondering this new Jewish "opportunity" in America, the (Reform) Union of American Hebrew Congregations finally established a permanent "Commission on Reform Jewish Outreach," as 1983 came to an end. Its declared purpose was to engage in active programs "to encourage both the non-Jewish parents in mixed marriages and their children, along with the 'unchurched,' to convert to Judaism—to become Jews by choice." This was a program which, for many years, had been ardently advocated by the president of the U.A.H.C., Rabbi Alexander Schindler. In his words, in addition to reaching the families of mixed marriages in order to convert the non-Jewish partners or children to Judaism, "this was also a program for those without a religious preference who may want to consider Judaism as one of the alternatives to make their lives meaningful."[10] Indeed, it may yet prove to be the first organized and active attempt at Jewish proseltyizing in the history of the diaspora. Not since the times of the Pharisees had such a view taken hold of any part of the Jewish community.

For Christians "to choose to be Jewish" represents essentially a *religious*, not an *ethnic* decision—as the act is generally understood. To search for "Jews by choice"—this, too, was another example and signal, since 1967, that the American Jew was prepared to embark upon a new-style emancipation: one that would discard the self-alienating attitudes of the older emancipation of west-Europe, and the more recent one in America itself. Neither a slave to the whims and dictates of others nor walled off from ready contact with his environment, he is in an unparalleled position to write a new chapter in the history of diaspora Judaism—not only as an enclavic, defensive member of an ethnic minority.

And in a most paradoxical way, his earlier troubled concern with what America thought of him as a Jew, his once poignant need to be sustained from the outside in his acceptance of inner Jewish values, have been largely responsible for his new assurance, at long last, that now, *if he wills it*—not others—he is free to be himself in a newer and freer America.

These new confidences and new freedoms provide a challenge to the religious institutions—one which, considering their earlier history in America—they may not yet be prepared to meet. What future, then, for Judaism in America?

NOTES

1. Ahad Ha-'Am, *Selected Essays*, translated (from Hebrew) by Leon Simon (Philadelphia: Jewish Publication Society of America, 1936), pp. 193–194.

2. Jacob Katz, "Misreadings of Anti-Semitism," in *Commentary*, July, 1983, p. 43.

3. André Foucalt, writing in Les Oeuvres Libres (1938), p. 310. Quoted by Hannah Arendt, "From the Dreyfus Affair to France Today," in *Essays on Antisemitism*, Koppel S. Pinson, ed. (New York: Conference on Jewish Relations, 1946), p. 192.

4. Ludwig Lewisohn, *The American Jew: Character and Destiny* (New York: Farrar, Straus & Company, 1950), p. 15.

5. For an unusual view of the anxieties and tensions within the French community of the time, and the conflicts between its Ashkenazic and Sephardic sectors, see Frances Malino, *The Sephardic Jews of Bordeaux: Assimilation and Emancipation in Revolutionary and Napoleonic France,* (University of Alabama Press, 1978), especially pp. 60–111.

6. That, for many members of the second generation, Jewish education had negative results is borne out by a study of Jewish intermarriage in Greater Washington, D.C. This investigation shows that among all second-generation Jews in that city in 1956 the rate of intermarriage was 10.2 per cent. These 10.2 per cent, who showed such marked signs of assimilation, comprise almost three times as many men who had received some Jewish education as those who had had no Jewish education at all! In the third generation, however, Jewish education had positive, not these negative, effects. (See also Chapter XIII.)

7. Milton M. Gordon, "Assimilation in America: Theory and Reality," in *Daedalus,* Spring, 1961, p. 282.

8. Leo Bogart, *The Response of Jews in America to the European Jewish Catastrophe, 1941–1945.* Unpublished M.A. thesis, University of Chicago, p. 46.

9. For a report on conversions to Judaism in the United States, see an unscientific, inconclusive, but pioneering study of this phenomenon by David M. Eichhorn, "Conversion: Requirements and Results" in *Intermarriage and Jewish Life* (ed. W. Cahnman) (New York: The Herzl Press, 1963), pp. 11–121. See also Theodore I. Linn and Associates, *Rabbi and Synagogue in Reform Judaism* (New York: Central Conference of American Rabbis, 1972) pp. 395 ff. (See also Chapter XIII.)

10. Reported by the *Jewish Telegraphic Agency News Report,* December 5, 1983.

PART FOUR
The Changing Religious Scene

CHAPTER IX

The Evolution of the Synagogue

IF THE AMERICAN CITY BECAME THE "NEW FRONTIER" OF THE MID-nineteenth century and the European immigrants its builders, then, a century later, a still newer frontier was being pioneered by their great-grandchildren—suburban America. About seventy-five million "ex-urbanite immigrants" have already made their way to the cities' proximate hinterland of towns and villages. Younger American families continue to leave the pavements behind and put themselves down some-where nearby, where they are sure that the grass grows greener and their children will grow taller, despite the fact that a smaller number have also been returning to the "rehabilitated cores" of several larger cities.

The Jews of America share abundantly in this new nomadic experi-ence. Of their total number of almost six million, over four million live in or near the largest cities: New York City, Los Angeles, Chicago, Philadel-phia, Boston, Newark, Cleveland, Washington, D.C., Baltimore, and St. Louis; and in retirement or resort communities in the southern and western "Sun Belts." And there, and in the other metropolitan centers they populate, there was every indication that they bulked even larger in the migratory flight to the suburbs than the other members of the gen-eral population.

If, as we have noted, the general impact of American opinion was a major positive factor in fostering a new approach to his emancipation, then the increasing suburbanization of the Jew has been of even greater influence in forcing him to rediscover the sources of his significance as a Jew. "In moving from the city to suburb," wrote one perceptive Jewish suburbanite of the fifties, "we had, if only subconsciously, a vision of a less 'Jewish' existence . . . a running away from the ghetto, however plush-lined. . . . Still in seeking a less 'Jewish existence,' no matter how subtly expressed, we find in Suburbia a more 'Jewish existence.'" In the city, he explains, "we had found it unnecessary to think seriously of ourselves as Jews." Paradoxically, in the densely-populated Jewish neigh-borhoods of the cities, Jews could live and die without ever—or barely ever—entering a synagogue. There, too, the proportion of synagogue members was always the lowest; most of the congregations were small and in the east-European Orthodox style. But the new environment of the suburbs created a new Jewish need: they were now required to revise their old concept of themselves as Jews:

It is the village neighborliness—the same neighborliness that permits a "good morning" to any man seen at the station more than twice, and most of the women; an occasional beer with the man next door; a joint effort with the man across the street in clearing the leads and the gutters—that builds the first pressures toward membership in the synagogue. The man next door may go to Immaculate Conception, the man across the street to St. Luke's, and the man on the other side may spend his Sundays at Lee Hills Country Club, but this man is a Jew. He knows it, his neighbors know it, and the other Jews in the community know it. Some positive action seems indicated.[1]

That positive action became symbolized in the new American Jewish phenomenon: the active participation in synagogue life by all the members of the young Jewish family. For the youthful matron, the boyish father, and in the synagogue religious school and clubs for the growing children, there were welcome places waiting.

A new role thus opened for the synagogue in America, as the social, cultural, and religious center of the Jewish community. In the course of its long history, the synagogue, of course, had been all these things before. But then, in the past, it was set into a framework in which each of these significances—the social, cultural, and religious—meant things vastly different from the suburban, or for that matter the urban, American community of the twentieth century.

In what ways had it been different, and in what ways would it become still more different in an America that was different?

When contemporary American Jews refer to their synagogue as a temple, they are in error. There was only one temple in Jewish life, and that is spelled with a capital T. The Temple in Jerusalem, which was destroyed and rebuilt only to be destroyed again, had a Biblical mandate. How it came to be built, maintained, and operated was fully described in the Bible. A full set of laws and practices was minutely formulated to govern the institution of the Temple, whose plan and purpose were divinely preconceived.

The synagogue, in contrast, had a much humbler origin. It came upon the scene as a human accommodation to the circumstances of Jewish history and grew into significance only after the Temple had been destroyed. Ironically, however, while the exile of the Jews to Babylon brought the downfall of the Temple, the same historic event was responsible for the molding and shaping of the synagogue.

But neither did the Temple spring into existence all at once. It emerged instead out of specific historical experiences, and finally became the primary religious focus for Biblical monotheism, strong enough to resist the powerful and all-pervasive forces of Baal-worship and the other varieties of Canaanitish polytheism. Shrines, high places, altars of all kinds had for long centuries been established throughout the country; local, private, and regional sanctuaries abounded, each with a Levite and a priest to serve in it, and all in the name of the God of Israel. But not without the obvious danger: the assimilation of the Canaanitish religious practices into the cult of Israel. The central sanctuary, when it was finally established by Solomon in Jerusalem, in some measure was able to retard the many pagan movements that had flourished all over the land.

Even before Solomon, David had wanted to establish the Ark of the Lord in a fixed place so as to pave the way for the erection of the Temple as the symbol of permanence, in a city that was to be regarded as permanent and eternal. David was unable to carry out his plan, but Solomon, his son, completed the task and erected the Temple in Jerusalem. In so doing, he helped to free the ritual practices of Israel from heathen influence. Once the Ark was permanently enshrined in the Temple, it ceased to be a portable sanctuary, constantly subjected to the local influences of its earlier homes—as at Shechem, Shiloh, Mizpah, Beth-el, and other regions. In Jerusalem, only the priests and their assistants, the Levites, could perform the rites of worship ordained by Biblical tradition.

The people now came to Jerusalem to offer their gifts. They came from afar to Mount Zion, at great effort and expense. Each day, mornings and afternoons, there were sacrifices on the altar; Temple precincts were particularly thronged at the time of religious pilgrimages when families from all over the land converged upon the central sanctuary. Since the Jews at that time were primarily an agricultural people, these pilgrimages were related to the harvest calendar. They came at the beginning of spring, at the time of the first harvest in early summer, and again at late harvest time in the fall, each time to seek God's blessing and to thank Him for a season of abundance.

The Temple Solomon erected was elaborate and well built; it had taken seven years to complete. Its woods were from the forests of Tyre: the cedars and cypresses of Lebanon. Its glitter and brilliance were rich to behold: "Solomon overlaid the house within with pure gold; and he drew chains of gold across the wall before the Sanctuary; and he overlaid it with gold. And the whole house he overlaid with gold, until all the house was finished; also the whole altar that belonged to the Sanctuary he overlaid with gold." (I Kings 6:21–22). The splendor of the building was matched by the rich aura that surrounded the Temple service conducted by the levitical choir and orchestra, whose tones overflowed the chambers.

One can imagine the magnetic hold such majesties must have had upon the popular mind. Yet, despite the influence of the Temple in

Jerusalem, not until the reign of King Josiah (638–609 B.C.), more than three centuries after Solomon had built it, were the last idolatrous vestiges of the local shrines and high places finally eradicated. Josiah purged the pagan-tainted regional altars and at last the nation had one central sanctuary whose religious practices could be preserved from local deviations. Ironically, this very centralizing of all sacrificial worship in the single, national sanctuary helped give rise to the synagogue, a new and different religious institution, long after the Temple had been destroyed.

It is likely that, following Josiah's reforms, those who lived at some distance from Jerusalem, with difficult access to a sacrificial altar, sought to draw near to God in other ways. Since neither altar nor priest was permitted to function outside the central sanctuary in Jerusalem, they and their descendants (who were exiled to Babylonia after the destruction of the First Temple in 586 B.C.) sought to bind themselves together in religious devotions that would tie them, at least sentimentally, to the Temple, its services, and its ritual practices. We can picture them gathering in their homes on the sacred day of the week, the Sabbath, to read to one another from the scrolls of the Law and the writings of their prophets. After reading these texts someone might lead in prayer, perhaps using the very psalms that were part of the Temple service. Still others might interpret some portions of the sacred texts, relying upon the oral traditions that had customarily been handed down from father to son.

When Ezra returned with the Babylonia exiles, he resolved to make Scripture the basis of national life. He convened a public assembly, unconnected with the Temple service and away from its precincts. Ascending a wooden dais, he opened the Torah scroll and read it before the gathering for six hours, with interpreters explaining the passages to the people. This solemn act symbolized a regiving of the Torah to Israel. From that time forward, the emphasis shifted from the centrality of the priests to the people themselves; from the place of worship and instruction to the gathering of worshipers, the congregation itself. This is the *edah*, which the Torah understands as a religious congregation of ten Jews, regardless of its location or its organizational structure. Wherever they assembled—in private homes, at the city or water gate—it was their religious purpose, not the place of worship, which was now made paramount.

Out of such new needs and conditions the synagogue arose. From the very start, it centered around the congregation rather than a building or a site. In contrast to the Temple, it was humble and simple, for it had no fixed place or form. Whenever ten or more family heads gathered, they could give democratic expression to their desire to pray and to study; the *edah*—the congregation—was now supreme, not the priests. While the

Bible contains elaborate descriptions of the sanctuary that was to become the Temple, and of the role of its officiants, the priests and Levites, the synagogue grew without plan or design, without an established hereditary and hierarchical clergy. Yet in no way was it an institution of protest or of rebellion that claimed for itself the role of the Temple; it was, instead, conservative and preservative. Thus, its prayer services were modeled after the Temple service and were recited twice daily, mornings and evenings, at the time of the sacrificial offerings. Later, after the Temple's destruction in A.D. 70, the synagogue liturgy was even broadened to include the recitation of daily prayers for its restoration. And as a perennial reminder of the supreme sanctity of the Temple, the orientation of the meeting place was always to be toward its former place in Jerusalem. Even the furnishings of the synagogue could not imitate some of those in the Temple: there was no altar in the synagogue because sacrifices were not part of its service; there could be a *menorah* (candelabrum) but it could not be of seven branches, like that of the Temple, but only of five, six, or eight. Even its music could not suggest the majesty of the Temple tones; instruments were prohibited, partly because the synagogue was mourning the destruction, but principally, not to emulate the Temple style. The synagogue awaited the day when the Temple would be rebuilt and the sacrificial system re-established. Yet, even when Solomon's Temple was replaced by the building of a Second Temple, the synagogue did not disappear. In Jerusalem alone, the city of the Temple, four or five hundred synagogues continued to thrive and something new was added to the Temple itself: a chapel for prayer! While it saw itself as a temporary parallel to or substitute for the Temple, the synagogue was, in fact, a dynamically new and altogether unique religious creation—the response of the Jewish spirit to the changing environment.

Ezra's public reading of the Law must have helped to set the future patterns for the synagogue service. From that time forward, the reading of Scripture became a characteristic feature of Jewish public worship. In the course of time, too, a homily became an independent part of the service, by means of which the congregation became acquainted with all the Biblical books not read as an integral part of the synagogue service. The synagogue thus served not only as a place of prayer *(beth-tefillah)*, but also as a house of study *(beth-midrash)*. It is no small wonder that from the German word for "school" *(schule)* came the Yiddish word for "synagogue" *(shul)*. As early as the first pre-Christian century, Philo of Alexandria had explained the nature of the synagogue in just such terms to his Greek-speaking neighbors: "Schools of practical wisdom, self-control, manliness, uprightness, and other virtues are opened every seventh day in all cities. In these schools the people sit decorously, keeping silence and listening with the utmost attention out of a thirst for refreshing discourse, while one of the best qualified stands up and instructs them in what is best and most conducive to welfare, things by which their whole life may be made better."

In addition to being a house of prayer and instruction, the synagogue building also served as a public center where matters of public concern could be aired. Courts of law met in its rooms, heard testimony, administered oaths, and proclaimed judgments. Strangers to the community were welcomed into its hostel, the poor were invited to received alms there, and community philanthropies were administered by its councils. In time, these communal functions of the synagogue became so integrated with its religious and cultural purposes that, by the Middle Ages, the practice had developed whereby one could interrupt the services in order to inform the entire community of wrongs and injustices not yet redressed. The strong emphasis placed by the synagogue upon the human needs of the congregation rather than upon the house in which it met was responsible for the fact that its architecture became a matter of relative indifference to the Jewish community. But while it lacked the external splendor of the ancient Temple, it did become something the Temple never was: a community center, not an ecclesiastical stronghold. It served not only as a place of prayer and study, but as a house of meeting: a *Beth Kenesset.*

In spite of its conscious effort not to become the surrogate of the Temple, even before the Temple's destruction the synagogue had attained an independent position as the seat of religion of a different character. As a result, far from destroying the Jewish people after the fall of the Temple, the Exile helped to strengthen their aspirations to universalize their faith. In this process, the synagogue played a pivotal and crucial role: it accompanied the people wherever they went and helped bring them closer to their God, even in the remotest parts of the Diaspora. The Jewish people never forgot Jerusalem—the synagogue saw to that—but neither did they die for lack of a national center. The synagogue took the place of the Temple, the study of Scripture replaced the cult; it was this religious continuity that kept the Jews spiritually alive through the centuries. The synagogue had succeeded in universalizing the religious teachings of what, in the hands of the Temple priesthood, had become a national cult, with a single, national religious center.

But without the development of the rabbinate as a new and parallel institution in Jewish life, the synagogue would have been bereft of the rationale and ideology necessary for its universalism. Today, synagogues and rabbis are institutionally united; at the beginning of the Christian era their developments paralleled one another but had not yet converged. The priests who had ministered in the Temple had also been the interpreters of Jewish law, not as expounders but as judges. With the destruction of the Temple and the consequent waning of the priesthood, leadership began to fall into the hands of those who could act as judges.

By reason of his knowledge of the law and his technical abilities as a student of jurisprudence, the scribe began to assume the importance once held by the priest. Politically, too, the scribe enjoyed the support of the strong Pharisaic party.

The Pharisees were united on religious grounds, differing on many points with the Sadducees. However, economic and political factors were even more important than ritualistic or legalistic differences in causing a division between these two sects. The Pharisees were a people's party; the Sadducees represented the last remains of priestly vested interests. It is therefore understandable why the scribes, who had no priestly connections, would be helped to leadership by the Pharisee party.

With the reorganization of the schools after the destruction of Jerusalem, the scribe was not called rabbi, a title for what we might call the "diplomaed doctor of the Law." The growth of the educated class as the teachers and expounders of the law became more and more pronounced, and they began to judge as well as to expound. When, finally, the teacher also became the official judge, the importance of the priesthood was greatly diminished. For in that Jewish society it was the judge who exercised wide powers and who enjoyed top status.

The Pharisee rabbis did not deprive the priests of the special prerogatives Scripture had given them as experts in the laws of purity and sacrifice. But these lay teachers began to fashion Jewish life in such a way that priests and Levites were no longer really indispensable to a living Judaism. The synagogue continued to carry out its major functions without priests, just as Judaism could itself survive without the Temple. Now, the schools became the focal point of the community and in some ways the academies were even more significant than the synagogue itself. For as the Pharisees made more insistent claims to leadership in the religious as well as the secular fields, they attained the necessary authority to mold both the sacred and the profane aspects of Jewish community life. The destruction of the Temple was the last straw; it helped to bring about the disappearance of a professional priesthood upon which the community had depended. While the schoolmen or rabbis were not yet the spiritual leaders of specific congregations or synagogues, as in our day, in many ways they were even more important as leaders of the total community. From the schools they legislated and planned the total content of all of Jewish life—the style and the program of the synagogue as well.

In Second Commonwealth days, religious and civil authority came to be vested in the hands of the Supreme Court, the Sanhedrin, whose members could now be non-priests. Yet they had to have certain "credentials" in order to participate in its deliberations. These could be granted only to duly authorized scholars, and this need ultimately led to the institution of ordination *(Semikah)* as a prerequisite for admission to the Sanhedrin. Thus lay scholars were now fully established in their right as the authoritative expounders of Scriptural law and as rabbis they became the pre-eminent judges and "rulers" of the people.

The Talmud, which is the work of these rabbis, reflects the wide gamut of their communal suasion. Its new interpretations of Judaism reveal how those lay scholars were preparing the way for Jewish survival in circumstances that might otherwise have destroyed the Jewish people and their way of life. Although shorn of their land and national sovereignty and bereft of their central sanctuary, Jews no longer required a national theocracy. Under Pharisaic influence and leadership the Jewish people now became an international religious community: the synagogue, though not yet led directly by the rabbis, was already prepared by them for the day when it would become the portable sanctuary for Jews everywhere. At its core, then, the story of the beginnings of the synagogue and of the rabbinate is really a story of social and religious adaptability—the creative response of Jews and Judaism to new and often hostile environments.

As Jews spread throughout the Roman exile and moved across the European continent, they took their portable sanctuary with them. In medieval Europe they lived apart from their Christian neighbors, yet their inner communal life constituted as an autonomous corporation served their total human needs. In these circumstances, the synagogue became an adjunct to the general Jewish community, and not the private province of either interested or devoted individuals. The rabbinate, the schools, and the charities also came under the single, central control of the elected officials of the community.

Still, it was the synagogue that remained the most important center of the community. Several other houses opened on what was known as the "Synagogue Square": the abattoir, the public baths, the dormitory for transient Jewish lodgers traveling across the continent. During the day, the synagogue quarters were used as schoolrooms for the children, and at night as a meeting place for the community council and its various committees: the loan society, the bridal-dowering society, the free-burial society, and the like. For many Jews the "Synagogue Square" was probably the closest thing they had to the lost patrimony of the Holy Land.

Even the rituals of the synagogue were co-opted, as it were, into the service of the community interest and welfare. Nonpayment of taxes, immoral conduct, rebellious action, and other infringements of communal regulations were punishable by the most censorious weapon available to the medieval Jewish community: the culprit was simply denied the right to participate fully in the services of the synagogue. When vital community matters pressed for discussion, the synagogue service itself was interrupted, and then, following the "secular" interlude required by the communal interest, the sacred worship continued, naturally and unselfconsciously, as if public discussion were indeed an integral part of the divine service. The officials of the community also transformed the synagogue service into a regular rallying point for the various charitable enterprises under their control: collections took place each day, and coin boxes and plates were passed around before and after the daily services, morning and evening.

Nor was the medieval synagogue only a place for the serious. Jewish life abounded with many opportunities for private celebrations of religious moments: betrothal collations, wedding parties, circumcision feasts, and the like. As the most significant possession of the community, the synagogue was ideally constituted to serve as a social center for the public celebration of religiously associated events in the private lives of its members. Yet, once again, even these personal activities were "socialized"; they too came under the jurisdiction and control of the community council. The host was required to pay a head-tax for each of his guests—taxes earmarked by various communities for different social services—for schools, for indigents, or for any other of their ongoing budgetary requirements. And those whose social appetites led to conspicuous or over-demonstrative celebrations which exceeded the norms of the community were penalized by special "sumptuary taxes" levied by the ruling elders.

Medieval Jewry, the nation within a nation, used the synagogue as the national center for its welfare state. Education, religion, social welfare, charity—indeed, all their human needs—found their base in the synagogue, so that ultimately nothing Jewish and nothing human was alien to it. When, however, the medieval Jewish community started to break down, as the spirit of emancipation rose, inevitably the synagogue would be radically altered. In America, as we have seen, Jews from the very first lived in an emancipated community, and from the very first, too, the American synagogue was different.

America offered a new and challenging situation for Jewish communal organization. In America, separation of church organization from the state was a social reality. While the earliest American synagogues were, in effect, the equivalents of the "Jewish community," they were, nevertheless, voluntary groups, enjoying complete congregational autonomy. Even when they became more numerous, after the arrival of west-European Jews in the 1850's the tendency continued: each congregation remained a law unto itself.

Those who then came from the provinces and lands of western Europe already had a foretaste of the breakdown of the structure of their traditional medieval community. On the eve of emancipation, the Jewish communities of Europe, and particularly those of the West, had already been influenced by the dissolving forces of the absolute state, early capitalism, and the rise of Jewish enlightenment. With the granting of civil rights to the Jews of France and to the Jews of Germany, the scene was completely set for the final dissolution of the organic and autonomous Jewish community. For the first time in European history, as we have seen, Jews enjoyed equal rights before the law, were permitted to hold public office, and were granted full rights of national citizenship. For many Jews, such a revolutionary circumstance rendered the continuation of a Jewish corporate community useless, unnecessary, and even fraught with possible danger.

The period that saw the final demise of a self-sufficient Jewish community also saw the rise of the congregation as an autonomous unit. Although civil rights were being granted, the complete absorption of Jews into the Christian population was still unattainable. Jewish separation now was a fact caused not by the Jewish desire to remain apart, but primarily because the group attitudes of the German and French populations required it. Yet the newly emancipated Jewish group ardently strove for recognition as status equals.

To justify their separation they could find only one rationale, and that was religion. As the doctrine of separation of church and state began to be asserted and recognized, it became quite possible for nationals of the same country to differ along lines of creedal alliance and still be regarded as loyal citizens of the state. Jews realized then that they, too, could retain a *formal* allegiance to the religious principles of Judaism, while discarding the communal and national ties that seemed to them a political hindrance to complete civic acceptance.

If Jewish religion, divorced from communal and national associations, was to become the principal criterion of Jewish identity, it then followed that the congregational synagogue was the institution best to express this new alignment. The *congregation,* and not the *community,* was to become the unit of Jewish self-government and expression, the means whereby individual Jews could form and retain their Jewish identity. The rise of the congregation to its new position as the "mirror of the Jewish universe" represented an inversion of earlier Jewish community life. Theretofore the synagogue had been the hub of the Jewish community, but it was completely communal in nature and it served as the instrument of communal will. Now that Jewish community life, as experienced before, was non-existent, to the superficial observer it may seem that little had changed in terms of the synagogue program. But the synagogue's activities were now carried on *in its own name,* and its functions were the concern of each autonomous congregation. It is this aspect of its nature that is basically different from its medieval forerunners and marks its flowering in America as a major departure in Jewish history.

In spite of their professed orthodoxy, the earliest American synagogues were far removed from European orthodoxy, *if only as a result of their social structure.* Now that each congregation was completely self-governing, it could sanction whatever deviations from the older religious practices is deemed wise or necessary. Additionally, the very nature of the oldest settlers was conducive to uncritical religious innovations. As noted previously, not only were the earlier east-European arrivals (prior to 1920) principally the *proste*—or simple, low-status folk—whose élite religious leaders had mainly stayed behind, but the same description applied to almost all of the earlier German-Jewish immigrants as well. Many were essentially young adventurers, without too much education. Moreover, there were not yet uniform prayer books, nor local theological seminaries to help standardize rabbinical practices, nor even a congregational union to unify the diverse and varied procedures of the local synagogues. Valiant efforts were undertaken in the last quarter of the nineteenth century to establish a single, national association of synagogues which, at the least, might have provided American Jews with a voluntary congregational equivalent of the authoritarian European corporate community. This program to establish a single, coordinated form of "American Judaism" failed, ostensibly because its initiator, Rabbi Isaac Mayer Wise, sought to mold it to his own Reform ideology. But doubtless of equal importance in accounting for their failure to establish a central authority in an all-inclusive organization was the self-conscious American temper of these congregations already evident at so early a moment in their new world experience. Their reluctance to give up their autonomy and their willingness to retain a loosely organized, virtually improvised pattern of congregational life were very much in keeping with the decentralized structure of the dominant American religious culture: Protestantism.

If before the 1880's it was difficult to bring the Jewish congregations of America into a single, over-all synagogue union, after those years it would be impossible to do so. The vast number of east-European Jews who then came to America represented a wide variety of local religious and cultural patterns. While all these regarded themselves—and each other—as Jews, they did bring with them the local partisanships, and the fierce *landsman* loyalties of their Polish, Lithuanian, Ukrainian, Galician, Hungarian, Rumanian, or Russian cities, towns, and villages. The synagogues they formed were actually what sociologists call "ethnic churches." This type of religious institution, as we have seen, was founded in America by other immigrant groups, too—by Scandinavians, Germans, Slovaks, and many others. But among east-European Jews of the early twentieth century their "ethnic church" was not only a means for the preservation of the larger Jewish culture, but also served as a vehicle for transplanting to America the unique subculture of the particular European region from whence each of these different Jewish groups hailed.

The impact of Suburbia on American religious life, and particularly upon the synagogue, has been of major proportions, as we have had occasion to note. But this development is little more than a continuation, although with new implications, of the changing environmental influences that have been constantly shaping the form and the function of the American synagogue since the beginning of the century. These social ecological influences have, in fact, paralleled closely the life span of the three Jewish generations of east-European descent whose American history began less than a hundred years ago. Students of urban immigrant life describe these influences in terms of areas of settlement. The area of first settlement is the city district, usually hard by the downtown business center, which is inhabited by the first generation: the greenhorns who are just off the boat. The area of second settlement is the district populated by many of these immigrants soon after their children—the second generation—are born. It usually consists of a series of neighborhoods of small and cheap homes rather than of tenement houses, and its physical improvement over the area of first settlement clearly and visually reflects the advancement of its dwellers to higher rungs of the social and economic ladders. The area of third settlement is the new neighborhood, often near the edge of the city limits, where the children or the grandchildren, the members of the third generation of the immigrants, move. It is uniformly middle class, and both in the life-style of the householders and in the physical structure of the houses reflects a highly acculturated, economically established American community.

If we were to use these areas of settlement as gauges and indexes of values and not merely of physical mobility, we would understand better how and why the contemporary American synagogue had been transformed into a new social and religious institution. And we would discover, too, that the new American synagogue community is as much—if not more—a response to the new sociology of America as it is to two thousand years of synagogue history.

The twentieth-century synagogue in the area of first American settlement was virtually a transplantation of its *shtetl* counterpart: the pre-emancipated prayerhouse of east-Europe. It was small in size, intimate in the extreme, and decorum in prayer was considered to be nothing less than an aberration of western Jewish emancipation, if not a sign of Christian influence. There was no preacher, no sermon, no school, no cultural program, no social welfare, no membership organization beyond the informal handful of regular worshipers. Those who came to pray or to study were largely *landsmen* from the same European communities who joined together at daily and Sabbath services; no membership chairman sought out as prospective members those who were not already worshiping together. In retrospect, we can understand the paradoxical nature of their difficulties: by refusing to adapt their synagogue to the new environmental influences, they succeeded in making it both irrelevant and anachronistic. The synagogue they established here presupposed the medieval structure of the corporate Jewish community, which was the only kind of Jewish community they had known. But, of course, such a presupposition was only an illusion; no such community existed in America. Thus, their synagogues were destined to be nothing more than prayer or study halls, to be by-passed by the general Jewish community whose vital center was focused in the host of new secular, ethnic organizations soon to rise.

In contrast, before the 1880s the American synagogue had indeed achieved a significant status: it had become the equivalent of the total Jewish community. Even though the congregations had then refused to band together into a comprehensive, national union, individually, they were the effective centers of local Jewish life across the country. But ironically, the pious east-European immigrants who followed, and who settled in the new American "ghettos," the areas of first settlement, reduced the synagogue to little more than a prayer house whose ineffectiveness as a community institution helped pave the way for the rise of secular-mindedness in their children.

For the historical reasons we have already examined, east-European Jewish immigrants had a built-in middle-class potential even before they attained that status in fact. As a result, their social mobility was even more rapid than many other immigrant groups who arrived at the same time. Before too long, many first-generation Jewish immigrants moved to areas of second settlement. But they still were not ready to grapple with problems of handing down their religious tradition in the new environment. For even in the second settlement area the congregational atmosphere retained most of the features that had been part of the synagogue in the first neighborhood. Worship was still primarily its fundamental function—worship, that is, by the older males, and not by family groups. Even the study circles associated with the prayer services had been reduced quantitatively and qualitatively. The advanced lay scholars who had peppered such intellectual activities in the east-European *shtetl* synagogue, it appeared, had either not come over to America or still remained in the older settlement area, or were, perhaps, losing their interest in such exercises. As a result, what did remain of these Talmudic study groups in the second settlement synagogue was merely a faint spark of a former fire; the discussions were becoming less learned, the participants less numerous.

Continuing the same patterns of activity characteristic of the first settlement synagogue, the congregations in the area of second settlement still concentrated on the general *shtetl* style. They remained unwilling to add to their program activities that could, at the least, compensate for the growing decline in the habits of worship or study, or which, at best, might attract new and young blood to prayer and learning through cultural or social programs. If to this inner failure one adds the increas-

ing estrangement of many second-generation American children from
the ethnicism of their parents, which the synagogue and Judaism symbolized, it is not difficult to see why the congregation of that time and
place had hardly any impact upon the growing generation. The older
women, it is true, were now brought closer to it by means of the Ladies'
Auxiliary, which functioned primarily as a fund-raising arm of the congregation, without a voice in its management or program. But for the
other members of the family, and particularly the younger members, the
synagogue of the second settlement area was attended only on High
Holy Days: three days a year. Aside from such special "state occasions," it
stood as a lonely, little-frequented relic of the past. For most second-
generation Jews it had become something of a museum, containing ancient, even beautiful memories—but only memories, nothing more.
Their parents were unwilling to forget, and they were not anxious to
remember.

Into this vacuum a new and typically American institution entered—
the Jewish Community Center. As early as 1854, in Baltimore, a Young
Men's Hebrew Association was founded, and by the end of the century
similar community centers had been organized in many other cities.
Then, with the coming of the east-Europeans, the "uptown" German
Jews established settlement houses for the "downtown" immigrant newcomers, to teach them English, proper Western manners, and, in addition, to offer them supervised recreational activities. Both the older
Jewish "Y" and the newer settlement houses served as the forerunners of
the Jewish Community Center or Y.M.H.A., which became exceedingly
popular and widely spread in the 1920s and 1930s, and which still continues to offer the American Jewish community a variety of recreational
and cultural opportunities. Its avid acceptance by the members of the
second generation was a reflection of the synagogue's failure to attract
them. Living as most of them were in areas of second settlement (which
were predominantly populated by Jews) they required a neighborhood
center, but they sought one that did not emphasize the religious side of
their Jewish lives. To be sure, the "Y" attempted to offer them Jewish
"cultural" activities: youth clubs, forums, discussions, and reading circles. But for most of those who joined it was the gymnasium or the
swimming pool that served as the feature attraction.

By 1948, however, these Jewish Community Centers, affiliated in a
country-wide association with the National Jewish Welfare Board, were
moving toward a re-examination of their role as Jewish centers. The
very people who, two decades earlier, were emphasizing the American
democratic aspects of the "Y" to the neglect of its specific Jewish functions were now seeking to assert that its principal purpose was to serve as
"an agency of Jewish identification," which provides a "common meeting
ground for Jews regardless of doctrinal, ritual, political, or social views."

There was nothing unusual in this self-revaluation: for an institution that had undergone a series of transformations since its first days in America, it was surely proper to review its contemporary role—certainly since by then the Center Movement encompassed over 150 member agencies in local communities throughout the country. But there can be little doubt that the major cause for its new orientation toward more Jewish programming was the result of the amazing new hold that the synagogue was coming to have upon the community, once Jews moved to areas of third settlement.

In the areas of first and second settlement, the synagogue was little more than another small Jewish association among the many others. It was the *Hevrah,* the Jewish association, that became the accepted and popular vehicle of their multi-organization community. There were east-European associations in America for almost every individual fancy and purpose: burial societies, benevolent societies, loan societies, *landsman* societies, family societies, and still more of the like. And the worshiping congregation centered in the synagogues of the first and second areas of settlement were formed as still other associations—for those who were religious-minded. Sometimes, an association would itself create its own associational synagogue; thus benevolent associations, lodges, or burial societies often built prayer halls to serve the members of their own organizations.[2]

But in the area of third settlement, something new happened. For virtually the first time in their history, Jews who moved to those neighborhoods would be living in sections predominantly non-Jewish. It was this fact above all others that helped to account for the transformation that now came over the synagogue in these new areas of settlement. To achieve status as coequals with their Christian neighbors despite the paucity of their numbers in the area, Jews required a center for Judaism, and not only for Jewishness. In this new environment, then, the synagogue had to be more than just an association; it had to become *the* center for the Jews of the neighborhood. Fortunately, the idea of the "synagogue center" had been proposed, as early as 1918, by Dr. Mordecai M. Kaplan. His aim was to make the synagogue into more than a hall of worship for small and special-interest groups by adding to it all the communal social, recreational, and cultural functions that had characterized the "Y." Kaplan, indeed, began to preach the importance of reaching out to the unsynagogued and the secular Jews, of bringing them back to Judaism by means of a synagogue center that would encompass the entire gamut of Jewish communal interests. Even those congregations which did not espouse Kaplan's religious philosophy of Reconstructionism (see next chapter) eagerly adopted his program for the vitalization of the synagogue in the new milieu, in the role of synagogue center. Before long, *shuls* (synagogues) had pools, and those who formerly swam in the "Y" now had a religious center to which they streamed. In any case, the losing battle in which the synagogue in America had been engaged for so many decades now seemed destined for new victories.

In what is sometimes the area of fourth settlement, Suburbia, the synagogue center has, in fact, reached its zenith, as *the* community center of the new and youthful families who usually make up its constituency. It becomes the meeting place for all Jewish organizations: the lodges, the Zionist groups, the charity associations. It serves as the social center for the teen-ager and frequent dances, parties, and bull sessions are conducted in its youth lounge. It is the scene of family celebrations, and catered luncheons, receptions, and dinners fill its public rooms on the occasion of weddings, confirmations, Bar-Mitzvah celebrations for thirteen-year-old boys, or Bat-Mitzvah, the counterpart for the adolescent girls. On weekday afternoons and on Sundays, its schoolrooms are filled with children studying Hebrew, Bible, and Jewish history, and in the evening and weekends the children's clubs, Boy Scout and Girl Scout Troops. Its men function as a social unit in organizations known as Men's Clubs or Brotherhoods, and they perform a variety of special services for the congregation in addition to their bowling leagues, breakfast groups, and dinner meetings. The women, too, are extremely busy. But no longer are they relegated to the fringes of congregational management. They sit as full-fledged members of the governing boards, shape synagogue policy through their own organization, the Sisterhood, and usually are the effective force in molding the school and youth programs. Each congregational subgroup—the youth, the men, and the women—participates in the regional synagogue organizations, sponsored by their particular religious movement in Judaism—Orthodox, Conservative, or Reform—and beyond the region as well in the national synagogue organizations. In all, the synagogue center of today, in Suburbia or in third settlement urban areas, keeps the whole family occupied and knits communities together in shared purpose across the country.

Yet for all this activity, it is often difficult to relate those who participate in these programs to the religious ideology a synagogue is supposed to represent. In the smaller communities, a much greater percentage affiliates with a synagogue than in the larger ones. Still, even after balancing them together, the national average of the affiliated is something less than fifty per cent—about 2,700,000 souls out of a total of 5,750,000 Jews in America. Ironically, sometimes, as a mark of their community-mindedness (or affluence?) some families join more than one congregation, with different religious ritual systems and ideologies.[3] An observer of suburban congregational life described some aspects of the confused process:

Young married couples, recently settled in a suburb look first for fellow-ship and friendship. They decide that they "ought to have some kind of a Jewish club, maybe even a Jewish center, like a Young Men's and Young Women's Hebrew Association." Enthusiastically, they set out to establish the center, only to discover that soon the religious educational needs of their very young children will have to be met. And "how can that be done without a Rabbi or teacher?" After much cogitation and self-examination they agree that they really need an institution that will provide for the children's religious needs, as well as for their own social and fellowship interests. They conclude that a religious institution can provide for social as well as educational needs. Hence, they expand their original concept to include a synagogue. Now they have blue-printed a synagogue-center—an all-inclusive organization which will serve the needs of these young families.[4]

But what kind of synagogue is it to be? Orthodox, Conservative, or Reform? The answer to this question is usually resolved in nonideological fashion: by popular referendum or by means of the politics of compromise. "We asked our organizers," reports one typical group of Jewish suburbanites, "What kind of synagogue they wanted. Some thought it ought to be Reform; others wanted an Orthodox synagogue, and a great number wanted the Conservative. We figured that the Conservative was the 'middle of the road' and *would not offend any group in the community*. So we called it a Conservative synagogue."[5] (Italics mine.)

It often did not really matter what "they called it." For, Jews, particularly these third-generation-returnees, could not altogether shake off their secularity—nor, as "good Americans" did they feel the need to do so, even when, in the 1950s and '60s, they joined those new suburban synagogues, in their multitudes. Their worldliness—as well as their material successes—led them in the direction of a new phenomenon in Jewish religious history—the establishment and maintenance of giant-sized, corporate-like congregations. By the 1970s, as noted, it was estimated that there were some 4,500 Jewish congregations in the United States with a combined population of about 2.7 million men, women and children. Amazingly, however, virtually one out of every two of these families was a member, in fact, of only some 300 "suburban" congregations—the giant, middle-class-oriented congregations, that had now become their vogue. Many of these bordered on, or surpassed 2,000 families.[6] It was the new power and authority of these 300 synagogues that had set the style for almost all the others: cultural activities and learning programs may have abounded, but the essential values of associating as members were social, not religious. They were also costly "clubs" to join—which tells us much about the *reasons* for joining: almost all of these mammoth congregations had annual budgets of half-a-million dollars, or more.

As the 1970s began, however, there were definite signs—if only among an extremely small minority of younger families—that some were seeking a more authentic personal Jewish experience than their parents had ever bothered to think about. As children of *arrivistes,* who had to prove to themselves that they had indeed succeeded, their generation had no need for, nor did it find fulfillment in, the exaggerated, and often extravagantly oversized, mammoth congregations of their suburbanized parents. Indeed, they were rebelling against all of this, and unexpectedly willing to experiment with the very old, whilst rejecting the tinselled, middle-class novelties that had repelled them.

But they were the counter-culturalists in search of their own, more genuine Jewish selves. Some remained on the sidelines of the organized community, still shy of the large or established congregations, or bored by their old labels; others were founding or joining smaller, more intimate and less-denominated cultural and spiritual fellowships, which were known as *havurot.*[7]

Once, as we have seen, a humble synagogue served as the portable sanctuary of the Jews, an adaptation to the new environment in the face of the Temple's demise. Though it hoped for the Temple's restoration, in fact it became the replacement for the Temple. It was made to serve new functions, as a House of Study and a House of Meeting. But it continued to be a sanctuary.

Then, brought to America, it kept the earlier, smaller Jewish communities alive, but fell into unpopularity when the east-Europeans turned instead to their associations, their new organizations, their neighborhood centers.

Now, it has again returned to the center of Jewish interest and preoccupation. But has this new birth of Judaism come about for no different a reason than the new burst of interest in Jewishness—the impact of American psychology and sociology upon the Jew in America? Has the synagogue become an accepted fashion among Jews, because American life says yes? Have Jewishness and Judaism successfully merged in the synagogue center for reasons that have little to do with their intrinsic meanings? Does the contemporary American synagogue possess religious ideologies that flow out of Jewish thought and theology, or has it become primarily a respectable "survival center," the major beneficiary and principal vehicle of the "new ethnicity"?

Three major religious movements have grown up here: Orthodoxy, Conservatism, and Reform. What does this development in America say to the questions we have raised?

NOTES

1. Harry Gersh, "The New Suburbanites of the '50s," in *Commentary,* March, 1954, pp. 218–19.

2. For a fuller discussion of these associations in America, see Isaac Levitats, "The Jewish Association in America," in *Essays in Jewish Life and Thought* (eds. Blau, Friedman, Hertzberg, Mendelsohn) (New York: Columbia University Press, 1959), pp. 333–349.

3. A typical example is the Jewish community of Omaha, Nebraska. As of December 31, 1962, its Jewish Federation reported the total number of Jews in Omaha as 6,969, of whom 3,664 were married and 898 were single adults. Of the total adult population of 4,462, only 860 were not affiliated with a synagogue, and of these, 36 were newcomers who had arrived in Omaha as of January 1, 1962. Of those affiliated with congregations, 90 were members of two congregations, and 10 were members of three congregations!

The largest congregation in Omaha was the Conservative synagogue with 801 members; the Orthodox (Beth Israel) was next with 591 members; the Reform Temple was third with 469 members; and a smaller Orthodox congregation had 33 members. (In each case, married couples are counted as one membership.)

See *Community News Reporter,* January 24, 1963, Vol. II, No. 4 New York, Jewish Telegraphic Agency. See also *American Jewish Year Book* (Philadelphia: The Jewish Publication Society of America, 1973) Volume 74, p. 282.

4. Albert I. Gordon, *Jews in Suburbia* (Boston: Beacon Press, 1959), pp. 96–97.

5. *Ibid.*

6. I estimate that approximately 1.2 million Jews (in 1970) were affiliated with these giant synagogues, each of which consisted of 1,000 or more families. My estimates are based on the raw data for the year 1970–71, of synagogue population and finances provided by Daniel Elazar. The numbers I have employed are based upon extrapolations from Elazar, in addition to observations of the scene—economically and demographically—in 1983. None of these numbers can be precise, but they are offered to provide the reader with a basis for empirical judgment. See Daniel Elazar, *Community and Polity: The Organizational Dynamics of American Jewry,* (Philadelphia: The Jewish Publication Society of America, 1976), pp. 72–3; 272; 305–6; 403 (notes).

According to the "National Jewish Population Study," it was indicated that "fifty three per cent of the national sample reported no formal membership in a congregation. The remainder were affiliated with Reform congregations, 14 percent; Conservative, 23 per cent, and Orthodox 9 per cent. It can be assumed that the proportion affiliated was greater outside of New York City." See *American Jewish Year Book.* 1973: p. 282.

7. For a fuller discussion of the "*Havurah* movement," see Stephen C. Lerner, "The Havurot," in *Conservative Judaism* (no. 24) September, 1970, pp. 178–87.

CHAPTER X

Denominationalism American-style

IF BY THE 1980s SOME AMERICAN JEWS HAD BEGUN TO SEEK NEWER, MORE intimate, and smaller-scaled religious fellowships, this mood was a far cry from the dominant spirit of their parents in the 1950s. In that earlier decade, Jews were busy "moving up" in every way possible. Part of that movement included a radical change in their religious geography. As they made their way from the crowded city cores to the open spaces of exurbia, they also began building new and larger synagogue buildings.

Powered by the prosperity following World War II, and ably assisted by a crop of successful and creative Jewish architects—congregations were emboldened to purchase large tracts of land. Enough of those tiny, competitive, scrubby synagogues downtown, they were told. The time had now come to do what Americans do: to "think big." And so they changed the physical map of Judaism, as monumentally scaled, imposing synagogue "plants" became the rage, with the aid of outstanding designers like Eric Mendelson, Percival Goodman, Louis Kahn, and other notables. In suburban Philadelphia, Jews invited the celebrated architect Frank Lloyd Wright to create a daring building for them, which he did, conceiving it as a "travelling Mount Sinai."

In the emancipated climate of the new world, where the question of "being Jewish" seemed to have been transformed into a personal, individual option, synagogues would be regarded as "private organizations." Because Jews now lived in the midst of fellow citizens—not estranged but inter-connected—who comprised a "nation of belongers," some joined as members of synagogues, sometimes even whimsically and thoughtlessly. And because America was also dedicated to the principles of *laissez-faire* and the entrepreneurial spirit, Jewish congregations, too, came under the same spell of privatism. They were the personal affairs of their own members.

It would follow, then, that the private proprietary rights of most Jewish congregations in America could almost never be called into question—certainly not by non-members. They came to regard their own rules and regulations as transcending Jewish history and custom, as if they were "divine rights of property"—their new Torah, which others, outside of their walls, could not tamper with. Like so many other American clubs and associations, they considered that their real purpose was principally for the enjoyment and benefit of their own members. They did not feel called upon to justify or to rationalize their actions, style, or programs—except to their tight membership islands. And even these shifted with the moving sands of the joiners; as neighborhoods changed, members came and went, and with their coming and going, earlier stances and postures were rapidly altered. Thus, almost overnight, Orthodox synagogues became Conservative; Conservatives were made over into Reform, and on and on the "conversions" went. Like America itself, one could hardly look for philosophical consistency among those whose lives were ruled by pragmatics.

As the Jew became more deeply rooted in America, he expressed his historic apartness through the building of religious edifices which, while separate, are "separate but equal." More and more, the Jewish institution of religion was an acceptable symbol of legitimate democratic difference, and in a society which thinks of itself as religious, the synagogue building has become a public sign of the rootedness of the Jew in the broader culture. It is a valuable and valid spiritual address. However, it is also a sign of cultural and possibly even of religious loss. In a Christian society, the church does not exhaust Christianity: it acts principally as the ritual and social center for the faithful or the would-be faithful. The state, however, rightly or wrongly, continues to think of itself as the embodiment of Christian values and hopes. Within the Jewish community, the synagogue does not (indeed, as we have seen, never did) comprise all of Judaism. Always, the synagogue depended upon the schools, the community welfare systems, the living religious law, and most significantly, upon the home life, for its support and strength.

But in America synagogues burst their historical seams, and, instead of remaining institutions subordinate to the total Jewish community, became independent, self-governing congregations. They did so in the name of an ideology: the democratic principle of voluntary association. Here, different groups of Jews could read and interpret the religious tradition as they saw fit, and they could depart from both the traditions and the authority of the community by founding religious congregations after the spirit of their own choosing.

Indeed, Jews in Europe were not completely free to make their own Jewish choices even *within* their own religious community: the state had the right to intervene in all internal Jewish matters. In Russia and Germany, for example, Jews were regarded in law as members of a closed and monolithic religious community, without any inner divisions or denominations. In this connection, it is instructive to note that when Rabbi Samson Raphael Hirsch of Frankfurt-am-Main wanted to break off from the "official" Jewish religious community—which was Reform—in order to organize a separate Orthodox *gemeinde,* or community association, he had to wait many years for the passage of a special Act by the Prussian Parliament until permission was legally granted him and his followers by the state. This "Law of Secession," known as the *Austrittsgesetz*, was passed only in 1876, and it finally permitted a Jew to leave his local congregation without having to leave Judaism altogether. In its day, this government law granting *Orthodox* German Jews the right to secede from *Reform*, and to establish their own "separate Jewish religious community," was hailed as a momentous victory for religious freedom. In America, of course, such a law would have been unthinkable: the right to associate freely was regarded as a fundamental liberty open to all Americans, religious or not.

Indeed, America became the home of denominational Judaism for many of the same reasons that Protestantism here became something other than it had been in the Old World. One cannot fully appreciate the transformation that the synagogue was to undergo in response to the American environment without relating it to the "revolution" in the historic life of the church that American Protestantism represents. In contrast to their European predecessors, Protestant churches here have been characterized largely by a spirit of voluntary cooperation on the part of likeminded laymen. By and large, their concerns are the concerns of the laity and not those of the clerical leaders. As a result, in America, Protestant church life has been tied into social and political interests covering a broad range of activities that were never considered to be part of the concerns of the church in Europe.

This lay-dominated church life has given rise to another special characteristic of American Protestantism—congregationalism. True, the "high" Protestant churches are officially governed along episcopal lines, giving the impression that they are centrally organized. In practice, however, in virtually all American Protestant churches the basic programs and activities are centered in the life and the choice of the individual congregation. It is the local church—not the bishops, the synods, or the church presidents—that is the effective molder of congregational life. While the external controls of these central, super-congregational authorities can often be invoked in favor of certain policies and principles, in practice, the key to the successful coordination of church activity lies in the voluntary cooperation of members of the local congregation.

It is in the soil of voluntarism and pluralism that denominationalism grows, and America was to be fertile ground indeed. Protestants saw America as a place for diversity and cooperation and turned their backs on what they believed was the old, not the new, way—the way of centralized, authoritarian, clerical control. This American Protestant spirit has bred the rugged individualism that is the hallmark of denominationalism.

Yet denominationalism in American Protestantism has given rise to an indifference to theological and creedal matters. The emphasis of "a denomination" is always more upon "group survival" than upon specifically religious issues. Moreover, while the denominational church is concerned with the traditions, customs, and the life-style of its own group, and with preserving these in order to maintain its special identity, its major emphasis is upon blending with the national culture. The result, according to church historian Wilhelm Pauck, is that "American Protestantism has become, and still is, a social-religious movement . . . and a social-political movement." "Indeed," he goes on to suggest, "American Protestantism has become a middle-class movement in part in connection with its own understanding of itself, and in part through its active participation in American social-political life. The outlook of Protestants is determined largely by the interests of the middle class, and not necessarily by concerns that are identifiable as Christian."[1]

All of these factors can be seen in their Jewish unfolding, too, in the development of the American synagogue. Here, new adjectives were devised—Orthodox, Conservative, and Reform—and, often, these became more important to their followers than did Judaism, the substantive they modified. Denominational Judaism was born in America. Does it, in fact, represent a deeply motivated and meaningful use of the principles of diversity, pluralism, and voluntarism, or is it governed mainly by social, cultural, or economic factors? Has denominationalism served as a contribution to or a diminution of Jewish religious thought and ideology?

Some answers will emerge from an examination of the history, the ideology, and the educational enterprises of these three Jewish denominations in America.

Reform. Reform was a revolution in Jewish life, and at its inception it was a revolt of the layman. In parts of western Europe, as we have seen, a small number of rabbis permitted themselves to express new religious ideas at their rabbinical conferences. As a group, however, it was laymen and not rabbis who spearheaded the fight to organize Jewish life along these radical lines. The reasons are obvious: laymen were affected by the emancipation in realistic fashion, while many rabbis never directly felt its impact. It was the layman who was in close contact with the commercial world and who came to have new associations in the non-Jewish community: trade rights, economic guarantees, war, and peace had direct bearing upon his day-to-day life. He was living on wider highways of life, and he felt the impact of external forces more than the cloistered and secluded scholar who lived according to the dictates of ancient forms of social control, the laws of the Bible and the Talmud. Any attempt to receive widespread authoritative adjustment from medieval-style rabbis was apparently hopeless. Laymen had to seek such adjustment on their own.

Most students of Reform Judaism see in it only philosophical, theological, or ritualistic implications. They look upon it only as a religious movement. But it was also a social phenomenon, just because it was fostered by laymen. Seen in this light, Reform represents a movement that resulted in, if it did not consciously espouse, communal reform as well as religious change. It helped to destroy the last vestiges of communal control and rabbinical sanction. In place of a central Jewish community, it fostered the rise of Jewish congregationalism, and in the process granted to laymen rights in purely religious matters, which they never before possessed. Never before had religious control passed into the hands of men who were neither equipped nor sanctioned by Jewish tradition to exercise it.

In the late eighteenth century, the Jewish laymen's program in Europe began very humbly and without fanfare in the area of the school. Their first thought was to institute teaching reforms whereby the very young would be given broader insights into modern culture, along with their religious training. Lay teachers were engaged and advanced ideas taught. Yet these efforts still remained weak and ineffective. They would become more widespread and acceptable only when the men who stood behind them—the new-style lay leaders—would achieve status as officials of congregations. It was in Germany that they first moved into power, and it was thus that Germany became the birthplace of Reform Judaism. The new consistorial decrees of the French and German governments were fully in keeping with the theory of the lay reformers. They helped the early Reform laymen achieve their desire to overthrow the autonomous Jewish community. For the decrees made it clear that in the future the Jews must not regard themselves as a separate group within the state, but, like all other religious groups, should be culturally assimilated by the nation of which they were a part. Rabbis and teachers were reminded, at every opportunity, to cultivate loyalty to the Fatherland. They were also told to teach that military service is a holy duty, and that, in the performance of this service, the Jew is to be freed from all religious observances that are in conflict with his civil duties. The new and rising lay leaders were fully in accord with these views, and were anxious to assert the principle that the Jew and the Jewish community had a single goal: usefulness to the state.

While these views of the functions of Judaism had their birth in Germany and France, it was America that became the true home of Reform. Here, no struggle for emancipation animated Jewish efforts; Jews began life in America as political equals. Yet the lay proponents of radical Reform in nineteenth-century American Judaism were religious pioneers without a theological program. To be sure, they espoused certain rabbinical platforms and enunciated certain principles of progress. Seen in retrospect, however, their viewpoints were essentially pragmatic. Facing the new political situation created by their American nationality and citizenship, they had to improvise a new series of responses, as members of a separatist religious community. In such a circumstance, one could not expect them to have been consistent with their own "theories," or, indeed, to have been theoretical at all.

In a way this had to be so. The problem of adjusting their outlook to the American scene was the problem of the Jewish citizen who lived in a paradoxical community. On one hand, for the first time he resided in a democratic community in which there was official separation of church from state. How then could he justify social separatism, or indeed any separatism beyond the scope of ritual and theology? Yet he knew very well that this society was dominated by the Christian tradition, and so, willy-nilly, as a Jew he continued to remain alienated from the total community. This made him as aware as ever of the need to seek common cause with his coreligionists even in matters apart from the purely religious. Thus, while he fiercely asserted and believed in his American nationality, he could not completely give up a hold on his ties to the Jewish community. This resulted in a somewhat disjointed "Reform" approach: it was radical in its desire to adjust traditional Judaism to American ways of life, yet it lacked a theological platform for its religious program.[2] It was a Reform movement but not a Reformation.

The very first attempt at Reform in America came about in 1824 in Charleston, South Carolina, when a group of forty-seven members of that city's congregation petitioned for certain changes in the synagogue ritual. Characteristically, they requested that as "in the Catholic, the German and the French Protestant churches" the "principal parts, [of the Jewish service] and, if possible, all that is read in *Hebrew,* should also be read in *English* (that being the language of the country), so as to enable every member of the congregation fully to understand each part of the service."[3] When their memorial was rejected by the congregation's elders, they founded a new group, The Reformed Society of Israelites. For lack of the required rabbinic leadership, this new congregation withered. Yet it did succeed in projecting a new religious approach in American Judaism, for Reform societies were to be founded some years later in Baltimore, New York, Philadelphia, and Chicago that successfully launched new Reform congregations, when they found rabbis whose views coincided with their own. Essentially, these were groups desiring most of all to practice a form of Judaism that would appear to be as American as all the other religious groups in the country.

In the first half of the nineteenth century, American rabbis who subscribed to these views were hard to come by. There was only a handful of pioneers: such men as Rabbis Max Lilienthal, Isaac M. Wise, David Einhorn, Samuel Adler, Bernard Felsenthal, and Samuel Hirsch. Nor could even these few agree among themselves as to the direction Reform should take. In 1856, a rabbinical conference was held in Cleveland purporting to represent all shades of American rabbinical opinion. It ended in conflict, however. There was no general agreement among the non-Reform rabbis present, and two factions arose among the Reform: those from the eastern states were more moderate, those from the West, more radical. The spirit of the Cleveland conference continued to plague the Reform group for some years—not only the ideological clash, but the confrontation of personalities; and the sectional differences between East and West remained as obstacles to unity. But the American rabbinate was itself a new and different Jewish institution and it would be several decades before it would develop its own self-confidence in the new environment. So, too, the elaboration of a coherent rabbinical ideology, as distinct from the practical reforms desired by the laymen, would develop only as the slow product of the rabbinate's reaction to the new time and the new place.

By the 1870s, the American rabbi-reformers came to see it as their task to adjust Jewish theology to the accepted scientific theories of their day, theories which, to some religionists, were patently subversive of traditional religious thought and practice. For some decades, they had been unsuccessful in their attempts to establish an academic and theological center that would serve as a rallying point for Reform, where American Jews could train their own rabbis in the light of American conditions, without continuing to rely upon those prepared in Europe. Finally, in 1875, under the leadership of Rabbi Isaac Mayer Wise, the Hebrew Union College was founded in Cincinnati. Wise had hoped that this seminary would, in fact, serve as the single rabbinical school for all the settled American Jewish congregations, irrespective of their earlier religious orientations. In America, he believed, Jews would produce their own unique expression of Judaism—the specific American religious style, or *Minhag America,* as he called it—much as Babylonian, North African, Spanish, and Polish Jewries had done before. Such an American Judaism would be committed to moderate reforms, in the spirit of the age and the place. He was rebuffed in these efforts at uniting all these congregations into a single comprehensive religious movement, because not all of them could accept his ideology nor his hopes as theirs; they were not as willing as he seemed to forget the religious experiences and outlook that they had brought to America from Europe. When these others did not join with him, the Hebrew Union College was led by these circumstances to become, not *the* center of American Judaism but *a* center, not the ideological symbol of Judaism in America but the citadel of Reform Judaism in America. Within a few years, it had assumed the posture and stance of a denomination. By becoming more and more self-conscious of its own Reform "ideology," it put pressure on the nonaligned congregations to do the same. Before long, two new denominations were born in America: the Conservative and the Orthodox.

In November 1885, a turning point was reached; a conference of Reform rabbis was convened in Pittsburgh by Dr. Kaufman Kohler to draw up a definitive expression of their views, and to formulate a fundamental set of principles, a "theology" to guide the new Reform denomination. Yet, of the eight points of the platform, only one dealt with a purely theological problem. The other "principles," in one way or another, were really expressions of their new American situation and the new democratic milieu in which they lived. The primary concerns of the Platform can be seen from these excerpts:

The Platform declared that "Judaism presents the highest conception of the God-idea"; it spoke of the "consecration of the Jewish people to its mission as the priest of the one God" and claimed "that the modern discoveries of scientific researches in the domain of nature and history are not antagonistic to the doctrines of Judaism." Its intention was to "maintain only such ceremonies as elevate and sanctify our lives, but reject all such as are not adapted to the views and habits of modern [Western?] civilization." Judaism was a "progressive religion, ever striving to be in accord with the postulates of reason." Since Christianity and Islam were "daughter religions of Judaism," the "Platform" expressed appreciation of "their providential mission to aid in the spreading of monotheistic and moral truth." "We acknowledge," the Platform framers added, "that the spirit of broad humanity of our age is our ally in the fulfillment of our mission, and therefore we extend the hand of fellowship to all who co-operate with us in the establishment of the reign of truth and righteousness among men." Finally, they proclaimed, "in full accord with the spirit of Mosaic legislation which strives to regulate the relation between rich and poor, we deem it our duty to participate in the great task of modern times, to solve on the basis of justice and righteousness the problems presented by the contrasts and evils of the present organization of society."

The "Pittsburgh Platform," it is true, possessed no binding character, but it did serve as a central focus of those ideas which were to echo from American Reform pulpits for the next half-century. Its major emphases were drawn from the sociological impact of America, rather than the theological resources of Judaism. In the preaching of such men as Rabbi Joseph Krauskopf, who in 1883 was among the first four graduates of the Hebrew Union College, we can hear the longing of the new American rabbi for the emancipation of Judaism from its outlandish, outmoded oriental cloak, coupled to the fervent wish to re-fit it into a garb better suited to the Western American environment. Like many of his contemporary Reform colleagues he called upon his congregation to:

. . . observe what little progress the Israelite has made in his religious unfolding since he started upon his westward journey. His heart and mind, when at service, are still in the Orient. He still builds his synagogue in the oriental style of architecture, and its Holy of Holies he places in the East, in imitation of the heathen temples consecrated to the Sun, and towards that side he turns his face in prayer, in the belief that from that quarter God will turn a readier ear to his supplications. He still prays in the language of the East, even though he may not understand a word he says. Though far away from the Oriental climes and environments, he still repeats prayers that had a meaning there, but are out of place here, prayers concerning sacrifices, which he no longer brings, concerning the kind of oil to be used for his Sabbath lamp, neither of which are any longer used by him. He prays for an abundance of rain at a time when a little less than we usually get at that season would not come amiss. He prays for a speedy return to the Orient, without really meaning a word of it.[4]

Rabbi Krauskopf was critical not only of the Orthodox whose "oriental" ways he felt were out of keeping with American life, but of some of the customs still observed in the Reform synagogue. He contended that the progressive congregations were not as yet sufficiently Westernized:

Are we so very sure that we ourselves have kept pace with the westward strides of civilization, that we have completely emancipated ourselves from all obsolete and obstructive orientalism? Does not the objection raised against the use of antique hand-written parchment-scroll, insead of the simple modern book of print, apply to us? Does not the objection against the use of Hebrew, of a language unintelligible to almost all the worshippers, apply to us? Do you not still force your poor children in your Sabbath schools to study this language of the East, though you know that they will not learn it, that, for the little time they can devote to it, they cannot learn it.[5]

Indeed, he went still a step further. He sought to free the Jewish congregation in America from all traces of foreign influence. He asked why it was necessary to add "yet another foreign language . . . the German, which, however necessary it may have been for our German-born grandparents and parents, has ceased to be with us?" He was willing to sanction "a little Hebrew" in the service, "in deference to the position it once held as the Holy Language, and as a memento. . . . But why German?" he asked. "Has it any greater merit before God than the language of our own blessed country?"[6]

This effort to cast aside the traditional rituals and liturgies was regarded as a necessary step toward the Americanization of Judaism for it was clearly linked to the desire of ridding their religion of its outworn and irrelevant "orientalism." In this approach, the rabbis were clearly on the side of their laymen. In a second area, too, their "philosophizing" made practical sense to their congregants: Judaism, they were teaching, was a universal, not a "national religion." The "mission theory" as a rationale for Jewish survival in the Diaspora, a concept developed and heightened by the Jewish antinationalists of western Europe, became an important and useful doctrine for the American Reform rabbis. It offered them a twin platform: they could, with one basic approach, negate Jewish nationalism as the motivation for Jewish life while defending the need for integration into the American context in all matters save religion. If Jews were to remain a community apart from the majority, it was only for religious and theological purposes. These seemed to be the only safe and sure reasons suitable to the new environment.

In America the mission idea was given even further significance. It became, as it were, a theological support for the extension of the political concept of democracy. While in other lands it had been the habit of each religious group to claim that only its way was the right way, that none who held another creed could be saved, the feeling of the American Reform rabbi was that "in our time and especially in our country such views are being rapidly outgrown . . . for independent thinkers uniformity is impossible." The rabbi of New York's Temple Emanuel, Dr. Joseph Silverman, went even further. For him the "millennium was not far off." He said:

> Better days are coming. Men come in personal contact with one another in business, pleasure, society, lodges, clubs, hotels; they meet in schools and academies and charities, on the forum, in the assembly halls, in the press, stand side by side in a thousand various walks of life and recognize that they are all alike. They throw off their theologies, and religion, pure and simple, makes them one. Catholics, Protestants and Jews commence to recognize one another as men and brothers, women and sisters, children of "Our Father" in heaven.[7]

It was in connection with their third basic principle that many of the new Reform rabbis came into conflict with their laymen. Their abandonment of the "priestly" rituals led them to stress the "prophetic" ethical strains in the tradition as their primary religious goals. In their eyes, Judaism's genius was as a prophetic religion of social justice. Yet, ironically, the very reforms that they had introduced into congregational life had the effect of converting their synagogues into Jewish replicas of respectable and affluent Protestant churches, whose social outlook was anything but radical or progressive. In many, not only had the major service been transferred from Saturday to Sunday morning, but hardly any of the specifically Jewish characteristics were visible. Hebrew prayer was virtually eliminated in favor of English. Cantors no longer chanted the liturgy but were replaced by an organ and mixed choir, in which non-Jews were often employed as professional singers. Head coverings and prayer shawls were gone. The older practice of seating the women out of sight in a special section was abandoned in favor of family pews. Indeed, the entire design of the synagogue interior, which had always before focused upon the centrality of the Torah lectern, to emphasize the transcendent importance of Sacred Scripture, was now altered to shift attention to the preacher and the pulpit. Thus, in sight and in sound, in form and in content, the Reform temple seemed little different from a typical, prosperous urban American Protestant congregation.

Moreover, a strange paradox was developing. By 1890, the Reform movement was easily the most dominant and best organized religious party in the American Jewish community. Even some leading Eastern congregations that had once opposed the Hebrew Union College and later attacked the "Pittsburgh Platform" were changing their earlier loyalties and moving into the new camp. Yet this was an age of rational religion and irreligion, and the institutional strength of Reform was no gauge of the religious loyalties of its followers. In fact, judging from the sermons of even the more radical Reform rabbis, the movement seemed to be decaying from within; it lacked verve, vitality, and commitment. Dr. Solomon Schindler, a prominent Reform rabbi in Boston, was ready to give up even his radical innovation of Sunday services. "Sunday services," he said, "are not a failure because they are held on Sunday, but because people do not care for *any* services, and as it is here, it is, I suppose, in other cities." "On Saturday," his lament continued, "they say they should not be expected to attend—their business prevents. . . . On Friday evening, they say, they are not in fit condition to listen to an earnest discourse because they are tired. . . . Sunday is entirely out of the question. . . . *Après nous le déluge.*"[8]

Religious loyalties were weak. Despite the attempt on the part of the Reform rabbis to meet the intellectual challenges, by seeking a harmony between science and Judaism, they were continuously confronted with what Dr. Max Landsberg of Rochester called "the coldest indifferentism." Yet even his call and that of his colleagues for greater religious enthusiasm was more sociological than theological in its motivation. If Jews, he said, would identify themselves and their aspirations with "their priestly mission among mankind" and not "lower themselves in the eyes of their own servants," religious loyalties "would so influence our conduct as to raise us up in the eyes of our fellowmen and remove prejudice against us from their minds."[9] But these rabbis were captives of their own methodology and viewpoint. Even in their attempt to inspire a return to Judaism, they seemed unwilling or unable to utilize tools other than the "practical," the "reasonable," or the "socially and culturally acceptable."

Yet, the religious indifference of their congregants was not checked, but fostered, by many of the reforms of their rabbis. Even some of their contemporary theologians, in assessing the direction that the Reform movement had been following until the mid-1930s, now believe that without a change in its course, sooner or later Reform Judaism would have collapsed. "In its endeavor to be 'rational,'" says Dr. Jakob J.

Petuchowski of Hebrew Union College, Reform "proceeded to banish every element of the 'irrational' from Judaism. . . . But the moment you make your commitment to God dependent upon the outcome of your reasoning, there is at least tacit admission that it is possible for your reasoning to take a different course and lead you to an entirely different destination."[10] So, too, by their dramatic emphasis upon ethics over against ritual, the rabbis made worship seem unimportant and irrelevant. And their denial of the religious significance of the laws of the Torah left each individual on his own, free to make his own choices. Thus, the "religious community" was not even a community any longer, but a chance combination of religiously indifferent individuals.

In addition to these built-in ideological paradoxes, another major reason for the religious weakness of Reform Judaism during its first half-century can be traced to its inadequate educational program. The "Pittsburgh Platform" mentioned not a word regarding what it believed Reform congregations should do in the area of religious education. In time, the Protestant Sunday School became the model for the Reform temples. Convened on Saturday or Sunday mornings, the children were often exposed to but one or two hours of teaching by amateurs who were equipped neither by training nor scholarship to do more than tell "Bible stories" or recount a few chapters in Jewish history. Hebrew was rarely taught, the Talmud never, and even the Bible was reduced to a series of tales for children, rendered in English, but rarely studied as religious literature. Perhaps the clearest index to the failure of this kind of education to kindle the light of religious leadership is the fact that most of the outstanding Reform rabbis of this century were neither the products of Reform Jewish homes nor of Reform educational background. As youngsters growing up in the homes of their east-European parents, many had received the traditional religious training in Hebrew, Bible, and Talmud, before entering the Hebrew Union College to embark on their professional careers.

It is difficult to speculate at this remove what might have become of Reform Judaism in America without the massive influences of the east-European Jewish immigration. By 1920, Reform was stagnant and its future problematical. "In the nick of time," says Reform theologian Petuchowski somewhat sarcastically, "Reform Judaism discovered Jewish 'peoplehood.' After Revelation and *halachah* [Jewish religious law] had fallen victim to the grinding mills of Reform dialectics, 'peoplehood' came along to hold the Reform movement together."[11] But the concept of peoplehood, which is another way of speaking of Jewishness, was not "discovered" by Reform alone; it invaded the entire American Jewish scene in the wake of Hitler. Indeed, Jewishness, as we have seen, came to the aid of a faltering Judaism in America, and not only to the Reform movement.

Some historians of Reform Judaism, as well as spokesmen for other Jewish movements, make much of the influx of Jews with east-European backgrounds into the Reform movement with the passing from the scene of the older German-Jewish generation. They see in this phenomenon the principal basis for the changes that Reform was to adopt, beginning with the mid-1930s. But though there is obvious truth to this assertion, it does not explain enough. Why did Jews of east-European background leave the traditional synagogues in the first place? What were they seeking, as Jews, in moving over to Reform?

There are no easy answers to these root questions, but two points can be noted, which go beyond and even contradict the usual explanations. In the first instance, as we have previously noted in some detail, the second-generation Jew of east-European descent was no longer at home in the "ethnic synagogue" of his parents. Indeed, for many of these folks, Judaism itself was not really at home in America. The Reform movement represented the most liberating option available: it was thoroughly Americanized, virtually de-ethnicized and denationalized, and its religious requirements were least demanding: almost "rational," almost Protestant. Far from bringing the "peoplehood" concept with them, some second-generation east-European Jews embraced Reform by the 1930s and the early 1940s, just because it appeared to reject this ethnic value of their parents' synagogues. They were escaping from, not advancing toward, Jewishness.

Moreover, it was only the Reform temple that offered an educational program for their children most congenial to their desires. The traditional synagogues of the day paid little or no heed to the religious education of girls, and thus, by default lost many of their parents to the temples: for in America the role of the woman had become something quite other from what it was in Europe. But more importantly, the Reform Sunday Schools, with their minimum time demands—one or two hours on a morning in which children were already free from public school—and their concentration upon instruction in English, seemed to suit the needs of those second-generation parents who themselves had chafed under their childhood burden of long hours of study of a "foreign language," Hebrew. For some second-generation Jews of east-European background, Reform had thus become what Rabbi Isaac M. Wise had hoped it would become: the Jewish religious synonym for America and the American way. Wise, however, had seen this as an advance, as a positive Jewish development; these folk, on the other hand, were motivated by other, less constructive, Jewish desires—to retreat from Jewishness.

It was only when Jewishness began to revive, after the full impact of Hitlerism was felt by American Jews, that the Reform movement and its east-European components, like the other movements in American

Judaism, began to awaken from its moribund state. Ironically, for Reform, Jewishness, which it had long sought to by-pass, now came to the rescue of its Judaism. At a convention in Ohio, in 1937, the Central Conference of American Rabbis, the national association of Reform rabbis, adopted a new set of principles, far different from the "Pittsburgh Platform" of 1885. This program came to be known as the "Columbus Platform," after the city in which they met. While these rabbis still proclaimed their belief in Judaism as a progressively developing religion, and restated their conviction that some of the laws of the Torah had lost their binding force, nevertheless they made bold to assert that they now regarded the Torah "as a depository of permanent spiritual ideals" and as "the dynamic source of the life of Israel." But most important of all was their rejection of the classical Reform position that had regarded the Jews as a religious group alone, and their dramatic espousal of the Zionist position: "In the rehabilitation of Palestine, the land hallowed by memories and hopes, we behold the promise of renewed life for many of our brethren. . . . We affirm the obligation of all Jewry to aid in its upbuilding as a Jewish homeland by endeavoring to make it not only a refuge for the oppressed but also a center of Jewish culture and spiritual life." And this view was now possible because of their newly found affinities to the unsynagogued and the nonreligious sector of the Jewish world. Of those they could now say: "We recognize in the group-loyalty of Jews who have become estranged from our religious tradition, a bond that still unites them with us."

It may seem strange to intrude upon a discussion of Reform Judaism with a recitation of the thought of a Conservative rabbi. Yet the principal thinker most responsible for giving Jewishness a new respect and a new religious significance in American Judaism was Professor Mordecai M. Kaplan. In 1934, two years before the "Columbus Platform," Dr. Kaplan, a leading Conservative rabbi and a member of the faculty of the Conservative rabbinical school, the Jewish Theological Seminary of America, had published an American Jewish classic, his *magnum opus, Judaism As A Civilization.* Although Kaplan never intended to substitute Jewishness for Judaism, he placed so important an emphasis on the concept of Jewish peoplehood that to some he seemed to project the folk over the faith. Secularists and secularism in the Jewish community were to be accorded their full honor and given equal treatment with the religionists, he claimed, for "the religion of a people is *but a phase* of the entire life of that people and determined by the forces, social, economic, and cultural, inherent in its life. . . ."[12] (Italics mine.) This new emphasis upon the social and cultural aspects of the Jewish civilization, as being equally as valid as the religious expression of Judaism, served to justify the new Jewishness and to give it new spiritual significance. But what is often overlooked is the fact that Kaplan's program—"Reconstructionism," as he called it—had a vital and direct impact not only upon the Jewish secularists nor upon the Conservative rabbis—his students at the Jewish Theological Seminary—but upon the future shape and content of Reform Judaism. While Reconstructionism was originally intended as a program for all American Jewish life, Dr. Kaplan's close connections with the Conservative movement made it appear that his disciples had been associated with that group alone. But it may yet be history's verdict that Kaplan's most permanent beneficiary was not Conservatism, but Reform. He did criticize Reform "as based on a misconception of the very nature of a religion like that of the Jewish people."[13] It had sought to maintain the faith without the folk. But once this misconception could be overcome—and by 1948 it would be—Kaplan's "people-centered religion" was linked to a theology to which Reform could subscribe and could easily accept. For in addition to all that he did to give Jewishness an honored place within Judaism, he was offering what Reform needed most: a rationalist-humanist, twentieth-century substitute for its nineteenth-century "Darwinian theology," and within a Jewish framework, to boot.

Kaplan, as we shall see, shored up Conservatism, too, in the 1930s and 1940s, by providing it with a sociological rationale for reconstructing the meaning of old ritual laws and customs. These he regarded as the *social sancta* of the people of Israel, the religious forms evolved by the Jewish nation in their spiritual quest, not as fixed, final, or revealed statutes. For the Conservatives, the emphasis had always been on the corpus of tradition, and not upon theology; their big religious questions were always related to the dilemmas caused by a wish for ritual change within historical continuity. Kaplan's "Reconstructionism" gave them a rationale for conserving the traditional religious practices of Judaism. But the Reform movement, in addition to this "new sociology," required most of all a new theological ground, one which would replace their outdated "God-idea" of the last century, yet still suit the rational temper of their liberalism. By coupling a scientifically oriented theology to an ethnocentric religious emphasis, Kaplan's reinterpretation of the meaning of God for modern man—a naturalist rather than a supernaturalist outlook—provided Reform even more than Conservatism with a program it could now wholly appropriate.

Indeed, Dr. Stephen S. Wise, the American Jewish leader who most dramatically typified the new-style Reform rabbi of the twentieth century, twice offered the presidency of the Jewish Institute of Religion to Dr. Kaplan.[14] In 1922 the Institute was founded in New York by Dr. Wise to ordain rabbis "liberal in spirit, wherein its teachers and students are not committed to any special interpretation of Judaism."[15] Despite this nondenominational approach, the Jewish Institute of Religion was considered by most Jews as a second Reform seminary, by the side of the

Hebrew Union College in Cincinnati, and indeed, in 1949 it finally merged with it, with Dr. Nelson Glueck of Cincinnati as President. Yet its "liberalism" was virtually identical with Dr. Kaplan's, and while he never left the Conservative faculty of the Seminary, the very fact that the Institute turned to him, albeit unsuccessfully, is a clear indication of the significant impact his teachings had on the new-style American Reform movement.

By and large, today, in terms of personal religious practice and observance of customs and rituals, there really exists a basic American common denominator: laxity, compromise, and nonmeticulous concern with the comprehensive regimen of religious conduct which the tradition requires. Despite a "return to tradition" which became evident among many Jews in the 1970s, a "religious consensus" still permeates all three Jewish denominations in America—with the exception of a small minority within Orthodoxy—a consensus based upon the survivalist motivations of Jewishness rather than on fundamental religious commitments to Judaism. Thus, Reform Jews are often not distinguishable from their Conservative or even many of their so-called Orthodox brethren by the way in which they personally observe the tradition, as they had been in the nineteenth century.

For many years the principal hallmark of American Reform Judaism was its liberal "social gospel"—clearly borrowed from late nineteenth and early twentieth century Protestant churches. Indeed, the high point of its "Pittsburgh Platform" of 1885, as we have seen, was the strong belief that it was the "duty" of the movement "to solve on the basis of justice and righteousness the problems presented by the contrasts and evils of the present organization of society." But this penchant for social outreach, once the special preserve of Reform Judaism, came to be espoused in later years by both the "mainline" Orthodox as well as the Conservative movement. As these other Jewish religious groupings became acculturated American citizens, what special territory could then remain as the unique domain of the Reform group? This was the question even some thoughtful Reform Jews—rabbis and laymen alike—would be asking themselves, particularly after the onset of the 1960s. Would Reform continue to content itself merely with its old-style "social justice programs" or "interfaith activities?" Would it be satisfied to remain traditionless and spiritually inert, passively accepting the conventional notion that its temples merely served as respectable (but soulless) retreats for those Jews who were escaping from the commitments of piety and serious religious education?

Indeed, in 1972, an official self-study of the movement stunned even some of its most passionless members. It reported: "More than one in three (of our) congregants, aged 20 to 24, is now married to a spouse who was born non-Jewish (and) one in four of this age group is married to a spouse who has not converted . . . on every issue of Jewish identity on which they were questioned, Reform youth seem to be more detached from Judaism and Jewishness than their parents."[15]

The official Reform body, the Central Conference of American Rabbis, was apparently disturbed as much by the *conduct* of almost half of its own rabbis; that self-same study had also reported that 44 per cent of the Reform rabbis were officiating at marriages "without conversion." As a direct result of these findings, at its next annual convention, in June, 1973, the C.C.A.R. resolved to urge its members not to perform mixed marriages any longer, and generally to close the widening gap between themselves and non-Reform rabbinical groups. Increasingly ever since, the Reform rabbinate has been undertaking serious efforts and mounting special programs aimed at revitalizing Sabbath observance in more traditional ways and intensifying the home celebration of the festivals, with the stated objective of bringing their congregations "back to the tradition." More and more of these temples were also adopting the wearing of skull-caps, as well as of prayer-shawls, and introducing daily religious services, as required by tradition—for the very first time.

Its traditional antinomian heritage had also made Reform indifferent to the need to provide its followers with "rules" or even authoritative "guides" to ritual conduct. This older attitude is now being surpassed by a new interest in the traditional lifestyle. Reform guides to ritual practices are beginning to appear in increasing numbers. There are even "official" Reform *responsa*—legal "briefs" based upon Talmudic *halakah*—in growing numbers. Reform is moving "to the right" along with the other two religious denominations, despite its more liberal stance. Nonetheless, Reform congregations could not match the amazing success of Conservatism, which—at least until the early 1970s—was the fastest growing movement in American Judaism. It was Conservatism which had stressed the *practice* of the tradition, even while it remained flexible in theological matters. The amazing congregational growth of Conservatism in the period following World War II is perhaps the most eloquent proof of the truth of our earlier suggestion that Judaism in America is increasingly powered by the sentiments of Jewishness—the desire to be regarded as Jews. These survivalist, ethnic desires were seeking religious expression—and they appeared to find a congenial home in Conservative Judaism.

Conservatism, with its emphasis upon the norms and the ways of Jewish life and its general avoidance of novel theological commitments, was thus uniquely the product of America, and its particular history and widespread acceptance in a very short space of time tell us much about the nature of the American Jewish situation, in general.

Conservatism. "Practical Judaism," it often seems, might be a better name to describe "Conservative Judaism" in America. Somehow, this description does justice to two significant if antagonistic attitudes that have been the major hallmarks of this movement. At once, the word "practical" rings out suggestions of its pragmatic, compromising, and nonideological tendencies, which, if its critics are to be believed, have been the cornerstone of its success as an "American religious movement." The meteoric rise of Conservatism is the result, it is often claimed, not of any intrinsic Jewish ideology, but rather of the social and economic forces of America itself. When contemporary suburbanites choose to join a Conservative and not a Reform or Orthodox congregation, they are not motivated, say the sociologists, by a religious decision to join a religious movement. Rather, their choice reflects different considerations—considerations that are the product of the prevailing American environment. If, indeed, any Jewish motivations are at work, they are at best ethnically oriented: they represent a decision in favor of Jewish continuity. When third-generation descendants of east-European immigrants decided in favor of Conservatism, it is claimed, they were making a "practical," not an "ideological" decision: to continue to relate to Judaism in a Jewish way, in a way which they believe most closely approximated a balance between the Jewish life-style of their parents and the way of Jewish life they were prepared to offer their children.

But there is another meaning to "practical Judaism," a meaning that some of the major ideologists of the Conservative movement had adopted as the basis for their religious commitments to it. Dr. Louis Ginzberg, dean of Talmudists the world over, and from 1902 until his death in 1954 the leading scholar on the faculty of the Jewish Theological Seminary of America, regarded "practical Judaism" as the hallmark of his school and its true religious purpose:

> One may, for instance, conceive of the origin and idea of Sabbath rest as the professor of Protestant theology at a German university would conceive it, and yet minutely observe the smallest detail of the Sabbath observances known to strict Orthodoxy. For an adherent of this school *the sanctity of the Sabbath reposes not upon the fact that it was proclaimed at Sinai,* but on the fact that the Sabbath idea for thousands of years found its expression in Jewish souls. It is the task of the historian to examine into the beginnings and developments of the numerous customs and observances of the Jews; *practical Judaism* on the other hand *is not concerned with origins,* but regards the institutions as they have come to be. If we are convinced that *Judaism is a religion of deed, expressing itself in observances* which are designed to achieve the moral elevation of man and *give reality* to his religious spirit, we have a principle in which *reforms in Judaism* are possible.[17] (Italics mine.)

Here we have a fundamental statement of the importance of the "people of Israel" to the religion of Israel. The people were the carriers of the tradition, and Ginzberg was anxious to retain the historical flow of the tradition: thus, "reforms in Judaism" but not a creedal, denationalized Reform Judaism. Like Dr. Solomon Schechter, President of the Seminary (1902–1915), Dr. Ginzberg and other products of east-European Jewish scholarship wished to preserve the historical integrity of the Jewish people. What the Reform movement held out as a new hope, they saw as a disruption and a discontinuity. For the followers of Isaac Mayer Wise were seeking to build an American Judaism, while they believed it necessary and possible to build Judaism in America. Hence their repeated emphasis upon the practice of Judaism as an historical way of life, and their disinclination to focus upon "theology," old or new, as a major preoccupation. Judaism, they steadfastly maintained, is not a church or a religious denomination to which Jews had been converted. Thus, "theology" as such, abstracted from the practiced religious and cultural life of the people, had never played a key role in its history. Of course, said Schechter, Judaism had a theology, "but the true health of a religion is to have a theology without being aware of it."[18]

In the service of these ideas, Schechter formulated his well-known phrase, "Catholic Israel"—the universal synagogue—by which he intended to deter American Jews from what he regarded to be the ultimate destination of Reform: a narrow Jewish sectarianism, rather than the embodiment of historical Judaism on American soil. Ironically, not too many years later, in 1918, even before Reform was itself ready to "rejoin" the Jewish people, one of its own great rabbis, Dr. Stephen S. Wise, was sounding the same warning. "Reform," he cautioned, "if it become as it is fast becoming a Jewish sect, may for a time survive as a sect. But it will cease to be Jewish, as every Jewish sect has passed, save for the Pharisaic, which was not a sect, but a vital movement of a people in the interests of national as well as religious self-preservation."[19]

It was not a fear that Reform might fail, but that it would indeed succeed in its comprehensive program to "Americanize" Judaism, which was responsible for bringing Schechter to the new world in the first place. As an organized effort in America, Conservative Judaism really began as a frightened response to the "Pittsburgh Platform." Prior to 1885, when the "Platform" was promulgated, a number of traditional congregations were still linked to Isaac M. Wise's country-wide synagogal association, the Union of American Hebrew Congregations, despite the fact that his personal inclinations and those of his seminary, the Hebrew Union College, were those of Reform. For some decades, the members of the "Historical School"—rabbis with traditional tendencies—had cooperated with those of Reform views, in the belief that a single, united effort would best serve the interests of all American Jews. But when the leading rabbis of the Union came out four-square in favor of such sweeping, radical views, a strong counter-Reform action was set in motion. What during the nineteenth century had only been a point of view shared in common and was only loosely joined together by the name "Historical School" was now to become the harbinger of the Conservative Judaism of the twentieth century.[20] Led by Rabbi Sabato Morais of Philadelphia, who became its first president, a dozen or so leading eastern congregations formed The Jewish Theological Seminary Association a few months later. In their constitution's preamble they set down the urgent reasons for their action, reasons which clearly spelled out their opposition to Reform:

> The necessity has been made manifest for associated and organized effort on the part of the Jews of America faithful to Mosaic Law and ancestral traditions, for the purpose of keeping alive the true Judaic spirit; in particular by the establishment of a seminary where the Bible shall be impartially taught and rabbinical literature faithfully expounded, and more especially where youths, desirous of entering the ministry, may be thoroughly grounded in Jewish knowledge and inspired by the precept and example of their instructors with the love of the Hebrew language and a spirit of devotion and fidelity to the Jewish Law.[21]

But not even these noble sentiments could stand up to the rising tide of Reform that swept America before the turn of the century. By 1900, after the Seminary had been actually functioning for thirteen short years, its future was very much in question. There can be little doubt, if hindsight is to be trusted, that had not east-European Jews begun to come to America in such massive numbers, the spiritual map of Judaism in America would have been quite different: it would have been Reform, without interruption, from coast to coast. But the sheer numerical weight of the new immigrants, who came from countries where Jews were still unemancipated, changed all this. It was then, in 1902, that Dr. Solomon Schechter, a noted Jewish scholar born in Rumania but then teaching at Cambridge University, was invited to come to New York City to head a reorganized Jewish Theological Seminary of America. Like his unsuccessful predecessors, Schechter saw it as his principal task to stem the swing to Reform. The Seminary, however, has thrived and flourished since his coming, but it probably would have had a much more difficult if not impossible road to travel if, along with Schechter, there had not then also arrived hundreds of thousands of east-European Jews.

These east-European Jews to whom the message of Schechter and his Seminary colleagues was addressed proved to be both a source of strength and of frustration. On the one hand, their "integrity" as Jews had not yet been sundered by the inroads of Western emancipation; their Jewishness was unimpaired and nondivided. Thus, Schechter's attack upon the sectarianism implicit in the Reform movement of his day could find echoes in their own thinking. "The pioneer," he warned, "is too easily carried away by catch-words. . . . Such war-cries as 'Progressive Judaism,' 'American Judaism,' and 'Reform' have all the same charm for him in the spiritual world, as the advertisements of patent medicine and universal remedies usually exercise upon his mind in the material world."[22] He would therefore not turn his Seminary into a denominational center, nor would he try to make its congregational union—the United Synagogue of America—which he founded in 1913, into a new movement or section in the religious life of American Jews. He spoke of the "conservative spirit," the "conservative tendency," the "conservative standpoint"—but not of the "Conservative Movement," and surely not of an adjectival, denominational, Conservative Judaism. It was his earnest conviction, moreover, that such an attitude toward historic Judaism was also thoroughly in keeping with the American spirit. "If there is a feature in American religious life," he said, "more prominent than any other it is its conservative tendency. . . . The large bulk of the real American people have, in matters of religion, retained their sobriety and loyal adherence to the Scriptures, as their Puritan forefathers did. America thus stands for wideness of scope and for conservatism."[23]

These views and hopes were continued after Schechter's death by his successor, the American-born Dr. Cyrus Adler. Adler served briefly as head of the United Synagogue of America, and in 1915, after Schechter's passing, went on to become President of the Seminary. Like his predecessor, he hoped to rally the forces of tradition in America around the "conservative tendency," without establishing fixed, denominational patterns in their congregational life. He, too, drew upon American historical experience as a guide to his thinking. The United Synagogue of America, in his view, was "patterned somewhat after the very excellent model of the thirteen colonies which formed the Union, wherein we unite to promote the general welfare of our Congregations but not to force them into a mold so that all may come out exactly of the same pattern. We would not if we could and we could not if we would. . . ."[24]

But while Schechter and Adler appealed to the unifying elements of Jewishness still abiding within the east-European congregations, there were other factors at work that would frustrate their hopes. "The conservative tendency" would give birth to a Conservative Movement, and the movement, facing Reform on the left and Orthodoxy on the right, would inevitably seek to create a Conservative Judaism in the center. Schechter, Adler, and others like them had believed it possible that a proclamation of general loyalty to tradition could serve as a rallying point for all tradition-minded congregations, without requiring their detailed and full conformance to the whole of the tradition. In time, they believed, many members of these congregations, who really longed to practice and to observe the traditions, would do so, and the present chasm between their beliefs and practices would be bridged. Not only was it prudent to do so, they felt, but it was the moral duty of the United Synagogue to enroll as many congregations as possible. Ultimately, they believed, by the suasion of their joint association, and without coercion, these congregations would readopt the traditions they really loved, but which, in the environment of America, they had temporarily neglected.

The first and second generations of east-Europeans had lived out their lives, yet at the end of that time, what these men had supposed to be only a "temporary period of adjustment" seemed, in reality, to represent a permanent accommodation. The influence of Protestant America, with its emphasis upon the forms of public worship rather than upon Church Law or religion-in-the-home, had indeed played an important role in the shaping of Judaism in America. It was a different role, however, from the one Schechter, Adler, and their followers had anticipated. And as for that "conservative tendency" of Americans, which they had believed might influence Judaism here, its contemporary impact on Judaism was principally in ways which they themselves would have had to regard as negative. After all, their concept of the religious life was geared to the traditional view that the personal observance of Jewish laws and customs is pre-eminent, and the public worship secondary to private piety and learning. But the "conservative tendency" of the Protestant spirit of America had no such tradition to conserve. Not only was it itself antinomian, but its doctrinal emphases have led to more denominationalism in America, not to less. Thus, if the *Zeitgeist* of Christian America had any influence on Judaism here—and it did—it would tend to move Jews away from, not toward, the hopes of Schechter. Instead of "Judaism in America," as he had hoped, the Jewish religion here would become more pluralistic, not less, and it would seek to express itself not in one, but in several denominational, and, after 1945, even sectarian-Hasidic, forms.

Then, too, the growth of American secularism in the years immediately following World War I, which we have discussed earlier, endangered the whole Jewish enterprise. Beginning with the 1920s, and until the close of World War II, the future of Judaism in America was gravely in doubt. Among the Conservatives, the same indifferentism prevailed as within the ranks of Reform Jews. One man, Dr. Mordecai M. Kaplan, seemed to provide the only real ray of hope. A perceptive observer neatly summarizes Kaplan's place within that situation, from the inside of the Jewish Theological Seminary, looking outward at the general Jewish scene:

> Had it not been for the inventive and imaginative techniques which he [Kaplan] devised to rationalize the Judaism into which the Seminary was inducting its students, it might have lost—in those years of religious attrition, the late twenties, thirties and early forties—literally scores of future rabbis.

Mordecai Kaplan, unlike those who were to be his colleagues and very much like those who were to be his students, survived the same fires of uncertainty and skepticism through which he was literally to force his students to pass. . . . At the age of twenty-one he graduated from the Seminary and, after continuing post-graduate studies, both Jewish and secular, he accepted a call to an Orthodox pulpit. . . .

It is not unusual that Kaplan's own intellectual uncertainty should have been communicated to his orthodox congregants. . . . Within weeks of his decision to abandon the [Orthodox] rabbinate, he was asked by Solomon Schechter to succeed the recently deceased Joseph Asher as professor of homiletics, while continuing in his capacity as dean of the newly organized Teachers Institute of the Seminary. . . .

Mordecai Kaplan undertook to appraise the foundations, unfolding, and future of Judaism. In a generation in which Jewish scholarship was devoted to conservation and self-perpetuation, he had the daring to reopen pressing questions of doctrine and theology. . . .

Where Reform theology was still characterized by a Judaized neo-Hegelianism and Orthodoxy was intransigent, Conservative Judaism stood resolutely noncommittal and astride all positions. This uncomfortable stance had, however, marginal benefits. It attracted students who were sufficiently concerned with the survival of a traditional Judaism to be antipathetic to Reform and sufficiently acculturated to be unsusceptible of Orthodoxy. A student body existed for whom there were no real teachers but Mordecai Kaplan. In a very real sense Kaplan—opinionated, passionate, and unrelenting—gave both his students and his institution a hard time. He renovated Judaism while he taught it; he exploded convictions while he formulated his own; he disabused Judaism of cherished theological illusions while substituting equally debatable doctrines.[25]

His naturalist theology appealed not only to the humanist-minded layman, but especially to his rabbinical students, most of whom were not a little influenced by the raging secularism of the day. In addition, his view of Judaism as constituting a "religious civilization" in which the nonreligious, cultural components had a significant place helped give the synagogue generally, and the Conservative synagogue in particular, a new assessment of its possibilities. Kaplan saw no division between the sacred and the secular in Jewish life. Thus, it would no longer do for a Jewish congregation to devote itself only, or even primarily, to public worship. To justify itself as a bearer of a "civilization," it had also to satisfy the aesthetic, the cultural, the educational and the social needs of its constituents. And just as the synagogue had need to deal with what might formerly have been regarded as secular concerns, so the nonsynagogal Jewish agencies—the Y.M.H.A., or Jewish Center, the Zionist organizations, and the various relief and welfare groups—were to be regarded as performing significant "religious" roles in the perpetuation of the Jewish civilization. The Jewish community, Kaplan insisted, was an "organic community," not a conglomeration of separatist, unrelated organizations and societies. Thus, more than any other single man or movement, Kaplan succeeded in dramatizing the essential unity of Jewishness and Judaism in an age when neither was virile enough to "go it alone." It was this aspect of his Reconstructionist program, more than all others, which won him an admired and respected place among the nonsynagogued. Paradoxically, this acceptance by those beyond the synagogue helped to boost his importance and influence in the eyes of those who were still in the synagogue, and, particularly, those in the Conservative synagogue—for though their hearts were still in the synagogue, they, too, were often secular-minded.

Theologically, however, things were different. Kaplan never did succeed in winning over the Conservative group to his position, and as we have seen, his radical departures from the traditional God-views were much more in the spirit of the Reform movement. But while the Conservatives rejected his "theory," they often adopted his "practice"; they did not accept his theology, but they appropriated his sociology as it related to "practical Judaism." Ironically, Kaplan's naturalist theology constituted so radical a break with the Jewish tradition that if, in fact, the Conservatives had adopted it, such a step would inevitably have made their movement what Kaplan himself did not wish it to become: a denomination. Indeed, this is what had made Reform in America into a denomination—its radical theological departures from the norms of Jewish historical experience. So too with Kaplan's theology: any group that would accept it officially as their own would necessarily stand apart from the others as a distinct party, following a distinct doctrine. Will it or not, any such group, supported by a unique doctrinal approach to Judaism so fundamentally at variance from the norm, must end as a denomination. That Dr. Kaplan realized this seems apparent from the fact that for a long time he refused to allow his followers to set up "Reconstructionist congregations" patterned along his avant-garde theological lines. He had preferred, all along, to fructify all Jewish communal life, rather than to institutionalize it still further. In this respect, his views coincided with those of Schechter and Adler, who also sought to avoid a "Conservative" Judaism because they did not wish to establish another denomination; in their view, Reform was already one too many. They, of course, derived their hopes from Jewish history, while Kaplan was motivated by the democratic concept of diversity-within-unity. They looked forward to the emergence of a single religious expression along traditional lines. He preached a pluralism that went beyond denominationalism.

During his many years as Seminary Professor, Dr. Kaplan was also head of a New York City congregation, which he founded. But he would not call it a "congregation"—he named it "The Society for the Advancement of Judaism"—and he was not called its "Rabbi" but its "Leader." Thus, as late as 1946, Dr. Kaplan was still urging his former students, graduates of the Seminary who were now members of the Rabbinical Assembly of America, the national Conservative rabbinical association, to shun denominationalism, as he had. He made his impassioned plea in an address entitled "The Rabbinical Assembly at the Crossroads":

> Shall we function as a third congregational denomination to be known as "Conservative"—or shall we function as a non-denominational body dedicated to the furtherance of American-Jewish life as a whole? . . .
> The congregational approach implies that the basic unit of American-Jewish life should be the voluntary group of families, which is organized for the purpose of worshipping in common. . . .
> The communal approach implies that the basic unit of American-Jewish life is the Jewish people which is mediated through the community of all American Jews. . . . The principle underlying this view is that the community of all Jewish interests, and not merely those served by congregations, constitutes the matrix of Jewish life, Jewish values and Jewish religion. . . . The center group, by reason of certain advantages which inhere in the avoidance of extremes, holds the key to the future of American Judaism. . . .
> Some of our rabbinic colleagues are of the opinion that the interests of Judaism would best be served if the Rabbinical Assembly were to use its newly won power for the purpose of solidifying the center group. It should bring into sharp relief the specific principles and practices that differentiate it both from the Orthodox and the Reformist parties. . . .
> I am convinced, however, that it is of the utmost importance for us to guard against our justification for existence as a distinct body upon the particular theological or ritual changes we may adopt. That might give us a superficial show of strength, but it would actually incapacitate us for a much more vitally needed service to Judaism. . . . Instead of envisaging the Seminary as the authoritative front for such theological and ritual changes as we want to see introduced into Jewish life, we should aim to transform it into an agency for the conservation of Jewish life itself . . . *by placing the Seminary at the service of the whole of Jewry.*[26]

But the die was already cast. Ironically, this very moving plea for nondenominationalism was published in the magazine of the Rabbinical Assembly, which for some time had been bearing the telltale name, *Conservative Judaism*. Not a tendency, or a school of thought, but a religious denomination.

Denominationalism was inevitable, however. It was thrust upon Conservatism, as upon the other groups, by the sheer force of the general American as well as the specific Jewish environments. Kaplan's theoretical analysis, moreover, just could not stand up to the realities of Jewish life in America—realities which, in addition to the inner group dynamics, were largely caused by the economic, social, and religious factors of America itself. (Indeed, even his own Reconstructionist movement would slowly become more denominational. First, there had developed a national Federation of Reconstructionist Congregations and Fellowships, with its own *Reconstructionist Prayer Book*. Then, in 1968, the Reconstructionist Rabbinical College was established in Philadelphia, and the stage was set for the birth of a *fourth* Jewish denomination!)[27] His desire to transplant the historical nondenominational "organic Jewish community" to American soil did not fit in with the American sociological landscape. In calling for the reconstitution of the Jewish civilization in America, he was, in effect, seeking to preserve more than the "Jewish civilization," but also to establish it corporately and institutionally here as a nation within a nation. But the triple melting pot was inexorably at work, and more and more Jews were coming to see American Judaism not as an aspect of the Jewish civilization but as a variant and valid expression of the American civilization, just as other Americans regarded their own faiths. By the 1970s, as will be seen later, the new ethnicity, coupled to a growing re-traditionalizing of religion in America, would make Jews more aware of their self-interests as members of their own community. Still, Reconstructionism seemed destined to remain a very small denomination among the officially synagogued.

Moreover, from the days when the "Pittsburgh Platform" was first promulgated down to the present, a succession of pressures within the Jewish community has imperiously led all those who could not accept such reforms to seek their own separate common cause. When the Seminary was first established in response to that "Platform," it sought to prove that Judaism in America need not stray from too many of the ancestral traditions. But under Schechter it attracted only those of the east-European community who were themselves sufficiently acculturated to seek American-trained, American-oriented rabbis. Indeed, it was this American accent and this prospective Americanizing influence of the Seminary that propelled a number of nontradition-minded lay leaders of the Reform group—such wealthy philanthropists as Jacob Schiff, Louis Marshall, Felix Warburg, Daniel and Simon Guggenheim— to help reorganize and finance it in 1902, thus enabling Solomon Schechter to be brought from England. In sociological terms, even in those early days under Schechter and despite its claim of representing "Catholic Israel," Conservatism was, in effect, the "reform movement" of the acculturated east-European congregations. That this was clearly understood even then helps to account for the fact that a number of congregations who had been part of the older Seminary broke away from it immediately after its reorganization. They made it known that they would not regard the graduates of the Seminary as having the authority of rabbis, thus making it clear that they did not accept the "traditionalism" of the Seminary as sufficiently traditional. It was too westernized, too scientific, too American. Thus, willy-nilly, now from the right, as before from the left, pressures were put upon the Seminary and the United Synagogue that forced them into a self-conscious middle-of-the-road position.

Conservatism was attracting those second-generation east-European Jews who were still sufficiently traditional to identify with a synagogue, but whose Americanization had progressed too far for them to remain within the synagogue of the first-settlement area. Some of these, to be sure, were leaping even farther, and in a single jump away from Orthodoxy were landing in the Reform temple. Most, however, would not venture that far, and in the Conservative synagogue found a spiritual home that was much closer to their family sentiments and nostalgias. But the fact that they had made the leap was, in itself, an index to their desire to be emancipated from some of the traditional forms and to seek a more acculturated expression of Judaism in America. Here again, in spite of the intellectualizations and rationalizations of Seminary ideologists who tirelessly warned against drastic innovations and reforms, those who made up the membership of the congregations clearly believed that, in moving over to Conservatism, they were adopting a new form of Judaism. This made them increasingly self-conscious of their Conservatism, more and more anxious to justify their new place, and more and more concerned with the telltale question: "How is Conservatism different from Orthodoxy and Reform?"

This anxiety, of course, inevitably led them to a greater self-awareness, which is the stuff of which denominationalism is made. At the close of World War II this mood was heightened even more, as a revived Jewishness brought new waves of enthusiasm to Judaism, and novice suburbanites poured into newly built synagogues. But because, as we have seen, many of these young, third-generation families did not join a Conservative congregation as a result of having been converted to Conservative Judaism, paradoxically they were all the more eager, in rationalized afterthought, to convert their prior emotional or sociological reasons into an ideological system.

And then, to unite all these forces that were molding Conservatism into a religious denomination, there was the important matter of fund-raising. In its early days, when the Seminary was still the "ward" of the affluent Reform philanthropists, the members of these synagogues were not called upon to support the central institutions of Conservatism. In their minds, they were members of a local synagogue, not of a national congregational movement. But in the 1940s it became clear that the children of those Reform benefactors were no longer Seminary-minded and the earlier sources of income were no longer available. Guided by the administrative genius of its new president, Dr. Louis Finkelstein, the Seminary turned to the individual members of its congregations for personal support. This new base, made possible by the growing Jewish middle and upper classes, not only helped to develop a series of new programs and institutions under the national aegis of the Seminary but became the firm foundation of denominationalism for the Reform and Orthodox groups as well. Local Jewish Federation or Welfare Funds, which controlled the central fund-raising apparatus in each of the communities, while committed to the proposition that the over-all communal interests were indivisible, unwittingly, however, contributed to the growing spirit of sectarianism, too. They placed primary emphasis upon the "overseas" needs of the Jewish people, on refugee rescue and rehabilitation, and rallied the whole community behind this effort. In the process, however, they made it clear that funds for the support of the American seminaries, theological colleges, and religious movements were not the concern of the total community, but only of private persons, their local partisans in the various denominational synagogues. As a result, a "gentlemen's agreement" was fostered: the Seminary would be careful to solicit primarily members of its own congregations, as would the Reform Hebrew Union College and the Orthodox Yeshiva University. The net effect of all this was to be seen in the new denominational spirit that swept the Jewish community. Now, individual members of hundreds of congregations all over the country were made to feel that they shared a movement in common with hundreds of thousands of others. They had everything but a national membership card to prove it, and that too would soon be supplied.

Nevertheless, the ideological problems remain unresolved. Conservative Judaism, today, no less than in the days of Adler, in the infancy of the United Synagogue of America, is more a denominational coalition than a singleminded movement. "Tradition and Change" is the way their leaders still describe their fundamental allegiances. But how much "tradition" and how much "change"? In effect, like all of Gaul, Conservative Judaism "in three parts is divided." On the right, it has a group of congregations and rabbis who are virtually indistinguishable from the Orthodox. They are firmly committed to *halakah,* the authoritative body of Jewish law, as the norm for Jewish religious practice, and are exceedingly reluctant to sanction or to accept any major deviations. On the left, there are those who are deeply influenced by Reconstructionism, and who come closest to the Reform position, in that they wish to go beyond the traditional laws in search of new forms.

Oddly enough, in one important respect both the rightists and the leftists are unwittingly motivated by similar moods: the desire to recapture the lost spirit of east-European Judaism. Kaplan's disciples, as we have seen, had sought to reconstitute in America the social solidarity of the organic community of Poland and Russia, and they attributed spiritual meanings to this. The rightists were deeply influenced by the poetic teachings and writings of Dr. Abraham J. Heschel, a member of the

Seminary faculty until his death in 1973. Heschel, a Polish neo-Hasid, began where Martin Buber's philosophizing left off, and attempted to weave those mystical, east-European insights into the habit and regimen of traditional Jewish religious observances. While he spoke in theological terms, his major contribution had been his ability to evoke a mood of, if not a return to, piety—the piety of the east-European *shtetl*. Whether this romanticized piety is, in fact, a realistic possibility for Jews in America or whether it is only a transient, nostalgic substitute, which the revived Jewish folk-feeling in America has temporarily lighted upon, remains to be seen.

The largest majority, however, remain in the center. They accept the body of *halakah* as normative for Jewish religious life, but they also believe that by means of research, scholarship, and a piously oriented probing of the tradition's intent and meaning, changes can indeed be made, but only in accordance with the "due process of the law." Of all three groups, they remain most conscious of their "Conservative" label and wish to avoid the partisanships of the extremes.

The Conservative movement continued to be the fastest growing Jewish religious movement until the late 1960s, when it became apparent that many American Jews were either almost wholly ethnically-oriented, or, if religiously inclined, more intent on a clearer-cut traditionalism than that of "tradition with change" which Conservatism had been advocating. As a result, there was some movement to the right in Conservative quarters, accompanied by a great deal of inner soul-searching, and what has been described as the "development of a kind of Conservative *anomie*." One astute observer explained:

> During the 1950s and '60s the *yeshivot* multiplied in number, size and fundamentalism; the Orthodox rabbis became even more intransigent; the influence exercised by Orthodoxy in Israel became clearer; and Orthodox synagogues established themselves in upper-class and upper-middle-class areas. Even Hassidism was transformed from an antediluvian curiosity into a movement which—it was said—had much to teach modern man. The net result was that the Conservative understanding of the American Jewish present, together with the Conservative expectation of the American Jewish future, became confounded.[28]

Nevertheless, the Conservative "coalition" has held together very well; it did not fall apart, even if the rate of the movement's growth in the populous metropolitan areas of the Northeast did begin to show signs of flattening out. What, indeed, keeps the three distinct groups within Conservatism together?

In the first instance, there exists, of course, a minority of genuinely motivated and thoughtful laymen, who despite their present religious differences do see in Conservatism the best opportunity for the slow evolution in America of an authentic yet indigenous Judaism. They are willing to work together and to wait together, despite their obvious disagreements. In addition, one must not minimize the tremendous influence exerted upon all sectors of the "Conservative coalition" by the Seminary and its learned faculty. And the Rabbinical Assembly, too, consisting principally of the graduates of the Seminary, is a potent factor in harmonizing the often disparate elements in the movement. Its disciplined loyalty to the *Alma Mater* helps to moderate conflicting attitudes that might otherwise be irreconcilable.

By the 1980s, however, a number of new fissures were beginning to become publicly visible. Many of these were the results of pressures both from within and beyond the movement to come to terms with issues that were being raised by Jewish feminists. For some years before, many of these questions of ritual style had been dealt with locally, by congregational rabbis and boards, and, as a result, they did not disrupt the "coalition" of right-wing, centrist, or left-wing synagogue units, in the various parts of the country. These had to do with the full participation of women in the public prayer services; as well as their being counted, on a par with men, as equals in various ritual, liturgical and religious rites. The really knotty question, raised by the feminists and their allies, had to do with the ordination of women as rabbis. Yet this was an issue that could only be resolved by the powerful Faculty of the Seminary, and not left, as were the other questions, to the decision or discretion of Conservative rabbis or their congregational boards: they simply did not have the right to ordain anyone, male or female. Ordination of women had by then, become an accepted practice among the Reform and Reconstructionists. But the Conservative movement held a variety of differing views on this matter, and the all-powerful Seminary faculty had remained divided on the question until late in 1983, when, in an historic and courageous decision, it voted to accept women candidates for ordination beginning with the academic year of 1984.

As a movement, Jewish feminism was a relatively new phenomenon which surfaced in 1971 when "Ezrat Nashim" ("The Ladies Gallery") was founded as its earliest public voice. This was probably the first tradition-oriented group of women in Jewish history which publicly sought the *equality of women within Judaism.* It consisted principally of women who had grown up in the schools and youth movements of Conservative Judaism. In 1972, they appeared before the convention of the Rabbinical Assembly to expound their novel views. They regarded themselves as "internal critics, or the 'loyal opposition' (and) were less vulnerable to accusation of self-hatred of the kind often levelled at such Jewish women as Betty Friedan and Shulamith Firestone, and others like them."[29] Since that time, an umbrella organization of many groups, the "Jewish Feminist Organization," was founded, setting as its goal "nothing less than the full, direct and equal participation of women at all levels of Jewish life, communal, religious, educational and political."[30]

The issue of full participation of women in the ritual life of the synagogue is of little consequence to the Reform group, because of its basic inattention to the stringent requirements of *halakah,* the Jewish religious law. From the Orthodox, these women's groups could hardly expect much encouragement, for they rigidly regard the religious tradition as changeless. Indeed, even their more moderate spokesmen had opposed the proposed Equal Rights Amendment, claiming that its passage into law would contribute to the destruction of the fabric of family life. Clearly, the Conservative Movement, with its emphasis on "tradition *and* change," and its prior acceptance of mixed-seating at services, in addition to the local innovations introduced by many of its congregations in connection with the participation of women, would become the natural target of Jewish feminist concern. Dr. Robert Gordis, one of the distinguished members of the Seminary faculty had made a strong public plea in favor of such ordination:

> Today the Jewish community is acutely conscious of the threat to its survival posed by the defection and alienation of many of its youth, often the most creative and sensitive members. The agonizingly difficult task of winning their loyalty and commitment to Judaism would become far more difficult if the ordination of women were to be denied. They would regard it as a sign of the petrifaction of Judaism, a betrayal of its pretensions to ethical significance . . . we must conclude that their ordination is highly desirable, indeed a necessary element in any program designed to advance the health of Judaism and strengthen the survival of the Jewish community.[31]

Despite the fervor of his words, it would take three years more before his fellow faculty members would move away from their adamant position in favor of what they had once regarded as more traditional ways. But by 1983, the strength of Jewish feminist positions would ultimately win the day. By a lop-sided vote of 38 to 5, the Faculty voted in their favor, aided and abetted by a large groundswell of its own rabbi-graduates who were also largely in favor of accepting women as rabbis. After all, it was they who occupied pulpits throughout the country and were thus more likely to respond to pressures at the grass-roots level by the growing number of feminist supporters, among men and women alike. It remains to be seen, however, how many of those women who will one day graduate as rabbis from the Conservative Jewish Theological Seminary of America, will be called to serve as *heads* of congregations. (Since the first woman rabbi graduated from the Reform Hebrew Union College in Cincinnati—in 1972—some seventy others have similarly been ordained, both at that school, and by the Reconstructionist Rabbinical College in Philadelphia. Yet to date, most of these have remained in secondary positions, serving as assistant rabbis in larger metropolitan synagogues or temples, as youth directors, or as principals of religious schools—or they have left the rabbinate, altogether.)

That decisive step taken by the Seminary faculty could also be seen as a bold new attempt to reassert the role of the Seminary itself as the fountainhead of the movement. For many years, the "Conservative coalition," with its left, right and center—rabbis and congregations who could best be defined by the proximity or distance from Orthodoxy on the right or Reform on the left—regarded the Seminary as distantly aloof from the day-to-day religious lives of its congregational members across the country. Indeed, to many it appeared that the movement had outdistanced its own central institution—the Seminary itself—which seemed to remain where and what it was in the earlier days of the century: a great faculty of scholars, but one that was essentially Orthodox in practice, and uninvolved in either the great or small religious questions with which its own Conservative rabbis and congregations were grappling. "Tradition and change" was, it seemed, neatly divided: the congregations were involved in the problems of "change"; the Seminary, and its ivory-tower scholars, dealt only with "tradition." "By this vote," its Chancellor, Dr. Gerson D. Cohen, made bold to proclaim late in 1983, "the Seminary faculty has reasserted its religious leadership of the Conservative Movement—a leadership which is based on authentic scholarship, but it is not aloof from the daily lives of the laity. Further, in its action . . . the faculty has reasserted the commitment of our movement to pluralism . . . in its recognition that there are many ways of expressing one's religious convictions."[31a]

While many regarded this commitment to "coalitionary cohesiveness" as one of the hallmarks of Conservative Judaism, its right wing now saw this as one of its weakest points, and not as a mark of greatness, as Dr. Cohen had suggested. A vocal and beleaguered minority of Orthodox-oriented Conservative Rabbis made ready to do battle with its own Alma Mater. Conservatism had always been especially important in helping Jews whose lives were more powered by Jewishness than by Judaism, to find their way back to a synagogue. Many who had joined were not able to find a spiritual home in either Reform on the left, or Orthodoxy on the right—even though their own middle-of-the-road choices were rarely based on purely religious convictions. It was usually rather a question of style, emotion, and ambience—not ideology. By 1984, however, the Seminary's decision to ordain women as rabbis seemed to be just the issue necessary to stir a crucial ideological battle for the first time in the history of the movement.[31b]

The lack of ideological unity within Conservatism was compensated for by the growth of its institutional unity. By this, we do not merely refer to the obvious "sense of national belonging" and the "we-group cohesion" that result from the work of the country-wide lay arms, the submovements of the United Synagogue, which had grown up: the Women's League, the Federation of Men's Clubs, and the various young people's organizations. It is in the field of Jewish education that the greatest force for institutional unity has been felt. Since the turn of the century, the Jewish population in America has multiplied by a little more than five, while by 1958 the enrollment of children in Jewish schools had increased twelve times. In 1900, most Jewish children were still taught by private teachers. By 1925, schools had become the vogue, but, by and large, these were schools, known as *Talmud Torahs,* run on a central, communal basis, and not affiliated with any particular congregation. But by 1962, the scene had drastically changed: more than 90 per cent of the over six hundred thousand children then receiving Jewish education in America were studying in schools under congregational, not communal, auspices. Riding the crest of both waves, the greater interest in Jewish education and the popularity of the congregational school, was the Conservative group. The Reform movement was still married to the Protestant-type Sunday School, and the Orthodox groups still relied heavily upon the communal Talmud Torah, and failed to build up their own congregational schools. The Conservatives, on the other hand, had been placing their emphasis in the direction of supplementary afternoon schools where children studied for five or more hours a week, and were working together on the national and local level to raise the standards of teaching and learning in their own schools. Almost 40 per cent of all those attending Jewish schools in 1958 were the children of the Conservative congregations; the Reform followed with 28 per cent, and the Orthodox with 21 per cent. The other 11 per cent of those attending Jewish schools were not affiliated with any of these three Jewish "denominations." In addition, 60 per cent of the Conservative children were in the more intensive afternoon school, while 80 per cent of the Reform children were attending the once-a-week Sunday School.[32]

The statistical evidence alone supplies an important clue to the success and the unification of the diverse elements in the Conservative movement. While it was still unable to agree on the theological or ritual implications of "tradition with change," Conservatism did attract as members those families whose renewed sense of Jewishness urged them to seek more than a Sunday-School type of Jewish education for their children, although their religious commitments still did not reach such intensity that they would desire the ten- or twelve-hour-a-week Talmud Torah. In time, the preoccupation of the Conservatives with Jewish educational problems and concerns led to additional joint undertakings, which became institutional unifiers and hallmarks of their movement. Camps Ramah, the children's educational summer camping program;

the Leader's Training Fellowship, the special educational program for gifted teenagers; and the Conservative-sponsored Jewish Day Schools, known as Solomon Schechter Schools—all these educational efforts have tended to supply the Conservatives with a series of common undertakings that further federated their interests by means of operational loyalties.

But will these "operational loyalties" long be able to serve as substitute denominators of ideology and religious thought? Will a renaissance of Judaism follow upon the upturn in Jewishness, and literally force upon Conservatism an ideological affirmation that must spell out more clearly "just how much tradition and how much change"? Or will the typical American affection for "religion-in-general" find an honored and permanent place in Judaism, even while its adherents retain their nominal membership in any of the three separatist, denominational forms? (We shall see how this practice of "*civil* Judaism" had become pervasive by the 1980s.)

Some would respond to these questions by suggesting that the survival of Judaism in America is not really dependent upon the answers to such questions in the first place. Any religious movement in Judaism, they would say, which attempts to accommodate itself to the spirit of America, is destined to the doom of long-term failure despite its short-term success. Only a religious commitment to Judaism based upon the historic faith and without regard to environmental factors can endure historically. And one must not expect that such intense devotion can be experienced by the largest number of Jews. In things of the spirit numbers do not count. In every age and place there was a "saving remnant," a small but dedicated minority of Jews, whose supreme religious commitments were responsible for the survival of the tradition.

Generally, these were the sentiments of the third American denomination, the Orthodox. But is not America different even for the Orthodox? And is not "Orthodoxy" itself heterodox?

Let us see.

Orthodoxy. If our concerns were only chronological, we should have started this chapter with a discussion of Orthodoxy, and not left it for the last. For, as we have seen, the very earliest Jewish settlers in America were traditional in the European sense, which is what is usually meant whenever the word "Orthodox" is applied to Jewish religious life in America.

But American Orthodoxy, as a conscious religious movement, not as a natural component of the traditional Jewish community, was the third of the three denominations to emerge here. And its birth followed the patterns of the others: the historical sources of Conservatism were nurtured in Europe but it did not come to life as a movement except as an

American reaction to Reform. So, too, with Orthodoxy: its European roots go back to the soil of Babylonia, but only when Conservatism seemed to usurp traditionalism did Orthodoxy react in ways that were to transform it into a third religious movement.

Despite its name, as a result of its present status in America as a rival denomination, Orthodoxy has become quite different from what it was in any other land. "Most American Orthodox rabbis," an Orthodox leader wrote in 1955, "recognize that there has (sic) always been, and still are, different modes of Orthodox Jewish thought and practice, and that Orthodoxy has always admitted a great measure of innovation."[33] But not quite a hundred years earlier an "Orthodox" American leader thought otherwise. Said he: "If our religion be anything, it is as unchangeable as its source is eternal."[34]

What accounts for the difference in views? The answer can be summed up in one word, acculturation. One hundred years separate these two Orthodox rabbis, a century of Americanizing influences whose impact created not only the Reform and Conservative movements, but American Orthodoxy as well.

What, then, is American Orthodoxy?

It is surely a coat of many colors. Orthodoxy may never become the private way of life of more than a small minority of American Jewry, yet since its virtual evaporation by the time the 1940s had arrived, it has shown remarkable recuperative power, élan, and new vigor. It may be said to be sociologically the most interesting of all three denominations, even though by the 1980s it had become not only highly visible, but often strident, militant, and triumphalist. In many respects, the Orthodox in America have been buttressed by the monopolistic position which the "theopolitics" practiced in Israel has granted the Orthodox rabbinate there. Yet it is also apparent that the new sense of power experienced by contemporary Orthodoxy is the result of forces much closer to home: the growth of a more committed, religiously oriented Orthodox community that is reaping the harvest of innovative and successful educational enterprises it first began to initiate little more than a generation ago. It has also to do with the fact that traditionalism in America has come to have a respectable place, which is something first- and second-generation Jews did not always know or understand. Most of those who were members of Orthodox congregations a generation ago were, in effect, non-observant, "residual Orthodox," which is to say that the synagogue of their choice, which they did not attend often in any case, might just as well have been Orthodox—like the one they remembered their immigrant fathers and grandfathers attending.

Orthodox congregations today, however, reflect a changed constituency. Many members are graduates of day schools or Orthodox schools of higher learning. They, and others like them, are therefore not indifferent to Jewish observances as a system of personal behavior, as were those who had belonged before the 1950s. Moreover, since Conservative and Reform congregations are well-established and offer different choices, there is clearly a place for those who differ ideologically with these, and are seeking to practice a more traditional pattern of Jewish religious observance. As a result, many members of these congregations have actually become Orthodox in an ideological sense, and openly advocate the "principles" of a rock-solid, unbending, changeless Orthodoxy. And when thousands of folk like these are also college professors, biologists, physicists, mathematicians, and holders of graduate degrees, despite their relative small numbers, they can wield wide and lasting influence on many others less traditional than they. Additionally, the quality of many Orthodox academic institutions, literary and religious journals, and educational enterprises often exceeds the achievements of the other two denominations, and serves to attract new interest. Secularism, too, has been a "god that failed" for some, and as a result a new phenomenon began to surface in the 1970s, the *"baal teshuva"*, or "one who returns." These were young people, many of whom were disenchanted by the various drug and guru cults, and who lacked even an elementary knowledge of Judaism. But they "returned" to the Judaism they had turned away from in their spiritual ignorance, and began to study religious texts, and to pray in and join Orthodox communities.[35]

Yet, despite the facade of a common front of traditionalism over against the innovators of Reform and Conservative Judaism, Orthodoxy is far from being united. Nor do many of its disparate groups even share a common approach to the problems arising from modernity or life in a secular democracy. Sociologically speaking, the mainline, or "centrist" Orthodox (usually second or third generation in America) behave more in the fashion of a "church," while the ultra-pietists—many of them Hasidim, as we shall see—conform to the patterns of a "sect." Church groups are generally more acculturated to the society in which they live; sectarians tend to be principally enclavic. "Church types" try to meet the challenges of secularism of the larger community, as well as those from within their own faith. "Sect people," on the other hand, repudiate compromise, reject what they consider a hostile world, and prefer to live in isolation. Yet, together, they constitute the "Orthodox Jewish denomination."

A movement whose spokesmen "insist that they represent the one authentic Judaism, while other approaches are error, distortion, heresy or even pretense"[36] is hardly likely to recognize itself as constituting a "denomination." But the inexorable environmental factors of America have marked out this status for Orthodoxy, no less than for Reform and Conservatism. Indeed, even in its formative years in the late nineteenth and early twentieth centuries, when it deliberately sought not to regard itself as native to America, Orthodoxy could not avoid reacting to the new environment in ways that were destined to set it off from the other Jewish religious communities. Thus, its first organized response to Reform and Conservatism—doomed to immediate failure, by the way—was to invite Rabbi Jacob Joseph from Russia, in 1886, to serve as the "Chief Rabbi" of New York City. This program failed not only because of the opposition of the non-Orthodox congregations, but because the "Orthodox" were really not Orthodox; socially, culturally, and, one is tempted to add, religiously, they were heterodox. Then as now, wittingly or not, the Orthodox congregational groups were themselves the active beneficiaries of the pluralism available in the nonorganic, non-European, voluntary Jewish community of America.

Three American generations later, it still disdains the adjective "Orthodox," not because it has officially come to terms with heterodoxy and pluralism, but because it "insists that there is but one Judaism and giving it a first name makes it appear that other interpretations are equally valid." But such protestations are to no avail; they are idealized restatements of past European history, rather than a genuine reflection of the mood and manner of American Judaism. Indeed, the sober judgments of Dr. Samuel Belkin, then President of Yeshiva University, American Orthodoxy's foremost academic center, leave no doubt that for "mainline Orthodoxy" to succeed, it had to prove its relevance to America, not its estrangement. But the more it strives to influence America and American Jews, the more acculturated it must appear. And, in the light of our earlier analysis, the more "American" Orthodoxy becomes, the more denominational its status within a pluralistic religious community; and the more "non-Orthodox" it appears in the eyes of assorted groups of neo-pietists who prefer enclavic group life to acculturation.

Addressing himself courageously to the principles, problems, and programs of "modern," centrist, or mainline Orthodoxy in America, Dr. Belkin wrote:

> What is the central principle which underlies Orthodoxy or traditional Judaism?
>
> In my opinion, the essence of traditional Judaism is the indisputable faith that the Torah, the revealed word of God, is not a mere constitution or code, but that, as the law of God, it represents divine authority and contains the highest wisdom and loftiest truths, and that as such the divine law is sufficient for all time and should control and guide the entire life and destiny of our people. . . .
>
> I believe that Orthodoxy or traditional Judaism can succeed in converting a great majority of our people to our cause. The trend in America is toward a traditionally inspired Jewish community . . . our people . . . are ready to listen. . . .
>
> I believe that Orthodoxy or traditional Judaism needs to develop a

greater sense of organization. If we organize all our forces which stand for a positive approach to Jewish life, we can determine the essence of American Judaism for many generations to come. . . . A narrow-minded man may sometimes characterize American orthodoxy as un-American, only to discover that real Americanism means reverence for the Bible as the word of God, and obedience to the authority of Scripture—concepts which lie at the foundation of this country. . . .

I see religious Jewish life on this continent divided into three parts. One segment of the community argues that it is impossible for the Jew to continue to live the same kind of spiritual life in the United States as he had lived for centuries on the European Continent. . . .

The only way, in accordance with their thinking, that the Jew can survive on this continent is to develop an easy-going *translated Judaism,* a Judaism which requires no great sacrifices, a Judaism which may be acquired with little effort. . . .

On the other hand, there exists today a small segment of the Jewish community, which is extremely pious in theory and practice. This particular group feels that it can best live within the sacred heritage of Judaism if it ignores completely the contemporary environment, and *transfers,* without the slightest change, the traditional Jewish way of life that their forefathers lived for centuries on the European Continent. They refuse to conform to any modern standards even when such standards are not directly, or even indirectly, in conflict with the precepts of the Torah and our sacred traditions. This group is known not only for its extreme piety, but also for its extreme isolation from the larger part of the Jewish community. . . .

The Yeshiva [University] as the fountainhead of Torah learning in America, follows in the traditions of the Torah academies which functioned for centuries on the European Continent. It has been, however, the main aim of the Yeshiva [University] throughout its existence, not merely to *transfer* that tree of knowledge to the American soil. . . .

It is . . . the aim of the Yeshiva to *transplant* in the American cultural and social and democratic climate the tree of Torah knowledge and practice, which shall continue the Torah learning of ancient academies *and at the same time, be a particularly American product.* . . .

Our philosophy is one of integration and we firmly deny that our integration in the American community in any way implies the abrogation of even one iota of our sacred tradition. More than two generations of our people have been lost to us [to Orthodoxy] *because of the erroneous belief that there exists a serious conflict between our spiritual heritage and the American way of life, which is itself deeply rooted in Hebraic spiritual values.*[37] (Italics mine.)

This forthright and open embrace of America was indeed a new and a far cry from the life style of the older east-European Orthodox community in America. But in a sense, Belkin was turning his back on what he considered abortive and unrealistic attempts to perpetuate the tradition in America. The new-style "orthodoxy of the American-born Jewry is not new" to Jewish history, he maintained. In Spain, Italy, England, and Holland, unlike eastern Europe, he pointed out, Jews had integrated into the community without losing their traditional, "orthodox" religion.[38] Indeed, he made bold to proclaim at the very time that Jews were celebrating the Tercentenary of their American settlement in 1954, that American Orthodoxy was then really "not more than twenty-five years old."[39] But this American Orthodoxy was not the same as the Orthodoxy that the unemancipated east-Europeans brought with them from their native countries. In earlier decades, Jews in America thought of themselves as Russian-Jews, Polish-Jews, German-Jews, and the like. These national origins were now all but forgotten in an acculturated American Jewish community. Today, Jews denominate themselves differently: they are known to one another as Orthodox Jews, Conservative Jews, or Reform Jews. Applying Herberg's phrase, one may now say that American Judaism is itself a "triple melting pot."

Yet Belkin's view coincides with our earlier analysis when he linked the upsurge in Orthodoxy and its new awareness of America approximately to the time of Hitler. We have seen how, in that era, a slowly reviving Jewishness began to lead many to a new interest in Judaism. For some time, the road "home" meant going back to what they considered the only authentic religious source, Orthodoxy. While the Orthodox movement has since been rejuvenated, nevertheless, in Belkin's words, "more than two generations were lost" to it. But its dogged determination to survive those difficult years bequeathed to its contemporary leaders a foundation upon which they are rebuilding. Even a brief review of its struggle to keep alive gives us an insight into the remarkable ways in which an unemancipated immigrant community attempted to accommodate to the free environment of America, and how, in the process, it ironically created novel "American" institutions for the preservation of its "unchanging" faith.

By far the most important obstacle that tradition-minded Jews had to hurdle in the new world was the thorny question of education. In pre-emancipated communities of Europe, and particularly in eastern Europe, the organic Jewish community, the *kehillah*, as a state within a state, had made the school the cornerstone of its communal concerns. Indeed, these communal Jewish schools contributed much to the essential unity of medieval Jewry. It mattered little in which country Jews lived or what national languages they spoke: the curriculum of the Jewish school, the only school available to Jews, was virtually the same for all— the Bible and the Talmud. But in America the earliest Jewish congregations, bereft of a comprehensive communal superstructure and far too small and few in number, could not undertake any organized teaching programs. As a result, the teaching of Judaism soon became a matter to be left to the private discretion of parents, and what few teachers they could engage were woefully incompetent. In 1731 the Sephardic congregation of New York City, Shearith Israel, did embark upon a faltering experiment, which set a pattern for what, some two hundred years later, would become the most significant and unique contribution of American Orthodoxy. In that year an elementary school was organized, known as a *yeshiva,* which offered instruction in general as well as Jewish studies. (In Europe, and before that in Babylonia, a *yeshiva* meant something quite different. There it was an academy of higher learning, a seat of Talmudic study, which offered *semika,* or rabbinical ordination, to those who mastered its courses. In a sense, the appropriation in America of a word formerly reserved for schools of advanced adult study as the name for an elementary school for children tells its own story.) But the effort was not long lived, despite its subsidies from the government, as they were then given to all denominational schools in New York State. By 1803, a new school had to be organized at this congregation, the Polonies School, or Talmud Torah, which was established through a bequest of a Polish Jew named Meyer Polonies. After forty years or so of doubtful success, this school, too, had to close its doors.

By the mid-century, a new American institution had come upon the scene that was to capture the interest and attention of the Jews. This was the public school. By law, most public school systems were prohibited from offering religious instruction, and in the eyes of the Jews this was one of its most desirable features. However, the law was often circumvented, and many tradition-minded Jews entertained grave doubts as to the desirability of sending their children to schools where they might be exposed to subtle or overt proselytism. But their numbers in America were still too small, before the large-scale east-European immigration began, to warrant the expense of establishing a full-scale private system of Jewish schools. Inevitably, the public school was the winner, and the question of Jewish education remained as thorny as ever.

Nor did the large increase in the Jewish population deposited by the new east-European immigration waves help to solve the problem at first. Far from it. Most of these newcomers, the traditionalists and the secularized alike, saw the public school as a major vehicle for the adjustment of their children to the new environment. The very idea of a free educational enterprise in which all the diversity of Europe would emerge in a new American unity was most appealing to the great majority of Jews. Indeed, this early American Jewish heritage, which identified the public school system with the vital meaning of democracy and with the hope for a secure future here for all the downtrodden and oppressed, is still deeply imbedded in the psyche of many contemporary Jews. Even today, one cannot fully understand why the American Jewish community, the religionists among them, often appears to be defending what some others call the "godlessness" of the public school system, without an appreciation of what the public educational system has symbolized for Jews. It was America itself, the land of equality, the happy home of persecuted minorities, where children were free to be themselves, without fear of the lurking authority of church or parson!

But if Jewish children were joyfully to be enrolled in the public school, what to do about their religious education? The Reform group had solved that problem in accordance with their minimal religious commitments: they established congregationally sponsored Sunday Schools. The east-European traditionalists, however, were far too poor to support a congregational school, and besides, their small, first-settlement area "prayer halls" were really incapable of housing schools, in any case. But neither would they have anything to do with the Germans' "Protestant" Sunday School. Their embrace of the public school was a sign of their wish to forget—to forget the disabilities they had in east-Europe. On the other hand, they also wanted to remember—to remember and to retain traditions that the Reformers had shed long before.

Some engaged private teachers who taught groups of children in the various homes. Others turned to their European experience, and set up a *heder* (literally, a room) which, in its later American form, became the pattern for the future. The *heder* was a "private school," usually conducted in the home of the principal-teacher, and supported by monthly tuition payments of the parents. Except Fridays and Saturdays, children came for instruction every weekday afternoon and evening after their public school sessions, and on Sunday mornings, as well. Before long, associations were established on communal lines, by groups who were intent upon gaining wider public support for the *heder*. In time, in place of the one-room "private school" of the *heder*, the community-sponsored Talmud Torah, as these afternoon Hebrew Schools were known, came into being. Nevertheless, the poverty of most of these east-European families made it necessary for many of their children to be accepted without the payment of fees. The consequent lack of funds was a perennial plague that caused annual financial crises, and the school's physical accommodations could rarely exceed basement rooms in rented quarters.

Moreover, the constant need to broaden the program of the Talmud Torah by adding subjects relevant to the child's new experiences in America played havoc with the curriculum. In Europe, the principal subjects were Bible and Talmud. But, in America, new rationales for religious orthodoxy had to be developed: in Europe they learned to pray, simply by praying; here they had to be told about prayer and ritual, and then taught the skills. In America, too, a justification for the validity of Jewish culture in a non-Jewish environment had to be worked out: concerns never felt in the autonomous, pre-emancipated east-European community. Thus, courses had to be introduced in Zionism, Jewish history, current events, and music, in addition to instruction in the Hebrew language. Ironically, the multiplication of school subjects increased as the demand for a reduction in the hours of instruction grew. A vicious circle developed: the more acculturated the children and the parents became, the more necessary it was to add still newer areas to the curriculum: such subjects as comparative religion, the role of Judaism in a democracy, Jewish ethics, and the like. Yet as the generations became more conscious of their Americanism and more "modern" in their own eyes, the less time were they willing to make available for the Jewish school. As a result, despite its many successes in the face of great odds, the educational program of the Talmud Torah could often be accurately described as being "a mile wide and an inch deep."

Then came 1925. With the stoppage of mass Jewish immigration, the future of the Talmud Torah became even bleaker still. As long as new streams of east-Europeans were flowing in, the "downtown" Talmud Torah could be assured of enrolling large numbers of immigrant children whose traditional ties to Jewishness and Judaism were still vital and strong. They more than made up for those whose "Americanism" caused them to regard Jewish education as more and more superfluous. Then, too, as the first- and second-generation community gained greater economic stability, they moved to newer areas, away from the congestion of the immigrant downtown sections. There, large synagogues replaced the small prayer halls, and the community Talmud Torahs were soon to discover that most of these congregations—the Conservative synagogues in particular—now placed the education of the young at the very core of their program. They attached school buildings to their synagogues, engaged "Americanized" teachers, and in general sought to capture the faltering religious interest of the parents by centering their concerns in the children. The "community Talmud Torah" was left to the unsynagogued and to the Orthodox, many of whom remained "downtown" because their economic circumstances did not permit a move to the new areas.

The Talmud Torah, as a community instrument for Jewish education, was the invention and creation of the east-European Orthodox group, and yet the shifting social and economic circumstances had all but taken this institution away from them and placed it into the hands of Conservative congregations. By the 1980s, less than 10 per cent of all children receiving a Jewish education were attending afternoon supplementary schools under community, private, or noncongregational auspices. But without those earlier models that had been established by the Orthodox-inspired community Talmud Torah under trying, pioneering conditions, the pattern for the contemporary congregational Hebrew School would not have been available. Indeed, this contribution of Orthodoxy in America is not restricted to the Hebrew Schools of the Conservative congregations alone. Many Reform temples moved away from their one-day-a-week Sunday School and added midweek after-public-school classes in Hebrew language as well.

But in a way, the general decline in Talmud Torah education and its loss by Orthodoxy to the non-Orthodox congregational school served it as a blessing in disguise. As we have seen, the educational effectiveness of the Talmud Torah program was already seriously impaired by the 1940s. Not the Talmud Torah, said some visionary Orthodox educators, but a more intensive school was now needed. What they had in mind was an American-style *yeshiva*, a private, all-day Jewish-sponsored school which could teach not a part of, but "the whole child." Within a few years, this Orthodox-inspired educational movement would make still another contribution to American Jewish life, whose influence would be widely felt by the whole community. But here again the later success of the Jewish day school movement as an increasingly acceptable pattern in America owed much of its vitality to the struggling efforts of the first generation Orthodox east Europeans. Only a half-century later, its phenomenal growth had become one of the great positive "surprises" of American Jewish life. It would reflect the "rise," not the "decline," of Orthodoxy's *influence*, if not its *pervasiveness* in America.

After 1945, when the day school movement began to show its first signs of real growth, its antagonists—which included most of the non-Orthodox educators of the time—had largely predicted its ultimate failure and doom. It appeared to be "too Orthodox," even "un-American." By 1962, however—less than twenty years later—of a total Jewish student population of almost 600,000, some eight per cent were then attending the burgeoning day schools. The intensification of Jewish schooling in America continued to increase by leaps, as day schools flourished and grew, year by year: in 1977, it was estimated that from the eight per cent of only fifteen years earlier, the rate of day school attendance had jumped dramatically to twenty-two per cent; and by 1980, these percentages had climbed still higher to twenty-eight per cent. By 1983, it was reliably reported that over 100,000 students were enrolled in day schools and *yeshivot*. Of these, about ninety per cent of the students were in schools organized by the Orthodox—about one third of which were "ultra-pious" or *Hasidic yeshivot*. Yet, by then there were also almost ten thousand children studying in the recently established Conservative day schools, and many hundreds in similar schools which some Reform temples had also begun to organize.[40]

This phenomenal growth as an "all-denominational" enterprise appears even more remarkable when one considers the difficult history of day school education, from the days of its first establishment, in the last decades of the nineteenth century. A group of east-European immigrants in New York City boldly decided then to found the first American *yeshiva* for elementary school children, in the era of free public education. This school, Yeshiva Etz Chaim, represented a conscious effort to offer children a comprehensive educational program of general studies within the framework of a Jewish religious school. Only a handful of parents stood behind this major pioneering effort, but the school authorities held fast to their program nevertheless. Their hand was to be strengthened immeasurably some years later, in 1915, when the full weight of the leading Orthodox rabbis and laymen was placed behind their work. In that year the Rabbi Isaac Elchanan Theological Seminary, forerunner of the Yeshiva University of today, merged with Etz Chaim, and to its elementary school a high school was added, known as the Talmudical Academy. These, together with the higher educational program of the Elchanan Theological Seminary, formed a more complete school system. Later, in 1928, this growing institution reached out still further and established a degree-granting academic college, called Yeshiva College. These achievements for Orthodoxy were accomplished under the helm of the President of Yeshiva College, Dr. Bernard Revel, whose passing in 1943 brought Dr. Samuel Belkin to his former place. Then, in 1945, Yeshiva College became Yeshiva University, and ever since, new undergraduate schools, including Stern College for Women, postgraduate and professional schools, a School of Social Work, and the Albert Einstein Medical School have marked a dynamic new era for American Orthodoxy.[41] It would not likely ever become a dominant majority, but increasingly—and especially since the 1970s, as we will see—its role as an aggressive and creative minority, made it into an exciting and dramatic religious community which has contributed far beyond its small numbers to the rise of the *new* Jewish identity in America.

Ironically, the founding of the Rabbi Isaac Elchanan Seminary, whose later history is so intimately tied to the success of contemporary, acculturated American Orthodoxy, was in its time a reaction to the acculturated east-European traditionalists. It will be remembered that those who could not accept Isaac Wise's American Judaism reacted by organizing the Jewish Theological Seminary in 1886. The story was repeated a year later, when a group of east-Europeans founded a third rabbinical school, and thus a third religious movement, as a mark of their dissatisfaction with the traditionalism of the Seminary's east-Europeans. In effect, however, this new division was really not the result of a clash in religious ideology but of cultural orientation. The disparities between those who broke off to establish the Isaac Elchanan school and those who followed in the path of the Seminary are "symbolized in two words which the respective groups used for Jewish study: *Lernen* (learning) and *Jüdische Wissenschaft* (the science of Judaism)."[42]

Fifty years later, however, the leaders of Isaac Elchanan and its Yeshiva University were to speak differently. "In all of its activities," they said then, "Yeshiva University will seek to foster . . . harmonious growth, in which the bases of modern knowledge and culture in the fields of art, science, and service, are blended with the bases of Jewish culture, so that it students may . . . develop as informed and devoted sons in the spirit and faith of Israel, able to recognize the essential harmony of life."[43] A remarkable paradox emerged, discernible, however, only in the retrospect of almost a century of Americanizing influences. The success of the Yeshiva University and its impact upon the growth of Orthodox day schools is directly related to its urgent desire to appear as American as the other two Jewish denominations.

But the growing popularity of Jewish day schools today must not blind us to the fact that for many years in the past, and perhaps for many yet to come, grave objections were to be raised to this educational movement. As early as 1908, Dr. Samson Benderley, a professional Jewish educator, expressed the concern of many:

> Shall we withdraw our children from the public schools and establish schools of our own as the Catholics are doing? This plan . . . should be banished from our minds. . . . What we want in this country, is not Jews who can successfully keep up their Jewishness in a few large ghettos, but men and women who have grown up in freedom and can assert themselves wherever they are. A parochial system of education among Jews would be fatal to such hopes.[44]

Objections such as these were raised in those decades when first- and second-generation east-Europeans were concentrating heavily on their Americanism. In parochialism they saw a threat to their acceptance as equals and this attitude prevented the day-school movement from making much headway. By 1935, American Jewry could point only to 17 day schools with a total enrollment of forty-five hundred children, and all but one of these schools were located in New York City. But beginning with 1945 and the new return to Jewishness, an amazing phenomenon began to unfold: new day schools were being formed, in quick succession, all over the country. Thus, in 1958, a national educational survey showed that there were 214 of these schools from coast to coast, 78 of them outside metropolitan New York.

This amazing growth continued at a quickened pace into the 1980s, with the lion's share of the newer day schools—there were about 400—springing up outside of the Greater New York area. Indeed, there were already day schools from coast to coast—at least one in virtually every Jewish community with a population of 5,000 or more. Increasingly, high schools were also added on, and they comprised a student population of over 15,000. This reflected the unheralded demand of over two-thirds of their elementary school graduates, who elected to continue their secondary education under Jewish auspices.

Yet, when several Reform temples also began to establish day schools in the 1970s, even the Orthodox must have realized that although their influence was contagious and penetrating, other social and educational issues were also at work as some liberal and progressive congregations began to copy what they themselves had always rejected as "pure Orthodoxy." Which is not to say that many of these self-same extrinsic factors were not also at work in the proliferation of both Orthodox and Conservative day schools, too. Many purely Jewish concerns were at issue in all three camps: increasing dissatisfaction with the supplementary education offered in many afternoon or Sunday schools; concerns over the "alienation" of Jewish youth; and the growing rate of intermarriage. It was felt that an intensive Jewish education in a Jewish environment could help provide solutions to these and related problems. (A study of Jewish community leaders, however, as late as 1959, had revealed that more than two-thirds of them still opposed day schools on ideological grounds.)[45]

Yet, it was also becoming clear that the increasing social and economic mobility of middle-class Jewish parents, coupled to a new phenomenon—the loss of Jewish confidence in the public school—gave the burgeoning day school movement even greater impetus. By the late 1960s, public schools were coming increasingly under attack, particularly after they were forcibly integrated by means of bussing. Nor could municipal budgets continue to maintain proper standards for their schools; as a result, the pursuit of excellence was inevitably abandoned by a growing number of public educational systems. Many of these problems were directly responsible for the rapid growth of private schools under church or secular auspices across the country, and in the process, the Jewish day school movement benefitted immeasurably, as well. Regardless of the genetic roots of their motivations, Jewish parents of various religious persuasions were clearly adopting a form of Jewish experience which the Orthodox community had fostered, and with which, it alone, had long been identified. In this and in other areas, since the 1960s, Orthodox steadfastness seemed to have won admirers, if not always adherents.

Indeed, the synagogues of the Orthodox are not nearly as popular with American Jews as their successful day school movement would seem to indicate. Studies estimate that only forty-seven to fifty per cent of the country's Jews are affiliated with any synagogue. Thus, approximately 2,700,000 men, women, and children are members of all congregations, said to total approximately 4,500. Of these, the Conservatives are believed to comprise about 900 congregations with a total population of almost fifty per cent, or about 1,200,000 souls; the Reform have close to 800 temples, with a total of about thirty per cent of the affiliated—or about 850,000 adherents; and the Orthodox, who claim to have the largest number of congregations—about 3,000—account for slightly more than twenty per cent, or about 650,000 members. Despite the Orthodox claim of having the largest number of congregations, it is likely that there are less than 300,000 *fully-observant* and committed Orthodox Jews in the whole country, which would account for little more than four per cent of all the Jews in America—and less than half of their own synagogue members.[46] The Orthodox picture is even more sharply reduced outside of Greater New York City: religious observance in full Orthodox fashion is almost nonexistent in the smaller communities. In cities with under 100,000 Jews, it is usually the Conservative and Reform congregations which form the largest and dominant groups.

Orthodoxy thus presents a picture of both light and shadow. What it lacks in numbers, however, it more than makes up in zeal, ardor, and commitment, as we shall soon note in greater detail. Nevertheless, by the 1980s, in terms of numbers, and as a synagogue movement, it was still not gaining appreciably over the Conservative and Reform groups. Indeed, some of their congregations were voting to secede from the movement and were moving over to Conservatism. There was increasing dissatisfaction with Orthodoxy's refusal to countenance the introduction of family pews and its continued insistence upon segregating the women in special sections—usually in the upper balconies of the synagogue. But the democratic environment of America was so compelling that even tradition-minded Jews felt the need to abolish this ancient practice. The widespread adoption of "late Friday evening Sabbath Services," which until the 1970s had served as the effective displacement of the Saturday morning Sabbath service, was still another feature of the American Conservative synagogue that appealed to those traditional elements who sought to accommodate their religious life to their economic needs. Many Jews were unable, rather than unwilling, to leave their shops and factories on Saturday morning in order to be present in the synagogue. But they were able to attend the Conservatives' "Late Service" on Friday evening.

Then, too, there was the serious problem of the dietary laws. To be sure, by the 1960s kosher food had become "big business" in America. Indeed, the extent of its successful penetration into the general economy can be attested by such reliable reporters of the American market place as *The Wall Street Journal.* Its headlines have proclaimed the news that "Kosher Label Covers More Name Brands from Aspirin to Pizza."[47] A subheadline, however, was more revealing: "Gentiles Help Boost Sales of Matzo Balls." The president of a major kosher delicatessen producer, explaining the 20 per cent jump in sales of his company's products since 1961, reported: "Non-Jews have broken the ice in trying kosher foods and they're responsible for a large part of our sales gains."[48] And an executive of a food consultant organization suggested that "Kosher foods show signs they may become as popular as Italian foods. Matzo balls may replace pizza yet."[49]

Yet, despite these external gains, there is increasing evidence that in terms of personal observance, the dietary laws were not nearly so popular. In fact, they had been flouted officially by the organized Jewish community itself until a more self-conscious and vocal Orthodoxy began to boycott these events with increasing effectiveness in the late 1960s. Dinners sponsored by the comprehensive communal charity, the Welfare Fund and Federation, which for a long time were not served in accordance with the dietary laws, began to observe them, only after it became counter-productive not to do so. (Some observers have noted that with the huge increase in the targets set for these Israel-oriented fund-raising campaigns beginning with 1967, it was deemed improper to alienate any segment of the community, in order to reach those campaign goals). After World War II, a number of Jewish hospitals, built with capital funds collected from all sections of the Jewish community, the Orthodox included, openly refused to run kosher kitchens for their patients on the grounds that their institutions were "nonsectarian." (Insistent Jewish patients would, of course, be offered kosher food, but only "on request.") Increasingly, the few kosher restaurants that had always been found in the larger metropolitan areas were forced to close because of a growing scarcity of customers. Fewer and fewer Jews were "100 per cent kosher": more and more of those who may have retained some semblance of the religious dietary practices in their own homes—for nostalgia's sake?—consistently disregarded them in public. They had developed a double standard, a "domestic" and a "foreign" policy, which were at variance. At home, it was *gefilte fish,* which helps to explain the tremendous upsurge in packaged and processed kosher foods in food-market sales across America. But away from home it was shrimps and lobsters, which helps us understand why so few kosher restaurants have survived.[50] Indeed, the observance of Kosher food laws even inside Jewish homes was also in continuous, precipitous decline. By 1984, it was reliably reported, "every week another [Kosher butcher] shop closes in New York. In 1940, there were 3,800 Kosher butcher [shops] in all five boroughs [of New York City], today there are around 400."[50a] The "nonobservant Orthodox Jew," that uniquely American phenomenon, was everywhere in sight.

Yet the vitality of Orthodoxy—as a movement, if not as a personal way of life—could again be measured not merely in terms of synagogue affiliation but rather as a catalytic force for the conservation of more positive attitudes toward "Jewish culture." Many of the parents who were sending their children to Orthodox day schools were themselves non-Orthodox, or nonobservant Orthodox. What impelled them to make what seems so anomalous a decision? Surely, as earlier noted, there were a number of extrinsic reasons: the Jewish day school, for some, was better than the overcrowded metropolitan public schools (as in New York City); for others, it was preferred because it was a "private school" with small classes, where personal attention was possible; for still others, it was a practical solution to the problem of Jewish education that obviated the necessity of sending their children to public school by day and, again, to Hebrew School in the late afternoon.

Yet one must not discount the positive and impelling forces also at work in the Jewish community of America since World War II, and more especially with the rise of the "new ethnicity" at the close of the 1960s.

A growing desire to rediscover the lost self-esteem that characterized the second generation manifested itself in a country-wide urge for more and better Jewish education for their children. "I want my child to have the Jewish education I didn't get" was a refrain one could hear from coast to coast. Nor was there as much of the fear of parochialism which, ironically, had dominated the immigrant mentality decades earlier. These parents were looking for their roots and not escaping their lineage. Thus, more and more the assumption was that the private Jewish day school was neither alien nor foreign to America. Nor should this school, many parents came to feel, be compared with the Roman Catholic parochial school, which was ranged against the "godlessness" of the public school and dominated by a church hierarchy. A goodly number of those who now sent their children to Jewish day schools agreed with Rabbi Joseph Lookstein, a leading Orthodox protagonist of progressive day-school education. "The all-day school," he said, "is not intended to insulate the Jewish child against the environment. The world is not represented to him as an alien world. Nor is the school world within an exclusively Jewish one. America is as much a part of the child's life at school as Judaism is part of his life as an American. . . . There he learns that America wants him to be a good Jew and that Judaism commands him to be a good American."[51]

The success of the day-school movement continues to buoy up Orthodoxy.[52] Yet, in comparison with the rapid rise of Conservative and Reform congregations since World War II, the rate of development of new Orthodox *synagogues* has been disappointing. Where, then, would the graduates of Orthodox rabbinical schools go to serve? "From the synagogue toward yeshiva," suggested one of their leading spokesmen. "The largest Orthodox rabbinical seminary in America" (Yeshiva University), he correctly predicted in 1956, "will soon graduate one hundred rabbis every year, and even if many Conservative synagogues employ these new rabbis, at least half will almost certainly enter the teaching profession or Jewish social service."[53]

The paradoxical nature of such a future cannot be overlooked. On the one hand, at least part of Orthodoxy's destined role is to help build up the Conservative movement with rabbis trained in their own rabbinical schools. On the other hand, those Orthodox rabbis who will enter "the teaching profession" will often serve in Orthodox day schools where children of nonobservant Orthodox parents predominate. Yet, paradoxes such as these continue to shield the principal surprise: the new vitality of Orthodoxy, in its own right; but even more, as a creative catalyst for *all* Jews. The "new ethnicity" had found a welcome home among the Orthodox, and from within their camp it also found its way to other Jews outside their fold.

Yet even the day-school movement itself poses serious future problems to Orthodoxy. In earlier decades the Orthodox had pioneered in the community Talmud Torah, only to see it overtaken by the congregational Hebrew School, usually under Conservative auspices. The high tuition costs, too, will continue to militate against the acceptance of the day-school program by many members of the American Jewish community. (By 1984, many schools were charging over $2,500 per annum.) An awareness of this built-in difficulty has already led some Orthodox leaders to counter the heretofore unanimous American Jewish position on "church-state" matters by indicating, in their desperation, a desire for state support of parochial schools. One such extremely influential leader, Rabbi Menachem M. Schneerson, head of the Lubavitcher Hasidic movement, clearly stated his stand in favor of federal or state aid to parochial schools in an article which the Catholic magazine *Commonweal* reprinted with glee. Said Rabbi Schneerson:

> The principle of separation of church and state should not be misconstrued or distorted to mean a denial of religion. . . . Our Yeshivoth and Day Schools must daily turn away tens, if not hundreds, of children for lack of money and facilities. Annual tuition fees must run very high, and this is the only deterrent to many parents who cannot afford it. And this assistance [state aid] could at least to a certain degree immediately improve this condition. . . . The obvious conclusion from the above is that it is the moral duty of every Jew to do his utmost to make federal aid to the secular departments of parochial schools a reality, in order to strengthen and expand the Yeshivoth and Day Schools. . . .[54]

Since the writing of these words by the "Lubavitcher Rebbe," in 1962, even some "acculturated Jews"—especially those who are parents of day school students—have adopted this still-minority Jewish view.

From their point of view, there may be no other way out of the inevitable obstacles placed by mounting budgets in the way of day-school development and expansion. Yet, this issue is bound to involve the Orthodox groups in acrimonious and prolonged debate with their many opponents in the Jewish community. An official espousal of this position can further mark them off as a denominational community within the larger Jewish grouping.

But one major ideological problem seems to be looming on the horizon, which may yet prove the most difficult of all for Orthodoxy to meet. During the leaner years of the day-school movement, most Orthodox leaders, as we have seen, were content to identify this intensive form of Jewish education with the best interests of America, and with the Jewish child as an American. More recently, however, the stress seems to be away from the Jew as an American, and from the purposes of the day school as a contribution to democracy. "Maybe some of them are too 'narrow minded,'" said one Orthodox leader of these schools, pointing with pride, not dissatisfaction, to what he considered to be the true Orthodox approach. He said further:

> Maybe some of them are too "bookish" and have no patience with their neighbor's point-of-view. Maybe we are going back to "olden times" in our emphasis on the subject-matter, but we *are* producing more students for our higher Yeshivot. Maybe we have not as yet given the world more Hebrew writers and poets. But, primarily, we're more interested—quite frankly—in Talmidei Hahamim [religious and pious scholars]. . . . Perhaps we have engendered some conflicts between parents and children. But, at the same time we have restored to American Jewry the historic devotion to "The Book"; to the Hebrew language and to the Jewish way of life![55]

These are, indeed, authentic Orthodox sentiments: they reflect the basic religious concerns of the tradition—piety, religious scholarship, and concentration on the inner, spiritual essentials of the Jewish faith. But whether these alone can succeed as rallying points for the American Jew at this point in time is very much moot. For all his new self-awareness and his proud ethnic consciousness, the American Jew is still very much the American. He *is* interested in his neighbors; he opposes "narrow-mindedness"; his educational values go beyond preoccupation with books—even religious books—alone. Moreover, with very few exceptions, American Jews are passionately committed to higher secular learning, and their large numbers on the university campuses—both as students and faculty—attest to their essential unwillingness to accept these sectarian Orthodox views. Indeed, most mainline, centrist Orthodox families would also reject a view that accepted only a "parochializing" education for Jews, by disallowing children to attend non-Jewish colleges or universities, as the Orthodox ultra-pietists insist.

The strength of the Orthodox day school movement may indeed be ensured for years to come, but one is tempted to speculate whether, in fact, the history of the Talmud Torah in America may not be repeated in the future. Will Orthodoxy serve more as an indirect influence upon the other two denominations than as an independent and isolated force for the multitudes? Is it destined to remain a relatively small minority, despite its protestations of "authenticity" and its claim to be the "real" Judaism?

What often seem to militate against the strength of Orthodoxy are not only the environmental factors of America but the environmental factors of Europe, which still prevail in its midst here. While the Conservative and Reform movements have but one rabbinical seminary, one national rabbinical association, and one national congregational union, Orthodoxy in America has not yet shed its Old-World diversity and regionalism. Earlier, we described the largest and most significant of the Orthodox schools, the Yeshiva University, whose alumni together with those of the Chicago Hebrew Theological College finally formed their own Orthodox rabbinical association, known as the Rabbinical Council of America. But there are literally scores of smaller and medium-sized higher *yeshivot,* schools which train men for the Orthodox rabbinate. And many of these smaller Orthodox rabbinical groups go their own way and have little to do with either the Yeshiva University or the Hebrew Theological College of Chicago, counting them as too liberal, too modern, too acculturated. Thus, while Orthodoxy's congregations may still represent the largest number of individual synagogues in the United States, most of them are small, unrelated, and proprietary in nature. Even the Union of Jewish Orthodox Congregations, organized in New York City in 1898, cannot claim the undivided loyalty of many of these, despite the fact that it claims to represent almost three thousand congregations in the United States.

Oddly enough, contemporary Orthodoxy has become more and more heterodox. If the Conservatives are divided into three wings, so, too, are there at least three groups among the Orthodox: the "modern Orthodox," the "traditionalists," and the "ultra-traditionalists."

The "modern Orthodox"—or the "mainliners"—find their center in the institutions which have grown up around the Yeshiva University, and their Americanization has gone forward about as far as it can go. The "traditionalists," however, see in the Americanization of Orthodoxy a threat to the foundation of the "true faith." While many who may be called "traditionalists" have themselves received higher secular education, most, however, reject attempts to relate Judaism to modern life as nothing more than a series of untraditional, unsuccessful, secular excesses. They therefore look with disfavor upon any attempt to compromise the ritual. Instead of apologizing for the unworldliness of their religious commitments, they make much of their desire to live out their spiritual destiny four-square within the tradition. Indeed, they tend to regard the "modern Orthodox" synagogue as too acculturated, too compromising, too contrived, and they see little to commend it over a Conservative congregation.

The "ultra-traditionalists," on the other hand, consist of groups that emigrated to America from central and western Europe after 1933 and brought with them a conservative religious tradition which had been preserved for generations. For the most part, they were skilled workers or professional men, and they lacked neither the intellectual resources nor the modern experiences that were denied their east-European brothers who had settled here a half-century earlier. It is not surprising, therefore, that they tend to be suspicious of Orthodox institutions which pre-date their own arrival here. Since most of these are controlled by those who are now third generation members of "modern Orthodoxy," the "ultra-traditionalists" have been busy developing a network of religious institutions of their own.[56]

This pattern of excessive individualism was made even more unmanageable after the Second World War, with the coming to America of some thousands of Orthodox survivors of the east-European holocaust. Many of these are *Hasidim*, sectarian pietists, whose specific religious loyalties are offered only to their own rabbi—or "their *Rebbe*"—and who are considered as ultra-Orthodox, and separatist, even by other Orthodox Jews. They think of themselves as *Obgehitene Yiden*, the Guardian Jews, and are therefore most zealous and meticulous in performing all the prescribed commandments. They are concerned not at all with America, but with their version of Judaism alone. As a constant reminder of this, they take care that they may always be externally identified as *Hasidim* by wearing clothing they consider to be traditionally Jewish. They cut an unmistakable medieval European figure with their full, unshaven beards, their long black outercoats topped by broad-brimmed felt hats, which are often exchanged on the Sabbath for circular fur caps.

Hasidim tend to live in their own cluster-communities which center in enclavic neighborhoods such as Brooklyn, New York (the Williamsburgh and Crown Heights sections), where their *Rebbes*—the "reigning" heads of their particular sect—have chosen to live and to establish their "world headquarters." The two principal Hasidic dynasties are the Satmarer and the Lubavitcher, the former hailing originally from Hungary, the latter from pre-revolutionary White Russia. Both claim many thousands of adherents the world over, for whom their *Rebbe*'s word is regarded as virtually divine. They seek his approval and advice for most of their major personal decisions, ranging from marriage to occupational and business choices. There are smaller *Hasidic* sects as well, some of which are the Gerer, Bobover, Tasher, and Belzer—the names referring, again, to the east-European towns where the ancestors of the current dynastic heads—the founding *Rebbes*—originally held sway. With the notable exception of the Lubavitcher, most of these groups pay little heed to non-

Hasidic Jews, and outside of their own ranks play virtually no role in the life of the organized Jewish community.

The Lubavitcher, on the other hand, have been the most outgoing and aggressive; they are involved in the life of Jews everywhere—even behind the Iron Curtain, in "subterranean" cell groups. In the United States, they are the most high-profile of all *Hasidim*, mounting public campaigns for donning *tephillin* (phylacteries), distributing *matzot* on Passover, and even placing prominent billboard and newspaper advertisements urging Jewish women to kindle the Sabbath candles regularly, and to perform other *mitzvot*. Unlike most other *Hasidim*, the Lubavitcher also have a favorable attitude toward *aliya* (immigration) to Israel. They tend to support Israeli government actions which move in the direction of claiming all the "biblical territories" for a "Greater Israel" of the future.

The other influential *Hasidic* group, the Satmarer, is profoundly anti-Israel. They take the position that a secular Jewish government is an obstacle and a deterrent to their religious dream, the advent of the Jewish Messiah, who, when God is ready, will come to establish in the Holy Land, the divine—not the secular–human—kingdom on earth. They oppose the Lubavitcher on this, and other grounds, as well. As a result, violent altercations have taken place between them in their Brooklyn neighborhoods, which have not helped the cause of *Hasidism*, in other Jewish quarters. Additionally, from time to time, the Satmarer have initiated large-scale public advertisements which denounce the State of Israel as a secular impostor and a bane to the religious. While both of these *Hasidic* groups engage in major programs of Jewish education, and maintain important religious publications programs, their continuing inter-group disputes do not help the cause of Orthodoxy.[57]

While fully-observant Orthodox Jews of all styles and varieties constitute little more than three per cent of the country's Jewish population, they provide students of religion and society with an important example of the efficacy of a dedicated minority and its capacity to wield influence beyond its own boundaries. Since the late 1960s, there have been noticeable shifts within American Orthodoxy—and world-wide, too—on matters of private and public piety and religious rigor. These have been characterized as clear moves "to the right." They also reflected a more uncompromising interpretation of *halakah*, or Jewish law, and their increasing unwillingness to accommodate either to American values, or to modernity, in general. While there were no signs of any massive "conversion" of American Jewry to its camp, Orthodoxy, however, played a dynamic role as a catalyst in re-traditionalizing many Jews who still claimed membership in Conservative or Reform congregations. And at the base of all these unfolding phenomena, there was a quizzical paradox: relative to the total Jewish population, the number of Orthodox was not increasing, while in a remarkable way, it exhibited all the signs of a spiritual resurgence. How does one account for this apparent contradiction?

It had become a truism to describe American Judaism in generational terms: The majority of Orthodox Jews were members of the first generation, while the same could be said of Conservative Jews and the second generation; and Reform Jews and the third generation. Each generation, it seemed, had its separate "religious preference." Yet, there *are* first generation Reform Jews, and there *are* third generation Orthodox Jews. What were many of these "third generation Orthodox" like? One careful observer described them in these terms:

> The data from a number of community surveys suggest that many first generation American Jews who identified themselves as Orthodox in the past were not observant of Jewish law in their personal lives; they certainly didn't observe the law in accordance with Orthodox criteria. They may have identified themselves as Orthodox out of sympathy with Jewish tradition, for familial or social reasons, out of their affection for an Orthodox rabbi, or for any other number of reasons. This is much less true of second, probably even less true of third generation Orthodox Jews in America. Whereas fewer Jews identify with Orthodoxy today (1979), those who do so are far more committed to its norms. I don't mean to suggest that Orthodoxy's numerical decline is attributable solely to the decline in the number of non-observant Orthodox; but this is certainly an important factor. *I'm not sure whether it was the move to the right which led the non-observant Orthodox to feel increasingly uncomfortable, or whether their numerical decline opened the way for Orthodoxy to move to the right. I suspect both processes took place.*[58]

Yet, there appears to be little doubt that the Orthodox "move to the right" also coincided with the changing *zeitgeist* in the world, in America, and in Israel, as well. Liberalism was in decline, and neo-conservatism and right-wing politics were in the ascendancy by the mid-1970s. Orthodoxies of many sorts had come into a new vogue: in Christianity, the "evangelicals" were gaining favor over the "ecumenicals"; in Israel, the Orthodox rabbinate was increasingly seen to be *the* authority, *par excellence,* and *world-wide,* in matters of Jewish faith and religious practice; in Islam, too, there was a universal resurgence of Koranic authority. And Roman Catholics in the 1980s, under Pope John Paul II, were not subject to the liberalizing tendencies which had prevailed only twenty years earlier in the Church of Pope John XXIII.

In the world of American Orthodoxy, in addition, relative affluence had allowed many day school graduates to spend their late teens and early twenties in a traditional yeshiva, where they engaged in Talmudic and rabbinical studies. As Charles Liebman attested: "Such young people are isolated from the rhythms and routines of life that tend to shake the foundations of a strictly Orthodox outlook. They become more thoroughly socialized to the 'rightist' orientation which characterizes the Yeshiva world. When they leave the Yeshiva, they influence others within the Orthodox community; particularly since the superior knowledge obtained in Yeshiva provides them with status."[59] A related phenomenon—the several thousands of *baalei teshuva* (returnees to Judaism) whom we have previously described, gives added strength to Orthodoxy. They, too, adopt the strictest interpretation of the religious tradition, often discarding the allurements of the drug cult, the radical-left political youth movements, or similar enticements. Like the yeshiva students, they, too, serve to influence both old and young by their total commitment to the full Orthodox style. Though joined together by different backgrounds, both these groups of younger people have an extended outreach to many others: they often serve as an inspiration for emulation that is far more potent than their relatively small numbers might normally suggest.[60]

Indeed, these younger people may well tip the scales for Orthodoxy. Investigators who believe that the number of Orthodox may decline in the near future also believe that the proportion of their young to the old will increase at the same time. This paradox may not be unrelated—at least in part—to the powerful new sense of Jewish identity which is developing among many members of the "baby boom" generation—a generation more open to demonstrative ethnic espousals than the one which preceded it.

Often third or even fourth generation Americans practicing this ethnically powered, non-centrist form of Orthodoxy differ from their older precursors in a major and crucial way: they have learned to compartmentalize their lives into two realms, the sacred and the secular. Actually, many of those who joined Orthodox congregations before the 1950s had found it difficult to accommodate their undifferentiated American secularity to the rigors of Orthodoxy's inwardness and insularity. As a result, as we have seen, they either left Orthodoxy, or had invented "modern," or centrist, Orthodoxy. These more recent, latter-day traditionalists, who were born for the most part after World War II, have adopted a different stance. It is based on their novel, dualistic approach: when it comes to their private religious preference, they rule out "America"—and its culture—as irrelevant. They act on the principle that one's Jewish religious practices need not be in harmony with, nor accommodate to, the demands of society, science, or the reigning culture of the day. They are thus willing to accommodate to their time and place in all other realms, save the religious. For them, Jewish religious law is divine, and it is regarded as unchanging, and universally applicable, in time and space. This view was undoubtedly the product not only of new pride in, or knowledge of, their religious traditions, but the beneficiary of the new ethnicity: they could now assert their religious preferences by means of a fiercely loyal and uncomplicated Jewishness. They had an "ethnic right"—in the new ethnic America—to religious exoticism. In a word: in ways not always clear to themselves or their spokesmen—their revitalized Jewishness was retraditionalizing their Judaism.

As a result, they turned away from the centrist, less ethnic position of earlier leaders like Samuel Belkin, denying their claim that true Orthodoxy can be made "modern," or that it regard "integration into American life" as a prime spiritual goal, in order to capture the hearts of American Jews. In support of their rigid commitments to ancient Jewish law, they point to the fact that for purposes as diluted as those of "modern Orthodoxy," there are the Conservative or Reform movements, which "less authentic" Jews are free to choose; at their own peril, of course. Ironically, however, their triumphalist position—that only Orthodoxy is *truly Jewish*—since it is non-accommodating, also appealed to some members of Conservative and Reform congregations, thus affording this fervent style of Orthodoxy, spawned since the 1960s, much more weight than its numbers would suggest. As noted earlier, many non-Orthodox, whose *new* Jewish identity was rooted in similar "compartmentalist" views, were probably influenced—wittingly or not—by these bold and new attitudes of those younger than they, some of whom were even their own children. All were products of the validity of "genuine self-expression" accorded them by the "new ethnicity."[61]

Indeed, one study of the Conservative movement in 1979 suggested that there had already been a gain in members for Orthodox congregations, as a result of a small outflow of their members who had opted for Orthodoxy. The same report also projected a possible decline in membership in Conservative congregations in the coming decades. It further speculated that the larger number of its less traditional members could move over to Reform—or even cease to affiliate with any synagogue—while its smaller, more right-wing component might leave in order to join Orthodox congregations. "If that prediction proves accurate," an Orthodox sociologist announced, "it may realign the denominational patterns of American Judaism in such a way that eventually, Reform could become the largest branch; Orthodox, the second largest; the Conservative, the smallest."[62] Yet, such a suggestion may be gratuitous: Conservatism was still alive and widely pervasive in America. Despite Orthodoxy's increasingly high profile, the enthusiasm of its supporters, the multiplication of its institutions, and the support it received from its "establishment" in Israel, its actual membership had not increased by the 1980s.[63]

What must be emphatically added, as well, is that the spirit of "right-wing Judaism" had overtaken only the three established denominational institutions—the synagogues and the temples. Less visible to the eye, but powerful and ever present, nevertheless, are the dominant life-motifs of the largest majority of American Jews. They may not call themselves "Reconstructionists"—certainly, they rarely belong to the handful of Reconstructionist congregations that do exist. But they are indeed practicing what may be called "Civil Judaism," spurred by that self-same "new ethnicity" we have already described. "Civil Judaism" is nondenominational and cuts across the lines of many Jewish institutions and even synagogues, and in its basic spirit, if not in precise ideological terms, it is closely akin to Reconstructionism. It might be argued that for all practical purposes most members of Conservative and Reform congregations—and some, even within Orthodox synagogues—are also "civil Judaists."

Yet, if you asked the average American Jew, what "Civil Judaism" is, he would probably retort that he had never heard of it. But many Jews are living within its shelter, even though they may belong to one of the three major denominations or to none of them. What have all these "civil Judaists" in common, and why is their lifestyle, at base, the truest common denominator of what most American Jews believe or practice in these last decades of the century?

It was only in the 1980s that the idea of a "civil Judaism" began to attract the attention of students of Jewish life. When we set down the attributes of this "form" of Jewish belief and behavior—and these can only be examined by means of empirical behavioral studies—we come close to viewing Jewish religion in America as Mordecai Kaplan had been describing and advocating it. The most succinct statement of the core beliefs of this "civil Jewish faith" appeared in 1981. It lists the following fundamentals:

1. "A commitment to Jewish group survival as a 'sacred' value and a validation of Jewish existence as the fulfillment of a 'mission' or 'destiny' which calls for the exemplification by Jews of the ethical values of responsibility, justice, and compassion."

2. "Civil Judaism" more specifically affirms eight major tenets:

   a. "The unity and distinctiveness of the Jewish people."

   b. "The resultant responsibility of each Jew and of the Jewish community collectively for the security and welfare of all Jews."

   c. "The centrality of the State of Israel as symbol of this unity and mutual responsibility."

   d. "The enduring value of the Jewish tradition and the importance of its perpetuation."

   e. "The persistence of threats (both internal and external) to the survival of the Jewish people and tradition."

   f. "*Tzedakah,* understood both as philanthropy and more broadly as action on behalf of social justice and welfare, as a primary mandate of the Jewish value system."

   g. "The virtue of active participation in the broader society and the compatibility of such participation with 'good Jewishness.'"

h. "Theological pluralism: the relative insignificance of classical theological concerns and the affirmation of individual conscience as the ultimate arbiter in matters of religious practice, belief, and lifestyle."

Arching above all of these concerns is "the deep feeling of Jewish community—of a unity of destiny and experience which binds Jews together at a level beyond" their personal or social differentiations. Central to the "mysticism" of Civil Judaism is the State of Israel as the positive symbol of the myth of death and rebirth; this idea lies at the heart of contemporary Jewish self-understanding in North America. "What American 'civil' Jews support so vigorously is a mythically potent Israel . . . which . . . acquires its powerful hold on the attentions of these Jews, by virtue of a myth and meaning system which transcends its own reality . . . though the 'real' Israel may not correspond precisely to its (mythic) image among American Jews."[64] Virtually all these factors helped to reinforce the new *group-conscious* Jewish identity in ways that were almost completely absent from the American Jewish scene, prior to the onset of the 1970s and the rise of "status politics" in America.

Indeed, many observers claim that apart from the very small minority of fully observant Orthodox Jews, there is a single American Judaism today. Nevertheless, despite their many similarities in the private and personal religious practice of their adherents, the inevitable growth of denominationalism has served to sharpen their self-awareness and to make the distance separating them artificial but nonetheless real. In this respect, denominationalism has intensified institutional loyalties and rivalries too often confused with a religious ideology. The time may yet come, however, when out of the present welter of competing religious institutions a further deepening of religious loyalty may develop. Judaism has never feared diversity in religious expression. But this was so because, cutting through the varieties of religious expressions, there was a basic common denominator, a unity founded on supreme cultural and religious literacy.

The danger in America arises out of the fact that there still exists a common lack of knowledge of the history, development, and meaning of Judaism even among many of those who are in the synagogue today. This is the special challenge that faces the American rabbi—a challenge his historical predecessors hardly knew. But the rabbi, too, is different in America.

NOTES

1. See Wilhelm Pauck, "Our Protestant Heritage" in *Religion and Contemporary Society*, Harold Stahmer, ed. (New York: Macmillan Paperbacks, 1963), pp. 110–12.

2. See Stuart E. Rosenberg, "Some Attitudes of Nineteenth-Century Reform Laymen" in *Essays on Jewish Life and Thought* (ed. Blau, Friedman, Hertzberg, Mendelsohn) (New York: Columbia University Press, 1959), pp. 411–421.

3. Quoted in David Philipson, *The Reform Movement in Judaism* (New York: Macmillan, 1907), pp. 462–463.

4. Quoted in Stuart E. Rosenberg, *A Time to Speak* (New York: Bloch Publishing Co.), p. 53.

5. *Ibid.*

6. *Ibid.*, p. 54.

7. *Ibid.*, p. 55.

8. See Stuart E. Rosenberg, "The Jewish Tidings and the Sunday Services Question," in *Publication of the American Jewish Historical Society*, Vol. XLII, No. 4 June, 1953, pp. 372–383.

9. Quoted in Stuart E. Rosenberg, *A Time to Speak* (New York: Bloch Publishing Co., 1960), p. 65.

10. Jakob J. Petuchowski, "The Limits of 'People-Centered' Judaism," in *Commentary*, May, 1959, p. 389.

11. *Ibid.*

12. Mordecai M. Kaplan, *Judaism As a Civilization* (New York: Macmillan, 1935), p. 124.

13. *Ibid.*

14. In his autobiography Dr. Wise writes with a tinge of great regret: "Twice the presidency was offered to . . . Dr. Mordecai M. Kaplan, one of the finest creative minds of the American Jewish community. The institute had very good reason that the offer would be accepted. But for reasons that had never quite come to light, Professor Kaplan, after a long and trying period, including weeks and even months of indecision, appeared to find it impossible to accept." See Stephen Wise, *Challenging Years* (New York: G. P. Putnam's Sons, 1949), p. 136.

15. See I. Edward Kiev and John J. Tepfer, "Jewish Institute of Religion" in *American Jewish Year Book* (Philadelphia: The Jewish Publication Society of America, Vol. 49, 1947–1948), p. 92.

16. See Theodore I. Linn and Associates, *Rabbi and Synagogue in Reform Judaism* (New York: Central Conference of American Rabbis, 1972) pp. 395, 400.

17. Louis Ginzberg, *Students, Scholars and Saints* (Philadelphia: Jewish Publication Society of America, 1928), pp. 206–207.

18. Solomon Schechter, *Aspects of Rabbinic Theology* (New York: Schocken Books, 1961), p. 12.

19. Quoted by Salo W. Baron, *A Social and Religious History of the Jews* (New York: Columbia University Press, 1937), Vol. II, p. 254.

20. For a fuller description of the way in which "Historical Judaism" unwittingly emerged into Conservative Judaism, see Moshe Davis, *The Emergence of Conservative Judaism* (Philadelphia: The Jewish Publication Society of America, 1963).

21. *Jewish Theological Seminary Students Annual* (New York: 1914), p. 17.

22. From his address at the Founding Convention of the United Synagogue of America, in 1913.

23. Solomon Schechter, *Seminary Addresses* (New York: Burning Bush Press, 1959), pp. 48–49.

24. *Report of Proceedings of Annual Meetings*, United Synagogue of America (New York: 1915), p. 19.

25. Arthur A. Cohen, *Anatomy of Faith* (New York: Harcourt, Brace & Co., 1960), pp. 37–39. Used by permission.

26. Mordecai M. Kaplan. "The Rabbinical Assembly at the Crossroads," in *Conservative Judaism*, April, 1946, Vol. 2, No. 3, pp. 1–6, Used by permission.

27. Describing its own metamorphosis, *The Reconstructionist* (May 17, 1963, p. 25) recalls: "As is well known, for many years Reconstructionism was regarded by its leaders, its followers and its critics as a 'school of thought.' . . . Since 1959, however, when Dr. [Ira] Eisenstein took over the leadership of the [Reconstructionist] Foundation, he has been pressing for the adoption of a more active type of program, including the establishment of agencies and institutions which would embody the ideas and concepts of the movement . . . those identified with Reconstructionism are now convinced that if the philosophy and program of Reconstructionism is to have a fair hearing by American Jewry, they will have to be translated into the kind of terms which will render them part of an actual *movement*."

For a penetrating critique of what the author calls the partial "failure" of Reconstructionism as a living movement, or denomination, see Charles S. Liebman, "Reconstructionism in American Jewish Life," in *American Jewish Year Book* (1970) (Philadelphia: Jewish Publication Society of America) pp. 3–99, but especially pp. 57 ff.

28. Marshall Sklare, "Recent Development in Conservative Judaism," in *Midstream*, January, 1972, p. 10.

29. Anne Lapidus Lerner, *Who Hast Not Made Me a Man*, reprinted from the *American Jewish Year Book* (1977), American Jewish Committee, New York, 1982, p. 6. See also Susannah Heschel, (ed.), *On Being a Jewish Feminist*, Schocken Books, New York, 1983.

30. Lerner, *op. cit.* p. 6.

31. See his "The Ordination of Women," in *Midstream*, August/September, 1980, p. 31.

31(a) "Message from the Chancellor," in *Seminary Progress*, Vol. 28 No. 1, November, 1983, p. 1.

31(b) By early 1984, however, a small group of Conservative rabbis had banded together—virtually as "a movement within a movement"—to challenge this crucial decision of their own Alma Mater. In their broadside, addressed to their own colleagues in the Rabbinical Assembly—and to laymen as well—they denominated themselves as the "Union for Traditional Conservative Judaism . . . in the spirit of Solomon Schechter." They announced "the formation of a new organization in the Conservative Movement dedicated to the traditional ideas on which the movement was founded . . . If you believe that Conservative Judaism should remain true to its historic mission . . . then you are not alone . . . join us . . . build for the future."

It remains to be seen whether such open activism on the part of the Movement's small right-wing would succeed in achieving its stated goal "to bring Kashrut observance, Shabbat observance, the traditional liturgy, Torah study . . . back to the centerstage of Conservative Judaism"—without seriously dividing the Movement, or causing this vocal minority to read itself out of Conservatism altogether. Any one of these possibilities could have far-reaching effects on the vital balances that had maintained the "Conservative coalition" for so many decades.

32. See Uriah Z. Engelman, "Jewish Education," in *American Jewish Year Book* (Philadelphia: Jewish Publication Society of America, 1960), Vol. 61, pp. 127–149; for 1962 statistics as reported by the American Association for Jewish Education, see *Community News Reporter* (Jewish Telegraphic Agency), Sept. 13, 1962.

33. Emanuel Rackman, "American Orthodoxy," in *Jewish Life in America* (ed. T. Friedman and R. Gordis) (New York: Horizon Press, 1955), p. 33.

34. Rev. Samuel Isaacs, Editor of the *Jewish Messenger,* describing Orthodoxy in America in his journal of March 13, 1857.

35. For an intriguing study of this phenomenon, as it relates to young American Jews who went to Israel, and "return" to Judaism as "*baalei teshuva,*" see Janet Aviad, *Return to Judaism: Religious Renewal in Israel,* University of Chicago Press, Chicago, 1983.

36. Emanuel Rackman, "What Is Orthodox Judaism?" in *Jewish Heritage,* Vol. 2, No. 3, Winter, 1959–60, p. 5.

37. Samuel Belkin, *Essays in Traditional Jewish Thought* (New York: Philosophical Library, 1956), pp. 36–70 *passim.* Used by permission.

38. *Ibid.,* p. 43.

39. *Ibid.,* p. 59.

40. See Alvin I. Schiff, in *Jewish Education,* Spring, 1977, pp. 14ff; also his data in *Jewish Education,* Summer, 1980, pp. 5 ff. See also *American Jewish Year Book* (1983) p. 73.

41. See Jacob L. Harstein, "Yeshiva University: Growth of Rabbi Isaac Elchanan Theological Seminary," in *American Jewish Year Book,* Vol. 48, 1946–1947 (Philadelphia: The Jewish Publication Society of America, 1946), pp. 73–84.

42. Moshe Davis, "Jewish Religious Life and Institutions in America" in *The Jews* (ed. Louis Finkelstein) (New York: Harper, 1949), Vol. I, p. 391.

43. Jacob L. Hartstein, *op. cit.,* p. 84.

44. See Samson Benderley, "Jewish Education in America," in *Jewish Education,* Summer, 1949, Vol. 20, p. 81.

45. Sixty-eight per cent of community leaders across the country were of the opinion, as recently as 1959, that a Jewish day school was not in the best interests of America, or its Jews, because it was divisive, insular, and parochial. See Alexander Dushkin and Uriah Engelman, *Jewish Education in the United States,* American Association for Jewish Education, New York, p. 29.

46. Daniel Elazar, *Community and Polity: The Organizational Dynamics of American Jewry,* Jewish Publication Society, Philadelphia, 1973, pp. 71–73; 403. Compare with Charles Liebman, who, writing in 1979, suggested that fully-observant Orthodox Jews may actually number as few as 175,000—about 3 per cent of the Jewish population. See his "Orthodox Judaism Today," in *Midstream,* Aug.–Sept. 1970, p. 20.

47. *The Wall Street Journal,* April 8, 1963. The article reports: "About 2,000 products of more than 400 companies are now turned out . . . under the supervision of the Union of Orthodox Jewish Congregations. This compares with only 1,000 products and 225 companies four years ago. . . . Food items certified as Kosher by the Union range from Heinz soup to Carlton House nuts, from Milady's blintzes and Mother's gefilte fish to Hung's mushroom chow mein and Original Kosher Krispy Pizza."

48. *Ibid., The Wall Street Journal,* April 8, 1963.

49. *Ibid.*, Richard Jacobs, vice-president of Joseph Jacobs Organization, a marketing consultant firm that specializes in Kosher food products.

But if "matzo balls replace pizza," Italian marinara sauce may yet replace "old-fashioned horse-radish"—which *used* to accompany *gefilte fish!* An advertisement in Jewish periodicals (see, for example, *United Synagogue Review,* Summer, 1963, p. 28) beckons Jewish readers to try:

"Italian 'Chrain' [Yiddish for Horse-Radish]

"What has Buitoni done to gefilte fish?

"Nothing, except to provide you with a unique and delicious alternative to old-fashioned horse-radish: Buitoni Marinara Sauce. This zesty and tangy Italian 'sauce of the sea' brings out all the subtle flavors of gefilte fish. And it never makes your eyes water! . . . *Everyone will love this perfect alliance between full-bodied Italian sauce and the traditional favorite.*

"You can serve this delicious change-of-pace sauce . . . with peace of mind. Buitoni Marinara is Ⓤ Kosher and Pareve. . . ." (Italics added.)

50. In an interesting study of "Emerging Culture Patterns in American Jewish Life," Abraham G. Duker makes the following observations about the way in which food reflects trends of "Jewish acculturation and deculturation":

In many places the kosher restaurant is being replaced by the "Jewish style" or "kosher style" restaurant. There is also ample evidence of transculturation in this area. Just as spaghetti has become part and parcel of the menus of many American restaurants, dishes like borsht, potato pancakes, and blintzes are served in general restaurants in the larger cities, signifying the Jewish contribution to the general American cuisine as well as the numerical weight of the Jewish middle and upper classes. The Passover season presents a most interesting period in observance and semi-observance, with cafeterias and restaurants in New York serving both Matzah and bread as well as non-kosher dishes in Passover style. . . . Interestingly enough, delicatessen of the type which is considered as being typically Jewish food, can serve as a good example of American acculturation. Delicatessen was comparatively unknown in the East European milieu. In this country, Jews adopted it from the Germans in such a thorough fashion that it became identified as a Jewish dietary component. . . . More bizarre adaptations showing strong acculturation influences are the use of "Kosher Bacon," the common term used for "beef frye," parts of beef resembling bacon in appearance and as some would have it also in taste. The kosher Chinese noodles also belong in this category.

As evidence of the indiscriminate intermixing of both kosher and non-kosher foods in the "Jewish-style" restaurant, Duker describes the menu of a Cleveland restaurant, dated June 10, 1949:

Not only do "Stuffed Kishke," "Shrimp Cocktail," "Chopped Liver," "Gefilte Fish," "Pickled Herring," and "Creamed Herring" appear on the menu among the apppetizers with Baked Virginia Ham Sandwich and Kosher Corned Beef Sandwich on the sandwich list, but there is also a special *Kosher Korner* in which the following dishes are listed: "Cottage Cheese and Sour Cream; 2 Cheese Blintzes with Sour Cream; Chopped Liver w. Potato Salad; Corned Beef and Eggs; Assorted Cold Cuts with Potato Salad & Sliced Tomato." The reader will note not only the mixture of kosher and non-kosher meats, but also the indiscriminate combination of meat and dairy dishes in *Kosher Korner.*

See Duker's essay in *Publication of the American Jewish Historical Society,* No. 39, Part 4, June 1950, pp. 376–378. Used by permission.

50a. The report was offered by the president of the American Federation of Retail Kosher Butchers and quoted in the *New York Times* May 30, 1984, p. 15.

51. Joseph H. Lookstein, "The Modern American Yeshivah," in *Jewish Education*, Vol. 16, May 1945, p. 13.

52. See David Singer, "The Growth of the Day School Movement," *Commentary*, August, 1973, pp. 53–57.

53. Emanuel Rackman, "From Synagogue Toward Yeshiva," in *Commentary*, April, 1956, p. 356.

54. Rabbi Menachem M. Schneerson, "An Orthodox Rabbi's Plea for Parochial School Aid," in *The Commonweal*, September 28, 1962.

55. Joseph Kaminetsky, "Evaluating the Program and Effectiveness of the All-Day Jewish School," in *Jewish Education*, Winter, 1956, Vol. 27, No. 2, p. 48.

56. For an interesting treatment of these groups see Charles S. Liebman, "A Sociological Analysis of Contemporary Orthodoxy," in *Judaism*, Summer 1964, pp. 285–304.

57. For interesting social studies of these groups see: Israel Rubin, Satmar, *An Island in the City*, Quadrangle Books, Chicago, 1973; William Shaffir, *Life In a Religious Community*, Holt, Rinehart, Winston, Toronto, 1974; George Kranzler, *Williamsburg: A Jewish Community in Transition*, Philipp Feldheim, New York, 1961; Solomon Poll, *The Hasidic Community of Williamsburg*, Free Press, Glencoe, 1962; Herbert Weiner *9½ Mystics*, Holt, Rinehart, Winston, New York, 1969.

58. Charles Liebman, "Orthodox Judaism Today," in *Midstream*, August-September, 1979, p. 20.

59. *Idem.* p. 21.

60. See Janet Aviad, *op. cit.*

61. Chaim Waxman, "The Fourth Generation Grows Up: The Contemporary American Jewish Community," in *Annals of the American Academy of Political and Social Science*, March, 1981, pp. 82–3. Waxman refers to a controversial study by Charles S. Liebman and Saul Shapiro, presented to The Convention of the United Synagogue of America, (1979): *A Survey of the Conservative Movement and Some of Its Religious Attitudes.* It must also be noted in this connection that the older phenomenon of Orthodox congregations "converting" to Conservative, had slowed down, but had still not completely abated by the early 1980s.

62. Harold S. Himmelfarb, "Patterns of Assimilation—Identification Among American Jews," *Ethnicity*, September, 1979, pp. 249–67.

63. Jonathan S. Woocher, "The 'Civil Judaism' of Communal Leaders," *American Jewish Year Book: 1981* (Vol. 81) Jewish Publication Society, Philadelphia, 1981, pp. 149–169; but especially pp. 149; 168–9.

CHAPTER XI

The Rabbi: Past and Present

RABBI MEANS TEACHER, AND THE VERY FIRST RABBIS WERE JUST THAT. Today, the rabbi lives in a different world, controlled by a new range of circumstances and environmental conditions.

Is he still a teacher? In what ways has he met the challenge of the American religious milieu? How has he adapted his functions to the changing structure and the new demands of Jewish religious life in the new world?

First, however, a look at his historical predecessors and antecedents. The ancient rabbis were essentially lay scholars and not the spiritual leaders of specific congregations and synagogues, as in our day. It was in the schools that they forged and shaped the moral, religious, and cultural content of Judaism, and their remarkable contribution is still regarded in observant Jewish circles as the authoritative way of Jewish religious life. The Talmud, the repository of their spiritual labors, still remains the fundamental and classical work of post-Biblical Judaism, and contemporary students training for the rabbinate must seek to master it in order to qualify for ordination.

The history of rabbinical ordination goes back to the period before the beginnings of Christianity, when it was the custom of each master of the Law to authorize his own students to teach publicly, by laying his hands upon them. Through this visual ceremony rabbis were granted the modern equivalent of a diploma: a transference of pedagogical authority from master to pupil. The rabbi was ordained by his teachers, but ordained by them to be as one of them: a teacher of adults.

If the modern rabbi, unlike the Talmudic sage, sometimes seems more like an institutionalized, parochial cleric than a free-ranging, scholarly philosopher of religion or teacher of ethics, it is because he has been "clericalized" by the force of historical circumstances. As Jews came to live in a Christian society, they tended to reflect something of the sociology of parish life. And not only in the last few generations; the process had begun as early as the Middle Ages.

While the world of the medieval rabbi was not quite the same as his modern successors, neither was it any longer like that of his ancient predecessors. He was no longer the "scholar-king" of the Jewish community, as was his Talmudic counterpart, nor did he enjoy the uncritical, universal understanding and support of the community. Already sprouting in his world were the seeds of a future secularistic democracy, and there were the beginnings of the "rabbi-as-civil-servant," controlled by a community bureaucracy intent on its own lay dominion. When rabbis were laymen, as were the earliest, no division of life into ecclesiastical and secular spheres was possible. Inevitably, once rabbis were clericalized, made into professional religionists, they were ranged against the leadership of those who claimed higher power than the scholars: their lay electors.

What was the world of the medieval rabbi like? A glimpse of his universe may help explain some of the insoluble, frustrating dilemmas of the modern rabbi, who must often play the part of a clergyman while recognizing that a rabbi should essentially be a teacher.

The rapid migration of Jews in western Europe in the fourteenth and fifteenth centuries caused great confusion within the Jewish community. Little long-range community planning could be carried out under such circumstances. The effect of the Black Death upon the Jewish community was long lasting; many communities were impoverished and destroyed, town development was curtailed, group and family relationships broken up. Thus, leadership was difficult to come by.

Harassed by this anarchical state of affairs, the rabbis of this period felt obliged to assist those communities in extreme need of spiritual leadership by helping them to make a proper choice of their religious leaders. This set in motion, for the first time in Jewish history, the institution of what may be called a rabbinical diploma, which certified that the recipient had been examined by a competent rabbinical authority and been found qualified to arrange and supervise complicated matters of marriage and divorce, and authorized, as well, to organize and administer a religious academy *(yeshiva)* for the advanced training of mature scholars. The official title carried by the rabbi in accordance with the wording of the diploma was *Morenu:* "Our Teacher." "Our" referred to the adult community, not to children, for the elementary teaching of the young was undertaken by others, although under the rabbis' supervision.

The demands of rabbinical work became such as not to afford the rabbis ample time to engage in any other occupation. The tradition had to give way to the exigencies of a troubled and difficult time. There was no avoiding this development of a full-time professionalized rabbinate. And it is because of this professionalization that the rabbinate became something it never was before. The rabbi, heretofore the chief lay scholar in a community of lay scholars, became a clergyman.

Beginning with the fourteenth century, the century that first saw the rise of the professional rabbi, the rabbi regularly attended the wedding ceremonies in his community as a religious official, receiving some fee for his services. Before this time, the marriage ceremony was performed either by a member of the bride's or groom's family, close friends, or a distinguished member of the community. To this day, Jewish law makes no requirement that Jewish marriage be performed by a religious official of the community. Yet the requirement at the beginning of the fifteenth century that only the rabbi, or someone delegated by him, might perform the wedding ceremony was enforced as a community enactment and was strictly followed. The absorption of this function into rabbinical prerogative was clearly the result of the beginnings of the assimilation by the rabbi of the functions of the Christian clergy.

In many ways, however, he still retained the unique features of his office and would not effect the role of the Christian clergyman until centuries later, in America. The medieval rabbi was not yet a parish worker; little pastoral visiting was done by him. This function was performed by the laity in general, and in many cases by the lay heads of the community. He still retained his traditional position of teacher and scholar and was, as in earlier times, linked with the school. Nor did the rabbi feel himself attached to any single synagogue in a city possessing more than one. On the Sabbath he would usually worship in the oldest and most respected synagogue of the city. There, he was given a special seat next to the Holy Ark. During the week he seldom visited any synagogue, preferring to pray either at home or in the school with his students, prior to beginning the day's studies.

The rabbi was still not a leader of synagogue ritual, nor was he a liturgical official, as he has become in America. True, he still decided all problems of ritual and liturgy, but he did this as a scholar who was best acquainted with Jewish law and tradition, not in the capacity of a synagogue official. While in the early days of rabbinic professionalization the rabbi did come into closer alignment with the school as its official administrator, he had not yet merged his office with the functions of the synagogue. The medieval community had granted him a new title— "Rosh Yeshiva"—head of the Talmudical academy, but in no real way made him head of the synagogue. The medieval synagogue remained a *communal* institution, controlled in most instances by the lay officialdom of the Jewish community.

Still another area of competence and authority occupied the medieval rabbi's special talents: he was the judge of the community. Jewish law prevailed in all countries of the dispersion, and since legal authority was the basis of the *Morenu* diploma, the rabbi was called upon to exercise his powers of interpretation in both civil and religious law. No situation among Jews that required litigation would be brought to a non-Jewish court. Thus, a variety of problems, ranging from the interpersonal to the commercial, were laid before the rabbi for his decision. It was principally as a result of such a condition that the medieval rabbi, in many ways, was still able to retain his pre-eminence as the authoritative religious leader of the community in spite of the fact that he had become a professional civil servant.

The medieval Jewish world had made him into a civil servant-clergyman. But the modern Jewish community would make the rabbi into something even different—the Jewish counterpart of a Protestant minister. The desire for emancipation caused Jews to seek to assimilate non-Jewish thought and institutions into their religious and communal life. But for such hopes and aspirations the medieval rabbi, like the medieval Jewish community, would never do! They may not have been ready to say what kind of rabbi they really wanted, but the Jewish candidates for emancipation seemed to know very well what kind they did not want. Pointing their fingers at the rabbis they saw around them, their criticism revealed a desire to revamp the style and the structure of their religious institutions, to make them conform to Christian procedures:

> For the welfare of your community you do nothing; you do not teach them the fundamentals of religion, you do not supervise the education of their children. You preach no moral sermons, you do not visit the sick at heart or prepare the dying for repentance. . . . No communal matter ever comes before you; you deal only with the butchers and the cooks, rendering decisions on forbidden foods.[1]

Never before in Jewish history had the laity expected the rabbi to act as pastor and counselor, nor considered it necessary for the rabbi to be a "preacher." Fundamentals of religion were left to the elementary teachers in the Jewish schools. The rabbi was the judge, the scholar, the academic philosopher, and, in the medieval community, an ecclesiast, serving under the control of the autonomous lay council. Now the spirit of emancipation was sweeping across western Europe, and he was to become something new altogether.

Certainly, under this scheme of things a new type of rabbi had to be prepared; the traditionally trained rabbi was not fitted for this new office. Nor was he prepared to shed his traditional prerogatives, as judge and jurist, and submit to a lay-controlled congregation in matters purely religious. Without seminaries to train them, modern rabbis were self-developed during the early decades of the nineteenth century. Yet by the middle of the fourth decade there was a sizable number of rabbis in the West who had received a general education and were personally imbued with the modern spirit. Despite the fact that seminaries of the modern type were not yet in vogue, the number of new-type rabbis slowly increased and they began to exert a more direct influence upon the development of Jewish religious life. It was particularly their competence in fields of general knowledge that helped the rabbis regain their position as the leading spokesmen of their community.

In America, where Jews began life in a state of emancipation, the rabbinate was cast into a modern mold from the start. Even the traditional functions of the traditional rabbi were different, and after several decades here, even the east-European Jews in American came to look for a new type of rabbi. As lower class immigrants who had arrived without the benefit of a general education they came to seek rabbis who would excel their constituents in secular as well as in Jewish knowledge. Since learning—and now secular learning, in particular—was still a mark of status among the Jewish group, this factor inevitably assisted the rabbi in regaining some of the prestige he had lost in Europe, by helping him to become a new kind of leader of the Jewish religious community. In the dogged attempts of many immigrants to achieve rapid Americanization, and particularly in their desire to entice their American-born children to an "American Judaism," the acculturated rabbi served as a key figure. An English-speaking, university-trained Jewish clergyman could lend status to their group and could function as their respected "Minister-at-large" and "Ambassador to the Gentiles."

The rise in America of the modern rabbinical seminary also helped project the rabbi into new community prominence. The schools developed certain standards of theory and practice, which tended to centralize the religious organization of the community. Officially, each congregation and its lay leaders were still supreme, yet, as a result of the central position occupied by the three major seminaries devoted to specific schools of religious thought, at least certain segments of the community were taking the first steps toward a united action that would transcend the limits of localism.

As each of the groups in Jewish religious life, Reform, Conservative, and Orthodox, organized their seminaries, congregations began to turn to them for rabbinical leaders. The seminaries also helped to foster the rise of congregational unions, which, in turn, looked to their spiritual godfathers for inspiration and guidance. Although these congregational unions were ostensibly led by representative laymen, the rabbis of each group were the real motive power behind them. The seminaries also established departments to facilitate the placement of their graduates, and this, too, helped to diminish the power of independent congregational bodies. While the ultimate government of each congregation was still in the hands of the local governing board, the fact that the seminaries represented a source of supply of a recognized type of rabbinical leader helped to strengthen the hands of the rabbinate in general. No longer in isolation, no longer dependent upon the individual congregations for status, to a large extent the rabbi began to regain his pristine position within Jewish life. Although he still remained a congregational official, nevertheless he gained significant sanction and support from his own religious movement, as crystallized and centralized in its seminary.

The seminaries helped to develop the modern functions of the rabbinate, too. By shaping the education of their graduates, and by incorporating in their curriculum courses similar to those taught at theological schools of Christian denominations, they assisted in defining the modern functions of the rabbinical office. More and more, the rabbinate assimilated the role of the Christian clergy. The rabbi, in the modern period, became the pastor, the educator, the preacher, the confidant, the mental healer, the case worker, the psychologist, the administrator, and the public relations man of the Jewish community. With the assumption of those duties, however, he still has not regained his former role, that of judge and lawgiver. (Among the ultra-pious, as well as the *Hasidic* sects, as already noted—where there is no effort to accommodate to Protestant American models—their spiritual leaders still "rule," and remain preeminently what they always were—scholar-judge-saints—no different from their medieval predecessors.)

Yet there are signs on the horizon to indicate some kind of consolidation of rabbinical duties. The new rabbinical duties described above have developed over a period of years when the Jewish community in America had not begun to train specialists in fields other than the rabbinate. Today, social workers within the Jewish community have come into their own. Administrators and fundraising experts are finding their place within the professional Jewish orbit. Trained educators and educational directors are, in many cases, replacing rabbinical leadership.

The ancient rabbis were the lay teachers and guides of the total Jewish community. The modern American rabbi has become but a staff member, albeit "chief of staff" of a private Jewish membership club, the synagogue of the twentieth century. He no longer really "belongs" to the whole community, or even to the "whole" synagogue; he is but the paid official of one denominational group, which is often in serious competition with the "other" synagogues: the rival claimants to religious domination. As a competitive staff head, he is expected to offer better and more efficient service to "his" organization than the other staff heads in the community. Indeed, this is the way in which his effectiveness as a rabbi is often measured.

That the modern rabbi is expected to emulate the pattern of public behavior of the Christian clergy is so apparent that it needs no elaboration here. But in the very nature of a rabbi's calling and training his tasks are essentially scholarly, not ecclesiastical; pedagogical, not liturgical. He is not ordained in the synagogue or by the synagogue, in order to serve the synagogue, as is the case among Christian religious groups. He is called to serve as a "Rabbi in Israel": a teacher of his people, nothing more, but surely nothing less. The greatest of the Jewish prophets, Moses, is still known as *"Moshe Rabbenu,"* not priest, cleric, or ecclesiast, but "Moses, our Teacher." It is in this role that the modern rabbi is least known, perhaps, because most American Jews are no longer willing students of Judaism.

The modern rabbi has inherited some of the institutional frustrations caused by this historical change. In most seminaries, his training still follows the older lines of classical Jewish education. He is required to master materials intended to prepare him to act as communal judge and chief scholar. Indeed, the major emphasis of the curriculum in most Jewish theological schools is upon a scholarly orientation to the biblical and Talmudic literature. His dilemmas and frustrations arise out of the fact that he is now called to serve a Jewish community no longer conversant with these materials on the level of advanced scholarship. He will discover the first day he steps out of the seminary and into his synagogue that his congregants do not require a scholar-educator as much as they need an expert elementary teacher for adults. Most Jewish adults who comprise the membership of his congregation are not part of his scholarly world. Once, the rabbi's functions were geared to lecturing and teaching on a "graduate" level, when in earlier days his constituents lived within a solitary cultural island. Today, when the study of Judaism has become an "optional elective subject," for his people are part of many worlds beyond that of the synagogue alone, he must first seek to teach them the barest, most minimal, elementary subjects. No longer can he take for granted their knowledge of the Hebrew language of the Bible, the Aramaic of the Talmud, their mastery of the medieval philosophers, or their understanding of the theological ideas of Judaism. This may explain why, increasingly, students enrolled at the rabbinical schools at both the Conservative Jewish Theological Seminary of America as well as the Orthodox Yeshiva University are attending these schools for purposes of higher Jewish education—perhaps to teach at American university departments of Jewish studies—rather than to enter the rabbinate in order to serve a Jewish congregation.

The rabbi's dilemma is heightened for still another reason. Like other areas of our society, the modern synagogue has a tendency to be child-centered. Adults can be successfully persuaded to spend much of their spiritual energy in lavishing their attention upon the religious needs of children. While the majority offer lip service to the significance of adult education, only a minority of them seem willing to invest the time and the effort required to make an education program culturally significant. When they do commit themselves to programs of study, it is likely that they will be willing to expend only peripheral and marginal efforts in that direction. As a result, the modern rabbi is forced, if he is to succeed as a teacher, to deal with adults by adopting methods congenial to modern circumstances, even if they were never before undertaken in the Jewish past.

Nor are these academic frustrations the only obstacles to his fulfillment as a Jewish religious leader. Most American rabbis, at least before the 1950s, had come out of family backgrounds that differed greatly from the lifestyle of the congregants they were called upon to serve. Until then, most Conservative and Reform rabbis had been raised in lower-income Orthodox and scholarly families. Their entry into the rabbinate, it was expected, would not only raise their material standard of living, but would also afford them, they hoped, the possibility of retaining and deepening their lifelong habits of Jewish devotion, piety, or their personal delight in the study of Jewish culture. Some, to be sure, were also drawn into the rabbinate more by their loyalty to Jewishness than by their uncritical acceptance of the Judaism that was then being practiced in these congregations. In any case, their strong Jewish attachments were usually the product of homes far less-acculturated than those which made up the membership rosters of their congregations. Since the late 1950s, these earlier characteristics of the Conservative and Reform rabbinate have altered dramatically.[2] Today, almost all of their constituents who were ordained since that time are themselves the products of their own respective denominations. Indeed, there are now even Orthodox rabbis who are children of Conservative or Reform parents, or of parents who had no religious affiliation at all—representing a change of 180 degrees, which the new Jewish identity of more recent years had helped to effect.

In historical perspective, too, not only has the rabbinical calling been reshaped, if not reduced, but the territory of the rabbi's concern has been sharply rolled back. In the ancient community, he was teacher and master of all; in the medieval world he slowly came under community rule, was often made into nothing more than a pawn in the hand of the city's bureaucrats; in our time, his boundaries have been further restricted: he is not even a symbol of *the* synagogue, only of *a* synagogue. As a result, he is identified by others, and inevitably has come to identify himself with only part of a community: the religious part. A new dichotomy thus enters American Jewish life, a dichotomy that has its roots in the medieval world of the rabbi—the religious ranged against the nonreligious, the sacred against the secular. More and more, the rabbi has been forced into becoming an official protagonist of the synagogue, as if the synagogue were a thing apart from the community.

The modern American rabbi may impart the traditions of the Talmudic rabbis, yet he knows that although he bears their title, he cannot be like them. The world of the ancient rabbis has passed, and can never return. And this, because the medieval rabbi was made into a professional clergyman—something Hillel and Akiba were not. Little wonder, then, that the modern rabbi cannot even be like his medieval colleagues. In America today, he is expected to be just like his Protestant and Catholic counterparts. And if Hollywood's outspoken voice is an indication of the real but unspoken desires of many Americans, all three are expected—if they are to be successful in their congregants' eyes—to measure up to a new description. Who, in fact, is the successful American minister? "He's a first name kind of guy. . . . He's everybody's kind of guy. . . . He's a lovin' kind of guy. . . . He's God's kind of guy. . . . He plays baseball with kids."[3]

Indeed, it has been maintained, that despite the multiplicity of community roles which the American rabbi had earlier assumed, by the 1960s, he was no longer a leader, for he had been unceremoniously dropped out of the power structure of American Jewry and virtually left out of the decision making process. Rabbis, one careful researcher commented, were still being "consulted out of deference to their position and stature, and with the knowledge that their cooperation (was) necessary for the execution of many policies, but we seriously doubt whether a lay leader would relinquish his own vital interests or change well-established community policy on the advice of a rabbi."[4] An even stronger description of the low estate to which the rabbinate had fallen by that decade, was offered by another scholar, an astute observer of the religious scene. Documenting the precipitous rabbinical descent then clearly discernible, he wrote: "Formerly judge, administrator, holy man, scholar, and saint, as time passed these roles and tasks passed into the hands of others, better equipped for them because of community position, economic power, and public acceptance. The rabbi was left to preside at circumcisions, weddings and funerals, to 'conduct' religious worship, which in traditional synagogues, meant to announce pages and tell people when to stand up and sit down, to counsel the troubled and others marginal to the life of the community, and to teach the children; in all, a slightly ridiculous figure, a medicine man made obsolete by penicillin."[5]

All of which opens up a series of grave issues which seriously call into question the future calibre of the American rabbinate. Unlike the hard economic times of earlier generations, when rabbis, like many of their professional congregants, had minuscule incomes, the lowest beginning salary for recent rabbinical graduates now ranges upwards from $30,000 per annum. (Academics are now paid far less than most novice American rabbis.) More to the point: until the 1950s, stringent occupational limitations had faced even the brightest Jewish students, effectively debarring them from the higher echelons of business and finance, and closing them out altogether from many of the free professions in both the arts and sciences. Today, on the other hand, the American scene is fairly dotted with bright and youthful Jewish achievers of many kinds: from university presidents to bank presidents; Jewish scientists, politicians, financiers, entrepreneurs, artists, writers, and high technologists abound. None of these need any longer struggle to be seen, heard or heeded.

In new circumstances such as these, it became highly questionable whether rabbinical schools and seminaries could attract the best of the Jewish students—those who could truly become outstanding leaders in the world of arts or sciences, if they so chose. A new and fairly startling question arose: Would the American rabbinate become merely a nesting ground for the second best—for those possessing a "civil-service mentality," who would merely seek sinecures, holding down "respectable jobs" as "respectable religious bureaucrats"? Or would some of the by-products of the new Jewish identity serve as a counterweight to all of this. After all, by the 1980s, rabbis were beginning to serve congregations in whose midst there were thousands of new-style Jews. Many of these had, by then, benefitted from intensive day school education themselves. Others also had the valuable opportunity of having studied Judaism as part of their American university training—as we shall soon see. Still others were involved in serious study-encounters as part of a host of Jewish-Christian dialogue groups across the country. As a result of these and other more spiritual exposures to Judaism, they were able to see their rabbis in a much different light than was the case with their own parents or grandparents, who had needed surrogates to "live out" the Judaism which they never knew or had forgotten. The younger synagogue members, beginning with the 1980s, no longer needed rabbis, as did their parents, to serve as their "ambassadors" or religious spokesmen. Thanks largely to their own revitalized Jewish identity, intellectuality was beginning to be given its long-neglected place of honor and significance within congregational life, almost for the first time in America.[6]

The rabbis of such "new Jews" could only benefit from these changed and welcome circumstances. They may not become saints again—or even judges—as once they were. But there is new hope that they may yet recapture another central feature of their historic role: they may once again become Jewish *scholars*—understood, and even respected by their congregants for that *Jewish achievement* alone!

NOTES

1. M. A. Ginzburg, *Ha-Moriah* (A collection of essays in Hebrew), (Warsaw, 1878), p. 46.

2. See Charles S. Liebman, "The Training of American Rabbis," *American Jewish Year Book*, Vol. 69, 1968, (Philadelphia: The Jewish Publications Society, 1968) pp. 3–112.

3. From the national advertisements for the movie *A Man Called Peter,* based

on the book by Catherine Marshall describing the life and work of her husband, the late Rev. Dr. Peter Marshall.

4. Kenneth D. Roseman, "Power in a Midwestern Jewish Community," *American Jewish Archives*, XXI, No. 1 (April, 1969), pp. 81–82.

5. Jacob Neusner, *American Judaism: Adventure in Modernity*, (Englewood Cliffs, N.J., Prentice Hall, 1972), p. 39.

6. See my *The Real Jewish World: A Rabbi's Second Thoughts*, (New York: Philosophical Library, 1984) pp. 61–225.

PART FIVE

The American Jewish Way: Its Influence and Future

CHAPTER 12

Canadian Jews and Their American Cousins

Is the style of American Jewish life an aberration, without serious effect upon Jewish history and its future, merely a short-run phenomenon without influence upon other Jewries? Or does it serve as a model and paradigm other post-emancipation liberated Jewish communities can follow, and upon which they can base, *mutatis mutandis,* their own accommodations to modernity?

Many writers and scholars, when discussing the spread of American Jewish influence beyond its country's borders, inevitably point to Israel as a prime example of a free "cultural exchange": Hebraic culture in the homeland flows westward and fructifies Jewish life in America, while lifestyles and cultural patterns that have been "made in America" are exported to, or at least, appropriated in, Jersualem. Depending on the critic's point of view most of the "culture" from America that has been adopted by Israelis is either "very good" or "very bad" for them. The range of American influence is extremely wide: it runs from films and television, fashions and foods, and styles of leisure-time activity to the courses, curriculum, as well as the architecture of Israeli universities—not to mention the increasing "dollarization" of their economy, the "anglicization" of their language and literature, or the "coca-colaization" of their social and cultural expectations. To be sure, as a consequence of massive American political and economic aid to Israel since 1967, the latter often appears, in the eyes of some, to have become a satellite, if not a colony, of the United States.

Yet, all of these examples, in addition to many more that could be catalogued, are actually aspects and reflections of *American* life and culture which can also be found to have penetrated other—near or remote—parts of the world, not excluding the Far East. The issue which concerns us here is whether American *Jewish life and culture* serves as an influence in the life of Israel? To this question, the answer, in broad and general terms, would have to be in the negative. Indeed, Israeli religious and cultural leaders object strenuously to some of the accommodations American Jews have made to their non-Jewish environment, both in their religious and cultural styles. Predictably, these are regarded as clear examples of the way in which the diaspora—even the American dias-

[233]

pora—acts as a corrosive agent, eating away at "Jewish values," and leading to assimilation. American Jews, they contend, display the same signs of religious defensiveness as did the German Jews in the nineteenth century, who, in the popular Israeli view, distorted Jewish life by their "reforms." These Israelis react almost reflexively, falling back on their own stereotyped formula: what may seem good for Jewish religious and cultural life in America serves Israel in inverse proportion to the "benefits" these may appear to confer here or elsewhere.

If, therefore, one wants to examine the pervasiveness of "American-style" Judaism, it stands to reason that he look closer to home. Yet, if he surveys Jewish life in the western hemisphere, there is only one notable example he can find. Central and South American Jewries are still essentially European in their outlook and structures, despite the fact that they have resided in the new world in large numbers for more than half a century. On the northern doorstep of the United States there is a Jewish community—younger and often closer to the European experience than American Jews—yet one that does provide an answer to the question: how pervasive and influential is the Judaism that has grown up in America? Can it be successfully reproduced elsewhere in the free Jewish world?

The Canadian Jewish entity, while relatively small when contrasted to the Jewish population of the United States, *is* a sizable community by world standards, and does possess historical patterns that can illuminate the questions raised. It is of benefit to examine the growth and development of Canadian Jewry, however briefly, for this neighboring Jewish community often acts as a "mirror image" of American Jews, and reflects both their strengths and weaknesses in ways that can shed new and useful light on the meaning of, and the receptivity to, the American Jewish experience.

As a community, Canadian Jewry is essentially a twentieth-century phenomenon. In 1959, Jews were celebrating the 200th anniversary of their continuous settlement in the country, but in effect, as a developed and cohesive group, they are really a post-World War II community. Indeed, about 40 out of every 100 of its present members were not born in Canada, and half of these arrived after 1945. Compared to the American Jewish population, Canada's Jews show a very strong component of recent immigrants: more than twice the percentage—close to forty per cent in Canada, compared to probably less than twenty per cent in the United States.[1]

As the century opened, about 15,000 Jews were scattered across the country—a land area representing the world's second largest nation state. A few years later, in the early 1900s, pogroms in eastern Europe were responsible for creating an expanding Canadian Jewish community, which, by 1914, numbered over 100,000 souls—a sevenfold increase in fifteen short years. To appreciate these new dynamics, one must note that just 35 years later, even this number had doubled, and in the few decades since 1950, the Jewish population again grew from about 200,000 to about 300,000.

The addition of these 100,000 Jews is largely the result of clearly defined immigration "waves": first, there were the thousands of "displaced persons" from post-Holocaust Europe; then came thousands of Hungarian Jews who fled their homeland in the wake of the revolution of 1956; since 1957, more than 10,000 French-speaking North African Jews, mostly from Morocco, also arrived; over 22,000 Jews who had formerly lived in Israel have emigrated to Canada, mostly beginning with the 1960s; the mid-seventies saw the arrival of some 8,000 Jewish immigrants from the Soviet Union; and during that same decade an almost-equal number of South African Jews had made their way to Canada. Clearly, the Canadian Jewish community is far from being culturally homogeneous, monolingual or largely third- or fourth-generation, as is presently the case with a majority of America's Jews.

Since the turn of the century, the number of Canadian Jews has multiplied almost twenty-fold. Had this same mechanism been at work in the United States, its Jewish population would now number 20 million! In relation to other Jewish communities around the world, the Canadian group ranks seventh in size, after the United States, Israel, the Soviet Union, France, Great Britain, and Argentina. Within Canada, they are the third largest religious group, and the eighth largest ethnic group, but they constitute only about one and one quarter per cent of the total population. (In the United States, Jews comprise approximately two and three quarters per cent of the country's total numbers.)

From coast to coast, in the 1980s, twenty-five million Canadians inhabit, for the most part a narrow, hundred-mile band of land north of the United States with ten times the population. There are almost six million Jews in the United States—more than one-quarter the total population of Canada. Six out of ten of America's Jews reside in the metropolitan areas of four cities—New York, Los Angeles, Philadelphia, and Chicago. Each of these cities has a greater number of Jews than the 300,000 who live in all of Canada.

There is also the problem of space and distance. In all, the Canadian Jewish story is little more than a "tale of two cities"—Montreal with about 100,000 and Toronto with some 120,000 Jews. You have to travel one thousand miles westward to encounter Winnipeg's 15,000 Jews, and beyond the Rockies to the water's edge in Vancouver to come upon another 14,000. Unlike their cousins south of the border, there has been relatively little Jewish diffusion westward. More than three-quarters of the Canadian Jewish community are in the east, and most live within three hundred miles of one another, while the rest reside in small pockets and, with several exceptions, are thousands of miles removed from the nearest "large" Jewish center.

Canadian Jewry is also characterized by problems of time. To the obstacles emerging from its geography, there must also be added the problems emerging from its history. It is one of the youngest Jewish communities in the world, and immaturity and inexperience are characteristic of the young. Often lacking their own precedents, Canadians—Jews and Gentiles alike—have accepted foreign models which do not fully suit their own special needs. Yet, despite the ever-present temptation for most Canadians to do things "the American way," and despite the colossal influence of their neighbors to the South, there are certain built-in Canadianisms that have nevertheless persisted over the years.

Although the two "founding races" were politically equal, the dominance of the English over the French resulted in French-Canadian tension which made possible even greater self-awareness on the part of all the ethnic groups making up the "Canadian mosaic." Indeed, because it was a "vertical mosaic," with power centered at the top in English hands, all other Canadians were given added incentive to achieve more, both as ethnic communities who made up Canada and as Canadians proud of their own ethnicity. Professor Watson Thomson, addressing the Senate Committee on Immigration in 1946, described the Canadian mosaic in these terms: "British political wisdom, Jewish cosmopolitanism and realism, French lucidity of mind and expression, German emotional depth and capacity for work, Slavonic spontaneity and verve—all these are there in the riches of our Canadian life, and each set of qualities can be learned and assimilated by all." We need not accept his simplified descriptions to affirm the fact that a variety of cultural and community experiences is regarded as normal for Canada.

In effect, biculturalism has implied multi-culturalism—or, more correctly, cultural pluralism. A sociologist, Dennis H. Wrong, characterized Canada as being officially in favor of such programs at the very top level of government. "The Department of Citizenship and Immigration," he said, "prides itself on favouring 'integration' (implying a tolerance of cultural differences), rather than 'assimilation' (viewed as conformity to the majority of immigrants to Canadian life)." As late as April, 1970, in its fourth report, the Royal Commission on Bilingualism and Biculturalism, exceeding what could have been a mere literalism, a narrow interest in the two founding cultures alone, proposed that Canadian public schools help the nation's ethnic minorities maintain their languages and customs by offering courses where there is sufficient demand. It is necessary, the report maintained "to safeguard the contribution these languages and cultures can make to the quality of Canadian life . . . for the benefits of linguistic diversity accrue to Canadian society at large." The historian W. L. Morton summed up the general attitude in a single sentence: "Anyone, French, Irish, Ukrainian, or Eskimo can be a subject of the queen and a citizen of Canada without in any way ceasing to be himself."

These factors of Canadian life have until now served to impede the growth of a fully developed sense of Canadian nationalism. It has also made the application of the theory of the "melting pot," so widely accepted in the United States, a difficult if not impossible program for Canada. Distinctions of origin were kept to a minimum in the United States, whereas in Canada they are maintained not only in practice but even in law.

Immigrants arriving in Canada discover two major cultures, and cannot easily come upon a well-defined conception of Canadianism. They are not, moreover, exhorted to adopt a specific Canadian way of life; in any case, none exists as such. Nor does the frightening spectre of flag-waving superpatriots. In the United States, "melting pot" was once an ideal and a symbol of the American democratic conviction that no one should be disqualified from full participation in American life on grounds of ethnic origin or connection. Yet the melting pot, as it has actually worked out in the life and social habit of America, has, as we have seen, produced a "triple melting pot." The ethnic differences of many European immigrant groups have mostly been melted down, but those who continue to survive live on within the religious framework of the three major faith communities—Catholic, Protestant, and Jewish. These three religious communities have retained the residual flavors of the cultural and ethnic variations of the older immigrant groups in America. Yet, as noted earlier, a "new ethnicity" has been revived in the United States.

From the very earliest days in Canadian Jewish experience, however, things were very different. Canada was regarded in law—not only in fact—as a Christian country, and Jews numbered so small a minority in religious terms that there could hardly be an appeal from the fact of a Christian Canada. Nevertheless, as already noted, Canada did offer all ethnic communities that so desired, in law and in life, opportunities to foster their own life-styles in flourishing sub-cultures within the diverse mosaic of Canada.[2] Thus all facets of Jewish communal life which were anchored in the folk-spirit and the national-psyche found easy and acceptable accommodation in Canadian Jewish life. Zionism, the Yiddish language, theatre and press, and a host of other folk vehicles of the Jewish national spirit could never be regarded by the Jews of Canada as alien to their Canadianism. Jews in Canada who lived the folk-culture of Jewishness were respectable Canadians and did not need to join synagogues to achieve status as a community—as many American Jews had thought useful.

The fact that the Canadian Jewish community is, in reality, the product of the years following World War II is even difficult for historians to imagine. After all, the first Jewish "community" was established in Three Rivers over two hundred years ago. But of Canada's current Jewish population, almost half—over forty per cent—are foreign born, and the basic leadership group—because it is older—represents an even higher percentage of first-generation immigrants. A significant number of all of these have personally suffered the yoke of anti-Semitism and the Nazi oppression of Europe. Their views about all things Jewish—religious, communal, political—are still privately conditioned by their personal and recent experience as Jews who grew up in Europe.

It is important to note the peculiarly American pattern, however, because an analysis of Canadian ethnic survival reveals patterns of a very different nature. In the United States, the Jewish community has been at great pains to transmit those aspects of its heritage that were rooted principally in secular culture—Yiddish language and literature, social and communal organizations devoted to the preservation of folk-institutions, a Jewish language press and theater (whether in Yiddish or in Hebrew), Jewish school systems reflecting national-cultural rather than religious aspirations. This explains why political movements linked to Zionism had such difficulty winning over mass Jewish support until the period following Hitler and World War II. Then American Jews adopted Zionism not so much because they were converted to its political and cultural ideologies but rather as a humanitarian gesture—to resettle and rehabilitate Jewish refugees. Only later, with the rise and development of the State of Israel, were American Jews ready to accept the general aims of political Zionism as a national-cultural expression of Jewish survival.

Clearly, the ethnicity of Canadian Jews—their Jewishness—has helped to preserve their faith—their Judaism—and not vice-versa, as had been attempted in the United States. But the natural historical development was in the manner of the Canadian, not the earlier American way—the Jewish people, or nation, preserved the religious style. Had Jews not behaved that way throughout Christendom, they might long ago have been converted to the Church. Once they lost their sense of nationhood and had become only a religious faith-group, they would surely have gone over to Christianity in great numbers. A minority faith that is not linked to a folk and a people tends to be gobbled up by the majority. American Jews began to rediscover this only in the late 1960s.

The built-in ethnic awareness that Canadian Jews possess had helped to foster their religious attachments as well. Many Jews who arrived since 1900 were more conscious of their ethnic ties to the Jewish people than scrupulous concerning their Jewish religious obligations. Nevertheless, they preferred to regard themselves as Orthodox, not because they were always loyal to the religious tradition but because they believed that religious reforms were the way to cultural and ethnic assimilation. (A similar set of attitudes is also characteristic today of many secular Jews in the State of Israel.) "At the same time," according to the Royal Commission on Bilingualism and Biculturalism, "other Jews, who have themselves been given to the forces of assimilation, welcome the Orthodox arrivals (the Hasidim and other ultra-pietists who came after World War II) because they seem to guarantee the survival of traditional Jewry in Canada, without demanding any sacrifices on the part of those with less strict devotion to the traditions of their religion." Here again, without an ethnic base, this kind of vicarious religious transference could not function.

Some of the by-products of the peculiar brand of Canadian biculturalism have, however, placed obstacles in the way of the unimpeded growth and development of Canadian Jewish life. More than fifty per cent of the total population is Catholic, and the influence of that Church upon educational systems and structures in several provinces—most notably in Quebec—has tended to create special problems for Jews. Still another difficulty engendered by "biculturalism" is related to the fact that French-English dichotomies are also Catholic-Protestant divisions. Describing Canada, Dennis Wrong has said, "Religion as a way of life has been weakened; religion as an ideology has been strengthened." In such a situation, the tensions that emerge from these unresolved inter-group rivalries inevitably place the Jew squarely in no-man's land, subject to pressures from both sides and, for this reason, rarely capable of fully satisfying either group. Returning to Montreal after an absence of some time, Mordecai Richler, a Canadian-Jewish author, could still write in 1960:

> The first generation of Canadian-born children, myself included, were sent to *their* schools. According to *them*, the priests had made a tremendous contribution to the exploration and development of the country. Some were heroes. But our parents had other memories, different ideas about the priesthood . . . though we wished Lord Tweedsmuir, the Governor-General, a long life each Saturday morning in the Synagogue, there were those among us who also knew him as John Buchan, the author of thrillers riddled with anti-Semitism.
>
> Always, there was their history, and ours. Your heroes and mine . . . Back in Montreal . . . after an absence of seven years . . . as far as I can see it's still a matter of their Canada, and ours . . . though nobody is literally threatening my skin these days, I am, as a Jew, daily exposed to the possibility of small insults. This, even though my people have contributed beyond their numbers to the arts, sciences, and commerce in this country.[3]

Yet it was precisely during the 1960s that new developments in inter-religious understanding became visible in Canada. And most of these had been "imported from the United States." While America had not legally discouraged the development of plural ethnic and cultural communities, there had been growing up, as earlier noted, a warm-hearted tolerance among that country's religious groups. The developing irenic, egalitarian attitude of these faith communities, we saw, is directly traceable to the democratic institutions of America—the *secular* constitutional and political factors that have helped to foster religious if not cultural pluralism. Some of this attitude towards *religious* accommodation began to spill over into Canada, where native *cultural* pluralism could not of itself have begotten a pluralistic openness among the faith groups. Protestants and Catholics, Catholics and Protestants, a fifty-fifty balance of power; no more, no less: this was as democratic a religious *entente cordiale* one could expect in a nation which regarded itself as a Christian country.

Seen more and more as a representative modern religion, Judaism in Canada is being accorded growing attention, and gradually Canadian Jews are no longer regarded as members of an ethnic community alone but also as practitioners of a major world-faith, with a venerable and unbroken universal history. This awareness, from without, that Judaism is not merely a minority cultic deviation but a major world religion, has allowed Canadian Jews to add new dimensions to their older established foundations as an authentic cultural sub-community. Canadian Jewish religious institutions have thus been summoned to a new life and are coming into a significant period of growth and importance. There can be little doubt that this is part of a continental, and not purely Canadian, development.

More and more, Canadian Judaism thus tends to reflect the American Jewish scene rather than the European Jewish community. As a result, despite the ethnic diversity of Canada, the "community"-orientation of its earlier history, the central role played by the Canadian Jewish Congress as a "supercommunity of communities," and the various indigenous cultural factors already mentioned, Canadian Jewish life is increasingly shaped by influences that are shaping a North American Judaism. Inevitably, Canadian Jewry must reflect the North American environment, not the European. And there are many benefits, indeed.

In spite of the existence of numbers of assimilated Jews, still other American Jews have succeeded in permeating the general culture as Jews and as bearers of Jewish ideas and styles. Inevitably, this has built self-awareness and self-assurance as a community. And inevitably, as well, this self-confidence has spilled over to the Jews of Canada, whether they themselves have earned such inner strengths or not. To cite but one example: the amount of "Jewishness" prevalent in the general American culture helps condition Canadian Jewish cultural components. In the United States, Broadway plays or best-selling novels dealing with Jews have dominated the American cultural milieu for several decades. This condition reflects the American cultural scene and is not true of other

western countries. Yet, Canada, so very much part of American continental culture, also partakes of it, willy-nilly, despite the fact that the
native Jewish cultural component in Canada is much less visible, much
less numerous, and, on the whole, very much less decisive than in the
United States. In Central or even Western Europe, it would have been
inconceivable for literary reputations to have been made by writing
about Jews or by describing Jewish life for the stage. In French or even
in English Canada, it would have been hardly possible for a community
of less than 300,000 Jews to have caught the ear and the attention of
Christian neighbors who constituted 80 times their number. If people
like A. M. Klein, Mordecai Richler, Adele Wiseman, Henry Kreisel, and
other Canadians who wrote primarily about Jewish life have an eager
audience, part of the reason for the receptive attention they received is
surely related to the cultural impact Jewish authors had already established and pioneered for them in America.

There were many other unscheduled and unearned benefits Canadian Jews received as a result of their proximity to the Jewish community
of the United States. With the advent of space-shrinking jet planes, even
remote Canadian Jewish communities were on the American "mainline"; Jewish intellectuals, writers, teachers, and rabbis from America
were easily available to inform and inspire Canadians. They were as
accessible to the Jewish community of Canada as they were to the Jews of
Los Angeles, Chicago, and New York. The significance of their impact
cannot be measured in any ultimate historical sense. Paradoxically, however, in the short run they also helped to link Canadian Jewry to the
American-Jewish cultural world.

Over the years, hundreds of Canadian students have also been the
beneficiaries of various rabbinical seminaries and Jewish teachers' colleges in the United States. Some, of course, returned to Canada to serve
as rabbis and teachers while others were "lost," remaining to live and
work in the United States. On balance, however, the accessibility of these
American institutions has allowed for many important benefits to Canadian Jewry—benefits their own cultural life could not easily have produced independently.

While Canadian Jewry has benefited from many of these American
advantages, contrariwise, it has not always suffered from some of the
disabilities to which Judaism was often subjected in America. American
Jewish intellectuals, for example, could more easily opt out. Within the
melting pot, they could aspire to become humanists, secular democrats,
as well as other assorted varieties of nondescript libertarians. They could
spend a lifetime seeking to detach themselves from the Jewish community and to pass as "Americans." But Canadian Jews had fewer real
options for a non-Jewish existence. French Quebec offered them virtually none. Ontario, with its long-lived Orange tradition, was hardly more

hospitable, until very recently, to Jews who wished to opt out. Winnipeg's ethnic diversity, on the other hand, made pluralism fashionable and allowed Jews to follow their own cultural styles with as few inhibitions as, for example, their Ukrainian neighbors. By and large, Canadian Jews had neither the possibility nor the need to assimilate to other models of Canadianism. Their Jewish style of life was as "Canadian" as any other.

Moreover, the influences of European life linger on. This explains why many students of Canadian Jewish life and history often describe Canadian Jews as community-oriented, rather than congregation-centered. Their descriptions reflect an approach to Canadian Jewry which seeks to establish as certain fact that it is indeed closer in spirit to the Eastern-European Jewish community than to the newer American Jewish community south of its border. The survival of Yiddish as a "mother-tongue," the cultural vitality and activities of the various European *landsmanschaften*, and the continued existence of the *shtetl* life-style with its blend of religious values and practices, social structure and patterns of behavior, are often invoked as evidence of the validity of such assertions. "Congregationalism," too, as developed in the United States by Jews who had come from England and Germany (modern states with ethnically homogeneous societies) and who regarded themselves as nationals whose principal distinction from their fellow citizens was one of religion—is often viewed as alien to the spirit of Canadian Jewry.

It is true that the Canadian Jewish community is closer to the European environment, but this is not necessarily a *qualitative* relationship. It is "closer," of course, because of its more recent removal from the Old World to the New. To be sure, spatial and physical factors do affect mental and spiritual attitudes. Jews who have only recently come to Canada from Europe will obviously continue to think in terms of the environment in which they were raised and nurtured; their Jewish attitudes and ideologies will tend to remain "European" for some time. In 1981, it was said that "Canadian Jews are more 'Jewish' than American Jews. They speak more Yiddish, provide their children with more intensive Jewish education, make higher per capita gifts and relatively more visits to Israel, are more likely to be Orthodox and less likely to be Reform, and have lower rates of intermarriage." Yet even the writers had indicated that "Canadian Jews have only recently begun to attempt to emulate the political sophistication of their American counterparts, who have had much experience (and considerable success) in defending Jewish interests within the domestic political world . . . Canadian Jews are roughly one generation closer to the 'Old World' than are American Jews."[4]

To be sure, the statistical evidence for many of these assertions was very strong, at least as it related to the then-current experience. While retention of Yiddish is still stronger in Canada than in the United States, it is also showing signs of serious decline, as the older generations pass away. According to the Canadian Census of 1971, about 50,000 had claimed Yiddish as their mother tongue, and over half of these said that it was the language they spoke most often at home—approximately sixteen per cent and eight per cent respectively, of the total Jewish population then in the country. Yet by the time of the next census, a decade later in 1981, these numbers and ratios had been dramatically cut by more than 60 per cent—only 10,000 Jews in Canada were using Yiddish as their language at home by then. (Canadian Jews were thus going rapidly in the same direction as their American cousins—losing all traces of any Jewish tongue of their own.) Evidence regarding intensive Jewish education of the day school variety is stronger, however: by 1980 almost two-thirds of Canadian students enrolled in Jewish schools of any type were studying in day schools—about 13,000 out of a total number of 21,000. While comparable data for the United States, as we have noted, also reveal an upward spiralling of day school enrollees—by 1980 they still amounted only to twenty-eight per cent of the total number of students involved in Jewish schooling. The Canadian Jewish community could indeed boast more than double that rate.[5]

A day does dawn, however, in their lives or in the lives of their children, when the new and ever-present environment begins to gain the upper-hand, and many older accommodations yield to the irrepressible demands of contemporary surroundings. The second and third generations begin to parallel many of the patterns of American Jews. That is to say it appears inevitable that Canadian Jewry will reflect the North American, not the European, environment. We have even been bold to say the "North American" and not the "Canadian" environment, because the Canadian environment itself, among non-French speaking citizens in general, is also increasingly accommodating itself to the *continental culture.*

To be sure, the Old World and the centuries-old traditions forged there have fundamentally shaped Jewish life and thought in Canada. It is especially noticeable in the exceptional interest Canadian Jews pay to the Holocaust, and the messages they derive from it. It reminds them of their marginality and induces a heightened sensitivity to acts of anti-Semitism. Yet the strongest single influence on their future is likely to be the quality and style of Jewish life that is developing in neighboring United States. But the very same can be said of Canada and the Canadian people as well. The fact that Canada is a North American nation has taken a long time to sink in, and according to historian F. H. Underhill it did not actually take place until the "Revolution of 1940," when Canadians passed from the "British century" of their history into the "American century."

But many Canadian Jews had already understood this about twenty-five years earlier. At the end of World War I, while English Canadians were still making much of their British heritage and of the fact that Canada was a British country, the Jewish community was already turning away from London and federating with New York's Jewish organizations and movements. English-speaking rabbis no longer came to Canada only from London but also from the United States. Indeed, the stirrings which led to the formation of the American Jewish Congress were also felt there, and the organization of the Canadian Jewish Congress was the result.

In the case of the Canadians, it was the sudden awareness of their dependence upon the United States for military security at the start of World War II that for the first time made them see their country as a North American nation, as part of this continent and not of Europe. World War I had marked the end of the European era for many Canadian Jews. While they remained culturally related to the great European Jewish cities right up to the time of Hitler, America was the new land of rising democratic hopes, of pluralist cultural and religious possibilities, and after World War I, even of great Jewish scholars and the beginnings of great Jewish schools. It was natural for Canadian Jews to turn to America as a free and growing repository of their ancient culture. In this sense, Canada's Jews were first American—and only later, like many other Canadians, mildly anti-American—before they would be "Canadian." And even then, in the absence of a pervasive and unitary definition of "Canadianism," the pressure to conform, or to define one's Jewishness strictly on Canadian terms—as American Jews have often done regarding their "Americanism"—hardly played a role in their lives. (In Quebec, as we shall soon see, much of this would change, however.)

There are unmistakable signs that the "Americanization" of Canada in the socio-religious realm is indeed moving ahead, and while it has not yet grown to American proportions, the process cannot be overlooked. In addition to regarding Canadian Jews as members of an ethnic sub-culture, the general Canadian community increasingly views Judaism as a representative modern religion, alongside the other legitimate Canadian expressions of world-wide religious communities.

Moreover, during the late 1950s—lagging, in fact, just a few short years behind the precedents set by the American Jewish community—Canadian Jews began to establish new congregations in the suburbs. In the larger communities several old but weak and ineffective congregations amalgamated into major new religious communities. This process brought a new prominence to Jewish congregations in Canada. It was inevitable that many of these newer congregations would reflect the religious and educational needs of the second, and even the third generation Canadian Jew. This led to two related developments: the unprecedented rise of *non-Orthodox* congregations, and the appearance of the "congregational-school" alongside the older community-school often known as the Talmud Torah. Both of these phenomena were "borrowed" from America.

As the Jewish population of Canada increased, and the number of synagogues grew over the years, the scope of the congregational activities expanded to involve all members of the family. In 1935, there were 152 congregations in all of Canada—140 of these were Orthodox, mostly small; 9 were Conservative; 3 were Reform. This imbalance clearly reflected the European, not the American pattern. But by the 1950s there was a perceptible shift toward the "American-style," with a clear movement toward non-Orthodox synagogues. This happened either by the founding of new Reform and Conservative congregations; or by "switching"—some old Orthodox congregations changed their allegiance and became Conservative. By 1980, the total number of synagogues had increased to 217, with almost half of the additional synagogues listing themselves as either Conservative or Reform. The breakdown now was 175 Orthodox, 27 Conservative and 15 Reform congregations. Moreover, most of the 175 Orthodox synagogues were principally prayer-halls without educational systems of their own, the majority still lacking the services of their own congregational rabbi. On the other hand, virtually every Conservative or Reform congregation was, in effect, a very large "community," with a synagogue-center program of cultural and educational activities for the whole family supplementing the ritual and religious life of the congregation. Each Conservative and Reform congregation had its own rabbi, and almost all had schools and principals. Indeed, in Montreal, Toronto and Winnipeg, some Conservative congregations even conducted their own Day School programs, either on their own, or jointly with other Conservative synagogues in the area. That Canadian Jewish life was being increasingly shaped by influences molding a "North American Judaism" is reflected in the rapid growth of Reform and Conservative Judaism.

Yet, despite the growth of non-Orthodox congregations, Canadian Jewry, when compared to the United States still retained a more traditional stance, although it was slowly inching its way toward the American style. By the 1980s Canadian congregations were about 40 per cent Orthodox, while the Americans were only twenty per cent Orthodox; 45 per cent Conservative contrasted to 50 per cent in the United States, and only 15 per cent Reform to the Americans' 30 per cent.[6]

Until the Second World War, almost all of Canada's rabbis were European-born and trained, and reflected a European-style rabbinate. They were essentially communal rabbis, attached to several synagogues as learned teachers rather than as spiritual leaders and educational administrators. In good European tradition, they preached their Yiddish "sermons" but twice a year, and were often constrained to earn their livelihood in occupational pursuits outside the rabbinate. At the outset of the war, with European schools closed, and Jewish scholars and would-be rabbis no longer able to remain in that Nazi-dominated continent, three *yeshivot* were opened in Montreal, and one in Toronto.

But increasingly, even in Orthodox circles, Canadian congregations are served by rabbis who were born and trained in the United States. Over the years, more than seventy-five Canadian-born men have been ordained in various Orthodox rabbinical schools in the United States; several dozen have been trained in the Jewish Theological Seminary of America; and a smaller number have graduated from the Reform seminary in America. Most of these rabbis have remained in the United States and continue to serve American Jewish congregations. In a sense, this "Jewish brain-drain" to the United States tends to neutralize the major advances in Jewish identification and education within Canada in recent years, which have made it possible for Canadians to gain entrance into the various American schools of higher Jewish learning.

These factors—the lack of a modern Canadian rabbinical school; the importation of most Canadian rabbis from the United States; the absence of an effective country-wide union of Orthodox, Conservative or Reform rabbis or congregations independent of their American counterparts—lead to the inexorable conclusion that Canadian Judaism will increasingly reflect the design and structure of American Judaism, if not its substance, in all details.

It would, of course, be a mistake to underestimate the emotional ties many Canadians of British birth or parentage continue to feel for British institutions. But these are increasingly remote, and become highly visible principally when members of the British royal family make their "state tours" of the country. The "repatriation" of the Canadian Constitution from Westminster, in 1982, together with its newly-minted American-styled "Charter of Human Rights and Freedoms," have also served to highlight the real distance from Britain. In the case of French Quebec, the connection to the British homeland is a scandal, and remains an annoyance when it is not reminiscent of actual or imagined wrongs against the "French fact" of Canada. Many Quebecois find the Commonwealth linkage itself a hurtful reminder of an era of subjugation. On balance, therefore, Canadian society beyond Quebec continues to be diffuse and diverse, and has difficulty developing a clear focus of loyalty within itself.[7]

Ironically, when some American scholars examine these aspects of Canadian life—the centrifugal nature of its separate cultures, and the lack of a unifying *national mythos*—they express serious doubts about the survival of the Canadian union. Robert Bellah, for example, has noted that "Canada is unitary neither politically nor religiously. But pluralism in the Canadian case, unlike the American, has not aided in the development of a differentiated civil religion. The lack of revolutionary experience, the long history of special ties of English Canadians with England and English symbols of civil religion, and the existence of a large province that is linguistically, ethnically, and religiously distinct from the rest of Canada—all these conditions have militated against not only the emergence of a Canadian civil religion, but of any very clearly defined sense of national identity."[8]

Salo Baron has pointed out that anti-Semitism is more likely to develop and grow into a virulent strain in countries which possess a homogeneous national culture, rather than those made up of competing or disparate blocs of ethnic subcultures.[9] Surely, medieval European history offers eloquent testimony to the fact that when Throne and Altar were wedded, Jews became easy targets as "outsiders" who were singularly different. Seen from this angle of vision, therefore, the variegated, unformed and often hesitant nature of the Canadian national character is a factor that contributes strength to the psychic-structure of its Jewish community. Of late, Canadians have thought it possible to build a multicultural country on its bi-national base. In the process, Jews have experienced fewer survival tensions than their cousins elsewhere, who live in more monolithic, culturally homogeneous countries. Indeed, as the French redouble their efforts to survive in the face of the pressures of English culture and institutions which have engulfed the whole continent, other "non-Wasp" Canadian communities take courage, find fewer causes for self-negation, and sprout recurring hopes for their own creative survival.

It was not until after World War II that Canadians were willing to open their doors wide to immigrants who were neither of French nor British background. Jews, in particular, were virtually debarred from coming to the country in any appreciable numbers during the height of their agonies in Europe throughout the Hitler period. "During the twelve years of Nazi terror," it has been established, "from 1933 to 1945, while the United States accepted more than 200,000 Jewish refugees; Palestine, 125,000; embattled Britain, 70,000; Argentina, 50,000; penurious Brazil, 27,000; distant China, 25,000; tiny Bolivia and Chile, 14,000 each; Canada found room for fewer than 5,000."[10] And it was not much before 1971, when the official Multiculturalism Act was proclaimed as law, that in what had formerly been regarded as a bi-cultural (if not a bi-national) country, Canadians came to realize that the efforts to forge national unity on an English-French base alone could not be fully successful in a society which by then also consisted of many other ethnic cultures and traditions.

Yet, multiculturalism could not fully displace the older *mythos* of biculturalism. The structural division of the country into two parts—indeed, into two "separated," legal fragments—may also divide the Jews of

Quebec from those residing in the rest of Canada. The concern of French Quebeckers—separatists and federalists alike—for *la survivance,* their survival in the midst of an overwhelming North American, continental culture, was believed to offer possible "fringe benefits" to Canadian Jewry: by heightening concern for language and culture it could lead to a strengthening of Jewish group identity. There have been long years of Jewish anxiety over "French xenophobia," beginning with *la revolution tranquille*—the "Quiet Revolution"—which started in Quebec in the early 1960s. Later, the rapid rise in the 1970s of separatist-independentist feelings also led to two successive victories for Rene Levesque's *Parti Quebecois*—in 1976 and 1981—which gave Quebec "separatist-oriented" provincial governments. Nevertheless, there were still some who contended that a fully gallicized Quebec could help to engender an even greater sense of ethnicity among its Jewish population. It was believed that this new "French power" in Quebec would induce greater ethnic loyalties to Jewish identity—as "Black Power" had generated among American Jews, since the late 1960s. And as Montreal had always dominated the national Jewish landscape, a strong Jewish community there, it was also argued, would continue to insure similar vitality across Jewish Canada.

Ironically, some of this optimism was also fuelled by the obvious erosion of the tight control over the mind and heart—as well as the politics—of the Province, which had long been exercised by the Roman Catholic Church in Quebec. The "Quiet Revolution" had caused many French Catholics to distance themselves from the authority of the Church, and by late 1983, even its own bishops in Quebec were admitting that "the Church would never be what she was before the 1960s . . . In 1969, we had more than 80 percent of the Catholic population coming to mass every Sunday. Now, it's 25 percent." Despite the fact that over five and a half million Roman Catholics live in the Province, the Quebec Assembly of Bishops was also reporting to the Pope in Rome that the "glorious past" of the Church in Quebec had come to an end with the arrival of the Quiet Revolution, and with it had also come "an end to an era of tranquil assurance, of prestige and of unanimity" for the Church in Quebec.[11]

Nevertheless, Jews generally felt threatened—if no longer by the power of the Church, then by the new centralized state. In the period between the two national censuses of 1971 and 1981, the Jewish population of Montreal declined precipitously from close to 114,000 to about 100,000. This came about as a result of large-scale departures from Quebec to Ontario (mostly Toronto), Alberta, or British Columbia, all of them centers of American-styled, more-integrated and less-enclavic Jewish communities than had been the case in French-and-Catholic-dominated Montreal. (Some, of course, moved to the United States).

This movement away from Montreal represents much more than a geographical relocation elsewhere, considering that historically, it was always that city which had helped to establish the tone and set the style and pace for the rest of Jewish Canada. Montreal always had the country's most intensive Jewish educational system, the strongest advocates of religious Orthodoxy, the lowest rates of intermarriage, and the richest Yiddish literary and theatrical life. After 1981, it was sometimes suggested that a "certain stability has set in among Montreal Jews" and that "those eager to leave have already done so; those who remain have made their peace with the new Quebec."[12] Nevertheless, a survey of Jewish householders in 1978 would indicate otherwise. Even if there is no further movement toward independence on the part of Quebec, twenty per cent of the respondents under age forty said they would definitely or probably leave Quebec within the next five years. Moreover, this number increased to seventy per cent in the event that a province-wide referendum supported independence in some form. A referendum on this subject was indeed held in May, 1980, and failed by a margin of 60 to 40 per cent of the vote, *at that time*. However, the *Parti Quebecois* continued to hold out the hope that in future referendums, a clear-cut mandate for some form of independence for Quebec—perhaps in economic association with the rest of Canada—would, in fact, emerge. It can be expected that in such an eventuality, the emigration of Quebec Jews to English Canada, even if it does not reach the proportions of seventy per cent, will increase dramatically. Such a result might continue to heighten the possibility of greater conformity to a more Protestant, American-styled, "Wasp-oriented" Jewish community, for the rest of Canada, in the decades ahead.

The push toward the complete *francization* of Quebec, however, has actually resulted in two opposing trends among its Jews, neither of which supported the strengthening of Jewish ethnicism, as some had hoped. There was a determined effort to accommodate to the French language, culture and community, by those who were intent on remaining. For those contemplating the possible need to "escape" from Quebec to a place where ethnic loyalties—like those of the French—were a less dominating factor in their lives, there was a feeling of displacement and apprehension, which could not be said to serve as a creative Jewish lever. In either case, the cultural style and quality of Jewish life as hitherto known in Montreal, could be seen to be undergoing serious challenges to its integrity.[13]

There is yet another index of the concern Canadian Jews have over the shape of their future, and in this case, it runs parallel to the fears of attrition in numbers which are shared by many American Jews (See next chapter). For decades, Canadian Jews believed that intermarriage, while acknowledged as a challenge to their continuity, had posed no serious or special threat. Beginning with the mid-1960s, however, the rate of inter-marriage jumped dramatically to approximately 12 per cent, and has appeared to be increasing, moreover, at a rate of one per cent annually, since then. As a result, by 1983, intermarriage was thought to have reached a national average of close to twenty per cent. (From 1962 to 1972, however, *more than half* of Montreal's North African Jewish community were marrying non-Jews.) There was no comfort to be derived from the fact that the rates of Jewish intermarriage "south of the border" were estimated by some researchers to be almost double that of the national Canadian figures during the same period.[14] Nor, obviously, could there be any encouragement from the fact that compared to Canadian Protestants and Catholics, these very high intermarriage rates among Jews were relatively "low." The clear result of creeping "North Americanization"—if not Americanization—could be seen: the longer Jews are resident in Canada, the more likely it is that their Old World lifestyle will be cast aside. The increasing number of intermarriages among second-and-third generation Canadian Jews was also a mirror-image of the process that had already begun to express itself, in the American Jewish community which had, on the average, a head-start of a whole generation of prior settlement. And if an increasing number of younger Montrealers move away from their roots and homes—westward or southward—there is reason to believe that like their similar, mobile American Jewish counterparts, they too will demonstrate increasingly higher rates of intermarriage.

On balance, then, despite their differing histories, and the variations in the governance, laws, and customs of the two countries, immigrant Jews to both the United States and Canada seem to be subject to the same post-industrial sociology which applies in equal measure in both of their open societies. It seems fairly clear that in these circumstances Canadian Jews will continue to borrow heavily from the models and institutions which a vastly larger and longer-established community of Jews in the United States adapts, develops, or invents. And this, despite their desire to remain uniquely "Canadian." While one can expect that specific localisms will always endure in Canada, generally, Jewish life in that country seems to be substantially and firmly set upon the same rails and tracks as that of their American cousins, and if the two never completely intersect, it is only because they appear destined to keep moving along parallel lines.

NOTES

1. See Morton Weinfeld, "A Note on Comparing Canadian and American Jewry," in *Journal of Ethnic Studies*, Vol. 5, No. 1 (1977–78), p. 99.

2. With the passage of the "Multicultural Act of 1971," Canada adopted officially a designation that it was a "nation that is multicultural in a bilingual framework." A special Ministry of the federal Government makes substantial grants to assist cultural groups.

3. See Mordecai Richler, "We Jews Are Almost As Bad As the Gentiles," *Maclean's*, Oct. 22, 1960 p. 10; p. 82.

4. M. Weinfeld and W. Shaffir, "Canada and the Jews," in *The Canadian Jewish Mosaic*, ed. by M. Weinfeld. W. Shaffir, and I. Cotler, John Wiley and Sons, Toronto, 1981, p. 130.

5. See Alvin I. Schiff, "Jewish Continuity Through Jewish Education," in *Jewish Education*, Summer, 1980, p. 6.

6. See Stuart Schoenfeld, "Canadian Judaism Today," in *Canadian Jewish Mosaic*, ed. by M. Weinfeld, W. Shaffir and I. Cotler, John Wiley & Sons, Toronto, 1981, pp. 113–128. Compare with Daniel Elazar's accounting, *op.cit.*, pp. 71–73; 403. (*Supra.*)

7. See Kenneth D. McRae, "The Structure of Canadian History" in *The Founding of New Societies*, ed. by Louis Hartz, Harcourt, Brace & World, New York, 1964.

8. Robert N. Bellah and Phillip E. Hammond, *Varieties of Civil Religion*, Harper & Row, San Francisco, 1980, p. XIII.

9. See Salo W. Baron, "Changing Patterns of Anti-Semitism," in *Jewish Social Studies*, Winter, 1976, pp. 15 ff.

10. See Irving Abella and Harold Troper, *None Is Too Many*, Lester & Orpen Dennys, Toronto, 1982, p. X.

11. See *Toronto Globe and Mail*, November 28, 1983, pp. 1–2.

12. See, Harold M. Waller and Morton Weinfeld, "The Jews of Quebec" and *"Le Fait Francais"* in *The Canadian Jewish Mosaic, op cit.* p. 433. See also pp. 416–439.

13. See David Weiss, "Is There a Future for the Montreal Jewish Community?" in *Journal of Jewish Communal Service*, (1980) pp. 29–34. Also R. Wisse and I. Cotler, "Quebec's Jews: Caught in the Middle," *Commentary*, Sept. 1977.

14. M. Weinfeld, *op.cit. Journal of Ethnic Studies*, pp. 96–98. It should also be noted that intermarriage rates vary significantly from province to province. Based on the data provided by the Dominion Census of 1971, in ascending order, these were the results: Quebec, 8%; Ontario, 16%; Manitoba, 18%; Saskatchewan, 30%; Alberta 39%; British Columbia, 47%; the Atlantic provinces averaged approximately 50%. See Werner Cohn, "Jewish Outmarriage and Anomie," *Canadian Review of Sociology and Anthropology*, February, 1976, pp. 90–105.

CHAPTER 13

Towards the Next Century:
Problems and Prospects

THERE IS LITTLE DOUBT THAT THE ELASTIC AND CREATIVE AMALGAM OF
ethnicity and religion which American Jews created and fostered has
had a healthy influence. The "American Jewish style" has pervaded not
only other Jewries, but served also, as we have seen, as a model for other
Americans to emulate. The new buoyancy of the Jewish identity in
America which surfaced in the decades since the 1960s has, of course,
brightened the prospects for an even more creative group life in the
future.

Yet serious problems still abound—problems which can result in decelerating, centrifugal forces that may erode their new-found
cohesiveness as a free Jewish community in America. On the other hand,
the many positive gains that have only recently been achieved may continue to accelerate and thus increasingly serve as a countervailing, centripetal force leading to even greater spiritual capacity in the future. As
the next century looms on the near horizon, a nagging question persists:
On balance, which of these forces will prevail within American Jewry, in
twenty, forty, or a hundred years?

A good way to begin to take the measure of this crucial question is to
examine what has been happening in intellectual Jewish circles in
America. In the two decades preceding the 1960s, and in the decades
since that time, those two opposing forces have radically changed the
posture, as well as the balance, of this vital barometer-group. Traditionally, Jewish intellectuals have had the capacity of influencing the
views and the self-awareness of many other Jews, and the recent rise of a
new class of such élites—the Jewish academics—has an important bearing on the question. While they might not have aspired to such influence, the number of Jewish academics has been increasing so
dramatically since the late 1950s that they have become important and
powerful members of a sub-society, often described as the "new class"—
professions that deal with the world of ideas and their communication.
Indeed, in 1969, a survey conducted by the Carnegie Commission on
Higher Education showed that those who admitted to being Jewish comprised ten per cent of all university faculties in America, at the time.
Since there were then approximately 600,000 academics in the country,

this meant that at least 60,000 were Jews. Two years later, in 1971, Seymour M. Lipset reported that twenty five per cent of Ivy League professors were Jewish, although many of them were teaching in law schools or medical faculties.[1]

The very nature of this "new class" has often served to establish barriers between their fellow Jews and these academic-intellectuals; barriers that arise out of the sense of commitment they often have to their own sub-society, the "academic community." This community places demands upon them and exacts loyalties which can be strong enough to rival or transcend their ethnic or religious Jewish ties. As a result, it was not surprising that an astute observer of Jewish academics in the 1960s could report that the largest number of them "are not necessarily hostile to Judaism, but do not feel the least attachment to Jewish life," while there were relatively "few who have grown up in their Jewish attachments without growing out of them."[2]

What, then, were many Jewish artists, authors, scientists, and academics in their assorted varieties, thinking or saying about Jews, Jewishness or Judaism in the years preceding the rise of the "new ethnicity" in America? Have they remained at the same place on the pages of history, or have they moved on? Is the Jewish intellectual still locked into the position he had in the mid-1940s, when, in the words of one of them, his "very awareness of an inheritance makes for him inexpressingly poignant the double sense of being tied to, and having broken from, the past. *He has inherited the agony of his people; its joys he knows only second hand.*"[3]

In 1944, two well-known American literary figures of Jewish descent were asked to express their personal views of "their" community, Jews in America. Said Clement Greenberg: "Jewish life in America has become for *reasons of security*, so solidly, so rigidly, restrictedly, and suffocatingly middle-class . . . No people on earth are more correct, more staid, more provincial, more commonplace, more inexperienced; none observe more strictly the letter of every code that is respectable; none do so completely and habitually what is expected of them." And Alfred Kazin, with mock compassion, added the crushing coup: "What a stupendous moral pity, historically, that the Fascist cutthroats should have their eyes on him (the Jew) when he asks for so little—only to be safe, in all the Babbitt warrens."[4] Seventeen years later, *Commentary*, in dramatic and ostentatious display of the wounds joyfully sustained in their well-advertised flight from Jews and Judaism, sought out the new crop. What were the younger intellectuals, "these children of a neo-conservative age, the age of religious revival and the rediscovery of America," then thinking about their people and its heritage? Hardly anything pleasant at all, *Commentary* discovered. Notwithstanding all that had happened to both Jews and Judaism in the intervening years, nothing seemed to have changed. Like those who preceded them, these angry young men were still angry, and still wilfully out of touch with the vital sources of Jewish life in America. They still disliked the middle class in general and the Jewish middle class in particular. These were, as ever before, hostile to religion, against "Jewish parochialism," but equally opposed to even the normal commitments normal people have, lest they be accused of "chauvinism."[5]

There is increasing evidence, however, that world events—especially in the wake of the Arab oil embargo following the 1973 Yom Kippur War—as well as a slow turning away from its previous patterns of "knee-jerk liberalism" toward a more conservative stance, began to make important inroads into the Jewish intellectual community. Among many other of their re-assessments, these new moods would also cause some of them to view their own Jewish identity more positively.

Regrettably, relatively few field studies have examined these questions. It would appear important to gain insight into them, since Jewish college students constitute almost ten per cent of all campus communities.[6] In late 1980, however, an analysis of "Academy and Community," revealed that the *majority* of Jewish academics studied did maintain a sense of Jewish identity, as well as an attachment to the Jewish community. About three-fifths of these, while not disconnected from Jewish activities, did not accept the conventional wisdom that they were especially influential, and this may account in part for their inactivity, either in Jewish campus life, or in the wider Jewish community. On the other hand, the researchers also discovered something extremely revealing and evocative: two-fifths were actually "eager to 'break into' Jewish communal life," yet tended not to take an active role because they were convinced that leadership roles were virtually restricted to those with great wealth and power.[7]

Considering that the Jew "is no longer a guest in the newly emerging sub-society of the intellectual," the fact that Jewish academics by the 1980s were at all interested in "breaking into" the organized Jewish community is in itself quite remarkable. For, as Milton Gordon had written as late as 1969, "in the world or sub-society of the intellectual, ethnicity is not a very relevant issue either in structural or cultural terms. It is in these circles . . . that considerable primary group interaction takes place across ethnic lines, interfaith marriage is common, and the real melting pot in American life emerges."[8] If a new groundswell of interest in Jewish life on the part of many academics was emerging, much had indeed changed in less than two decades. Serious questions remain, of course: will room be made within the Jewish community to accommodate and encourage this new and unanticipated upsurge of interest? Or will the established Jewish order continue to revolve principally around fundraisers and remain locked into the same leadership patterns it has followed since the end of World War II?

In the older, traditional Jewish community, as enshrined in the *shtetl,* learning was considered even more important than prayer, and both were incomplete without *zedakah,* charity. In the *shtetl* it was customary to hear Jews say: "Praying three times a day does not make you a Jew. You have to be a Jew for the world. That means you have to do something for other people as well."[9] American Jews, as we have seen, have continued in this tradition of generosity. But often the methods they have chosen in pursuit of the ideal have been disturbing to the more sensitive among them, and seem to be a radical departure from the traditional style of Jewish life. Philanthropy often seems to be "industrialized" and geared to status-seeking, rather than as a mark of inner spirituality. The Jewish intellectual, as noted, tends to recoil from association with the Jewish community on these accounts. But he would do well to plumb the deeper motivations at work. One observer has linked the "new fund-raising" to the malaise of many American Jews, and his objective but understanding description gives us sympathetic insight into the problem:

> The American Jew is not fully accustomed to his new security and alternately revels in it and doubts it. Similarly, he has not learned to live with his prosperity and to relax with it. He needs more and he wants more. . . .
>
> This ambition is different from that which plagued Western European Jewry in the post-Emancipation years. That ambition was a craving for recognition by the Gentile community. Since the American Jew knows . . . that his quest for status within the general community has pre-defined limits, he intensifies his search within the Jewish group. Nowhere does this seem more clearly reflected than in Jewish community activities, both the pride of the American Jew and, in some degree, his shame. . . .
>
> He has aided European Jewry in building new lives in new lands and shown his solidarity with them and with the downtrodden everywhere. At the same time, these examples of utter generosity often mirror Jewish unsettlement, aimless competitive flux and hence a loss of Jewish moral growth and vitality. It is paradoxical that the events which most symbolize positive Jewish thought and action also disclose *a dilution of moral substance for the sake of recognition, status and outer splendor.* . . .
>
> The American Jew . . . works hard for Jewish groups, but much of his work seems prompted by considerations of conspicuous prestige. . . . He is both healthy and sick. The American Jew may be defined as a series of contradictions with the positive containing much that is negative and the negative, curiously, containing much that is positive. (Italics added.)[10]

If, in the eyes of the intellectuals, fund-raising could be regarded as "negative," it was one of those negatives containing much that is positive. The apparatus and network of groups participating in these campaigns did indeed play a crucial role in knitting together the whole community, across almost all religious and ideological lines. Secularists, Orthodox, labor and management—to mention only a few—were among the myriad of disparate groups who worked, side-by-side, in these mammoth community-wide efforts. Indeed, there are those who attribute to these projects many other lasting benefits in addition to the crucial financial aid produced. They regard it as the single most significant recruiter of lay leadership available to the community. Moreover, it has succeeded in involving, on a local as well as a national scale, more Jews, for sustained periods of time, than any other type of community enterprise. Observers also believe that the continuing success of these fund-raising drives— whether for Israel or for local community purposes—has also served as a means of impressing American public opinion with the cohesion, vitality, and unity of American Jewry. Most significantly, it has also been demonstrated that those who participate in and contribute monies to those large-scale community campaigns are usually heavily involved in Jewish life, and these fund-raising activities actually help to strengthen their further involvement in religious and cultural efforts within their own homes and communities.

Indeed, some leaders have warned that all of Jewish communal life in America may ultimately be diminished *if fund-raising drives decrease,* either in their intensity, in the number of donors, or in the size of the gifts themselves. One authoritative study suggested that:

> young people (under forty) are giving less often, professionals *do* give appreciably less than business people, and less identified Jews give less than their more involved counterparts. Since young people are increasingly turning toward the professions, and since Jewish involvement is to some unknown extent permanently lower among today's younger Jews, one can readily anticipate a decline both in the number of givers and in the size of their gifts . . . Thus, decreased giving means, all things being equal, less support for Jewish agencies, some unravelling of the organized community with greater factionalization, poorer recruitment of lay leaders for all aspects of Jewish organizational life, less opportunity for the average Jew to be induced to participate in a broad-based communal activity, and quite possibly dimunition in Jewish political influence.[11]

Despite the "negative-positives" of fund-raising, or of the fund-raisers themselves, Jewish life has always distinguished between the *means* of living, and the *ends* of living. No matter how crucial or central the amassing of these large amounts of Jewish-support money may be, the near-total equation of Jewish meaning with campaign goals and drives can lead to malaise and even to alienation.

It has been said that there are really only two kinds of Jews: those who are consumed by Jewish anxiety but succeed in denying it even to themselves; those who are troubled by Jewish anxiety but would never dream of denying it. Most Jewish intellectuals cannot empathize with the malaise of the middle-class American Jew because they are themselves afflicted with their own unique brand of Jewish restlessness and unsettlement. But they have played at the game of denying it, and thus did not always understand those Jews who still held on to their Jewishness or Judaism. In their case, the desire to avoid what they consider the Jewish community's extreme conformity to middle-class patterns had often succeeded in impelling them to adopt the extreme conformity of the non-conforming intellectual community. Both groups, however, seen in the perspective of historical Jewish experience, tend to emerge as *inau*thentic Jews. "The authentic Jew," said Will Herberg, "lives on two levels: as a responsible member of the historical community, and as a son of the covenant, a member of the trans-historical community of faith with which his destiny is inextricably linked. The authentic Jew is *in* this world, but never quite *of* it, never fully conformed or adjusted to the world in which he lives."[12] Weighed in scales such as these, neither the middle-class Jew nor the Jewish intellectual always measures up as authentic. The former had often adopted spurious adjustments that integrated him too glibly into a bland and unexciting cultural environment. Yet the Jewish intellectual in the new American era of ethnicity, if welcomed into a Jewish community more keenly aware of some of the causes of its earlier inauthenticity, may help effect a small revolution in its values, as the twentieth century draws to a close.

Some of the behavior of the American Jew, as we have pointed out, does produce strains of inauthenticity in him: in his too-easy adaptation to the environment, his assimilation of the baser rather than the nobler elements of contemporary middle-class practice. But these are, perhaps, passing phenomena in the American Jewish community, as they may be of American life itself. American Jews may be generous for the wrong reasons; but at least they are generous. They may sometimes band together for the wrong reasons; but, at least, they stand with one another, and do not seek to run away from themselves or their responsibility to one another. But what some intellectuals are not saying—perhaps because they are preoccupied with hypercriticism—remains to be said, however: Jews have bulked large as a group, despite their minority status in America, in the intellectual and scientific advancement of the nation.

The first American to win a Nobel Prize was a Jew, Dr. Albert Abraham Michelson, whose work in physics earned America this award in 1907. Since his time, scores of Jews, in various countries, have been awarded the Nobel Prize, and many of these have been Americans, including the father of the "wonder drug," streptomycin, Dr. Selman Abraham Waksman. In scientific fields, other Jewish names in America have become national by-words: Dr. Charles P. Steinmetz, the engineering wizard of General Electric; Dr. Abraham Flexner, the developer

of modern American medical school education; Dr. Albert Einstein, Dr.
J. Robert Oppenheimer, Dr. Edward Teller, and Dr. Isidor Rabi, interna-
tionally known physicists; Dr. Jonas Salk of polio vaccine fame; David
Sarnoff of R.C.A., the electronics expert. In the musical arts, the
achievements of Yehudi Menuhin, Jascha Heifetz, Vladimir Horowitz,
Leonard Bernstein, George Gershwin, Richard Tucker, Jan Peerce, and
scores of others are part of the cultural history of America. Jurists and
philosophers such as Morris Raphael Cohen, Louis D. Brandeis, and
Felix Frankfurter have made an indelible mark on the intellectual development of the law. Journalists of the stature of Adolph Ochs of the
New York Times and Joseph Pulitzer of St. Louis, plus many other first-
rate writers and dramatists of the Jewish faith, have imprinted their
names in the lists of the American unforgettable; not to mention less
known but no less significant Jewish contributors to America on the
university campuses, in the scientific research laboratories, the publishing houses, and the like. When the President of Notre Dame University
asked a conference of Catholic educators, "Where are *our* Einsteins,
Oppenheimers, and Salks?" he was, in effect, doing something many
Jewish intellectuals have refused to do: paying tribute to what the Jews
in America had achieved for America.

And in even more subtle ways, many in the Protestant religious communities were aware of the creative contributions which "Jewish
otherness" had made to the literary life—even more aware as observers
than the participants themselves. The irony was great: Jewish artists and
writers were leveling their critical shafts against "middle-class Jewishness" in America, when, in fact, all that seemed to remain of the earlier
Protestant dynamic here was a twentieth-century "middle-class American way of life." Sensitive Protestant thinkers were, in fact, somewhat
envious of Jewish otherness—it seemed to keep creative Jews alive, prevented them from becoming, as they felt most Protestants had become,
part of the unexciting, unimaginative wallpaper of the American social
setting. "Protestant is what one is if he does not take the pains to disassociate himself from the established background," sighed Martin E.
Marty. "The Jewish novelist (of the Saul Bellow era)," his lament continues, "as the uprooted, alienated, displaced urbanite formed the para-
bles of dislocation of the time. . . . But the Protestant writer is too much
at home to speak with interest of an emerging world."[13]

Seen from this angle of vision, the alienation of the Jewish intellectuals
was, indeed, more to be admired than the "cozy" attitudes to America
which most Protestants held—attitudes and platitudes which served only
to shore up a cultural monolith that was rapidly eroding. Perhaps their
alienation from Jewishness was really more a symptom of their cultural
aliveness and openness than these Jewish intellectuals knew—perhaps
more a recoiling from the boredom of Anglo-Saxon sameness than from

their own Jewish peculiarity. Perhaps, in fact, in their antibourgeois stance, Kazin, Greenberg, and their friends were more in keeping with Jewishness and Judaism, than they or their Jewish critics would allow. And perhaps in the newer unfolding of a pluralist America theirs would be the prophetic voice of a new spirituality—the historic voice of the alienated outsider.

Paradoxically, however, while the citations mentioned earlier reflect the massive contribution of Jews to American cultural life, they also highlight a glaring failure in *Jewish* cultural achievement of American Jews. In the European past the situation was reversed: many Jews had the benefit of higher Jewish learning, but were denied the possibilities of a general university education. In such circumstances, their cultural loyalties to Jewish life were firmly grounded in the roots of Jewish knowledge. While there has been a new and growing emphasis in the contemporary American Jewish community upon a more intensive elementary education, very few Jewish college graduates can boast of having received a higher Jewish education. It is already apparent that even their intensive elementary Jewish education cannot stand up to their new sophistication as college graduates; they rarely unlearn or relearn the Jewish materials they have been taught as children, in childish ways. Indeed, the more general learning they achieve, the more critical and secularized their thinking process grows. And if they have not complemented their new knowledge with an approach to Judaism equally adult and equally sophisticated, it is likely that they will forever identify its teachings only with the naïve and "primitive" meanings they were taught as children. Thus, the fact that American Jews will soon comprise a community consisting almost completely of college graduates poses new threats to their creative survival as a vital cultural group. Clearly, more strenuous efforts at developing programs to strengthen secondary and higher Jewish education are called for.

But in the 1970s the unexpected came to pass. One would not normally expect traditionally "alienated" Jewish students to be in the vanguard of a new revolution of Jewish awareness. Yet, it was precisely on the American college campus—in that decade—that vital signs of new Jewish identity-patterns began to sprout—even before these positive moods, centering in a strong espousal of Jewishness, had reached the hearts and minds of their own parents. As early as the 1950s there was evidence of a new interest on the part of a growing number of American universities in the field of Jewish studies, on a higher academic and cultural level. To be sure, the third oldest chair at Harvard University is the Hancock Professorship of Hebrew and other Oriental Languages established as early as 1764, and other universities in America, too, have long offered courses in Hebrew language and literature. For the most part, however, these were made available as part of a general theological grounding for future members of the Christian ministry. But with the growing use of Hebrew as a modern tongue, a number of secondary school systems in the East began to offer it as a language course that was acceptable for college entrance, alongside other modern foreign languages. Then, with the dynamic cultural rebirth in the State of Israel, this new American academic tendency became more widespread. Room was now made for Jewish studies, not as an aspect of pretheological Christian training but as a self-justified academic discipline.

By 1965, forty colleges and universities in the United States had established either undergraduate or graduate departments of Jewish studies as an integral part of their American program of higher education. Less than two decades later, even this major achievement was multiplied almost eight-fold: there were already over three hundred Jewish studies programs on campuses across the country, producing an average annual crop of Ph.D's of more than eighty young scholars.[14] These courses usually deal with four significant areas of Jewish scholarship: religion, history, language, and literature. The "Association for Jewish Studies," based at Brandeis University, was launched in the early 1970s to help set goals for these new courses, and to assist in raising the level of university teaching in these subjects. Founded with a membership of little more than two hundred full-time university teachers and researchers of Judaica, only a few short years later—thanks to the "explosion" of Jewish studies on the American campus—their numbers would reach almost one thousand. Local Jewish communities, too, have often assisted by supplying "seed money" for the program, or by endowing "Jewish chairs."

This "Judaica explosion," however, was not self-igniting, even if it was almost completely unanticipated. It became, by any standard of measurement, one of the brightest spots on the "Jewish map" of America. In 1966, a knowledgeable observer of the academic scene had cautiously indicated signs of growing promise, but even he could not have imagined the rising tide of interest that would begin to sweep across the Jewish academic community, only a short time later. The enthusiasm following the Six Day War in 1967, coupled to a surging interest in ethnic studies (principally Black, or Afro-American), affected Jewish students and professors, alike. Thanks to the combined efforts of the "Jewish studies networks" established by students on many American campuses, and an alert communal leadership, this dramatic acceleration of Jewish cultural achievement was effected. It should also be noted that the Jewish intellectual community—academics and administrators alike—heartily joined the rising groundswell created by these student activists who vigorously and successfully petitioned their faculties to incorporate Jewish studies into the regular curriculum.[15]

There was still another major achievement in which student activists played a decisive role and which helped to raise dramatically the consciousness of many American Jews. These efforts led to a new community "contagion," the national movement to rescue and redeem Soviet Jewry, which some even dubbed "the new Zionism." For many years, the established, mainstream Jewish organizations had been paying little heed to the possibility of getting Jews out of the Soviet Union. In the 1960s, following the lead of the World Jewish Congress, then led by Dr. Nahum Goldmann, these groups had taken the position that efforts to assist Russian Jews must not run afoul of East-West détente, and could even endanger the fragile minority-status of the close to three million Jews still living under tight Kremlin rule. Better, they contended, to let Soviet Jews stay where they are; it was believed more important to assist them in rebuilding their local cultural life, than to attempt to bring them to Israel. Only a very small number thought otherwise. A minuscule group of non-established Jews, spurred on by Jewish student activists on American campuses, began to agitate for Russian Jewish emigration. They staged public protests, and a variety of nonconformist demonstrations, and finally succeeded in getting this question placed high on the agenda of the national Jewish community. In due course, a countrywide body was established to coordinate all of these activities, and international Jewish conferences were mounted. From 1968 until 1980 almost 225,000 Russian Jews had been granted permission to emigrate to Israel by Soviet authorities. (Many later left Israel for the United States, Canada, Australia, and elsewhere, as we shall see). These achievements were phenomenal by any previous communal, or even international standards, and were, of course, aided and abetted by strong support from successive American governments and international statesmen committed to human rights. The Jewish community in America had succeeded in politicizing "a Jewish issue" and thus focused new attention upon itself as a cohesive and vocal "lobby." Yet the lessons for the organized Jewish community which emerged from the ceaseless efforts of those Jewish "outsiders" to politicize the Jewish establishment itself were also major and significant. The students and their newly allied cohorts—women's groups, academicians, writers, lawyers, and others—had succeeded in energizing and motivating a large section of Jewish America. Many who participated in these efforts were formerly inactive, half-hearted, or even alienated Jews. In the "Soviet Jewry movement" a new constituency of interested Jews was discovered—and not by mainstream Jewish organizations, but by the new "activists," led by the Jewish student groups.[16]

It is difficult to put a finger on any single event or to find specific and direct root-causes that might explain this second "Jewish explosion" of the 1970s—the redemption of so many Russians, virtually "written off" as Jews all the years before. The mood of détente, between America and

Russia, at the time, must have helped, as did the human rights provisions promulgated by international consent in the widely heralded "Helsinki Agreement." The Israeli government, too, played a significant role as a catalyst, in assisting the "agitators" (the so-called "new Zionists"), who fought the Jewish establishment in America long and hard, until it, too, adopted this cause as its very own. Yet, it should also be noted that the Holocaust—and the relatively quiescent role of American Jewry during the fateful years of 1933 to 1945—had begun to enter the minds and capture the hearts of the younger Jewish generation by this time, in ways their parents had not felt or even remembered.[17]

By the 1970s, at the very time the "Soviet Jewry movement" was coming into vogue, the Holocaust was also being recalled in new ways— actively, even militantly. There can be no doubt that these two phenomena were linked not only chronologically, but also thematically and psychologically. In 1981, looking back on the last decade, one observer wrote: "If the pace at which courses in Holocaust studies, special *yizkor* services, martyrs' memorials, lecture series on the Holocaust and a variety of research centers are multiplying is an accurate measure of communal interest, then the Holocaust has become a central item on the contemporary Jewish agenda. This spurt of interest, a phenomenon which began in the 1960s, is in striking contrast to the decades immediately following the war when the Holocaust was noticeable only by virtue of its absence from the spectrum of Jewish communal concerns."[18]

In 1979, even President Jimmy Carter had established the "President's Commission on the Holocaust." Yet, the new preoccupation with the Holocaust also had its critics. Some were fearful that "over-attention" to the Holocaust could, in fact, succeed in trivializing and commercializing it. Others were uncomfortable with "the way in which the Holocaust has become the single most visible aspect of the public life of American Jewry" and found it disturbing that "the Holocaust seems to be the issue that most easily confers an instant sense of identity and unity upon a fragmented community . . . (and) provides popular programming for synagogues and Jewish centers, fills university classrooms . . . (and) has been used as the most potent mandate—though a negative one—for Jewish survival."[19] There were also those who called it a "Holocaust Industry" or a "Holocaust Religion," and hoped that, instead, American Jews "*would learn how the Jews of Europe lived before they are forced to remember how Jews were gassed.*"[20] But the popularly accepted trend toward "Holocaust remembrance" had by then become a vigorous part of the new "civil Judaism"—both in America and in Israel—and a powerful element as well of the new Jewish identity in America.

Then, of course, there were also some anti-Semites who attacked the emphasis Jews were giving to the Holocaust because, as they speciously argued, it was really a myth created by Zionist conspirators: there was no

Holocaust at all! These anti-Jewish charges, as could be expected, only served to make the "Holocaust movement"—if one can call it such—an even more sacred and important function in the eyes of many Jews. The hostile response to the Holocaust must also be regarded as an indication of the success of the Jewish community in giving it a special public focus—one that had not been undertaken until some twenty-five years after the lurid and horrific events themselves.

It can be said, on balance, that these twin phenomena, the memorialization and sanctification of the Holocaust martyrs, as well as the effort to diminish the possibility of Russian Jewish obliteration, have served as accelerating, centripetal and unifying forces for American Jews, in more recent years. Both helped to create a new sense of belonging, based on an "interdependence of fate," to use the language of Kurt Lewin. Since 1967, immigration to Israel—*aliya,* or "ascent"—has also served as a new rallying point, although among a very much smaller number of Jews. In some ways, American *aliya* has a double entendre: it is a sign of both the success *and* failure of America Jewish life. Those who "ascend" to Israel usually do so because they are seeking a fuller Jewish existence than they believe America can provide. Yet, their pro-Jewish inclinations are inevitably the product of a positive spiritual experience that was given them, to begin with, by the voluntary and free society of Jews in America. They are not being "pushed" out of America, but "pulled" toward Israel. That pull was felt by people who grew up as self-affirming, and self-aware Jews, *in America.*

Indeed, this fact emerges even more clearly *after* they arrive in Israel, and may be said to be a major and under-current reason why from one-third to one-half of those Jews who do "make *aliya,*" return to America before the end of three years. It is, of course, not easy for them to adjust to Israel, which in many ways is still a developing society, beset with economic, social and political problems of great magnitude. Estimates vary widely but "according to official statistics, during the period of the British Mandate (1919–1948) some 6,613 American citizens immigrated to Palestine . . . They were attracted to the agricultural settlement of the land, to kibbutzim . . . By 1952 there were fourteen American kibbutzim, some settled by individuals who had fought as volunteers in Israel's War of Independence (in 1947–8)."[21] After 1956, *aliya* from America steadily began to increase, finally reaching an all time high in 1971, a year which saw over seven thousand American Jews settling in Israel. While almost 35,000 American Jews had come as immigrants to Israel from 1967 until 1982, the years following the peak set in 1971 have seen a falling off of new American settlers. Moreover, as indicated earlier, not all of these have remained.[22]

A significant study published in 1981 also noted the changing characteristics of the more recent American *olim* (immigrants): "Olim (now) tend to be young, aged under thirty; more women than men make aliya; more single than married persons make aliya . . . Compared to the American Jewish population, more Orthodox-affiliated individuals make aliya . . . and . . . a plurality of olim consider themselves to be religiously observant . . . They are characterized, compared to the American Jewish population, by a high level of Hebrew or Jewish schooling . . . Proportionally, Jerusalem attracts the most American olim; proportionally, Americans are over-represented on the kibbutz (compared to new olim, *in toto,* and to Israelis.)"[23]

A strange paradox was also emerging, one that had possible long-term effects on the nature of Israeli life, but which reflected, as well, on the future of the American Jewish community. If those from America who were going to live in Israel tended to be religiously observant, Israelis who were leaving their country to live in the United States during this same time period, were not of the Orthodox, but of the secularist variety.[24] It is estimated that by the early 1980s there were over 350,000 Israelis residing in the United States—approximately 100,000 of whom lived in the Los Angeles area.[25] (In Canada, they numbered over 25,000). Yet Israelis are often alienated in the United States and tend to be self-defined "sojourners" in America, preferring not to regard themselves as permanent "settlers." They also tend to be under thirty, born in Israel *(sabras),* and their numbers increase annually by about 10 per cent. Observers have noted their dilemmas:

> Like other non-Jewish sojourners before them, Israelis cling to their culture and are unwilling to organize as permanent residents in America. Even after many years in this country most never fully assimilate. They face a perpetual dilemma: they do not want to return to Israel until they have accomplished the tasks they set out for themselves—higher education, professional training, and accumulation of material assets. But as this situation is seldom achieved before developing an extensive personal network of connections and involvements, plans for returning become increasingly complex and vague. Yet Israelis continue to associate almost exclusively with people from their own group. Although they may remain abroad their entire lives, they rarely sever their ties with the homeland. They often go back home for visits, only to return to the country in which, more often than not, they still view themselves as foreigners.
>
> Part of the Israelis' reluctance to admit they have chosen a new home or might be in the process of doing so, results from the stigma attached to anyone viewed as an emigrant from Israel. If *aliya,* or immigration to Israel, is considered the ultimate Zionist injunction, emigration or *yerida* is looked upon as the ultimate betrayal of the Zionist cause. Furthermore, it constitutes desertion at a time when Israel is still struggling for a secure and peaceful existence. This long standing attitude both on the part of Israeli officialdom and the Israeli public at large, leaves Israelis abroad with an ever-gnawing feeling of guilt and a constant need to justify or rationalize their decision, or else to deny the intention of remaining abroad.[26]

None of these attributes or attitudes were calculated to make life in the United States Jewish community easy for the "descending" Israelis. American Jews, accustomed to assisting Israel, and often eager to do so, tend to be either ambivalent to, or even disdainful of, Israelis who leave their beleagured homeland. Lipset points out, moreover, that "the treatment of Israeli expatriates as nonpersons is most evident in demographic and other communal analysis and projections" undertaken by the American Jews, and "mention is rarely made of the fact that 5 per cent, or one in twenty Jews in the country, are recent settlers from Israel." Indeed, there were also other Jews from abroad who had come to live in the United States since 1967, and concerning whom little is known or administered to by the Jewish community. In addition to the Israelis, they included over 75,000 Russian Jews who arrived in the country since 1972; and other Jews from Argentina, Canada, Chile, Colombia, Cuba, Iran, Nicaragua, and South Africa.

As a result of this major influx of new Jewish immigrants—unprecedented in America since the Hitler period—it is believed that one out of every eleven Jews living in the United States in the 1980s was a relatively recent immigrant, with most having come barely a decade earlier. Such a large and diverse group of new American Jews—many of whom do not affiliate with local synagogues, schools, or other community institutions—serves as a centrifugal influence. Many of the 20,000 Iranian Jews who fled to America from Khomeini's rule, as well as the bulk of the Israeli expatriates, do not fully identify with the organized community, because they claim that they will one day—sooner or later—return to their own homeland. Whether these "sojourners" ever do return remains a question. Yet, considering their large numbers in relation to the total Jewish population, their negative mental attitude towards "joining up" as settled and responsible "American Jews," has a depressing effect on the whole community. It can also lead to serious defections from Judaism, in the next generation, despite the fact that the secular Israelis presently speak Hebrew, or still tend to commingle with their own countrymen. (A study conducted in 1979 suggested that about one-fifth of single Israeli immigrants had already intermarried in America.)[27] Iranians tend to more traditional Jewish ways and often send their children to religious schools, but Russian Jews remain marginal, and show few signs of "returning to Judaism," or discovering it in America.

The contrasts between these new Russian and Israeli immigrants of the 1970s and the older eastern- and central-European Jewish settlers who had arrived in the period between the two world wars are dramatic and striking. Their total numbers are approximately the same: close to 500,000 make up the aggregate sum of both of these two separate "immigration waves." Those who came from east Europe in the earlier part of the century were usually anxious to build a continuum in America of the vigorous Jewish life they knew in the old country. In many ways their efforts, and the institutions they founded, still inhere in the contemporary community, and their "Jewish works" survive in the organizations they built and molded. For the most part they settled in the populous Northeast, where they identified fully with their newly acquired citizenship and soon became active in the American political process, as well as in larger Jewish communal matters. Their physical Jewish presence was profoundly felt. They not only helped to invigorate the settled Jewish community, but also contributed to the building of the grass-roots of the Democratic Party, with which most of them were identified. This came about thanks to the outreach to these new immigrants by New York's Tammany Hall, and the other Democratic machines and city-bosses in places like Massachusetts, Pennsylvania, and elsewhere in the East. For the most part, their several children—they had a higher fertility rate than Jewish families of the 1970s or 1980s—married within the faith, and then went on to become the builders of suburban Judaism, at the close of World War II.

The Jewish prospects, however, for the half million or so Russian and Israeli immigrants of the seventies—many of whom have the same east-European forebears—are far different from those of the earlier immigrants who came during the inter-bellum period. The Israelis are also heavily concentrated in the Los Angeles area, in Florida, and in the sun belt region of the country, in addition to New York City. For the reasons already indicated, they are either not yet citizens, or, if some are, they do not bulk significantly in the political life of America as part of the "Jewish bloc." They remain marginal to the established community, and have not, to date, either founded major Jewish organizations, or influenced those that already exist.

The Soviet Jews in America have come, in the words of one of them, "from another planet." Apparently, Soviet authorities had granted a disproportionately large number of exit visas to assimilated and secularized Jews who hailed from the larger cities. These were people more likely to settle in the United States (or Canada) than the small-town Russian Jews, in whose home communities the inroads of communism and the ensuing assimilation patterns were less likely to have penetrated the Jewish population. Since Soviet Jews, unlike the Israelis, have no homeland to which they can return, they come as permanent settlers, not as sojourners. Yet, it remains unclear whether their assimilationist pattern, already so well-ingrained in the Soviet Union, will continue to grow in America as well, or whether it may be reversed. The question persists: by coming to America, and not going to or staying in Israel, have these Russian Jews also rejected Judaism, in addition to the Jewish state? It is too early, perhaps, to know; indeed, there is need for research into the long-term social-cultural consequences of both the Russian and the Israeli immigration. In any event, it is hardly likely that Russian immigrants to America of the last third of this century can or will play a positive role similar to that of earlier immigrants from east Europe. Indeed, they may very well contribute to the decelerating forces that are increasingly at work in the contemporary American Jewish community: by their detachment from organized Jewish life; their low birth rate; their lack of Jewish education and culture; and their general unwillingness to play a positive role as "givers" and not merely as "recipients," in the inner life of the community.

What, indeed, are the most significant, if infrequently discussed or noted, of these decelerating, corrosive forces at work in the American Jewish community toward the end of the present century?

First and foremost there is the issue of the "critical mass"—the basic question of Jewish numbers in the United States. Some scholars began questioning whether there will be, in fact, a substantial American Jewish community left, by the mid-twenty-first century. In 1977, one Jewish demographer, perhaps more in an effort to provoke debate than to make hard-and-fast predictions of the decline and possible fall of American Jewry, flatly stated: "When the United States celebrates its Tricentennial in 2076, the American Jewish community is likely to number no more than 944,000 persons, and conceivably as few as 10,420. This dramatic decline from a peak Jewish population in the United States of nearly 6 million was already in evidence during the Bicentennial."[28]

The two principal causes for this population erosion were said to be the declining Jewish birthrate, which was below the replacement level; and the increasing rate of attrition among American Jews, the rate at which Jewish-born persons give up their Jewish identity completely. Elihu Bergman, the demographer in question, was, of course, employing worst-case scenarios at every statistical turn of the road. The National Jewish Population study of 1971 had reported a Jewish intermarriage rate in the United States for the period of 1966–72 of 31.7 per cent, which represented an increase of 500 per cent from the 5.9% rate for the interval of 1955 to 1960. Using that base, and with devastating singlemindedness—well-suited for the initiation of such a polemic—Bergman then projected various future rates of Jewish intermarriage, well into the next century, and arrived at the population declines noted above. Yet a major flaw in his projections could be easily noted, even by equally pessimistic observers: every intermarriage had been equated with a defection from the Jewish community. Intermarriage, it can be said, is either a cause or an effect of assimilation; perhaps it is both. But not every Jewish intermarriage results in loss or attrition to the community: paradoxically, it can also be a source of additional recruits.

Little attention is paid to the fact that Judaism not only loses adherents in North America by means of apostasy, but that it is also on the receiving end of converts. According to published surveys, the total numbers, on both sides of the equation, tend to balance themselves out. For every million Jews who were born Jewish, 24,000 were said to have become apostates, while, of every million Jews currently considered Jewish, 21,000 had been converted to Judaism. In effect, this means that presently some 125,000 Jews have been lost to other religions (25% to Catholicism; 50% to various Protestant denominations; 25% to sects and cults). On the other side of the scale, however, more than 110,000 of the total present American Jewish population were not born Jewish. Most demographers neglect to take into account the little-noted fact that American Jewry not only has "exports," but "imports" as well. The attrition rate is thus not nearly as grave as they have portrayed it to be.[29]

Despite his dark prophecies, however, Bergman's essay on Jewish population erosion proved to be a useful contribution to a necessary debate. In the face of declining Jewish fertility rates which in the past decades had stood between twenty and thirty per cent below the national American average of 1.7, it became clear that it was Negative Population Growth, even more than increasing intermarriage rates, which was more certain to cause demographic decline. Accordingly, other researchers foresaw an American Jewish population of five million in the year 2,000; falling to four million by the year 2,025; then, to three million fifteen years later; and numbering only one and half million by the year 2,070. On the other hand, if Jewish fertility rates should move up to the present standards of American Protestants and Catholics—which appears unlikely, but possible—there could even be some Jewish population growth until the beginning of the next century, whereupon it would decline and then level off to less than four million.[30]

The major imponderable in all of these demographic predictions, it turns out, is profoundly linked to religious and community policy relating to intermarriage. Samuel Lieberman and Morton Weinfeld examined this problem in an unusual way:

Little quantitative research has been done on children of intermarried couples. However, it is known that many intermarried Jews, with or without conversion of spouse, continue to affiliate with the community, identify as Jews, and make some effort to pass on Jewish commitment to their offspring. Others, of course, do not. But consider the following proposition: as long as 50 per cent of the children of intermarriages remain Jews, there is no net effect on the size of the population, *regardless of the intermarriage rate!* Assume all Jews intermarry, and there are two children per family. If 50 per cent of the families remain "Jewish," so that 50 per cent of the offspring are "Jewish," we have no increase or decrease. If more than 50 per cent become Jews, the population in the next generation would increase! This points to the importance of the attrition rate in assessing the demographic impact of intermarriage, and in the centrality of competing definitions of Jewishness in the calculation of generational gains or losses.[31]

Things, however, were neither that neat, precise, nor predictable. As indicated, very little is known objectively about the *qualitative* side of intermarriage. Preliminary studies do indicate, however, that only about one-third of Jewish partners in mixed marriages view their children as Jewish, and even then, most of these children are rarely exposed to Jewish religious or cultural life. They are raised primarily without any ethnic or religious identification. One such investigation, whose findings were published in 1979, did report encouraging data relating to "conversionary intermarriages"—where the non-Jewish-born spouse adopted Judaism, usually prior to marriage—which "suggests steps the Jewish community might take to ameliorate the assimilationist threat inherent in intermarriage." Their research revealed that "on every index of Jewish attitudes and practices, couples whose born-Gentile spouses have converted to Judaism scored higher than other intermarried couples . . . Conversionary marriages compared favorably not only with mixed marriages, but with endogamous marriages as well. In the conversionary marriage, Jewish identity is not merely asserted; it is acted upon, particularly with respect to religious affiliation and observance. Thus, in some ways, there is more reason for optimism for Jewish continuity in families where the born-Gentile spouse has converted to Judaism than there is in the typical endogamous family . . . The not-insignificant minority of born-Gentile spouses—perhaps as many as 15 per cent—who did not convert, but expressed some sense of identification with Judaism, may also point up a valuable potential for the Jewish community."[32]

It was clearly in response to the growing need to reformulate religious policy concerning these matters that the American Reform rabbinate, the Central Conference of American Rabbis, declared at its national convention in 1983 that non-converted spouses of families within their own congregational orbit, who wished to follow Jewish religious practices, would be regarded as Jews, even if they did not formally convert. Conservative rabbis, too, while still insisting on formal conversion according to Jewish law, were also becoming less reticent about the subject, and although they did not seek out prospective converts or proselytize, they were establishing "conversion classes" for Gentiles planning to marry a Jewish spouse. The Orthodox rabbinate, however, remained indifferent to the problem of conversion, or ambivalent, at best. Since the Jewish tradition only considers conversion "pure" when it is done out of the love of God—not for personal gain, or even the love of man— many Orthodox Rabbis still regard a conversion for the purpose of marriage as one tainted with "ulterior motive," and therefore not fully acceptable, traditionally speaking. Yet, there were increasing signs that among the "modern Orthodox"—if not the ultra-right-wing pietists— these new concerns were also strong enough to make them rethink their older position.

Indeed, new policies seem to be called for on the part of all concerned Jewish entities which would change the traditional stance of discouraging prospective converts, or, at best, remaining merely passive about the problem. There appears to be a need to develop some active policy which will confront the fact that there is a growing group of "mixed-marriage spouses" who are not deemed Jewish according to religious law, but who do, nevertheless, feel themselves "to be Jewish"—albeit in a secular-ethnic way. One sociologist spoke for many when he recommended that a "new category of Jew" be recognized: it would consist of those who are members of the "people," but not of the "faith"; one might call it "ethnic conversion." He believed that there was much to be gained from this untapped source of persons who "are Jews through the alchemy of sociology, not of halakah."[33]

Many of the "demographic problems" facing the American Jewish community as the century draws towards its close are, in fact, related to issues not always connected to religion. It has been noted by many that Jews in America are often in the forefront of important "demographic revolutions." The rapid change in the role of women—the so-called sexual revolution—that were beginning to surface in the mid-1960s was only one of several serious issues which affected the stability and maintenance of the Jewish family. Additionally, Jews have the highest proportion of college graduates; are most disproportionately concentrated in relatively few major metropolitan centers; and for the most part enjoy high levels of social and economic mobility. They also display clear signs of attrition and reflect a condition where they are not replacing themselves. They constitute an aging community lacking in sufficient new births. In addition to the challenge of living in an open society, all of these factors must also be added to the rapidly accelerating changes in American marriage and family patterns which have been occurring all across the board among the general population. To be sure, these are *American* social changes of the greatest magnitude, yet for Jews they have especially ominous significance because they help to erode their long-standing tradition of family cohesiveness, in-marriage, and older marital patterns. It has been demonstrated, for example, that the "no-growth mode" already visible in the settled American Jewish community is not so much the result of smaller family size—those who do bear children usually have two or three—but is more closely linked to the new styles of delayed marriage, plus a radical novelty for Jews—the growing number of never-marrieds.[34]

Moreover, researchers who have carefully examined the distinctive differences always thought to be characteristic of "the cohesive Jewish family" have been finding these to be more modest than conventional opinion would have led one to believe. By the 1980s, Jews were still divorcing and separating from their husbands or wives at a lower rate than Catholics or Protestants, yet it seemed clear that they were already beginning to "catch up" with the growing rates developing in both these groups. Even among the Orthodox, and the ultra-pious Hasidim, divorce and separation were new factors virtually nonexistent in earlier generations. Single-parent families were also increasing among American Jews, as were alcoholism, desertion, and similar causes of family breakdown in the general population.[35] More and more, the celebrated qualities of traditional family life, always before a hallmark of their distinctiveness and spiritual strength—and often the envy of others—seemed to be eroding, especially among third- and fourth-generation American Jews. Jews were losing the assurance that their inner life would continue to mark them out as a unique people. Indeed, no amount of ethnic loyalty, vicarious pride in the achievements of Israel, or group solidarity in the face of real or imagined "threats to Jewish survival" were actually more threatening to the Jewish future than the steady collapse of the once-solid structure of their family life.

If these were some of the threatening problems within their interior realm, there were also serious political issues stemming from the "new Jewish demography" which affected their status as an influential American minority. In the longer range, these could indeed have significant bearing on both the "domestic" and "foreign" policies of the organized Jewish community. Their stance on important legal and social issues affecting their status as a religio-ethnic group was at stake. So, too, was their continuing effectiveness in successfully pleading Israel's cause, as a real or imagined "lobby" in aid of the Jewish state.

On the home front, "affirmative action programs," which by the 1970s had become part of the political landscape, were viewed by many Jewish leaders as an attack on the merit system. Jews in America have thrived, they believed, only when there was an absence of quotas of any kind. "Quotas are the most serious threat to Jews since World War II," said one leader, and "there is no more serious challenge to the American ethos than a quota system . . . The merit system had neither been invented by Jews, nor had it come into being for the sake of Jews . . . Unless certain of these tendencies are reversed (affirmative action plans to spur employment of Blacks, Hispanics, and other minorities) people who don't have jobs aren't going to get them. And people who have them aren't going to get promoted. It's an inevitable development, and the arithmetic is inexorable here. If the group is 3 per cent, the rest speaks for itself."[36]

The declining numbers of the American Jewish population could, in the future, put them at great disadvantage in a political climate influenced by these "affirmative action" quotas. There was a further threat, too. It stemmed from the movement of Jews out of the Northeast—with its large electoral college vote. For many years, Jewish leaders had been reticent about admitting to the reality of a "Jewish vote." But then, in relation to other minorities, their numbers decreased; their strategic location in populous Eastern states began shifting westward and southward; and these quota systems loomed as a large peril to their economic future. In response to all these new factors, many leaders began to call for an open re-examination of the political strategy of American Jews. Speaking for many, one of them offered these candid comments in 1982—words that would hardly have been put into print by any community spokesman in America, until the emergence of the new and braver Jewish identity in the 1970s:

> We must deepen and broaden our definition of Jewish issues. We must overcome our ambivalence in being perceived as an ethnic voting bloc . . . But, of course, observers of American voting patterns have known for some time that there is a Jewish voting pattern *and the very impression of our power has been a source of it.* Besides, why the shyness? Jews have been voting for candidates whose political platforms they deem compassionate of the needy, caring of the underdog, and which are critical of such socially baneful conditions as racism, discrimination and ultranationalism.
>
> This voting pattern has seen Jews vote against Jewish candidates and in favor of non-Jewish candidates when the former were viewed as less liberal than the latter. Moreover, Jewish voting singularly among ethnic voting patterns has been supportive of political platforms frequently at odds with economic interests of the relatively comfortable Jewish community. *All this by way of contending that there is indeed a Jewish vote and that it reflects favorably on our civic-mindedness.* But we are affirming something else, too. Does the candidate with soothing words for Israel have an understanding of the implications for Israel's security in an inadequate defense budget? Which candidate is the surer guarantor of peace, the candidate whose heart and rhetoric affirms it, or the candidate who confrontationally signals his preparedness to defend it?
>
> . . . in 1980 President Carter received 45% of the Jewish vote, a radical sea change in Jewish voting. Without commenting on the respective qualities of Messrs. Reagan and Carter, this stunning shift in our voting patterns, whether it be an aberration or a precursor of real change, is, we believe, a positive contribution to our real interests . . . To be sure, Jews constitute but 2.7% of the U.S. population. However, our actual percentage of the total vote approximates 5% and while even 5% is itself a small figure, given our (present) deployment in the major states and the electoral college system, the 1980 Jewish voting distribution augurs well for both Democratic and Republican future attentiveness. At least, quadrennially.
>
> Are we suggesting that liberals are no longer our trustworthy allies and that conservatives are?
>
> Hardly. But to the extent that liberals support state-sanctioned racist

criteria for participation in either the public or the private sector, they diminish us, diminish democracy. To the extent that in their sympathy for those who do not enjoy self-rule they are indifferent to the military-strategic implications for the United States and for Israel of a self-rule that is dictatorial or faces toward the Soviets, they are our and democracy's trappers.(Italics added.)[37]

Some observers have detected a move toward political conservatism among Jewish voters as a result of increasing concerns such as these. Indeed, since the early 1970s, important Jewish public figures—including editors and rabbis—had joined a variety of conservative-oriented foundations and think-tanks. As a result, there was a popular perception that most of America's Jews were moving to the political right. Yet there is no empirical proof to support such a view. On the contrary, as one scholar observed in 1981, "on issues concerning welfare, civil rights, women's rights, civil liberties . . . American Jews have been and remain liberal. While the country as a whole has moved right, Jews remain 'off the graph,' that is, they maintain their left-of-center position in the American political spectrum."[38] It remains to be seen, however, what their future political course may be, if increasing pressures are placed upon them to be more concerned than in the past with what they regard as their own self-interest.

"Self interest" is indeed a key word for the decades to come, and the knowledge of its proper ingredients is crucial for the *Jewish spirit,* not only for political strategy. For the American Jew of the twenty-first century will be the immediate heir of both the problems and the potentials we have been discussing. There are, of course, no sure answers or confident formulas. He will have to improvise and seek his own levels of adjustment to them. Yet no one who remembers the fate of the "crushing conformity" which was forecast for this unique Jewish community only as recently as the 1950s by many scholars and savants can be either sanguine or dogmatic about the shape of Jewish things to come in America. Both the unpredictable boons and the banes, which, as we have seen, began to emerge in the 1960s, are far from having run their full course. Yet there can be no escape from the dramatic ways in which Jews have changed course toward a more open and resurgent self-awareness of their group identity in the short space of less than two decades. And below the surface, too, there is now a new and profound stirring among American Jews, one that had not reached such depths before. They may yet surprise themselves and others and burgeon into fuller flower—if not as a more populous community, then as one more deeply-rooted in its own historic soil—as they "compartmentalize" their adjustment to America, and not merely accommodate mindlessly and pliantly, as was their earlier custom. What may superficially still appear to some mainly as a conforming, middle-class American community, powered principally by forces external to itself, may yet take its place by the side of the great Jewish communities of the past. If it does, it will be a testimony to the spiritual resources inherent in America, whose liberating influences will call forth a creative spiritual response from the Jews of America. If it does, moreover, then important and creative changes must inevitably take place in the institutional life of the American Jewish community: the rabbi may again become the scholar-teacher (if not the saint); the synagogue an intellectual center rather than a house of social meeting; the educational system may shift its emphasis to a deepening and heightening of outreach instead of concentrating on elementals alone; and the fund-raising apparatus, while retaining its "American efficiency," may come closer to the spiritual values of *zedakah*, to which it is now only superficially related. Paul Tillich has said that he did not believe "that a free society can be derived from any religion unless the religion has been profoundly influenced by the Jewish tradition."[39] The converse is equally true: when Jews are themselves spiritually free, they can free the Jewish tradition to help make it speak again in its historic and authentic accents.

As early as 1907, Dr. Israel Friedlaender, an east-European professor at the Jewish Theological Seminary of America, discussing the "problem of Judaism in America," offered his fellow American Jews a vision:

And when we thus try to penetrate the mist that encircles the horizon of the present, a vision unfolds itself before our mind's eye, presenting a picture of the future American Israel. We perceive a community great in numbers, mighty in power, enjoying life, liberty and the pursuit of happiness: true life, not mere breathing space; full liberty, not mere elbow room; real happiness, not that of pasture beasts; actively participating in the civic, social and economic progress of the country, fully sharing and increasing its spiritual possessions and acquisitions, doubling its joys, halving its sorrows; yet deeply rooted in the soil of Judaism, clinging to its past, working for its future, true to its traditions, faithful to its aspirations, one in sentiment with their brethren wherever they are, attached to the land of their fathers as the cradle and resting place of the Jewish spirit; men with straight backs and raised heads, with big hearts and strong minds, with no conviction crippled, with no emotion stifled, with souls harmoniously developed, self-centered and self-reliant; receiving and resisting, not yielding like wax to every impress from the outside, but blending the best they possess with the best they encounter; not a horde of individuals, but a set of individualities, adding a new note to the richness of American life, leading a new current into the stream of American civilization; not a formless crowd of taxpayers and voters, but a sharply marked community, distinct and distinguished, trusted for its loyalty, respected for its dignity, esteemed for its traditions, valued for its aspiration, a community such as the Prophet of the Exile saw it in his vision: "And marked will be their seed among the nations, and their offspring among the peoples. Everyone that will see them will point to them as a community blessed by the Lord."[40]

If America *forgets* the hates, the hostilities, and the hurts, and if, in the midst of freedom and relative affluence, Jews can *remember* their spiritual integrity and their need to contribute creatively as religious co-equals, this modern vision and prophecy may yet come true.

NOTES

1. Quoted in a dispatch of the Jewish Telegraphic Agency, April 21, 1971.

2. Daniel Elazar, "Involving Faculty in Communal Affairs," paper presented to Council of Jewish Welfare Funds, November 12, 1970.

3. Irving Howe, "The Lost Young Intellectual," in *Commentary*, October, 1946, p. 362; see also his "Spruceton Jewry Adjusts Itself," in *Commentary*, June, 1948, pp. 552–558.

4. Quoted in Norman Podhoretz, "Jewishness and the Younger Intellectuals" (Introduction), in *Commentary*, April, 1961, p. 307.

5. *Ibid.*, p. 309.

6. While Jews represent about 2.75 per cent of the total population, at least eight per cent of America's college graduates each year, are Jews. See R. L. Zweigenhaft and G. W. Domhoff, *Jews In The Protestant Establishment*, Praeger, New York, 1982, p. 19.

7. Albert G. Crawford and Rela Monson, *Academy and Community: A Study of the Jewish Identity and Involvement of Professors*, Institute of Human Relations, New York, November, 1980, p. 35.

8. Milton Gordon, "Marginality and the Jewish Intellectual," in Peter Rose (ed.) *The Ghetto and Beyond*, Random House, New York, 1969, p. 485.

9. Zborowski and Herzog, *op. cit.*, p. 230.

10. Lothar Kahn, "Another Decade: The American Jew in the Sixties," in *Judaism*, Spring, 1961, Vol. 10, No. 2, pp. 104–105; p. 111. Used by permission.

11. Steven M. Cohen, "Will Jews Keep Giving? Prospects for the Jewish Charitable Community," in *Journal of Jewish Communal Service*, New York, September, 1978, p. 69.

12. Will Herberg, "The Integration of the Jew in Contemporary America," in *Conservative Judaism*, Vol. XV, No. 3, Spring, 1961, p. 9.

13. Martin E. Marty, *Second Chance for American Protestants* (New York: Harper and Row, 1963), pp. 58; 64–65.

14. *Newsletter*, Association for Jewish Studies, Waltham, Mass., June, 1981, p. 2. By 1983, however, there were fears of shrinking enrollment "due in part to the precipitous decrease in the birth-rate in the early 1960s; part to the attraction of career goals in a shrinking economy." See *Newsletter*, Association for Jewish Studies, Winter, 1983, p. 1.

15. See David Silverberg, "Jewish Studies on the American Campus," in *Present Tense*, Summer, 1978, pp. 52–56.

16. See William W. Orbach, *The American Movement to Aid Soviet Jews*, University of Massachusetts Press, Amherst, 1979; also, for a personal account, see my

The Real Jewish World: A Rabbi's Second Thoughts, Philosophical Library, New York, 1984, Chapters 9 and 10.

17. A single but powerful example helps to sharpen this oft-forgotten point. Elie Wiesel, now the most celebrated American writer on the Holocaust, could not find a willing American publisher when he offered his first book for publication after arriving in New York from Paris, in the mid-1950s. Finally, he found a venturesome publisher and his first Holocaust book, *Night,* saw the light in 1960. See also his *A Jew Today* (New York: Vintage Books, 1979), pp. 17–23, where he describes how he became a writer, and the role of Francois Mauriac in launching him on a career as a writer of Holocaust books. Today, there is a willing reading public for books dealing with the Holocaust. Wiesel, himself, had contributed to the creation of this interest and this reading public. (See also the cover story "Elie Wiesel" in *The New York Times Magazine,* October 30, 1983).

18. Deborah E. Lipstadt, "Invoking the Holocaust," in *Judaism,* Summer, 1981, p. 335.

19. Paula Hyman, in *Moment,* April, 1981, p. 33.

20. Arnold Eisen, *idem.,* p. 31.

21. Kevin Avruch, *American Immigrants in Israel,* University of Chicago Press, Chicago, 1981, p. 35.

22. *idem.* pp. 35 ff.

23. Kevin Avruch, *op. cit.,* pp. 58–59.

24. It is entirely possible that owing to the selective character of emigration from and immigration to Israel from the United States there can be significant changes in the composition of the Israeli population. These point to some long-range effects on Israeli culture and politics which are linked to an increase in the Orthodox religious community, as well as to a stronger "nationalistic" element.

25. There are no precise figures. The U. S. Census of 1970 reported 100,000 people in families in which Hebrew was the main language spoken at home. The Jewish Agency in 1980 ("Lahis Report") gave the range as between 300,000 to 500,000.

26. Drora Kass and Seymour Martin Lipset, "Jewish Immigration to the United States from 1967 to the Present: Israelis and Others," in *Understanding American Jewry,* (ed. M. Sklare), Transaction Books, New Brunswick, 1982, pp. 279–280.

27. D. Elizur, *Israelis in the U. S.: Motives, Attitudes and Intentions,* Bar Ilan University and the Israel Institute of Applied Social Research, Jerusalem, 1979.

28. Elihu Bergman, "The American Jewish Population Erosion," in *Midstream,* October, 1977, p. 9.

29. See *Journal for the Scientific Study of Religion,* March 1980; also, Allen S. Maller, "Jews, Cults and Apostates," in *Judaism,* Summer, 1981, pp. 306–31.

30. See Samuel S. Lieberman and Morton Weinfeld, "Demographic Trends and Jewish Survival" in *Midstream,* November, 1977.

31. *idem.,* p. 29.

32. Egon Mayer and Carl Sheingold, *Intermarriage and the Jewish Future,* The American Jewish Committee, New York, 1979, pp. 29–31.

33. Egon Mayer, "A Cure for Intermarriage?" in *Moment,* June, 1979, p. 64.

34. See Calvin Goldscheider, "Demography of Jewish Americans: Research, Findings, Issues, Challenges," in *Understanding American Jewry,* ed. M. Sklare, Transaction Books, New Brunswick, 1982, pp. 1–55.

35. See Andrew J. Cherlin and Carin Celebuski, *Are Jewish Families Different?* American Jewish Committee, New York, 1982; Chaim I. Waxman, "The Family and the American Jewish Community", in *Understanding American Jewry*, ed. by M. Sklare, Transaction Books, New Brunswick, 1982, pp. 166–168.

36. Norman Podhoretz, editor of *Commentary*, the influential, neo-conservative magazine published by the American Jewish Committee. Quoted in Stephen Isaacs, *Jews and American Politics*, Doubleday, N. Y. 1974, pp. 168–169.

37. Nathan Perlmutter (and Ruth Ann Perlmutter), *The Real Anti-Semitism in America*, Doubleday, New York, 1982, pp. 282–284.

38. Chaim I. Waxman, *op. cit.*, p. 78.

39. Paul Tillich, "Freedom and Ultimate Concern," in *Religion in America*, ed. John Cogley (New York: Meridian Books, 1958), p. 282.

40. Israel Friedlaender, *Past and Present: A Collection of Jewish Essays* (Cincinnati: Ark Publishing Company, 1919), pp. 277–278.

Selected Bibliography

ABELLA, IRVING and TROPER, HAROLD. *None Is Too Many,* Toronto: Lester & Orpen Dennys, 1982.

AHAD HA-'AM. *Selected Essays.* (Translated by Leon Simon.) Philadelphia: Jewish Publication Society of America, 1936.

AMERICAN JEWISH YEAR BOOKS. Philadelphia: Jewish Publication Society of America, 1945 and following.

AVIAD, JANET. *Return to Judaism: Religious Renewal in Israel.* Chicago: University of Chicago Press, 1983.

AVRUCH, KEVIN. *American Immigrants in Israel.* Chicago: University of Chicago Press, 1981.

BALDWIN, JAMES. *The Fire Next Time,* New York, 1963.

BARON, SALO W. *A Social and Religious History of the Jews.* New York: Columbia University Press, 1958-

———. *The Jewish Community.* 3 vols. Philadelphia: Jewish Publication Society of America, 1942.

BECKER, CARL L. *Freedom and Responsibility in the American Way of Life.* New York: Vintage Books, 1955.

BELKIN, SAMUEL. *Essays in Traditional Jewish Thought.* New York: Philosophical Library, 1956.

BELLAH, ROBERT N. and HAMMOND, PHILLIP E. *Varieties of Civil Religion.* San Francisco: Harper & Row, 1980.

BOORSTIN, DANIEL J. *The Americans, The Colonial Experience.* New York: Random House, 1958.

BRYCE, JAMES. *The American Commonwealth.* 2 vols. New York: Commonwealth Publishing Co., 1908. Paperback, 2 vols. New York: G. P. Putnam's Sons.

CAHNMAN, WERNER J. (ed.). *Intermarriage and Jewish Life: A Symposium.* New York: Herzl Press, 1963.

CHERLIN, ANDREW J. and CELEBUSKI, CARIN. *Are Jewish Families Different?* New York: American Jewish Committee, 1982.

COHEN, ARTHUR A. *Anatomy of Faith.* New York: Harcourt, Brace & Co., 1960.

COMMAGER, HENRY STEELE. *The American Mind.* New Haven: Yale University Press, 1950.

Commentary Magazine.

CURTIS, JOHN SHELTON. *An Appraisal of the Protocols of Zion.* New York: Columbia University Press, 1942.

DAEDALUS. "Ethnic Groups in American Life," Spring, 1961.

DAVIS, MOSHE. *The Emergence of Conservative Judaism.* Philadelphia: Jewish Publication Society of America, 1963.

DOBKOWSKI, MICHAEL N. *The Tarnished Dream.* Westport: Greenwood Press, 1979.

DOMHOFF, G. WILLIAM and ZWEIGENHAFT, RICHARD L. *Jews in the Protestant Establishment,* New York: Praeger, 1982.

ELAZAR, DANIEL. *Community and Polity: The Organizational Dynamics of American Jewry.* Philadelphia: Jewish Publication Society, 1973.

FRIEDLAENDER, ISRAEL. *Past and Present: A Collection of Jewish Essays.* Cincinnati: Ark Publishing Company, 1919.

FRIEDMAN, THEODORE, and GORDIS, ROBERT (eds.). *Jewish Life in America.* New York: Horizon Press, 1955.

FUCHS, LAWRENCE H. *The Political Behavior of American Jews.* New York: The Free Press of Glencoe, 1956.

GINZBERG, ELI. *Agenda for American Jews.* New York: King's Crown Press, 1950.

GINZBERG, LOUIS. *Students, Scholars and Saints.* Philadelphia: Jewish Publication Society of America, 1928.

GLAZER, NATHAN. *American Judaism.* Chicago: University of Chicago Press, 1972. (Second Edition).

GLAZER, NATHAN and MOYNIHAN, DANIEL P. (eds.). *Ethnicity: Theory and Experience.* Cambridge: Harvard University Press, 1975.

GLOCK, CHARLES and QUINLEY, HAROLD. *Anti-Semitism in America.* New York: Harper and Row, 1979.

GLOCK, CHARLES and STARK, RODNEY. *Christian Beliefs and Anti-Semitism,* New York: Harper and Row, 1965.

GORDON, ALBERT I. *Jews in Suburbia.* Boston: Beacon Press, 1959.

GRAEBER, ISAQUE, and BRITT, STEWART H. (eds.). *Jews in a Gentile World.* New York: The Macmillan Company, 1942.

HALPERN, BEN. *The American Jew: A Zionist Analysis.* New York: Theodor Herzl Foundation, 1956.

HANDLIN, OSCAR (ed.). *Immigration as a Factor in American History.* Englewood Cliffs: Prentice-Hall, Inc., 1959.

HANSEN, MARCUS LEE. *The Immigrant in American History.* Cambridge: Harvard University Press, 1940.

HARTZ, LOUIS (ed.). *The Founding of New Societies.* New York: Harcourt, Brace & World, 1964.

HAWGOOD, JOHN A. *The Tragedy of German-America.* New York: G. P. Putnam's Sons, 1940.

HERBERG, WILL. *Protestant-Catholic-Jew.* New York: Doubleday & Co., 1955.

HESCHEL, SUSANNAH (ed.). *On Being A Jewish Feminist,* New York: Schocken Books, 1983.

HIGHAM, JOHN. *Strangers in the Land: Patterns of American Nativism, 1860–1925.* New Brunswick: Rutgers University Press, 1955.

———. *Send These To Me,* New York: Atheneum, 1975.

ISAAC, JULES. *The Christian Roots of Antisemitism.* Barley, England: The Parkes Library, 1960.

ISAACS, STEPHEN. *Jews and American Politics,* New York: Doubleday, 1974.

Jewish Social Studies (Journal), New York.

Journal of Jewish Communal Service, New York.

Judaism (Magazine), New York.

KAPLAN, MORDECAI M. *Judaism as a Civilization.* New York: The Macmillan Co., 1935.

KRANZLER, GEORGE. *Williamsburg: A Jewish Community in Transition.* New York: Philipp Feldheim, Inc., 1961.

LAVENDER, ABRAHAM D. (ed.). *A Coat of Many Colors: Jewish Subcommunities in the United States,* Westport: Greenwood Press, 1977.

LERNER, ANN LAPIDUS. *Who Hast Not Made Me a Man,* New York: American Jewish Committee, 1982.

LEVY, BERYL. *Reform Judaism in America.* New York: Bloch Publishing Co., 1933.

LEWISOHN, LUDWIG. *The American Jew: Character and Destiny.* New York: Farrar, Straus & Co., 1950.

LIPMAN, EUGENE J., and VORSPAN, ALBERT (eds.). *A Tale of Ten Cities.* New York: Union of American Hebrew Congregations, 1962.

LITTELL, FRANKLIN H. *From State-Church to Pluralism.* New York: Doubleday Anchor Original, 1962.

LURIE, HARRY L. *A Heritage Affirmed: The Jewish Federation Movement in America.* Philadelphia: Jewish Publication Society of America, 1961.

MALINO, FRANCES. *The Sephardic Jews of Bordeaux:* Alabama: University of Alabama Press, 1978.

MARTIRE, GREGORY and CLARK, RUTH. *Anti-Semitism in the United States,* New York: Praeger, 1982.

MARTY, MARTIN E. *The New Shape of American Religion.* New York: Harper and Brothers, 1959.

———. (ed) *Religion and Social Conflict,* New York: Oxford University Press, 1964.

———. *A Nation of Behavers,* Chicago: University of Chicago Press, 1976.

MAYER, EGON and SHEINGOLD, CARL. *Intermarriage and the Jewish Future,* New York: American Jewish Committee, 1979.

MEYERS, GUSTAVUS. *History of Bigotry in the United States.* New York: Random House, 1943.

Midstream (Magazine).

MILLS, C. WRIGHT. *The Sociological Imagination,* New York: Oxford University Press, 1959.

Moment (Magazine).

NIEBUHR, REINHOLD. *The Irony of American History.* New York: Charles Scribner's Sons, 1952.

NOVAK, MICHAEL. *The Rise of the Unmeltable Ethnics,* New York: Macmillan, 1972.

OLSON, BERNHARD E. *Faith and Prejudice.* New Haven: Yale University Press, 1963.

ORBACH, WILLIAM W. *The American Movement to Aid Soviet Jews.* Amherst: University of Massachusetts Press, 1979.

PARK, ROBERT E. *The Immigrant Press and Its Control.* New York: Harper and Brothers, 1922.

PARKES, JAMES. *The Conflict of Church and Synagogue.* New York: Meridian Books, 1961.

———. *A Reappraisal of the Christian Attitude to Judaism.* Barley, England: The Parkes Library, 1962.

PAWLIKOWSKI, JOHN T. *Catechetics and Prejudice.* New York: Paulist Press, 1972.

PERLMUTTER, NATHAN and RUTH ANN. *The Real Anti-Semitism in America.* New York: Arbor House, 1982.

PFEFFER, LEO. *Creeds in Competition.* New York: Harper and Brothers, 1958.

PHILIPSON, DAVID. *The Reform Movement in Judaism.* New York: The Macmillan Co., 1907.

PINSON, KOPPEL S. (ed.). *Essays on Antisemitism.* New York: Conference on Jewish Relations, 1946.

POLL, SOLOMON. *The Hasidic Community of Williamsburg.* New York: The Free Press of Glencoe, 1962.

RIESMAN, DAVID. (with NATHAN GLAZER and REUEL DENNEY). *The Lonely Crowd.* Garden City: Doubleday & Co., 1953.

ROSE, PETER. (ed.). *The Ghetto and Beyond.* New York: Random House, 1969.

ROSEN, GLADYS. (ed.). *Jewish Life in America.* New York: Ktav Publishing House, 1978.

ROSENBERG, STUART E. *The Jewish Community in Rochester.* New York: Columbia University Press, 1954.

————. *A Time to Speak.* New York: Bloch Publishing Co., 1960.

————. *The Bible Is For You.* New York: David McKay Co., Inc., 1961.

————. "Some Attitudes of Nineteenth-Century Reform Laymen," in *Essays in Jewish Life and Thought* (eds. BLAU, FRIEDMAN, HERTZBERG, MENDELSOHN). New York: Columbia University Press, 1959.

————. *The Jewish Community in Canada.* (2 vols.) Toronto: McLelland and Stewart, 1970–1971.

————. *The Real Jewish World: A Rabbi's Second Thoughts.* New York: Philosophical Library, 1984.

RUBIN, ISRAEL. *Satmar: An Island in the City.* Chicago: Quadrangle Books, 1973.

RUPPIN, ARTHUR. *The Jewish Fate and Future.* London: Macmillan and Co., Ltd., 1940.

SARTRE, JEAN-PAUL. *Anti-Semite and Jew.* New York: Schocken Books, Inc., 1948.

SCHECHTER, SOLOMON. *Aspects of Rabbinic Theology.* New York: Schocken Books, Inc., 1961.

————. *Seminary Addresses.* New York: Burning Bush Press, 1959.

SHAFFIR, WILLIAM. *Life in a Religious Community.* Toronto: Holt, Rinehart, Winston, 1974.

SHERMAN, C. BEZALEL. *The Jews Within American Society.* Detroit: Wayne State University Press, 1961.

SIMPSON, ALAN. *Puritanism in Old and New England.* Chicago: University of Chicago Press, 1955.

SKLARE, MARSHALL. *Conservative Judaism.* New York: The Free Press of Glencoe, 1955.

————. (ed.). *The Jews: Social Patterns of an American Group.* New York: The Free Press of Glencoe, 1958.

————. (ed.). *Understanding American Jewry.* New Brunswick: Transaction Books, 1982.

SOWELL, THOMAS. *Ethnic America.* New York: Basic Books, 1983.

STEWART, GEORGE R. *American Ways of Life.* Garden City: Doubleday & Co., 1954.

STROBER, GERALD S. *American Jews: Community in Crisis.* Garden City: Doubleday & Co., 1974.

TURNER, FREDERICK J. *The Significance of Sections in American History.* New York: Henry Holt and Co., 1932.

TELLER, JUDD. *Strangers and Natives.* New York: Delacorte Press, 1968.

WAXMAN, MORDECAI. *Tradition and Change: The Development of Conservative Judaism.* New York: The Burning Bush Press, 1958.

WEINER, HERBERT. *9½ Mystics.* New York: Holt, Rinehart, Winston, 1969.

WEINFELD, M; SHAFFIR, W; COTLER, I. (eds.). *The Canadian Jewish Mosaic.* Toronto: John Wiley and Sons, 1981.

ZBOROWSKI, MARK, and HERZOG, ELIZABETH. *Life Is With People.* New York: International Universities Press, Inc., 1952.

ZEITLIN, JOSEPH. *Disciples of the Wise.* New York: Bureau of Publications, Teachers College, 1945.

Index

Academic community, Jewish, 252ff.;
Judaica explosion, 260
Adler, Cyrus, 176, 179
Affirmative action, xiii, 32, 271, 272
Ahad Ha-'am, 117
Alberta, Jewish community, 248
Alexander III, Czar, 97
Alter, Robert, 33
Aluja, 209, 236f.
America, the new world and the old,
3–9; religion in, 6f. (*see also* main
entry: Religion in America); the
national character, 8f., 10–21; the
Puritan world, 10–13; the frontier
community, 13–15; recent national moods, 22–38; as Christian
country, 27–29; the land of promise, 49; destined to become a middle-class nation, 75; anti-
Semitism, 98–105; church-state
questions, 64, 103
"America First," 99
Americanization, 23–25, 51, 124–26
American Jewish Congress, 244
American Jews, ix, xii, 37; the new
world and the old, 3ff.; the second
generation, 20, 126; religious stirrings of the 1950s, 29; Israel-centeredness, 30, 86, 129; ethnicity,
33, 37; primacy of the individual,
34; the melting pot, 43–61, 194;
Jewishness and Judaism, 63ff.,
127, 129, 130–33; sacred *and* secular, 73–87, 238 (*see also* Secularism
in America); middle-class values,
76–81; the appeal of Zionism, 77;
the role of women, 79, 150, 185–
86, 202; population centers, 82,
137; *desiderata* for community leadership, 83; uniqueness of America, 92, 124; Christian-Jewish
relations, 108 (*see also* Interfaith
movement); separation of church
and state, 112 (*see also* Church-
state relations); in search of liberty, 124–33; number of affiliated,
152, 153, 201f.; denominational-

ism, 156ff.; return to tradition,
171; problems and prospects, 206,
252–75; "Civil Judaism," 213f.;
influence beyond U.S., 233; con-
tradictory elements, 255, 257; Nobel laureates, 257f.; what Jews
have achieved for America, 258;
"Soviet Jewry movement," 261f.;
the Holocaust, 262–63
Americans, beliefs and attitudes, 4–9,
12–13, 23–25; a "return to religion," 25ff.; secularism and religion integrated, 64
Amsterdam, 45
Anti-Semitism, 70, 91–116, 247; in
Russia, 66–67, 96–98; in Zionism,
69–70; religious basis for, 93–95,
103–5; in Germany, 98–99; social,
100; Black anti-Semitism, 109,
111; and emancipation, 118–20;
Jewish, 127
Apostasy, 268
Asch, Sholem, 74
Ashkenazim, 43, 44, 46, 55, 56, 57,
59
Assimilation, 132, 267
Association for Jewish Studies, 260
Atlanta, 83
Austro-Hungarian Empire, 50, 58

Baal teshuva, 191, 211
Babylonia, 55, 138, 139
Baldwin, James, 32
Baron, Salo, 247
Barth, Karl, 92
Belkin, Samuel, 192–94, 199, 212
Bell, Daniel, 36, 84
Bellah, Robert, 246
Belzer sect, 208
Benderley, Samson, 200
Bennett, John C., 104
Berdichevski, M. Y., 69
Bergman, Elihu, 267f.
Beth Kenesset, 142
Biculturalism, in Canada, 239
Bilu, 68
Black Death, 221

[283]